Defending the realm?

Defending the realm?

The politics of Britain's small wars since 1945

AARON EDWARDS

Manchester University Press
Manchester and New York
distributed in the United States exclusively by Palgrave Macmillan

Published by Manchester University Press
Oxford Road, Manchester M13 9NR, UK
and Room 400, 175 Fifth Avenue, New York, NY 10010, USA
www.manchesteruniversitypress.co.uk

Distributed in the United States exclusively by
Palgrave Macmillan, 175 Fifth Avenue, New York,
NY 10010, USA

Distributed in Canada exclusively by
UBC Press, University of British Columbia, 2029 West Mall,
Vancouver, BC, Canada V6T 1Z2

British Library Cataloguing-in-Publication Data
A catalogue record for this book is available from the British Library

Library of Congress Cataloging-in-Publication Data applied for

ISBN 978 0 7190 8441 6 hardback

First published 2012

Typeset 10.5/12.5pt Sabon
by Graphicraft Limited, Hong Kong
Printed in Great Britain
by MPG Books Group, UK

For Jennifer

Contents

Preface and acknowledgements

This book was born out of a growing frustration with the current state of conventional wisdom on the politics of British military intervention since the end of the Second World War.[1] It was spurred on by a belief that there has been a general failure amongst public servants and public intellectuals to fully appreciate the complex relationships between military commanders and civilian officials in Britain's 'small wars'.[2] If this failing were of purely academic concern it could quite easily be dismissed as a 'dialogue of the deaf' between the chattering classes. However, I have seen first-hand how this has had injurious effects on my own students' understanding of the role of the military instrument in serving government policy at the 'sharp end' of operations.

If that was not bad enough, skewed snapshots of Britain's post-war military interventions unfortunately seem to be informing the decision-making processes of policymakers, politicians and soldiers in today's global security environment.[3] This is worrying. If we do not have a firm understanding of the nuances of our own past, then how can we possibly make informed decisions, either in the present or in the future? *Defending the Realm* seeks to address this knowledge deficit by examining the historical record, as far as possible in light of the available archival source material and oral testimonies of those who were actually involved in Britain's small wars since 1945.[4]

Given my teaching responsibilities at the Royal Military Academy Sandhurst (RMAS), I have continuously sought to frame my lectures and seminars in the broader conceptual framework of strategic studies. An appreciation of the overlapping political, international, strategic and legal contexts within which British forces operate (and the lessons they have learned from this experience) is something Officer Cadets are expected to take away from the RMAS Commissioning Course. However, a hectic vocational-based training regime means that they are rarely afforded the opportunity to immerse themselves in this vast literature. Indeed, it was the absence of a single-volume strategic history of Britain's military experience in countering irregular adversaries[5] since 1945 that persuaded me to put pen to paper.

This book is also written with my other students in mind; commissioned officers who have soldiered in Northern Ireland, Iraq and Afghanistan. I only hope that it will enable these seasoned veterans to make sense of how their actions fitted into the 'bigger picture'. The ability of British military commanders to think conceptually and imaginatively, often under considerable constraints, is impressive. What is even more reassuring, however, is that they, like me, appreciate the importance of Field Marshal Montgomery's timeless aphorism that all 'uninformed criticism is valueless'.[6]

Defending the Realm, therefore, attempts to blend a close reading of the empirical data – the unpublished archives, interview transcripts and secondary sources – with a theoretical reflective account of the politics and strategy behind military events as they have unfolded on the ground. It applies a realist reading of Britain's strategic position in international relations since 1945. As such, it borrows heavily from the work of Hans Morgenthau, amongst others, who defined 'politics' as 'a struggle for power over men, and, whatever its ultimate aim may be, power is its immediate goal and the modes of acquiring, maintaining, and demonstrating it determine the technique of political action'.[7] Above all, this book attempts to bridge the gap between theory and practice at a time when, it is claimed, that 'we have all but lost the capacity to think strategically'.[8]

There are clear benefits of reading Britain's role in international security from a strategic perspective; as some defence professionals have observed, 'Strategic thinking is partly in someone's nature, but it is also a function of how we select, educate, train, stream and mentor the right people – nurturing them within defence and within wider government – to think at the right level and in a strategic way'.[9] This is echoed in the words of Professor Colin S. Gray, who articulates the view that 'education in strategy is a conceptual enabler; it is theory or education for practice'.[10] Moreover, it has also been necessary to situate these small wars in the broader historical context of the rapid decolonisation of Britain's empire, the Cold War confrontation between East and West, and, increasingly, amidst debates on the so-called 'changing character of conflict'.[11] However, what the book does not attempt to do is to provide tantalising detail about each of the eight cases examined. There are two main reasons why: first, it would be both impossible to do justice to the complexity of all of Britain's small wars since 1945 in a single volume, and, second, because it would be unwise for me to claim an encyclopaedic knowledge of each of the cases. The reader is, therefore, pointed in the direction of the expert literature on each case in the endnotes and bibliography.

The subject matter of Britain's small wars has fascinated me since I was a young boy, when I was privy to first-hand accounts of family members and friends who recalled, in vivid detail, their soldiering exploits in combating irregular opponents. One vignette from my own family history illustrates this well. My late great-uncle, Bill Graham, served in the 1st Battalion, the Royal Ulster Rifles, during the Second World War, landing by glider near Ranville in Normandy on D-Day. Within a matter of months Bill and his unit had probed deep behind enemy lines, advancing to contact towards the Rhine in a bid to secure the bridgeheads for Allied advance into Germany. At the end of the war he accompanied the Ulster Rifles to Palestine as part of the 6th Airborne Division, where he subsequently transferred into the Palestine Police, adapting his conventional war-fighting tactics to the rigours of Internal Security operations against Jewish terrorist and insurgent groups.

Like all good soldiers, Bill found that he could adjust his infantry skills and drills to fight what Montgomery once referred to as 'a lot of gangsters'. These 'gangsters', mainly found in the ranks of Jewish armed groups, nevertheless, proved formidable opponents for British forces in Palestine. Thus, Bill, like so many of his comrades, spent the remainder of his service as a battle-hardened soldier in an imperial policeman's uniform. Bill's story is indicative of the experiences of countless other British soldiers who found themselves having to adapt their big-wars skill-set to small-wars circumstances. In many respects Bill's personal story is reflective of the British military's ability to maintain a flexible and adaptable posture when applying armed force in the service of political aims.

I wish to thank a number of people for their advice and assistance during the research and writing of this book. It was my late grandfather, Jackie Graham, with whom I spent endless hours recalling 'wee yarns' about his brother Bill's military experiences. My father, James Edwards, has always been a constant source of encouragement in all of my work: he is my inspiration. My mother, Barbara, and my sister, Stephanie, make me feel at home each time I return from England. My brother, Ryan, also deserves a mention for keeping my feet firmly on the ground – even when we have bumped into each other amidst one of Britain's recent 'small wars'! David Ullah gave me an excellent first-hand account of his time in Aden in the 1960s, recalling vividly his experiences in Khormaksar, Crater and Radfan. His daughter Jennifer, my wife and soul-mate, has borne the brunt of my many days and nights toiling away on this book – and kindly cast her meticulous eye for detail over the entire manuscript. Jenny's continuing support for my intellectual pursuits is unparalleled and I dedicate this book to her with all my love.

My colleagues at Sandhurst have been outstanding in spurring me on in my academic endeavours. The RMAS Sabbatical Committee awarded me a term off in 2010 to complete much of the research and writing for this book. Drs David Brown, Martin Smith and Donette Murray recommended that I take additional time with the manuscript for quality-assurance purposes, and David and Donette kindly read over early drafts. My Head of Department, Dr Francis Toase, has been a huge supportive influence in all of my research endeavours, as too has his deputy Alan Ward. Tim Bean has been a fantastic friend and colleague, reading copious drafts enthusiastically and helping to hone my thinking over some well-earned 'brews'. Drs Ed Flint, Jenny Medcalf and Alieus Parchami also intervened to spur me along when a heavily 'kinetic' teaching load threatened to derail my research and writing. The RMAS Director of Studies, Sean McKnight, was excellent in approving (and, in many cases, helping to fund) my trips to the various archives, as well as to academic conferences to present findings from my research.

Colleagues beyond Sandhurst have also provided much support. Professors Graham Walker and Richard English facilitated my Visiting Research Fellowship at Queen's University Belfast in 2010–11. The Fellowship afforded me the intellectual breathing space to present research findings at guest lectures. Meanwhile, Dr Thomas Hennessey has been on hand to encourage me in broadening my intellectual horizons in our increasingly corresponding research interests. Dr Eamonn O'Kane kindly selected me to present a paper on the securitization of peacebuilding in Britain's 'new wars' at a convivial workshop at Falstad Memorial and Human Rights Centre, Norway, in June 2009, which fed directly into Chapter 8. Dr Cillian McGrattan kindly read over the manuscript and provided some invaluable criticism. I also wish to thank the editors of the scholarly journal *Small Wars and Insurgencies* for allowing me to use material from my article on the Army's counterinsurgency strategy in Northern Ireland. Moreover, the incredibly constructive feedback from Manchester University Press's two anonymous reviewers was extremely helpful in refocusing my attention on what I wanted to accomplish by writing this book. Tony Mason and the team at Manchester University Press have been terrific in permitting the deadline to lapse while I succumbed to a range of other academic pressures.

The assistance afforded to me by General Sir Roger Wheeler and Lieutenant-General Sir Philip Trousdell was invaluable. Billy Brown and

Jim Evans at PRRT in Belfast facilitated numerous crucial interviews with former members of the Royal Ulster Constabulary/Police Service of Northern Ireland, who included senior Counter-Terrorist officers, all of whom gave me candid insights into police-army cooperation at various levels. Together with an eclectic mix of people from police, military and paramilitary ranks, who cannot be named, I was provided a rare glimpse into the inner-workings of the strategic, operational and tactical aspects of Counter-Terrorist operations in Northern Ireland during 'our troubles' from all possible angles.

Without the assistance of a range of archivists and trustees of numerous collections across the UK the book would not have been written. Staff and Trustees at the Department of Documents at the Imperial War Museum, London; the Liddell Hart Centre for Military Archives, King's College London; the Special Collections section at the London School of Economics and Oxford University; as well as the National Archives, Kew, were also helpful. Staff at the Public Records Office of Northern Ireland searched out files relating to Operation Banner at a time of great transition for them. Last, but by no means least, I wish to thank Andrew Orgill, John Pearce, Ken Franklin and Mel Bird at the RMAS Central Library: without their assistance – and endless cups of tea – *Defending the Realm* would certainly have remained, to paraphrase Clausewitz, 'pointless and devoid of sense'.

The views expressed here are the author's and do not necessarily reflect the opinions of the Royal Military Academy Sandhurst, The Ministry of Defence, or any other United Kingdom government agency.

Notes

1 I was mindful while writing this book of Professor Lord Hennessy's caveat that one needs to '[b]eware conventional wisdoms; search for the lessons of history where you can find them'. Hennessy, Peter, *The Secret State: Preparing for the Worst, 1945–2010*, second edition (London: Penguin, 2010), p. 394.

2 'Small wars' are defined here as those conflicts which involve a state power and an irregular adversary, such as a terrorist or insurgent group.

3 For a similar argument see Porch, Douglas, 'The Dangerous Myths and Dubious Promise of COIN', *Small Wars & Insurgencies*, Vol. 22, No. 2 (2011), pp. 239–257. In a stinging attack on the mythology that has been built up around counter-insurgency, Porch (p. 253) argues that 'the certainty is that predictions for success of COIN doctrines anchored in mythologized history and selective memory are perilous propositions'.

4 There are a series of books on the history of Britain's small wars, such as Michael Carver's *War since 1945* (London: Weidenfeld and Nicolson, 1980);

Charles Townshend's *Britain's Civil Wars: Counter-Insurgency in the Twentieth Century* (London: Faber, 1986); Thomas R. Mockaitis' *British Counterinsurgency, 1919–1960* (London: Macmillan, 1990); Thomas R. Mockaitis' *British Counter-Insurgency in the Post-Imperial Era* (Manchester: Manchester University Press, 1995); John Newsinger's *British Counterinsurgency: From Palestine to Northern Ireland* (Basingstoke: Palgrave Macmillan, 2001); and more recently Benjamin Grob-Fitzgibbon's *Imperial Endgame: Britain's Dirty Wars and the End of Empire* (Basingstoke: Palgrave Macmillan, 2011). While Townshend and Grob-Fitzgibbon engage in a close reading of archival source material on Britain's small wars, the others do not.

5 'Irregular warfare is an exceedingly inclusive concept', argues Colin S. Gray, '[t]he noun matters more than the adjective . . . Irregular warfare is warfare between regulars and irregulars. As a general rule, please note the qualification, such warfare is between a state with its legally constituted official armed forces, and a non-state adversary'. Gray, Colin S., *Another Bloody Century: Future Warfare* (London: Weidenfeld and Nicolson, 2005), pp. 214–215.

6 Law, Bernard, Viscount Montgomery of Alamein, *The Memoirs of Field-Marshal the Viscount Montgomery of Alamein, KG* (London: Collins, 1958), p. 466.

7 Morgenthau, Hans, 'The Evil of Politics and the Ethics of Evil', *Ethics*, Vol. 56, No. 1 (October 1945), p. 14.

8 House of Commons Public Administration Select Committee, *Who Does UK National Strategy?*, First Report of Session 2010–11, 12 October 2010 (London: TSO, 18 October 2010), p. 3.

9 Newton, Paul, Paul Colley and Andrew Sharpe, 'Reclaiming the Art of British Strategic Thinking', *RUSI Journal*, Vol. 155, No. 1 (February 2010), p. 48.

10 Gray, Colin S., 'War – Continuity in Change, and Change in Continuity', *Parameters: The US Army's Senior Professional Journal*, Vol. 40, No. 2 (summer 2010), pp. 8–9.

11 Arguably, an understanding of history is important if we are to make informed judgements in the present. In the words of French philosopher Albert Camus, 'If, in fact, to ignore history comes to the same as denying reality, it is still alienating oneself from reality to consider history as a completely self-sufficient absolute'. Camus, Albert, *The Rebel*, translated by Anthony Bower (London: Peregrine Books, [1951] 1962), p. 252.

Abbreviations

AQI	Al Qaeda in Iraq
ATUC	Aden Trades Union Council
BLSC	Bodlein Library Oxford Special Collections
CDS	Chief of the Defence Staff
CENTO	Central Treaty Organization
CGS	Chief of the General Staff
CIA	Central Intelligence Agency
CIGS	Chief of the Imperial General Staff
COB	Contingency Operating Base
COIN	counter-insurgency
CPA	Coalition Provisional Authority
CT	Communist Terrorists
DFID	Department for International Development
EOKA	National Organization of Cypriot Combatants
FCO	Foreign and Commonwealth Office
FLOSY	Front for the Liberation of Occupied South Yemen
FNG	Federal National Guard
GOC	General Office Commanding
HUMINT	human intelligence
IED	Improvised Explosive Device
IISS	International Institute for Strategic Studies
IRA	Irish Republican Army
IS	Internal Security
ISAF	International Security Assistance Force
ISF	Iraqi Security Forces
IWM	Imperial War Museum
JAM	Jaish Al Mahdi
JDP	Joint Defence Publication
JIC	Joint Intelligence Committee
KAR	King's African Rifles
KAU	Kenya African Union
LCMA	Liddell Hart Centre for Military Archives

LSE	London School of Economics
MACA	Military Aid to the Civil Authority
MACP	Military Aid to the Civil Power
MCP	Malayan Communist Party
MPAJA	Malayan People's Anti-Japanese Army
MRF	Military Reconnaisance Force
MRLA	Malayan Races Liberation Army
NATO	North Atlantic Treaty Organization
NIO	Northern Ireland Office
NLF	National Liberation Front
NSC	National Security Council
NSS	National Security Strategy
ORBAT	Order of Battle
PIRA	Provisional Irish Republican Army
PORF	Popular Organization of Revolutionary Forces
ProExComm	Province Executive Committee
PRT	Provincial Reconstruction Team
PSO	Peace Support Operation
PSP	People's Socialist Party
RAF	Royal Air Force
RMAS	Royal Military Academy Sandhurst
RUC	Royal Ulster Constabulary
RUSI	Royal United Services Institute
SAA	South Arabian Army
SAS	Special Air Service
SBA	Sovereign Base Area
SDR	Strategic Defence Review
SDSR	Strategic Defence and Security Review
SIS	Secret Intelligence Service
TAOR	Tactical Area of Repsonsibility
TCG	Tasking and Co-ordination Group
TNA	The National Archives
TTPs	Tactics, Techniques and Procedures
UDA	Ulster Defence Association
UDR	Ulster Defence Regiment
UN	United Nations
UNP	United National Party
UNSC	United Nations Security Council
UNSCOP	United Nations Special Committee on Palestine
UVF	Ulster Volunteer Force
WMD	Weapons of Mass Destruction
WO	War Office

Introduction

> That questions of policy remain vested in the civil government must be loyally carried out. It is however the duty of the soldier to advise the Government and its subordinate officers as to the effect of the policy, contemplated or pursued, on military action.[1]

> All nations will continue to be guided in their decisions to intervene and their choice of the means of intervention by what they regard as their respective national interests.[2]

> War is an instrument of government policy: it is a means to a political end. The use of force is thus subject to political control. Political control of operations from the seat of government is much stronger today than it has been before; improved communications and the speed of political reaction to military events make a close control of operations by ministers inevitable, however remote the theatre. Political control may not affect the lower formations directly but it will certainly be an important factor for a higher commander and its effects will be felt throughout his command.[3]

A strategic history of Britain's small wars

Britain is often revered for its first-hand experience of waging 'small wars'. Its long imperial history, over the course of which this diminutive island-based nation once controlled territory covering approximately one-fifth of the world's surface and 25 per cent of its population, is littered with high-profile internal security campaigns, thus marking it out as perhaps the most seasoned practitioner of this type of warfare. Britain's 'small wars' typically involved fighting irregular adversaries, whether in the form of Communist insurgents in the bamboo-laden Malayan jungle, marauding Mau Mau gangs rampaging across Kenyan game reserves or Irish republican terrorists in the back alleys and rural hamlets of Northern Ireland. In contrast to 'big wars', which involve a conventional clash between uniformed armies on a clearly demarcated battlefield, small wars are fought by states against (typically clandestine) non-state adversaries and rarely lead to a definitive knockout blow being administered by one side or the other.[4] Often, small wars degenerate into protracted conflicts that threaten to exhaust the former while emboldening the latter.

Small wars have been an integral part of British military experience for hundreds of years. Indeed, one can trace the intellectual genealogy of formal doctrine (i.e. the guide to best practice) on battling irregular opponents to the work of British warrior-scholar Colonel (later Major-General Sir) Charles Callwell. Writing amidst the nineteenth-century *fin de siècle*, which coincided with the height of Britain's imperial prowess, Callwell defined 'small wars' as a term 'simply used to denote, in default of a better, operations of regular armies against irregular, or comparatively speaking irregular, forces'.[5] Nowadays, small wars have become synonymous with insurrection and the tactics of guerrilla warfare. Interestingly, the term *guerrilla* is itself derived from the Spanish *guerra*, and translated literally means 'little war'. However, in this book the term is taken to mean more than insurgency, as not all of the irregular groups detailed here sought to overthrow an existing government.[6] This is in keeping with Callwell's use of the term, insofar as 'in small wars guerrilla operations are almost invariably a feature of some phase of the struggle'.[7] That Britain has a long and distinguished history in this type of warfare was highlighted in the work of one of the best-known theorists of war, Colonel (later Major-General) J.F.C. Fuller. Writing in the shadow of the First World War, Fuller observed how:

> We, as the inheritors of a world-wide Empire, possess an all but unlimited knowledge of the nature of small wars; we have engaged in them for over two hundred years, and throughout this long period our difficulties in winning them have been very similar.[8]

Even though the types of combat experiences shared by state forces and their irregular opponents throughout the ages may have striking similarities, the political and military dynamics underpinning these armed engagements are rarely analogous.[9] Britain's armed forces therefore have had to remain vigilant, maintaining a flexible and adaptable posture in light of extremely fluid circumstances. Moreover, they have also tended to apply a model of counter-insurgency, since the 1950s, which has evolved from imperial policing tactics employed in far-flung colonies where the co-ordination of the joint civil–military response was vitally important in combating terrorists and insurgents.[10]

While this book details some of the tactical and operational dynamics underpinning how Britain fought these small wars, it is much more concerned with the wider strategic and political context within which they have been conducted.[11] This should come as no surprise as politics has always shaped the direction war takes and the kind of peace that comes once it has ended.[12] As Thomas Schelling prudently observed, 'Small wars embody the threat of a larger war; they are not just military engagements but "crisis diplomacy" '.[13] In other words, states have surreptitiously recognized the need to marshal all available resources towards ensuring success on the broader political front, of which these armed conflicts are the most accentuated elements. Schelling, a Noble Prize-winning economist, is often credited as being one of the leading lights of strategic theory, a conceptual framework of analysis that can trace its roots to the work of Prussian general and philosopher of war Carl Von Clausewitz, who did much in his posthumous masterpiece *On War* to explain the political connotations of war.[14]

'War', as Clausewitz famously declared, 'is the clash between major interests, which is resolved by bloodshed'. Yet war is more than this, as Clausewitz went on to argue; it is 'the continuation of political intercourse, carried on with other means'.[15] Despite the latter excerpt remaining Clausewitz's best-known dictum, many commentators misleadingly employ it to imply the culminating point of departure between 'peaceful' politics and 'aggressive' war. Rarely, though, is there a linear trajectory in armed conflict, wherein political intercourse, having been exhausted, simply runs its course and war takes over as a means of reaching a more decisive outcome.[16] In the sense that it is employed here, in the sense that Clausewitz himself understood it, war is understood as a dialectical process in which 'moral factors' and 'physical ones' interact, 'each penetrating and acting upon the other'.[17] Moreover, while the objective may very well be to recalibrate the equilibrium in favour of some idea of 'peace', war is continually shaped by politics and inevitably defines the peace which follows. Clausewitz illustrated this point well:

> Politics, moreover, is the womb in which war develops – where its outlines already exist in their hidden rudimentary form, like the characteristics of living creatures in their embryos.[18]

In other words, it is politics that gives war its purpose, which shapes its character, and which sets the preconditions for its termination.[19] Put more emphatically, argues Anglo-American strategic theorist Colin S. Gray, 'War is about politics, and politics is about the distribution of power – who has how much of it, what they do with it, and what the consequences are'.[20] For hard-headed realists, including renowned British historian Correlli Barnett, '[p]eace and war in history flow continually in and out of each other, alternative aspects of the single phenomenon of the struggle for power'.[21] It is in this violent competition between belligerents – when, arguably, power is in its rawest form – that we see the political essence of war most clearly.

The central argument of *Defending the Realm?* is that the politics of Britain's small wars have been shaped by the decline of its empire amidst a fundamentally anarchic international setting and the re-distribution of power,[22] just as much by the actions of military commanders and civilian officials 'on the spot' and the politicians and their apparatchiks formulating government policy in Whitehall.[23] This observation may seem glaringly obvious, but it nonetheless demands further scrutiny, especially since it can again lead to the mistaken view that politics is in some respects disconnected from warfare. In many ways, *Defending the Realm?* takes its cue more from the work of Antoine-Henri Jomini, Clausewitz's 'contemporary and rival',[24] than from the master himself, in so far as it posits the theory prominent in Jomini's writings that the phenomenon of war can be understood as a science more than an art, a process which requires much more than blunt force trauma and blood-letting to win the clash of wills between belligerents. Warfare also involves gaining a psychological edge, claims Jomini, insofar as 'other combinations not less important are absolutely necessary in conducting a great war, but they pertain more to the government of empires than the commanding of armies'.[25] Britain's handling of its security, whether amidst the *realpolitik* of the Cold War[26] and the decolonization of its empire, or, in the post-Cold War world, which Lawrence Freedman informs us is 'no longer . . . a dialectic between imperialism and socialism, but of order and disorder',[27] was carefully choreographed and more scientific, despite campaigning being characterized as chaotic and desperate.[28] Thus, Britain's approach to its small wars paid homage to Jomini's dictum that 'it is absolutely necessary to know that science . . . consists of a mixture of politics, administration, and war'.[29] Furthermore, these wars provide us with an opportunity to examine at close quarters how Britain managed its decline from 'great power' status at the end of the Second World War to its 'middling power' status by the end of the Cold War.[30] This is especially important given the tendency to see Britain as having been successful in these small wars and insurgencies, despite its loss of relative power in the world.

A uniquely British approach?

Britain's distinctive application of force has always reflected the truism that the political class make policy decisions in the build-up to war, while soldiers design and implement the military activities that will ultimately serve the political will.[31] Even though many commentators have scrutinized the drumbeat of warfare as it gathers rhythm and pitch in Whitehall or Westminster, few have analysed how these policy 'ends' as stipulated by the government are actually accomplished on the ground when military intervention becomes unavoidable. How civilian and military leaders set out to fulfil the obligations of policy by strategizing (i.e. applying military 'ways' and 'means' in the service of 'ends'), especially in battling irregular adversaries, remains the leitmotif of this book.

Therefore, this book is concerned with explaining how the complex, dialectical relationship between civilians and military commanders played out across all of the eight cases explored. In so doing it concentrates much more on how, why and with what consequences these conflicts were fought, and whether one can discern a uniquely British strategic approach – or 'way of warfare'[32] – to explain how ends, ways and means were related to one another in the prosecution of Britain's small wars. Gray explains this process more eloquently:

> Strategy is the bridge between politics and soldiering, but it is neither of those activities. Excellence in the military arts is no guarantee of superiority in strategy, which is why even an unblemished career in tactical and then operational levels of command provides no assurance of fitness for the highest of commands, where politics and force meet.[33]

Put another way, writes Hew Strachan, '[s]trategy is therefore the product of the dialogue between politicians and soldiers, and its essence is the harmonisation of the two elements, not the subordination of one to the other'.[34] There is much in Strachan's analysis that one might agree with. An important conclusion drawn by *Defending the Realm?* is that this dialogue was fundamentally important to the shaping of British strategy during the campaigns under study. It therefore frames discussion of Britain's small wars in their correct historical context and emphasizes the personal convictions and motivations of politicians and soldiers at the sharp end, just as much as the political debates over military intervention in London. It explores the politics of withdrawal in Palestine and Aden amidst growing Soviet and American influence in the Middle East, the sometimes-uneasy civil–military relations in Kenya, the appointment of a military supremo in civilian clothes in Palestine, Malaya and Cyprus, the failure of military primacy in Northern Ireland, as well as the strategic drift in Iraq, and the search for a more realistic (and limited) strategy in Afghanistan.

Full consideration is given throughout the book to the consequences of the political constraints placed upon the military by politicians, as well as the impact of the broader international context on each of the case studies. In this Clausewitz is no less explicit in his view that 'The main lines along which military events progress, and to which they are restricted, are political lines that continue throughout the war into the subsequent peace'.[35] Based on detailed research in the historical archives and the careful collation of eyewitness testimonies from those who fought in Britain's small wars, the book weaves together the complex strands of British strategy after World War Two. Indeed, the eight case studies were chosen primarily because it is in small wars, perhaps the most political form of military activity,[36] that one can see civil–military relations at their most strained, when decisions have been taken that tell us much about the strategy being followed, if any. The book also argues that, regardless of the political complexion of the party in office, successive governments have had to take into consideration both the challenges posed by a changing security environment and the political, economic and military reality of Britain's declining power in the world.[37]

More fundamental perhaps to the safeguarding of British prestige has been the need to preserve the corporate memory of our institutions of state. Here we see the experiences and memories of individuals who became involved in these small wars colouring the ensuing dialectical process of civil–military relations. Though they might not have been the most optimal or rational ones to apply in a different context, they were purely subjective points of view that influenced actions in subsequent campaigns. The British Army, for instance, has developed its own internal intellectual and doctrinal culture to capture its varying experience in modern warfare, typically undertaking such introspection that has been occasioned by a traumatic military crisis and the subsequent cathartic experience which follows.[38] Each generation has faced new adversaries and dutifully marshalled all available economic, political, diplomatic and military resources towards mitigating the threat to our national interests. It has been argued that the Army itself leans heavily on the 'lessons identified' from its past involvement in various theatres of war;[39] however, the Army has often had to learn lessons 'on the fly' to offset humiliating defeat in the face of a much weaker enemy.[40] Indeed, the culture of learning the lessons of the 'last war' has consistently influenced Britain's military doctrine, especially since the end of the Second World War. An early example can be found in the memoirs of one of the most famous British commanders, Field-Marshal Sir Bernard Montgomery. One of the first housekeeping matters Montgomery undertook when he replaced Field-Marshal Sir Alan Brooke as Chief of the Imperial General Staff (CIGS) in 1946 was to ensure that the soldiers under his command studied the 'conception of modern war'. He argued that 'a clear doctrine [had] to be evolved from the lessons from the past and to be taught throughout the Army'.[41] However, *Defending the Realm?* argues that it is the often-skewed snapshots of what have been unique circumstances and the misapplication of lessons in another totally different set of circumstances that has increased the likelihood of strategic failure for the British Army.[42]

The process of subjecting one's strategy to scrutiny underpins the drive by senior defence practitioners in the UK to encourage innovative thinking within the military. Some senior defence professionals have openly admitted that 'Revolutions and active debate both entail friction, and it is not in our organisational culture to welcome friction. But without friction, as basic physics tells us, there is no traction.'[43] The debate over Britain's need to encourage and nurture 'a community of strategically literate officials in Whitehall'[44] is ongoing, however, and this book is a contribution to our historical understanding of this process since the end of the Second World War.

For the historian fascinated by the ebb and flow of civil–military relations one does not have to see how the 'hidden wiring' of politics has infected all aspects of war, its termination and the peace that follows. As Barnett notes, 'The incidental unpleasantness of imperial retreat, like the pains of expansion earlier, fell not on the British at home, but on the army'.[45] The historical record is besmirched with examples of politicians who are prone to forget their impulsive reliance on the military to secure strategic goals, particularly at times when frugality – rather than strategy – has dictated the direction a small war has taken. How far unity of effort has existed in terms of civil–military relations in these small wars is perhaps a moot point. Arguably, as Frank Hoffman suggests, the contribution of civil–military relations to strategic effectiveness remains an 'underdeveloped area for military historians'.[46]

Traditionally, the distribution of power in Britain, as in so many other liberal democratic states, is hierarchical and the military instrument has been, therefore, always subordinated to the policy direction of a civilian government.[47] In Samuel P. Huntington's enduring words, '[t]he military profession exists to serve the state'.[48] As the question mark in the book's title intimates, the author remains sceptical about the health of civil–military relations when too rigid a model like that suggested by either Strachan, Huntington or Hackett has been followed. The conclusions reached in *Defending the Realm?* point towards a worrying trend: that politicians and military commanders have sometimes worked towards divergent ends in securing Britain's national interests. When this has happened, the inharmonious working relationship between civilians and the military has had an injurious effect on the utility of the military instrument. Admittedly, the jury is still out on whether recent operations in Afghanistan point to a new departure in the conduct of Britain's small wars. However, a report published in July 2011 criticized the way in which politicians placed constraints on the initial deployment to Helmand.[49]

Britain's changing strategic priorities

Britain's political aims in its small wars have been largely dictated by its wider strategic priorities. At the close of the Second World War the Soviet Union had been transformed from a partner in the fight against Fascism, to a competitor, and finally to a sworn enemy in the eyes of British defence planners. Meanwhile, the United States (US) was wary of the growing threat posed by Communism and sought to check its advance by sponsoring a Marshall Aid programme for those European countries that had suffered devastation during the war and which were seeking to reconstruct their societies.[50] The Truman Doctrine saw Washington provide aid to Greece and Turkey in 1947 in order to prevent these Mediterranean countries from slipping into the Soviet orbit. It was named after President Harry S. Truman, who continued to request further financial assistance from Congress, in the main because '[t]he overriding priority was to keep the power centers of Europe and Asia outside the Soviet orbit and linked to the United States'.[51] This continued to be the case well into the 1950s; the Soviet Ambassador to the US, Nikolai Novikov, dutifully reported back to Moscow that the aim of the Truman Doctrine, 'according to its advocates is to check "communist expansion"'.[52]

Against the backdrop of the US's rising power, Britain was anxious to construct her own grand strategy in order to shield her ever more malleable power from future Soviet aggression, though this had not been given much thought during the war, something greatly 'compounded by Churchill's lack of serious consideration of postwar planning'.[53] Moreover, the Second World War had exhausted the British war chest, bleeding it to the point of bankruptcy. It had no other choice than to apply for a loan from its American allies.[54] There were other structural handicaps too, Barnett reminds us, as 'a dream turned to dank reality of a segregated, subliterate, unskilled, unhealthy and institutionalised proletariat hanging on the nipple of state maternalism'.[55] Just as Britain was adjusting to the gloom, which would characterize much of the post-war period, the Soviet Union began to make inroads into its sphere of influence, particularly in the Middle East.

Taking note of a dalliance in British strategic interests, the Soviets moved quickly to capitalize on Britain's waning influence in the Middle East. One British diplomat, Christopher Warner, 'who had been optimistic about the post-war world, now concluded that the UK had been chosen by the Soviets for a political and diplomatic onslaught'.[56] A Top Secret assessment prepared by the Security Service, MI5, acknowledged how, eight months before the end of the war:

> This increased diplomatic activity is only the outward sign of Soviet interest in Middle East affairs. Secret diplomacy, commercial dealings, and espionage, in which every Power, great or small, engages – and which are not necessarily evidence of hostile intentions or moral obliquity – all play their part in the Soviet penetration of the Middle East.[57]

Britain nonetheless continued to maintain a tenuous foothold in the Middle East beyond 1945, despite Clement Attlee's Labour government remaining fixated on presiding over imperial decline and withdrawal from the region.[58]

Senior military officers 'on the spot', such as the Chief of Staff of Middle East Land Forces Major-General Harold 'Pete' Pyman, became increasingly alarmed by the challenge posed by the Soviet Union. '[T]he plain fact today', Pyman told an audience at the Army's Staff College in Camberley, 'is that unless the BRITISH COMMONWEALTH and the UNITED STATES hold the balance . . . RUSSIAN domination will prevail in the MIDDLE EAST'.[59] This view was shared by the CIGS in London, Field-Marshal Montgomery, who had been briefed on the intensity of Soviet penetration of the region by the Foreign Office prior to a visit to Moscow in October 1946. The Middle East was close to Montgomery's heart, given his wartime successes there, and as CIGS he actively sought to check the Communist advance in the region. However, the Army hierarchy remained hamstrung by Attlee, who, in his ideological pensiveness, lost no time in reminding his Chiefs of Staff that he had 'serous misgivings about their Middle Eastern strategy, which he thought far too costly and unnecessarily provocative towards the Soviet Union'.[60]

Responsibility for Labour's foreign policy outlook rested squarely on the shoulders of Foreign Secretary Ernest Bevin, who was further constrained, in what Attlee called 'the heaviest burden', by the realities of foreign and economic affairs being closely intertwined. Attlee recognized that even a region as important to British interests as the Middle East 'presented us with a very difficult problem . . . Britain had a long connection with this region, and vital strategic interests to sustain, interests which also concerned the Commonwealth'. Somewhat evasive in his memoirs about the purpose of government policy in the Middle East, Attlee later complained only that it was Britain's 'thankless task to try to reconcile many competing interests'.[61]

Having beaten Attlee at the 1951 Westminster general election, Churchill and his team could only lament what Labour had given away when they were returned to office.[62] By now decolonization was in full swing, resulting in the US 'taking over what remained of the old imperial hegemony of the former colonial powers. In return, it did not intervene in the zone of accepted Soviet hegemony'.[63] It soon became apparent that East and West were going to great lengths to keep the Cold War from going hot. As the risk of nuclear fallout increased, particularly after the Soviet Union acquired nuclear weapons in 1949, 'both superpowers plainly abandoned war as an instrument of policy against one another', opined Eric Hobsbawm, 'since it was the equivalent of a suicide pact'.[64] While one can certainly see the attractiveness of downplaying the risk of nuclear holocaust from a position of hindsight, the prospect did loom large in the minds of many public intellectuals, politicians and military commanders at the time. Some social scientists, like sociologist C. Wright Mills, were even prone to arraign the hopelessness of it all:

> War is no longer 'a continuation of politics by other means'. No political aims can be achieved by means of it. No truly 'national interests' of any nation can be served by it. No agenda that reasonable men can 'believe in' makes the preparation for war sensible or promises to achieve peace in the world.[65]

Doom-clad warnings were also reflected in the popular culture of the 1950s and 1960s, as spy novels flooded the market and Hollywood 'B movies' encapsulated the fear instilled in many people in the West that invasion and mutually assured destruction was just around the corner. For their part, the US and Soviet governments abandoned total war in favour of war by proxy. In places as diverse as Korea and Vietnam the superpowers sought to entice subversion, espionage and the financial recompense of friendly belligerents in order to weaken broader enemies.

Meanwhile, Britain had been advocating a position of coercive diplomacy since 1952. It was that year when Queen Elizabeth II ascended the throne, the Korean War had been raging for almost two years, and Britain tested its first atomic bomb. The acquisition of nuclear weapons signalled the turn towards a radical downsizing of the armed forces, while relying heavily on new and emerging technologies, later crystallizing in Duncan Sandys' 1957 Defence White Paper. It was thought that long-range weapons with devastating firepower could substitute bases and overseas territories. Yet it could not disguise the reality of Britain's strategic impoverishment. In Barnett's caustic words, Britain was in denial:

> All this in pursuit of a Middle East strategy that only made sense if the British were still a great power in the Indian Ocean. In the 1950s and 1960s British world strategy still followed the basic patterns of the nineteenth century: a chicken that had lost its head – India – but still ran round in circles.[66]

To make matters worse, the conflagration of nationalist insurrection was now gripping Britain's colonies, in large part actively fomented by the USSR, which presented its own direct ideological threat to British values. However, the much broader confrontation between the diametrically opposed blocs of East and West meant, as Professor Michael Howard observed, was 'between two sides with incompatible visions of world order, each believing that peace could be established only by the elimination of the other'.[67] Adhering to the rationality of the bipolar system often conferred upon them by strategic thinkers, the nuclear-armed states 'neither erupted into overt war nor ended with unilateral disarmament, but . . . softened with time', argued Howard, thus facilitating, first, Cold War détente after the death of Brezhnev and, second, its long drawn-out move towards termination.[68] In the meantime, Britain chose to align herself with the US policy of anti-Communism – though not, for obvious reasons, its anti-colonialist trappings – with varying degrees of success. Here Britain sowed the seeds of the ensuing strategic eclipse that would relegate her to the role of older, wiser Greek *consigliore* to the young, impetuous Roman emperor America.

There was tension too between politicians, civil servants and military commanders, particularly in terms of colonial security. Before taking over as CIGS from Field-Marshal Sir John Harding, General Sir Gerald Templer was awarded a sabbatical by the then Minister of Defence Harold Macmillan to write a report on colonial security. Templer had been lauded for his extraordinary skill in bringing the Communist insurgency in Malaya to heel, and his confirmation as the new head of the Army marked a hiatus in colonial security for Britain. Templer summed up perfectly the problem facing British imperialism in its latent phase, when he observed how 'One is reminded, firmly and correctly, that the Governors exist to govern, that the Colonial Office does not run Colonial territories, and that their job is to advise; if necessary, to exhort; but rarely, if ever, to command'.[69] Imperial hubris, seemingly, had not yet taken hold.

The Colonial Office maintained more than a healthy scepticism of Templer's fixation with reorganizing security and intelligence machinery in Whitehall at a time when Britain faced a double-fronted assault:

> The J.I.C. has in recent years concentrated its effort on (a) the 'hot war' threat from the Sino-Soviet bloc and (b) the so-called 'cold-war' threat. (a) is no doubt essential: but (b) has been pursued and interpreted in such a way as to make the J.I.C. completely myopic, and almost to ignore the essential field of (c) political developments unconnected or only indirectly connected with the 'cold war', but vitally affecting H.M.G.'s position in the world.[70]

A collective sigh rang out as they sensed an emerging tendency amongst the military hierarchy to see the Joint Intelligence Committee (JIC) 'as an instrument primarily of the Chiefs of Staff instead of the Ministers responsible for its Charter'.[71] In an ever-changing world, the Colonial Office nevertheless remained at the epicentre of political developments, as it struggled to manage the choppy transition from Empire to Commonwealth. As Labour, no more than the Conservatives, came to realize, calls for colonial independence had to be balanced against the malign intentions of world Communism.

For former US Secretary of State Dean Acheson, Britain was experiencing something akin to strategic flux. In perhaps one of his most famous remarks on Britain's imperial decline, he argued:

> Great Britain has lost an empire and has not yet found a role. The attempt to play a separate power role – that is, a role apart from Europe, a role based on a 'special relationship' with the United States, a role based on being the head of a 'commonwealth' which has no political structure, or unity, or strength, and enjoys a fragile and precarious economic relationship by means of the Sterling area and preferences in the British market – this role is about played out. Great Britain, attempting to work alone and to be a broker between the United States and Russia, has seemed to conduct policy as weak as its military power.[72]

While there is some dispute over the extent to which Acheson's remarks actually reflected US policy at that time, he was at least being consistent with his earlier complaint that 'Britain, which once had the training and capability to manage a world system, no longer has the capability'.[73] Responding much later to Acheson's remarks, historian Niall Ferguson pointed out that '[p]erhaps the reality is that the Americans have taken our old role without yet facing the fact that an empire comes with it'.[74] Political heavyweight Denis Healey may have been closer to the mark when he said that Acheson 'misled a generation'.[75] Whatever American motivations, the eclipse of British power had begun. That

Britain was losing the ability to project its power unilaterally in the world gave sustenance to its irregular adversaries as they sought to challenge its authority. Interestingly, as Anne Deighton points out, 'The quest to sustain the image and the reality of great powerdom through leadership, influence, and "punching above our weight" was part of the mentalité of British planners, the military, and the politicians'.[76] The illusion of great power status continued to colour the strategic outlook of British elites, particularly when faced with a mosaic of armed challenges in its colonial territories.

Britain's imperial retreat was in full swing by the 1960s. However, the independence granted to Cyprus after a four-year insurgency did not mark a clean break with British intervention. In 1964 Britain deployed a peacekeeping force, which was to become one of the longest-running UN commitments since the formation of the organization in 1945. Meanwhile, the rumblings of an anti-colonial movement in Aden would soon place Britain's Middle Eastern hub in danger. Sensing a groundswell of nationalist opposition, which was armed by weapons from the Soviet-backed Yemeni government, and facing an economic squeeze at home, Britain began withdrawing from its last foothold in the Arabian Gulf. By 1968, Britain had given up its east of Suez role amidst a deteriorating security situation. Denis Healey spoke for several of his Labour ministerial colleagues when he told MPs:

> We were very conscious that in some cases our imperial history might make the presence of our forces an irritant rather than a stabilising factor, particularly in the Middle East, where the events of 1956 still cast a long shadow.[77]

Healey's determination to limit defence spending to make it more affordable was based on the notion that Britain should play a leading role in Europe, rather than continue with its limited role east of Suez. Indeed, Labour's decision to curtail Britain's power and influence in the world would have long-term strategic repercussions. During the next decade and a half, argued Michael Dockrill, 'she continue[d] to be faced with the problem of reconciling her means to her less extensive but still onerous ends'.[78]

As it transpired, the 'economic dividend' expected by Labour ministers, like Healey, did not fully materialize. Indeed, the complete disregard for rumblings closer to home placed Harold Wilson's government on the back foot. Its claims to know nothing about the ethno-national conflict underpinning Northern Ireland society, prior to the flare up of the 'troubles' in the late 1960s, rang hollow.[79] While politicians publicly expressed surprise at the violence between Protestant unionists and

Catholic nationalists, defence planners claimed to have seen it all before and that they must, therefore, relate '[a]ttitudes and actions . . . to previous experience'.[80] Consequently, the tendency was to view the domestic schism between British citizens through a colonial prism, 'which the Northern Ireland position was rapidly in danger of becoming',[81] would have profound effects on the Army's intervention in the province. In any event, cabinet ministers had to 'walk a tightrope', Barbara Castle confided in her diary, as 'nobody wanted to take over political control, with all the trouble that implies – indefinite embroilment in Northern Ireland'.[82] Strategically, as Labour's 1975 defence review made clear, the main business lay in opposing the Soviets, not in providing a limited number of troops to a gendarmerie role in Northern Ireland. For Defence Secretary Roy Mason, the review was necessary in order to 'tailor our defence commitments and capabilities to our economic and political position as a middle-rank European Power'. There was no question that this could only be done 'by realistic planning for defence in the longer term so that political and economic realities always march in step'.[83]

Though defence policy played less of a role in the 1979 election, the Conservatives were officially committed to improving the capabilities of the armed forces.[84] As Francis Pym told MPs in February 1980:

> Our present intention is not to increase at as great a rate as the Soviet Union, but to ensure that we have an adequate capability to deter aggression and to preserve peace.[85]

The North Atlantic Treaty Organization (NATO) had been concerned by the build-up of Warsaw Pact forces and sought to persuade the other members to increase their defence spending. Pym continued:

> We want to increase our defence capability throughout the Alliance, and make our contribution. The increased imbalance is of great concern. At the same time, we would be wise to remember that we cannot go faster than the strength of our economy, and that is why we cannot increase our strength as quickly as some of us would like.[86]

Defence assumptions changed again in the early 1980s as NATO set about rebalancing its nuclear capabilities. For its part, the Tories decided to press ahead with the replacement of the Polaris force with the new Trident C-4 system. Talk of the eventual rundown of regular units in Northern Ireland would allow cuts to the size and shape of the armed forces. John Nott, Secretary of State for Defence under Margaret Thatcher, informed the House of Commons that Britain's strategic outlook would maintain a balance between its maritime and central force capabilities. 'The stark choice between the two', he informed David Owen, would be 'frankly unrealistic'.[87] In any event, Nott's proposals to reduce the Navy and Royal Marines would soon suffer a strategic shock, however, when Argentinean forces invaded the Falkland Islands on 2 April 1982. For the remainder of the 1980s the armed forces remained chronically under-funded and increasingly busy, confirming that, indeed, 'the history of British defence policy', as Lawrence Freedman once suggested, 'is an attempt to reconcile the mismatch between resources and commitments'.[88]

As the Berlin Wall crumbled in 1989, ministers at the MoD were telling their generals that there would never be another armed conflict in which conventional means would be needed on any sufficient scale.[89] Within weeks the Commander of the UK's 1st Armoured Division, General Sir Rupert Smith, had been sent to the Gulf to take part in military operations to liberate Kuwait. Britain's contribution to peace-support missions continued for the remainder of the decade, with contingent forces sent to Bosnia and Kosovo. Meanwhile, the security agenda widened, to include threats and risks beyond the ideological and geographically specific conflict between West and East.

Returned to power in May 1997 the New Labour government immediately commissioned a Strategic Defence Review (SDR), which one of its main architects, George Robertson, said would 'put the foreign policy priorities of this country first and then give a sense of clarity and direction to our forces as to how their roles can be properly and economically carried out for the future of our country'.[90] The SDR reaffirmed Britain's commitments to existing strategic priorities, suggesting that it had dealt with 'tomorrow's threats, not yesterday's enemies'. Robertson informed Parliament that:

> NATO remains the basis for defence and security, but, while the threat of major war in Europe is now a remote prospect, new threats confront us: terrorism; the international drugs trade; the proliferation of nuclear, chemical and biological weapons; information warfare; ethnic rivalries; population pressures; and the break-up of existing states.[91]

Though New Labour was later attacked for not forecasting the real threat posed by transnational terrorism, there was at least an acknowledgement that the end of the Cold War had altered the strategic context significantly. Nonetheless, it was the attacks in the US by Al Qaeda on 11 September 2001 that heralded a more profound transformation in the strategic context. The return of irregular opponents to the centrifuge of the British strategic calculus had begun.

New Labour's defence policy between 1997 and 2010 was characterized by its liberal interventionist outlook. For Tony Blair and Gordon

Brown, Britain's armed forces were 'a force for good in the world' and ought to be deployed only as an option of last resort. Contrary to this proviso, however, the armed forces were used as the first port of call, especially since, in Lawrence Freedman's words, the British 'attitude to the use of armed force was more confident and assertive, as exemplified by Sierra Leone'.[92] New Labour relied heavily on bayonet-cushioned diplomacy to impose its liberal interventionist policies. The shifting international context since the end of the Cold War had been noted in the SDR, which, above all, maintained that in order to protect Britain's national interests one needed to go to the problem in order to tackle it at its root cause. As such, defence-planning assumptions reflected the preference for expeditionary warfare, with the SDR stating that in terms of 'scales of effort' Britain could either 'respond to a major international crisis which might require a military effort and combat operations of a similar scale and duration to the Gulf War' or 'undertake a more extended overseas deployment on a lesser scale (as over the last few years in Bosnia) while retaining the ability to mount a second substantial deployment'. Although, crucially, it admitted that 'We would not, however, expect both deployments to involve warfighting or to maintain them simultaneously for longer than six months'.[93] There are multiple problems with such planning assumptions, not least that they assumed, wrongly, that short-term, one-off interventions would become something of a norm in the post-Cold War global security environment. Sadly, this was to prove overly optimistic, as the British soon found in the new battlegrounds in Afghanistan and Iraq.

Success or failure in Britain's small wars?

Acclaimed military historian Sir John Keegan once observed, about British forces: '[in] none of the dozens of small wars they have fought since 1945 have they been defeated'.[94] While this is broadly correct, Keegan overlooked the fact that Britain's armed forces have not always emerged victorious from these small wars either. Andrew Mack makes the point well:

> In every case, success for the insurgents arose not from a military victory on the ground – though military successes may have been a contributory cause – but rather from the progressive attrition of their opponents' political capability to wage war. In such asymmetric conflicts, insurgents may gain political victory from a situation of military stalemate or even defeat.[95]

Indeed, in only one of the case studies examined in *Defending the Realm?* – Malaya – can Britain claim a decisive win over its irregular opponent.

Rather, one can find much evidence to account for Britain's lack of 'political capability to wage war'. Nevertheless, the reversal of fortunes in Palestine, Aden and Iraq, for instance, cannot be solely attributable to the 'wobbliness' of politicians and civilian representatives. In some respects this would be to expunge the inertia displayed at times by Britain's military commanders, who failed to grasp Clausewitz's basic dictum that war is an instrument of policy:

> The first, the supreme, the most far-reaching act of judgement that the statesman and commander have to make is to establish by that test the kind of war on which they are embarking; neither mistaking it for, nor trying to turn it into, something that is alien to its nature. That is the first of all strategic questions and the most comprehensive.[96]

Looking at the often inharmonious civil–military relations across all of the case studies considered in this book, one can see how Britain has related ways and means to achieve its ends in a strategic conundrum which it faces every time force is countenanced. This was encapsulated most aptly by Field-Marshal Sir Alan Brooke, who recommended that the 'defence potential of the country can be continually kept under review and examined so as to ensure that the resources available are employed to the best advantage'. In perhaps the most revealing reflections on Britain's strategic outlook, he made clear that 'our foreign policy bears a direct relation to the strength available to support it'.[97] The significance of Brooke's words have lost none of their conceptual insight since they were first uttered.

Notes

1 Gwynn, Charles, *Imperial Policing* (London: Macmillan, 1934), pp. 13–14.
2 Morgenthau, Hans. J., 'To Intervene or Not to Intervene', *Foreign Affairs*, Vol. 45, Nos. 1–4 (October 1966–July 1967), p. 430.
3 Ministry of Defence (MoD), *Land Operations: Volume I – The Fundamentals, Part 2 – Command and Control*, Army Code No. 70458, Part 2 (London: MoD, 28 April 1969), p. 5.
4 This is certainly a theme explored in David Kilcullen's book *The Accidental Guerrilla: Fighting Small Wars amidst a Big One* (London: Hurst, 2009), pp. 31–32, 284, 292.
5 Callwell, Colonel Charles Edward, *Small Wars: Their Principles and Practice*, third edition (London: HMSO, 1906), p. 21.
6 It is also in keeping with M.L.R. Smith's argument that 'call it what you will – new war, ethnic war, guerrilla war, low-intensity war, terrorism, or the war on terrorism – in the end, there is only one meaningful category of war, and that is war itself'. See Smith, M.L.R., 'Strategy in an Age of

"Low-Intensity Warfare: Why Clausewitz is Still More Relevant than His Critics"' in Duyvesteyn, Isabelle, and Jan Angstrom (eds) *Rethinking the Nature of War* (Abingdon: Frank Cass, 2005), p. 52.

7 Callwell, *Small Wars*, p. 127.

8 Fuller, Colonel J.F.C., *The Reformation of War* (London: Hutchinson and Company, 1923), p. 193.

9 Gray, Colin S., 'War – Continuity in Change, and Change in Continuity', *Parameters: The US Army's Senior Professional Journal*, Vol. 40, No. 1 (Summer 2010), pp. 5–13.

10 Popplewell, Richard, '"Lacking Intelligence": Some Reflections on Recent Approaches to British Counter-Insurgency, 1900–1960', *Intelligence and National Security*, Vol. 10, No. 2 (April 1995), p. 348.

11 Much of the research and writing for *Defending the Realm?* was completed prior to the publication of Benjamin Grob-Fitzgibbon's interesting book *Imperial Endgame: Britain's Dirty Wars and the End of Empire* (Basingstoke: Palgrave Macmillan, 2011), which deals with Britain's post-war conflicts in Palestine, Malaya, Kenya and Cyprus. Where *Defending the Realm?* differs from Grob-Fitzgibbon's work is not merely in the broader sweep of case studies covered but also in its focus on the overlapping theme of British strategy in the Cold War and also in exploring the perennial issue of civil–military relations from 1940s Palestine to present-day Afghanistan.

12 In tune with Gray, I have yet to be persuaded that 'peace' is anything other than an unhappy compromise between irreconcilable political positions. On the general point of peace as a political condition see Gray, Colin S., *Another Bloody Century: Future Warfare* (London: Weidenfeld and Nicolson, 2005), pp. 338, 344. For further analysis on how this has manifested itself in the fragile peace maintained in Northern Ireland see Edwards, Aaron, and Cillian McGrattan, 'Terroristic Narratives: On the (Re) Invention of Peace in Northern Ireland', *Terrorism and Political Violence*, Vol. 23, No. 3 (June 2011), pp. 357–376.

13 Schelling, Thomas C., *Arms and Influence* (New Haven, CT: Yale University Press, [1966] 2008), p. 33.

14 For more on Clausewitz's indefatigable influence in strategic studies, see Clausewitz, Carl Von, *On War*, edited and translated by Michael Howard and Peter Paret (Princeton, NJ: Princeton University Press, 1989); Paret, Peter, *Clausewitz and the State* (Oxford: Oxford University Press, 1976); Gray, Colin S., 'Clausewitz Rules, OK? The Future is the Past – with GPS', *Review of International Studies*, Vol. 25, No. 5 (December 1999), pp. 161–182; Hauser, Beatrice, *Reading Clausewitz* (London: Pimlico, 2002); Strachan, Hew, *Clausewitz's On War: A Biography* (New York: Atlantic Books, 2007).

15 Clausewitz, *On War*, p. 75.

16 This is a point made by Rupert Smith in his paradigm-rattling book *The Utility of Force: The Art of War in the Modern World* (London: Penguin, 2005), p. 181.

17 Howard, Michael, *Clausewitz* (Oxford: Oxford University Press, 1983), p. 34. The subtle, almost Hegelian temperament, of Howard's reading of Clausewitz is something the present author finds particularly prescient.
18 Clausewitz, *On War*, p. 149.
19 Ibid., p. 605. Perhaps the most pre-eminent scholar writing on Clausewitz, Peter Paret, suggested that 'The bond between his political and military writings, which assume such different forms, lies rather in their common motive – the search for understanding . . . [which] enabled him to formulate the first theory of war that looked beyond the operational to include its political and psychological aspects, and . . . all time-bound and geographic standards'. Paret, *Clausewitz and the State*, p. 440.
20 Gray, 'War – Continuity in Change, and Change in Continuity', p. 6.
21 Barnett, Correlli, *Britain and Her Army, 1509–1970: A Military, Political and Social Survey* (London: Allen Lane, 1970), p. xvii.
22 The concept of anarchy is relatively benign in the work of neo-realist scholars, such as Kenneth Waltz. See his 'International Politics is Not Foreign Policy', *Security Studies*, Vol. 6 (1996), pp. 54–57.
23 Interestingly this is the reversal of the American experience written about so convincingly by Eliot Cohen, who pointed to the interference of statesmen in the business of war, which is often considered the preserve of military commanders. See his *Supreme Command: Soldiers, Statesmen and Leadership in Wartime* (New York: Free Press, 2002). For French philosopher Raymond Aron, 'The realm of politics is the arena in which individuals or groups, each having their own policy, aims, interests, and sometimes philosophy, come to grips'. See his *Democracy and Totalitarianism*, translated by Valence Ionescu (London: Weidenfield and Nicolson, [1965] 1968), p. 4.
24 Howard, *Clausewitz*, p. 24.
25 Jomini, Baron, *Treatise on Grand Military Operations or a Critical and Military History of the Wars of Frederick the Great as Contrasted with the Modern System Together with a Few of the Most Important Principles of the Art of War* (London: Trubner and Company, 1865), p. 460.
26 As noted in the preface, this book borrows from realism, arguably the predominant theory of international relations, in analysing Britain's role in the world. On the vibrancy of realist thought see Schmidt, Brian C., 'Realism as Tragedy', *Review of International Studies*, Vol. 30 (2004), pp. 428–429.
27 On the disorder anticipated in the wake of the collapse of the Soviet Union see Freedman, Lawrence, 'Order and Disorder in the New World', *Foreign Affairs*, Vol. 71, No. 1 (1992), p. 21.
28 For more on this process see Hyam, Ronald, *Britain's Declining Empire: The Road to Decolonisation, 1918–1968* (Cambridge: Cambridge University Press, 2006).
29 Jomini, *Treatise on Grand Military Operations*, p. 461.

30 For more on Britain's decline see English, Richard, and Michael Kenny *Rethinking British Decline* (London: Macmillan, 2000) and Chalmers, Malcolm, *Rethinking British Security Policy*, RUSI Discussion Paper (London: RUSI, 14 March 2008). The inevitability of British decline has been challenged by a political theorist influenced by the work of Hedley Bull and the English school of international relations. Morris, Justin, 'How Great is Britain? Power, Responsibility and Britain's Future Global Role', *British Journal of Politics and International Relations*, Vol. 13 , No. 3 (August 2011), 326–347.

31 For more on this point see Huntington, Samuel P., *The Soldier and the State: The Theory and Practice of Civil-Military Relations* (Cambridge, MA: Harvard University Press, [1957] 1985).

32 McInnes, Colin, *Hot War, Cold War: The British Army's Way in Warfare, 1945–95* (London: Brassey's, 1996).

33 Gray, Colin S., *Explorations in Strategy* (Westport, CT: Greenwood Press, 1996), p. 236. Strachan, Hew, 'Making Strategy: Civil-Military Relations after Iraq', *Survival*, Vol. 48, No. 3 (autumn 2006), p. 67.

34 Strachan, Hew, 'Making Strategy: Civil-Military Relations after Iraq', *Survival*, Vol. 48, No. 3 (autumn 2006), p. 67.

35 Clausewitz, *On War*, p. 605.

36 Many of the ideas on Britain's approach to coordinating civil–military machinery can be found in Kitson, Frank, *Bunch of Five* (London: Faber, 1977), p. 283.

37 Similar arguments have been advanced before, of course. See Pickering, Jeffrey, *Britain's Withdrawal from East of Suez: The Politics of Retrenchment* (Basingstoke: Macmillan, 1998), p. 177.

38 See Edwards, Aaron, 'Misapplying Lessons Learned? Analysing the Utility of British Counter-Insurgency Strategy in Northern Ireland, 1971–76', *Small Wars and Insurgencies*, Vol. 21, No. 2 (June 2010), pp. 303–330; Marston, Daniel, ' "Smug and Complacent?" Operation TELIC: The Need for Critical Analysis', *Australian Army Journal*, Vol. 6, No. 3 (summer 2009), pp. 165–180; Alderson, Colonel Alexander, *The Validity of British Army Counterinsugency Doctrine after the War in Iraq 2003–2009* (Cranfield: unpublished PhD thesis, November 2009); Ucko, David H., 'Lessons from Basra: The Future of British Counter-Insurgency', *Survival*, Vol. 52, No. 4 (August–September 2010), pp. 131–158. In contrast to the British approach of capturing lessons after a failure in military campaigning, it has been argued that the United States Army has avoided taking stock of its mistakes, particularly in the wake of the disastrous policy in Vietnam. See Nagl, John, *Learning to Eat Soup with a Knife: Counterinsurgency Lessons from Malaya and Vietnam* (Chicago, IL: University of Chicago Press, 2005).

39 For more on this process see Alderson, Alexander, 'Revising the British Army's Counter-Insurgency Doctrine', *The Royal United Services Institute Journal*, Vol. 152, No. 4 (August 2007), pp. 6–11.

40 The notion of 'learning on the fly' in modern interventions in Iraq and Afghanistan was coined by David Kilcullen in his book *The Accidental Guerrilla*.
41 Law, Bernard, Viscount Montgomery of Alamein, *The Memoirs of Field-Marshal the Viscount Montgomery of Alamein, KG* (London: Collins, 1958), p. 433.
42 A similar argument has been advanced by Douglas Porch in a recent article, 'The Dangerous Myths and Dubious Promise of COIN', *Small Wars and Insurgencies*, Vol. 22, No. 2 (May 2011), pp. 239–257.
43 Newton, Paul, Paul Colley and Andrew Sharpe, 'Reclaiming the Art of British Strategic Thinking', *RUSI Journal*, Vol. 155, No. 1 (February 2010), p. 49.
44 House of Commons Public Affairs Committee, *Who Does UK National Strategy?*, First Report of Session, 2010–11, HC 435 (London: TSO, 18 October 2010), p. 26.
45 Barnett, *Britain and Her Army*, p. 482.
46 Hoffman, Francis G., 'History and Future of Civil-Military Relations: Bridging the Gaps' in Murray, Williamson, and Richard Hart Sinnreich (eds) *The Past as Prologue: The Importance of History to the Military Profession* (Cambridge: Cambridge University Press, 2006), p. 250.
47 For more on this point see Hackett, General Sir John, *The Profession of Arms* (London: Sidgwick and Jackson, 1983), p. 174.
48 Huntington, *The Soldier and the State*, p. 73.
49 House of Commons Defence Committee, *Operations in Afghanistan*, Fourth Report of Session 2010–12, HC 554 (London: TSO, 17 July 2011), p. 24.
50 As Raymond Aron informs us, 'Dollars were undoubtedly used as a weapon against Communism and as an instrument in the policy of containment'. See his *The Imperial Republic: The United States and the World, 1945–1973*, translated by Frank Jellinek (London: Weidenfeld and Nicolson, 1973), p. 32.
51 Leffler, Melvyn P., 'The Emergence of American Grand Strategy, 1945–1952' in Leffler, Melvyn P. and Odd Arne Westad (eds) *The Cambridge History of the Cold War*, Volume 1: *Origins* (Cambridge: Cambridge University Press, 2010), p. 77.
52 *Arkhiv vneshnei polititiki Rossiikskoi Federatsii*, f. 489, op. 24"g", d. 1, p. 19, 1. 150. Cited in Narinsky, Mikhail, 'Soviet Foreign Policy and the Origins of the Cold War' in Gorodetsky, Gabriel (ed.) *Soviet Foreign Policy, 1917–1991: A Retrospective* (London: Frank Cass, 1994), p. 107.
53 Anne Deighton, 'Britain and the Cold War, 1945–1955' in Leffler and Westad (eds) *The Cambridge History of the Cold War*, p. 116.
54 Fraser, T.G., and Donette Murray, *America and the World since 1945* (Basingstoke: Palgrave Macmillan, 2002), p. 11.
55 Barnett, Correlli, *The Audit of War: The Illusion and Reality of Britain as a Great Nation* (London: Macmillan, 1986), p. 304.

56 Deighton, 'Britain and the Cold War', p. 119.
57 Ibid., p. 119.
58 The international policy pursued by Attlee's government can best be summed up as follows: 'In the field of Foreign Policy, in our relations with our fellow subjects in the Commonwealth and Empire and on the home front we have been guided by the principles of democratic socialism in which we believe.' Oxford University, Bodleian Library Special Collections (BLSC), *Clement Attlee Papers*, MS. Attlee Dep. 36, Fol. 65. 'Prime Minister's Speech to Delegates of the Northern Region Labour Party at Newcastle, 27 April 1946'.
59 King's College London, Liddell Hart Centre for Military Archives (LHCMA), Sir Harold English Pyman Papers, 7/1/4, 'Top Secret: Imperial Defence College Visit – Middle East Strategy' (n.d. June 1948?).
60 Kitchen, Martin, 'British Policy Towards the Soviet Union, 1945–1948' in Gorodetsky, Gabriel (ed.) *Soviet Foreign Policy, 1917–1991: A Retrospective* (London: Frank Cass, 1994), p. 124.
61 Attlee, Clement, *As it Happened* (London: William Heinemann, 1954), p. 174.
62 Attlee's successor as leader of the Labour Party, Hugh Gaitskell, later admitted to an audience at Harvard University in the United States that 'as a serious, realistic policy for Britain, "colonialism" is dead and can never be revived'. Gaitskell, Hugh, *The Challenge of Co-Existence: The Godkin Lectures, Harvard University* (London: Methuen, 1957), p. 95.
63 Hobsbawm, *The Age of Extremes*, p. 226.
64 Ibid., p. 229.
65 Ibid.
66 Barnett, *Britain and Her Army*, p. 481.
67 Howard, Michael, *The Invention of Peace: Reflections on War and International Order* (London: Profile Books, 2000), p. 76. A more nuanced interpretation of the Soviet conception of war and peace is provided by Peter Vigor, who argues that 'The Soviet Union will resort to peace with the capitalist countries either when, for one reason or another, an open struggle seems likely to be unprofitable; or when it has become desirable for the Soviet Union to break off a struggle in which she is already engaged, and to use the resulting "peace" as an opportunity to regroup, replenish and reinforce her armies'. Vigor, P.H., *The Soviet View of War, Peace and Neutrality* (London: Routledge and Kegan Paul, 1975), p. 196. This is in keeping with the Clausewitzian view that belligerents often remain locked in mortal combat with one another until one completely disappears.
68 Howard, *The Invention of Peace*, pp. 81–82.
69 Imperial War Museum, London, Department of Documents (IWM), General Sir George Erskine Papers, 75/134/4, Templer, General Sir Gerald *Secret: Report on Colonial Security, 23 April 1955*, p. 10.

70 Ibid.
71 The National Archives, Kew, London (TNA), CO 1035/1, Templer Report: Intelligence and Security Aspects, Committee on Security in the Colonies: Brief on Membership of the Joint Intelligence Staff, 1956.
72 Acheson, Dean, 'Our Atlantic Alliance: The Political and Economic Strands', speech delivered at the United States Military Academy, West Point, New York, 5 December 1962. Cited in Brinkley, Douglas, '"Dean Acheson and the Special Relationship": The West Point Speech of December 1962', *The Historical Journal*, Vol. 33, No. 3 (September 1990), pp. 599–608.
73 Acheson, Dean, *Power and Diplomacy: The William L. Clayton Lectures on International Economic Affairs and Foreign Policy* (Cambridge, MA: Harvard University Press, 1958), p. 6.
74 Ferguson, Niall, *Empire: How Britain Made the Modern World* (London: Penguin, 2003), p. 381.
75 Healey, Denis, *The Time of My Life* (London: Penguin, 1990), pp. 232–233.
76 Deighton, 'Britain and the Cold War', pp. 113–114.
77 House of Commons Debates (Hansard), 25 January 1968, Vol. 757, Col. 622.
78 Dockrill, Michael, *British Defence Since 1945* (Oxford: Blackwell, 1989), p. 98.
79 Edwards, Aaron, 'Social Democracy and Partition: The British Labour Party and Northern Ireland, 1951–64', *Journal of Contemporary History*, Vol. 42, No. 4 (October 2007), pp. 595–612.
80 Liddell-Hart Centre for Military Archives, King's College London (LHCMA), Sir Frank Cooper Papers, Cooper 5/1/3, 'Talk at Wilton Park, 18 July 1975'.
81 Wilson, Harold, *The Labour Government, 1964–1970: A Personal Record* (London: Weidenfeld and Nicolson, 1971), p. 696.
82 Castle, Barbara, *The Castle Diaries, 1964–70* (London: Weidenfeld and Nicolson, 1984), p. 701.
83 House of Commons Debates (Hansard), 6 May 1975, Vol. 891, Col. 1228.
84 Dorman, Andrew, 'Viewpoint – The Nott Review: Dispelling the Myths?', *Defence Studies*, Vol. 1, No. 3 (2001), p. 114.
85 House of Commons Debates (Hansard), 12 February 1980, Vol. 968, Col. 1252.
86 Ibid., Col. 1254.
87 House of Commons Debates (Hansard), 20 January 1981, Vol. 997, Col. 155.
88 Freedman, Lawrence, *The Politics of British Defence, 1979–98* (Basingstoke: Macmillan, 1999), p. 81.
89 Interview with General Sir Roger Wheeler, London, 23 February 2011.
90 House of Commons Debates (Hansard), 16 June 1997, Vol. 296, Col. 10.
91 House of Commons Debates (Hansard), 8 July 1998, Vol. 315, Col. 1073.

92 Freedman, Lawrence, 'Britain at War: From The Falklands to Iraq', *RUSI Journal*, Vol. 151, No. 1 (February 2006), p. 13.
93 MoD, *Strategic Defence Review*, Cm. 3999 (London: MoD, 1998), para 89.
94 Keegan, John, *The Iraq War* (London: Hutchinson, 2004), p. 165.
95 Mack, Andrew, 'Why Big Nations Lose Small Wars: The Politics of Asymmetric Conflict', *World Politics*, Vol. 27, No. 2 (January 1975), p. 177.
96 Clausewitz, *On War*, pp. 88–89.
97 LHCMA, Field-Marshal Lord Alanbrooke Papers, 9/1/5, speech to the Royal Empire Society on 6 November 1946 entitled 'Empire Defence'.

1

Drawing lines in the sand: evacuation from Palestine

> The British Government has declared open war on the Jewish people and its struggle for liberation. The Jewish Resistance Movement – the fighting Jewish people – will not submit.[1]

> On a Battalion level no officer or other rank should ever be allowed to negotiate with a civilian on matters of security, other than through the medium of a bullet. This was probably one of the most important lessons learnt in Palestine.[2]

> A political decision was needed in Palestine. What that decision should have been was not my business. But infirmity of purpose in Whitehall, and the lack of a clear political policy, resulted in the death of many young British soldiers; it was against those things that I fought. There is much to be learnt from a study of how the problem was handled by the Labour Government of that day – chiefly how *not* to handle such matters.[3]

Introduction

Britain was handed the Mandate for the former Ottoman territories of Iraq, Palestine and what became Transjordan by the League of Nations at the San Remo conference in 1920. The terms of the Mandate were officially agreed by Lloyd George's government in London in 1922. In Iraq, Britain administered the territory according to a treaty signed the same year, which created the 'fiction' that both were sovereign states.[4] Meanwhile in Palestine, under the terms and conditions of the Mandate, Britain was obliged to recognize the Jewish agency as 'a public body for the purpose of advising and co-operating with the Administration of Palestine in such economic, social and other matters as may affect the establishment of the Jewish national home and the interests of the Jewish population in Palestine'. The wording of the agreement was based on an earlier commitment by the British Government in the Balfour Declaration (1917), which envisaged 'the establishment in Palestine of a National Home for the Jewish people . . . it being clearly understood that nothing shall be done which may prejudice the civil and religious rights of existing non-Jewish communities in Palestine'.[5] The Balfour Declaration emerged amidst Britain's military campaigns against the Ottoman Empire in the Middle East during the First World War when, according to historian Tom Fraser, 'desperate to grasp at anything',[6] the British sought to reassure their Jewish allies that their support in the war effort would secure them favourable terms in peacetime.

Meanwhile, assurances had also been given to the Arabs. In 1917 the adventurer, expert linguist and eccentric British army officer T.E. Lawrence assisted in a successful revolt against the Ottoman Empire, which culminated in General Allenby's eventual capture of Jerusalem at the end of 1917. Reflecting on his own personal involvement in the Arab revolt several years later, Lawrence recalled how he faced a daily, uphill struggle in explaining British policy towards his Arab allies. Somewhat exasperatedly he mused:

> The war for me held a struggle to side-track thought, to get into the people's attitude of accepting the revolt naturally and trustingly. I had to persuade myself that the British Government could really keep the spirit of its promises.[7]

Lawrence's hopes were soon dashed. The British government had whipped up a potent feeling of Arab nationalism, which, although embryonic, would subsequently become one of the dominant ideological forces of the twentieth century. It was Britain's inability to keep its promises to either Arab or Jew which would hasten its inglorious withdrawal from Palestine in 1948 and severely damage its national interests in the Middle East. In fact it had created a paradoxical situation, largely because its policy was ad hoc and opportunistic.

Britain's experience in Palestine during the 1920s and 1930s was marred by deep antagonism between Arab and Jew, and hostility from within both communities towards the Mandatory Power. The rise of National Socialism in Germany from 1933 onwards quickened the influx of thousands more European Jews to Palestine, who by now had come to claim it as their spiritual homeland. The Jewish population more than doubled, rising from 175,000 in 1931 to 460,000 in 1939.[8] Feeling that their position was under threat, Arabs rose up and large-scale troubles broke out in 1936. Military reinforcements soon arrived and the rebellion was swiftly put down. A Royal Commission was established and visited Palestine to investigate the circumstances prompting the rebellion. In 1937 the Commission recommended partitioning the territory into two separate Jewish and Arab states.[9] Arab resentment at the British boiled over yet again into violence. It was another two years before the back of the insurgency was finally broken. Interestingly, British policy was criticized for adopting a more pro-Arab character. The gathering storm over Palestine, kept in check somewhat by the outbreak of the Second World War, soon broke as Arab and Jew turned to violence in order to attempt to settle their differences decisively. Britain had tried unsuccessfully to maintain an impartial stance but would soon find itself embroiled in a three-way conflict that threatened to tie it down for the foreseeable future.

Britain's Middle Eastern presence

On 22 March 1945 representatives from seven Arab states – Egypt, Iraq, Transjordan, Saudi Arabia, Syria, the Lebanon and Yemen – signed a pact establishing the Arab League. The key principles underpinning this new venture included 'the strengthening of friendship between the members, the co-ordination of their political action, and the safeguarding of their independence'.[10] The diplomatic overtures of the Arab League were of primary concern to Britain, particularly since the Labour government remained to be persuaded by the benefits of maintaining a strategic foothold in the region.[11]

While the cabinet remained divided on the issue of Britain's continuing involvement in the Middle East, *The Times* lost no time in extolling the virtues of the key role played by the British in maintaining the freedom of North Africa and Middle East during the Second World War. Its editorial suggested that the war 'has shown once again that no system of international security can be effective unless it embraces the Middle East. This area controls land, sea and air communications between the Mediterranean and Indian Ocean zones; and an aggressor who seizes it has both at his discretion.'[12] Importantly, the Middle East was the gateway for the safeguarding of British interests east of Suez.[13] British policy towards Palestine at this time, therefore, must be seen in the wider context of Britain's Cold War strategy, particularly in the Middle East. For the most part, politicians and high-ranking military officers tended to place varying degrees of emphasis on the course of action to be taken to counter-balance Soviet influence in the region. The latter saw their involvement in the region as a means to an end, in securing 'Oil in Iran, Iraq and Saudi Arabia and airports in North Africa',[14] while the former saw the only possible gains to be made by disengaging to avoid conflict.

The incoming Labour Prime Minister Clement Attlee faced a difficult juggling act: how to reconcile the wishes of the Arabs and Jews with Britain's own national interests. On the one hand, he was confronted with an animated pro-Zionist cadre among his senior ministers, such as Chancellor of the Exchequer Hugh Dalton and Deputy Prime Minister Herbert Morrison. On the other hand he had to deal with Jews fired up by Zionist zeal and who wished to establish a homeland in Palestine at all costs.[15] With the influx of Jewish immigrants after the war, the desire to construct a state aloft this sacred ground in Palestine intensified. Letters filled Attlee's in-tray on a daily basis from the Jewish Agency and other influential lobbyists. In one memorandum passed to the Colonial Office by Lord Rothschild,[16] the Anglo-Jewish businessman, lobbyist and peer recalled how several members of his family had visited the refugees on Cyprus and in Palestine. Their immediate concern was to seek an improvement in the living conditions of those refugees who had been liberated from the Nazi death camps. He impressed upon Attlee how:

> With few exceptions these Jews are intensely desirous of immigrating to some place where they can forget what they have been through. They turn to Palestine. Whether or not they will be allowed to enter Palestine is not known, but the whole problem hinges on the decision of the British Government to increase the quota of the Immigration certificates.[17]

Letters from prominent Jewish figures, like the Rothschilds, sought to apply pressure on the Labour government to lift the cap in the number of immigrants allowed into Palestine. They were not alone. Several influential members of the Parliamentary Labour Party and elected officials in the US sought to exert pressure on Attlee for more favourable terms for Jewish refugees.

In a rather embittered critique of what he saw as the ineptitude of current British policy towards Palestine, the Chairman of Labour's National Executive Committee (NEC), a professor of political science at the London School of Economics, Harold Laski, attacked the government's stance:

> The British Government ought to explain the weakness displayed – it has not explained it – to that dubious gangster the Mufti, and why, whilst the Anglo-American Commission was sitting, it thought fit suddenly to transform Transjordan into an independent state. It ought also to prohibit Brigadier Glubb, and similar advisers, from making pronouncements on British policy. Policymaking is the business, under the Cabinet, of the Colonial Secretary, and not of officers anxious to be regarded as the T.E. Lawrences of this generation.[18]

Laski and other pro-Zionist members of the NEC continued to lobby the government for 'a more advanced policy', but were disappointed when none was forthcoming.[19] In a far-ranging speech about Britain's policy towards Palestine at Lancaster House, Attlee impressed upon his audience how 'anything that affects the Arab peoples is a matter of interest to the British people and in the same way the destiny of Britain is, I believe, a matter of importance to the Arabs. We are associated in a natural partnership.' Attlee hoped that 'by frankly explaining our difficulties to one another and searching together for a solution [can be found] to which you and we can honourably agree'.[20]

Apart from the Labour government's steadfast commitment capping the number of Jewish immigrants entering Palestine, Britain lacked a convincing strategy. This was exposed by Jewish terrorists in the Mandatory territory itself, who accused Attlee's government of pursuing a policy of 'unparalleled callousness in trying to obstruct this work of rescue'. Ominously, they signed off on their statements by reminding London that '[t]he present bitter conflict is not of our making. We have been forced into it by the British Government.'[21] It was in the war of words that conditions were created within which Jewish insurgency and terrorism soon thrived, and which would ultimately shatter Britain's political will to remain in Palestine.

The rise of Jewish terrorism

A determination amongst both Arab and Jew to oppose British policy by force of arms had existed in Palestine for some time. The Army had earlier been dispatched to assist the Mandatory Power in quelling an Arab rebellion in the 1930s and again in the aftermath of the Second World War. Major (later Major-General) Charles Dunbar, who served with the 8 Para garrison in Tel Aviv in 1945, remarked how his battle-hardened soldiers found a worthy opponent in 'the Jews, especially the IZL [Irgun Zvai Leumi], who proved the bravest and most cunning guerrilla fighters I have ever met'.[22] Dunbar was almost in awe of his enemy, recalling how he admired their dedication and resilience. In his view it was 'a period of great alertness and constant vigilance' in which [w]e learned much about the techniques of IS [Internal Security], notably patrolling, the detection of mines and booby traps, self preservation and moral dominance'.[23] British units found themselves up against a determined enemy who would happily exploit any weakness or lack of imagination on the part of the Mandatory authorities. It soon became apparent that the British were 'at a loss to counter the insurgency'.[24] Dunbar's proficiency of British tactics, however, could not mask the growing friction developing in civil–military relations.

Unsurprisingly, the number of attacks by Jewish armed groups increased in the first few months of 1946. As Benjamin Grob-Fitzgibbon reminds us, despite the aggression, 'the security forces were, to a certain extent, restrained by government policy'.[25] Senior military officers were annoyed by the sluggish guidance being given from the political authorities in London. In many ways, the lack of direction had more to do with London's structural weaknesses, including the over-reliance on the advice from the senior civilian representative – the proverbial 'man on the spot' – than with any deliberate policy in Downing Street. As a result, although 'perceptive and well meaning',[26] the High Commissioner and Commander-in-Chief, General Sir Alan Cunningham, was an easy scapegoat. The truth was that the patent lack of strategic direction from London made matters worse and the whole campaign was at risk of being defined solely by the desperation with which British forces sought out their elusive and ruthless enemy, who seemed to blend seamlessly into the background. Indeed, it was the uncooperative attitude of the vast majority of the Yishuv which, in Cunningham's mind, gave rise to

> a situation in which a policeman is shot and lies wounded in the street beside a bus queue, no member of which will lift a finger to help him. The task of the security forces is made immeasurably more difficult by this attitude and by the impression which exists in the Jewish community that crime of this nature can somehow be eradicated without recourse to the police.[27]

Tensions between the British Army and Jewish insurgents soon boiled over in the wake of the murder of seven soldiers from the 5th Scottish Parachute Battalion in Tel Aviv on 25 April 1946. Nevertheless, the government 'continued to counsel restraint'.[28] Comrades of the dead soldiers took matters into their own hands and mutinied in Qastine Army camp, Tel Aviv. Dunbar later recalled how this 'was clearly an indication of the beginning of the soldiers' frustration against a series of political decisions which they knew instinctively were wrong and which resulted particularly through the policy of preventing Jewish immigrants . . . from entering Palestine'.[29] Although promptly brought under control by officers and NCOs, the episode flagged up the poor state of civil–military relations at the time.

Ernest Bevin, however, was uncomfortable with the rancour now evident within military ranks. The powerful Foreign Secretary chose to reassure the Labour Party, British troops and public opinion that the government had arrived at a policy, and it would now unfold in three phases:

> (1) to consult with the Arabs in order to arrange that in the interim there should be no interruption of Jewish immigration at the existing monthly rate; (2) after considering the ad interim arrangements of the Anglo-America Committee to explore, with the parties concerned, the possibilities of some temporary arrangements; and (3) to prepare a permanent solution for submission to the United Nations, and, if possible, an agreed one.[30]

It was aspiration, certainly, and the outgoing Chief of the Imperial General Staff (CIGS), Sir Alan Brooke, recommended that the troops be given a freer hand. Attlee was more circumspect and 'counselled restraint'.[31]

Responding, somewhat belatedly, to the murder of the British soldiers and the widespread destruction caused by the Hagana and Stern Gang in the first quarter of the year, Attlee gave the green light for Operation Agatha, which ran from 29 June until 1 July 1946. Its principal objectives were:

1. The occupation and search of the Jewish Agency.
2. The arrest of persons believed to have been implicated in recent terrorist activities.
3. The occupation and search of suspected headquarters and illegal armed organisations in Tel Aviv.
4. The arrest of members of the illegal armed organisation 'PALMACH'.[32]

Cunningham's General Officer Commanding (GOC), General Sir Evelyn Barker, presided over these renewed military operations. Jewish militant leader Menachem Begin was later to concede how Barker's move to clamp down on the Jewish Agency's headquarters had been 'very severe' and that '[d]efeatism raised its deathly head. People began to question our ability to fight the British regime.' Forced into a corner, the insurgents had little option other than undertaking 'a counter-attack in reply to Barker's heavy blows'.[33] Some 2,800 Jews had been detained in Haifa, Jerusalem and other towns across Palestine.[34] Hostility towards the British from within the Jewish community intensified in the wake of Operation Agatha, and the security situation deteriorated.

Sir Winston Churchill, who was by now Leader of the Opposition, wrote to Attlee upon completion of Operation Agatha to express his private thoughts on the troubles in Palestine:

> I should however like to make my position clear to you. Terrorism is no solution for the Palestine problem. Yielding to terrorism would be a disaster. At the same time I hold myself bound by our national pledges, into which I personally and you also and your Party have entered, namely the

> establishment of a Jewish National Home in Palestine, with immigration up to the limit of 'absorptive capacity', of which the Mandatory Power is the judge. I might hope we should agree upon this.[35]

Interestingly, Churchill, a known Zionist sympathizer, went some way towards recommending to Attlee that he should consider supporting the option of partition as a viable means of dealing with the warring factions. As the former Prime Minister noted, '[s]everal of my friends are far from abandoning Partition, and I am very much inclined to think this may be the sole solution'.[36] Responding to press attention on 1 July, Attlee said that, 'after consultation with the civil and military authorities in Palestine, His Majesty's Government authorised the High Commissioner to take all necessary steps to restore order and to break up the illegal organisations, including the arrest of individuals believed to be responsible for the present campaign of violence'.[37] He stressed the government's determination to oppose 'any attempts by any party to influence a decision in the Palestine question by force'.[38]

Jewish armed groups fed on the growing alienation and indifference towards the British. The three main groups were the Irgun Zvai Leumi (IZL), Hagana (meaning 'defence') and the Lohamei Herut Israel (LEHI, also known as Stern Group or by the British as the 'Stern Gang'). The Hagana was an illegal military force directed and financed by the Jewish Agency. Its remit was to protect Jewish settlements and to ensure the safe passage of Jews into Palestine. British military intelligence knew it was 'organised on a territorial basis', though its Palmach offshoot was more of a 'mobile striking force of "regular" troops liable to be stationed in any part of the country'.[39] The Irgun was much more of an irregular organization, while the Stern Gang, according to one intelligence officer, operated in 'cells, normally on a basis of threes, and in operations it would be most unusual for any member to know more than a handful of his colleagues. That is why they usually work in small numbers.'[40] While the broad outlines of the groups' ambitions and organization were known to British forces, specific intelligence about operations was less easy to come by. This was proven on 22 July 1946, when the Irgun bombed the King David Hotel in Jerusalem, which housed the Mandatory Power's administrative headquarters; 92 people were killed and 69 injured in the explosion.[41] As 'the dust settled from the King David Hotel bombing', writes Grob-Fitzgibbon, 'the summer in Palestine passed into autumn in a quieter manner'.[42]

In the weeks after the King David Hotel bombing, Cunningham drew heavy criticism from the military hierarchy in London, particularly from the CIGS, Field-Marshal Sir Bernard Montgomery, who privately berated him for his lacklustre performance as High Commissioner. Montgomery, in the eyes of one of those who served under him at El Alamein, 'was not a convivial man but he was a ready man, with a sharp eye and a sharp tongue, and he certainly made himself known'.[43] These were traits, he himself later admitted in his memoirs,[44] which would lead him into direct conflict with the Labour government over the issue of Palestine. His biographer Nigel Hamilton wrote of the Field-Marshal, 'Monty, zealous, irrepressible and even dangerous in his innocence about politics and diplomacy', had a tendency to rush 'foolishly in, determined to be the Commander-in-Chief towards who all soldiers looked for leadership, as well as a Chief of Staff capable of clarifying and directing Britain's military strategy'.[45] As Montgomery confided in an ill-tempered letter to the Colonial Office, 'We require there a man who has a firm and robust mentality, who knows what he wants, who will stand no nonsense, and who has the character to inspire confidence in others'. Complaining bitterly that 'the present High Commissioner had simply not cut the mustard', he continued, 'I don't know if you are aware of the fact that Cunningham was removed from command of the Eighth Army in the middle of a battle because he was quite unable to make up his mind what to do. That is not the sort of man we want in Palestine today.' Seeking to remedy the situation, Montgomery asked rhetorically, 'Do you really want a soldier as High Commissioner?' In his opinion, for he had a few, the 'whole matter seems to me to be getting very political. Would not a good civilian, who understands the political side of the game, be far better? However that is not my business.'[46] Given Montgomery's penchant for intrigue and his obvious position as Cunningham's superior, it is little wonder that the embattled High Commissioner relinquished his responsibilities as Commander-in-Chief in October 1946.

Political decision-making seemed to have stalled in London, leaving Cunningham exceedingly exposed in Jerusalem. That little progress had been made on either the political or diplomatic fronts did not deter Barker from flooding districts with greater troop numbers. Much later the historian Chaim Herzog claimed emphatically that a more 'formidable' Jewish resistance had occasioned the increase in Britain's military presence.[47] In its handling of the whole affair, the Labour Party did little to challenge that perception.

Labour's dilemma

Opening a two-day debate on Palestine in the wake of the King David Hotel bombing, the pro-Zionist Deputy Prime Minister Herbert

Morrison told Parliament how he '[d]eplored the fact that some of the victims of Hitler had carried away from the European ghettos the evils of intolerance, racial pride, intimidation, terrorism, and the worship of force'.[48] Morrison's ill-tempered comments exposed once again the fault-lines in Labour's internal policy. Arguably, what now united most Labour Party members on the issue was the urgent need to terminate the Mandate. Like the question of Indian independence, the Labour government had, at least in Attlee's eyes, 'to deal with a situation which we have inherited from our predecessors'.[49] One might have thought that British Labour, having both Arab and Jewish sympathizers in its ranks, would be in an opportune position to exert pressure on both sides of the dispute. Nevertheless, the differences of opinion undermined a unified approach and led some party members, like arch-critic of official government policy Richard Crossman, to articulate the view that Britain should now adopt a more pragmatic stance, not only towards Palestine but in colonial and foreign policy matters more widely:

> If she was to avoid the fate of France, she must evolve a foreign policy commensurate with her resources. To hold onto everything would be to lose everything. But equally to throw in her imperial responsibilities would be to create a most dangerous vacuum in the world balance of power.[50]

Crossman had previously served as Bevin's nominee on the Anglo-American Committee of Inquiry into the Problems of European Jewry and Palestine, which recommended that the Mandatory authorities admit of a further 100,000 Jewish refugees in April 1946. His comments angered Bevin, and the two men frequently clashed on the issue.[51] Labour's disquiet over Palestine may not have advanced her interests much, but it did unify and hearten Britain's enemies in the Soviet Union.

A top-secret Security Service assessment of Soviet influence in the Middle East concluded at the time:

> Although it now appears that Russia will in the long run support the Arabs in Palestine it is quite clear that at present the main object of Russian policy is to secure the withdrawal of the British.[52]

An earlier report had already warned the government that this was a sure sign of growing Soviet influence in the region:

> This increased diplomatic activity is only the outward sign of Soviet interest in Middle East affairs. Secret diplomacy, commercial dealings, and espionage, in which every Power, great or small, engages – and which are not necessarily evidence of hostile intentions or moral obliquity – all play their part in the Soviet penetration of the Middle East.[53]

The strategic balance in the Middle East served to colour British military thinking at the time, though it was not a sentiment shared by Attlee, who thought the region too politically combustible. Consequently, he avoided having to take any responsibility for the problem, leaving questions of diplomacy to Bevin, much to the chagrin of Army officers looking for clear Prime Ministerial guidance.

Montgomery again made representations to Attlee and the Cabinet, in which he urged more decisive action against the Jewish insurgents. The failure of the Jewish Agency to curb the terrorism of its dissidents in LEHI and Irgun, in the CIGS's opinion, bankrupted Cunningham's faulty approach. As a result of Montgomery's intervention, Operation Polly was approved; families and non-essential personnel were evacuated from Palestine and the authorities placed themselves on a 'war footing'.[54] Attlee was growing tired of the escalating violence. But no political formula had yet presented itself in order to facilitate disengagement. Colonial Secretary Arthur Creech Jones was left little choice than to pledge the government's full backing for the CIGS and GOC in their handling of ongoing military operations: 'His Majesty's Government will continue to give their unreserved support to the Palestine civil and military authorities in applying all possible measures for bringing a speedy end to these despicable evils.'[55] Having deliberated on the Anglo-American Commission's report, and recognizing that they 'had no power under the terms of the Mandate to award the country either to the Arabs or to the Jews or even to partition it between them',[56] the Labour government decided that the only real option open to them was to refer the matter of a solution to the 'Palestine problem' to the United Nations (UN), which Bevin eventually did in February 1947.

Meanwhile, on the ground, military operations took a more aggressive turn, due in large part to political complacency. Though garnering some success, 'the Zionist underground still held the initiative, choosing where and when to strike' mainly because of the continuing dearth of intelligence, which hampered more decisive counter-measures against the armed groups. After a bomb attack by the Irgun on the Goldsmith Officers' Club in Jerusalem, in which twelve soldiers were killed, Cunningham and his new GOC, Sir Gordon MacMillan,[57] imposed martial law on parts of Jerusalem and Tel Aviv on 2 March 1947. The large-scale cordon and search operation was subsequently judged a success by MacMillan, who saw the rounding up of terrorist suspects as a positive indicator in turning the war against Jewish terrorism. It was undertaken 'in order that the security services might search such areas thoroughly and apprehend persons implicated in the recent outrages'.[58] However, the operation was terminated two weeks later, in large part because it was thought that its continuation 'would only have resulted in antagonising unnecessarily the whole Jewish community'.

In his official report of the actions undertaken to disrupt the terrorist and insurgent groups, General MacMillan was careful to draw a distinction between 'Martial Law' and 'Statutory Martial Law'. While the former meant that a military commander could, if he wished, assume de facto control over all civil administration, the latter placed overall control firmly in the hands of civilians.[59] The Labour government became alarmed at the use of the term and promptly summoned Cunningham and MacMillan to London to explain the design of recent military operations. In positively Orwellian fashion, the terminology was hastily changed from 'Statutory Martial Law' to 'Controlled Areas' in an attempt to blunt its coercive edge. The use of emergency legislation continued to be a thorny issue in civil–military relations in the last days of the Mandate, reported Major-General Harold Pyman, Chief of Staff of Middle East Land Forces, who confided in his diary:

> The last thing in the world that we want to do is to give anybody the indication that either the Commander-in-Chief or General MacMillan is coming to the conclusion that the imposition of Martial Law is inevitable.[60]

On a related issue, those arrested for a raid on the Ramat Gan police station in Tel Aviv, including the Irgun member Dov Gruner, now faced a resolute GOC determined to make an example of them. MacMillan's decision to seek the death penalty undoubtedly intensified the conflict between Ben Gurion's moderates and the Jewish extremists such as the Stern Gang. The violence soon boiled over when the prisoners were hanged on 15 April 1947. As far as the British were concerned the executions had a dual-edged effect: as Pyman noted, the 'morale of the troops was [now] extremely high' and they 'had had a noticeable effect upon JEWISH TERRORISTS'.[61] There was no question that the executions galvanized support for the insurgents.

British prestige and authority were further shaken by the arrest of Major Roy Farran on 17 June 1947 for the kidnap of Jewish teenager Alexander Rubowitz. Farran, a veteran of Special Air Service (SAS) operations in the war, was tasked with a mission to 'actively' hunt down the dissidents.[62] MacMillan privately admitted that 'there is no doubt that the propaganda in connection with it probably fanned the flames of Anti-British feeling amongst the more extremist sections of the Jewish community'.[63] Whatever the circumstances surrounding covert operations in Palestine, David Cesarini has argued that the 'toxic legacy of the special squads contaminated British colonial policy for decades'.[64] Amidst this heightened atmosphere, two Field Sergeants were abducted and murdered by the Irgun.

It was clear that the battle of wills between the British security forces and the Jewish armed groups was moving to a new plane. In the Hagana's submission to the United Nations Committee on Palestine, it was pointed out that the 'The Jewish resistance movement is the Jewish nation organised for defence and struggle. [It] repudiates the moral and political foundations of British rule in Palestine.'[65] By now considerable pressure had been placed on the British government by the Jewish Agency in London and their allies in the government. Chancellor of the Exchequer Hugh Dalton, who admitted to having come 'to feel more and more strongly on this subject', sent a secret memo to Attlee in which he argued the case for withdrawal:

> I am quite sure that the time has almost come when we must bring our troops out of Palestine altogether. The present state of affairs is not only costly to us in man-power and money, but is, as you and I agree, of no real value from the strategic point of view – you cannot in any case have a secure base on top of a wasps' nest – and it is exposing our young men, for no good purpose, to most abominable experiences, and is breeding anti-Semites at a most shocking speed.

Although acknowledging that this could not be done overnight, given that Labour had yet to hear the outcome of the UN Mission's findings, he nonetheless spoke for many of his colleagues when he said:

> I appreciate that we cannot take decisive action until we have the U.N. Report, but I shall press once more, as soon as this last stage in the long drawn out affair is reached, for a decision in the sense indicated above. It is high time that either we left the Arabs and the Jews to have it out in Palestine, or that some other Power or Powers took over the responsibility and the cost.[66]

'That bastard Dalton',[67] as Bevin referred to his cabinet colleague at the time, was charged with funding the continuing engagement in Palestine, whilst carrying 'a very heavy strain'.[68] Even though Dalton was perhaps motivated more by his appreciation of prevailing economic conditions than his own political convictions, 'the strain of fighting for Britain's economic survival since 1945' clearly informed his strong views in the cabinet at the time.[69] 'Small concessions were made to my point of view', Dalton confided in his diary, 'But they were very small! We must come out of Palestine and heavily reduce our forces in Egypt.'[70] At a time when Britain's 'dollars were running out very fast', it was inevitable that Labour ministers would clash with military commanders.

Following its fact-finding mission to Palestine in the summer of 1947, the United Nations Special Committee on Palestine (UNSCOP) eventually returned to Geneva to discuss the dire situation; all agreed that the British Mandate should come to an end. The British immediately rejected UNSCOP's conclusions.[71] Arguably, the British had been anticipating an unfavourable settlement for some time. Nevertheless, they had maintained the fiction of even-handedness in the event of foreign intervention. It was thought likely that if the Arabs attacked the new Jewish state that Britain would restore order. The senior military intelligence officer in Palestine, Lieutenant-Colonel Dick Norman, briefed his colleagues on what he felt might happen:

(a) The Jewish state will be sufficiently well organised to defend itself against aggression from the Arabs of Palestine and Syria by the time the Mandatory has left the country,
(b) In the unlikely event of other Arab states being involved, it is probable that the Jewish State would have to seek assistance either from an ally or from the United Nations.[72]

Amidst all of this he pondered what safeguards Britain might wish to put in place; the response was not what he expected, insofar as London procrastinated over a decision. Whatever contingency might arise, however, the politicians were by now determined to withdraw.

There was a marked increase in tensions between Arabs and Jews in the wake of the publication of the UNSCOP report on 1 September. Writing home to his mother about his experiences, Norman thought that:

> Even if we do leave Palestine, the evacuation of all the troops will take quite a long time, so I shouldn't start banking on my moving elsewhere for several months at least. Anyway, the whole affair looks like getting bogged down at UNO unless somebody can persuade America and Russia to say something, and when they do, there'll be a lot of argument and, possibly, a stalemate.[73]

The UN report certainly inflamed Jewish and Arab opinion. However, stalemate was the last thing on their minds as both communities teetered dangerously on the brink of civil war.

The British decide to evacuate

Looking back on his time in Palestine, MacMillan told a packed conference at the Royal United Services Institute how, in the aftermath of the UN report:

> Thenceforth the local situation deteriorated rapidly . . . [The] disorders started with attacks by Arabs on the Consulates of the Powers which had voted against them and that the Irgun Zvai Leumi extremists and the Stern Gang soon renewed the murderous vendetta against British soldiers and police, which had diminished appreciably during the course of the Committee's deliberations.[74]

By mid-November the politicians had authorized the military to make arrangements for the evacuation of British forces. General Sir John Crocker, Commander-in-Chief of Middle East Land Forces, consulted Cunningham and the plan 'as formulated at the meeting was carried out almost in exact detail, that the Palestine government were in agreement and in step with the Army throughout up to the end of the Mandate and their departure on 15 May 1948'. As the plan made clear, the withdrawal was to be completed in three phases. First, British forces would withdraw from Gaza by 29 February. Second, they would withdraw from Jerusalem and parts of Samaria and Lydda by May. Finally, they would withdraw from the remainder of Samaria, Lydda and Galilee by 30 June. The final date for the withdrawal from the Haifa enclave was set for 1 August 1948.[75] This was easier said than done. After all, 70,000 military personnel, as well as 5,000 police and civilian officials, and approximately 210,000 thousand tonnes of stores, had to be moved out of Palestine.[76] It was a huge logistical undertaking and necessitated the military bringing in a retired senior officer to organize the operation. Interestingly, while it appeared that the civil and military authorities were 'in step', there is considerable evidence that the Colonial Office were slightly anxious that the withdrawal happen sooner rather than later. In a letter to the assistant Under-Secretary at the Colonial Office, Cunningham confessed, 'I am quite clear that in present conditions the sooner the Civil Administration ends the better. It now has no object, not much function and very little authority. I could however not yet say that it cannot go on.'[77] The Mandatory authorities were beginning to wobble.

Following an intensification of attacks against British policemen and soldiers in early January across Haifa, and further bloody clashes between Arabs and Jews in Bethlehem and other cities, *The Times* leaked a story that the Mandate authorities in Jerusalem 'considers it in the best interests that the British mandate should end before May 15', subject to an agreement with the UN that the termination could be brought forward by six weeks. For *The Times*, the alternative 'would be that Britain should remain indefinitely, assisting directly in the partition and trying to maintain order with all the forces at her command'. This, the newspaper speculated, would be 'a complete reversal of her declared policy and more than she could afford'.[78] While journalists may have latched onto the prospect of a more rapid drawdown in forces, the Chiefs of Staff were not persuaded by the need to terminate the mandate earlier than expected. They wished to follow a more deliberate plan, not a hasty one, in which British prestige could be managed, orderly and without losing face. A top-secret communiqué from General Sir Leslie Hollis confirmed as much:

> The Chiefs of Staff are adamantly opposed to any earlier termination of the Mandate. There is no military reason whatsoever why this should be done, and many [are] against it. The earlier the date of termination, the earlier will be established the conditions for conflagration in Palestine . . . The reason put forward for this change is because the administration can no longer carry out its responsibilities for the maintenance of internal security and the continuation of essential services.[79]

Much would now depend on the military's ability to implement the plan for withdrawal. Attention soon switched to Haifa, which would become the last battleground for British prestige in Palestine.

Major-General Sir Hugh Stockwell was the Commander of the 6th Airborne Division between August 1947 and May 1948, and a key figure charged with securing the Haifa bridgehead. Stockwell had overall responsibility for the Northern Sector of Palestine, which consisted of the two major commercial centres of Haifa and Galilee. Considerable insight can be gained into Stockwell's style of command from his correspondence with both his subordinates and the military chain of command. In one secret communiqué to his brigade commanders, he said that, in order to 'fulfil our task militarily we must at all times hold the initiative and impose our wills'. Unlike other sectors, Stockwell told his men, they were 'best aided in this by good intelligence, correct deployment of our troops and quick and accurate handling of our reserves'.[80] Stockwell showed real mastery in his leadership, running his sector in a fair and impartial manner, despite provocation from Jewish and Arab armed groups. He lost no time in asserting that he would 'take such measures as I consider necessary at any time to maintain law and order in the Sector under my Command'.[81]

Although British troops were to be concerned with de-escalating the armed conflict in preparation for withdrawal, they were not prepared to loosen their grip over the security situation. In the complex operational environment of Palestine, where two communities remained locked in a vicious cycle of violence, Stockwell grasped this more so perhaps than his fellow generals. That is not to deny that troops under his command did not occasionally engage in punitive actions. For instance, in a letter to MacMillan, an apologetic Stockwell wrote:

> I am so sorry that any impression is made to seem that the Army is not carrying out it's [sic] duties impartially. All ranks I know are endeavouring to give their best and to remain completely impartial in the carrying out of their duties.[82]

By now British forces were coming under increasing political pressure to manage the withdrawal in a more orderly fashion, despite the acceleration in Jewish terrorist atrocities against them, not to mention the indiscriminate bomb attacks against Arab civilians in bus stations, market-places and villages. In February 1948 alone over 50 British servicemen were killed; the total number of dead on all sides since November 1947 ran to 1,400 killed and over 3,000 injured.[83] Behind the scenes, British police and military sources admitted that casualties could be as high as 2,315 dead and 4,901 injured by the end of April.[84] Stockwell wrote at the time:

> The maintenance of law and order under the Mandate has become increasingly difficult throughout the NORTHERN SECTOR with the small forces at my disposal due to the mounting tempo of Jewish-Arab clashes, and it has been due in no small measure to the successful liaison and negotiations that my Officers have carried out that a major clash of this nature has not been precipitated earlier.[85]

At an operational level, the lack of sufficient forces to keep the peace was impacting negatively on the military's ability to maintain law and order. Stockwell privately admitted how, 'While endeavouring at all times, with the power at my disposal, to maintain the peace in my Sector', he had to balance in his own mind, 'the primary essential of a smooth and rapid evacuation of the British forces through the Port of Haifa'. As with his fellow military commanders, Stockwell's ultimate commitment was to 'uphold at all times British prestige'.[86] If that required firm action, as well as understanding, then Stockwell was capable of both. An intensification in violent clashes between Arabs and Jews made 6th Airborne Division's task much more difficult.

Palestine's civil war

The nature of the violence between Arabs and Jews was marked by the ease by which both sides resorted to 'guerrilla warfare accompanied by acts of terrorism'.[87] Historian Benny Morris informs us that there were two distinct phases to the civil war now under way between Arabs and Jews at this time. The first began in November 1947, when the British eventually announced their intention to withdraw, and concluded with the termination of the Mandate on the 14 May 1948, while the second began on the 15 May and ended in 1949.[88] The first phase was more distinctly terrorist in its character. Jewish extremists exploded a truck bomb in a crowded street in Jaffa, which resulted in the deaths of nine Arabs and the injury of seventy-one. One of the first reporters on the scene wryly observed how '[t]he Jews have thus struck the Arabs by the same methods as those so often used against the British'.[89] The Arabs appealed to the British authorities for better protection, but to no avail. The next day the Hagana blew up the Arab-owned Semiramis Hotel in Jerusalem killing a further twenty people and injuring many more. They later claimed the hotel served as the Headquarters of the Palestinian Nejada movement.[90] In the immediate aftermath of the bombing a leaflet drop across Arab towns and villages blamed Arab 'sniping, murder and robbery' for the violence, which it thought would not 'do any good to anybody'.

The irony of their own terrorist attacks on innocent civilians was lost on the Hagana, who went on to state 'remember that women and children, the old and the infirm, are in a permanent state of fear of retaliation to terrorist activity by the Arabs'.[91] Neither side was completely blameless. Fearing being overrun by the Jews, the Arabs had actually taken matters into their own hands. Arab snipers did indeed harass Jewish settlers, while also detonating bombs and mines on main roads near settlements. The largest attack by organized Arab forces came against the Hatikva Quarter in south-eastern Tel Aviv. On this occasion, British troops intervened and shot dead two members of the Hagana. Later, on 9 January, Syrian Bedouin troops attacked Kibbutz Kfar Szold in Upper Galilee, only to be repelled by the arrival of a British armoured-car column.

Meanwhile, the *Palestine Post*, a moderate Jewish daily, branded the actions of the British government 'farcical'. While careful to repudiate Jewish terrorist action, the local newspaper proclaimed, in somewhat stark terms, how:

> The Jewish people is [sic] fighting for its life and for the modest living space it has been allocated. The day has come for every Jew to defend himself, and defend himself doubly because the Government forces do not do so.[92]

Rumours quickly spread that the British were preparing to withdraw from Palestine earlier than expected and that US marines were to land to safeguard American institutions, something that deeply worried the Arab Office in London.[93] General Clifton B. Cates, the Commandant of the Marine Corps, later denied the rumours, re-emphasizing that the deployment of 1,000 troops in the Mediterranean was 'merely routine'.[94]

Paranoia now pervaded the minds of both Arab and Jew, who feared a vacuum once the British withdrew.

Terrorist attacks intensified as the British withdrawal grew closer. Tactics varied and included bombings, sniping, stabbings and shootings. Arabs retaliated by exploding a fifty-pound bomb in the main Bus Terminus in Haifa, killing one British policeman, one British civilian and six Jews; another twenty-five people were injured when the stolen van used to transport the bomb exploded prematurely.[95] Within twenty-four hours British soldiers were on the offensive in the town of Hebron, a short distance from Bethlehem, where 3,000 Arabs had surrounded Jewish settlements with the intention of purging their inhabitants. Six Royal Air Force (RAF) Spitfire aircraft were scrambled in support of the British operation, buzzing Arab gun emplacements in the mountainous belt of terrain which ran south down through the cities of Jerusalem, Bethlehem and Hebron. Mercifully, the British cordon held and the Arabs soon retreated. It would not be the last large-scale Arab offensive on Jewish settlements. In a particularly ugly reprisal for the Haifa bus terminus attack, Jewish terrorists blew up three Arab houses, killing eight children in an indiscriminate attack.[96]

The *Times* correspondent in Jerusalem was now reporting that amidst such an escalation in attacks the general 'opinion is growing here that Britain should leave as soon as possible'.[97] The deployment of British troops in Palestine was costing the taxpayer dearly, with a staggering £100 million pounds being spent between 1 July 1945 and 30 November 1947.[98] Moreover, in the seven weeks between 30 November 1947 and 18 January 1948, 20 British soldiers were murdered and 72 wounded, along with 14 policemen killed (40 wounded) and 8 British civilians (2 wounded); 345 Arabs had been killed and 877 wounded along with 333 Jewish and 633 wounded.[99]

By the middle of February violence again escalated, with a deadly attack on Jewish civilians in the district of Ben Yehuda Street. Fifty Jews were killed and seventy injured in co-ordinated explosions which ripped through the heart of this bustling shopping precinct, near to the Old City of Jerusalem. Amid the warbles of imminent attack sirens, rumours were rife that British troops had played an active part in aiding the Arab terrorists. The *Palestine Post* claimed to have *prima facie* evidence to support the theory that British soldiers either perpetrated the attack themselves, or at the very least colluded with Arab terrorists in the outrage, a difficult hypothesis to prove since militant Arabs and Jews were known to disguise themselves as British soldiers when planting bombs in each other's districts.[100] As the *Post* implied, the Government's

> very reluctance to institute an investigation into an act which more than any other incident of the past months may further strain the relations between the Mandatory Power and the people of Palestine is difficult to understand.[101]

In a statement, the leader of the Arab forces, Abdul Kader Husseini, claimed responsibility for the attack, which he said was in reprisal for an earlier 'basket bomb' attack in Ramleh.[102] Jewish terrorists wasted no time and responded with their own form of justice: several British soldiers were murdered and scores wounded.[103] A pattern of deadly violence followed in which the Stern Gang mined a train carrying British soldiers west from Cairo to Haifa: 19 soldiers and 8 airmen were killed, and 35 wounded. Many of the troops had been returning from rest and recuperation in Egypt. It was the largest single loss of life in such an attack since the Emergency began.[104]

Withdrawal

In many ways, the withdrawal from Palestine exposed an uneasy relationship between the military and politicians on the question of policy.[105] In a further embittered letter to the Minister of Defence, which attacked government inertia, General Hollis expressed his disdain for the lack of commitment on the part of British politicians, when he said: 'What the authorities in Palestine need is 100% backing and encouragement in fulfilling the present task and not indications that Government Departments begin to wobble from this policy when difficulties occur.'[106] While the picture was becoming more and more chaotic, Bevin moved to steady civil–military nerves on the matter:

> The situation in Palestine is so delicate that I feel it essential, if we are to keep our policy straight, that any public pronouncements, including the answers to any questions in the House on Palestine, should be cleared personally by the Minister of Defence, the Secretary for the Colonies, or myself (or in my absence by you). If this is not done, I feel that we may find ourselves in serious trouble, and I am sure that, in present circumstances, statements on Palestine should not be cleared between officials.[107]

Bevin was at last acting decisively. He advised the Cabinet in confident mood that British policy ought to 'explain and defend the policy which His Majesty's Government had pursued in recent months'[108] at the UN, using all possible influence to secure 'their observance and execution by both sides'. In a statement that perhaps said more about British interests than anything ese, he advocated that a Jewish state be

> set up in such a way as not to cause a continuation of chaos in the Middle East, i.e. we have sought a settlement including the existence of a Jewish state in which the Arabs could reasonably acquiesce and which they would not bend all their energies to undo.[109]

Bevin's determination to maintain a decisive stance undoubtedly chimed with those held by senior military commanders at the time. It was the Foreign Secretary's Middle East policy that the government now seemed to be following. Attlee remained nonplussed, later explaining his own position as follows:

> Most of the military were inclined to put too much weight on the Middle East as a base. They overlooked the political issues and the facts of Arab nationalism and insisted that we must hang on to it as a vital main support area. Monty did when he was C.I.G.S. He still had a hangover from the days when the Middle East was the essential link between our two great places of arms, Britain and India. But India had ceased to be a British Imperial place of arms and the Suez Canal had never been a particularly good waterway in war-time and the idea of the Mediterranean as a kind of covered passage for Britain had also been exploded. Monty over-emphasised the importance of the Middle East from the strategic point of view.[110]

In another departure from the previous position, Bevin's renewed grip on policy was marked by its emphasis on multilateralism. He remained convinced that a solution could not now be brought about by Britain alone:

> Efforts are already being made to encourage Egypt, Transjordan and Iraq, the three Arab states principally concerned, to concert their policy with regard to negotiations for the final settlement . . . Meanwhile, however, we cannot neglect taking the necessary precautions to safeguard vital British interests in the Middle East should fighting break out again contrary to our hopes.[111]

There was a feeling in the Cabinet that US support for the Jews could be attributed, at least in part, to 'the fear that unless they supported the Jews the latter would draw closer to the U.S.S.R.'[112]

Britain's wider strategic interests in the Mediterranean and Middle East led the JIC to see Palestine as a potential staging post for the spread of Communism in the Middle East, though it declared that the 'Russian star is likely to be no less attractive than the German'.[113] British intelligence assessments were suggesting that Soviet ambitions were to increase their influence in the region: firstly, 'by penetration of the Jewish Civil and Military Administration with a view to future exploitation' and, secondly, 'by immigration, illegal if necessary, of agents, propagandists and guerrilla leaders'. The Soviet Union's overarching aim, counselled the JIC, was to 'exploit Arab nationalism' and 'emphasise the sympathy of the Soviet Union with the Arab masses in their conflicts with the Arab ruling classes'.[114] Communism was considered wholly subversive and a constant threat to the balance of power in the international political system. Britain ought to be wary:

> The main intention of the Soviet Union in regard to the Arab World is to weaken our general strategic, political and economic position and thereby obtain for herself the opportunity to increase her own influence, and to further her strategic and economic ends throughout the area.[115]

Control over natural resources, including oil, and commercial trade routes, such as the Suez Canal, were of vital importance to British strategic interests. The withdrawal from Palestine, on the surface of it, appeared to have been made hastily and for short-term party political reasons, not according to the long-term strategic goal of containing the Soviet advance.

Operationally, the British had now failed in their bid to keep an uneasy peace between the warring communities,[116] despite the efforts of commanders on the ground like Hughie Stockwell, who strove hard to construct effective co-ordinating machinery.[117] The pressure proved too much for some officers, who complained bitterly about having to deal with 'a thoroughly non-cooperative, unscrupulous, dishonest and utterly immoral civil population such as the Jewish community in Palestine, who systematically and continually hide and refuse to give up to justice the perpetrators of murderous outrages', maintaining that 'reprisals are the only effective weapon to employ, saving time, money and unnecessary bloodshed'.[118] Such battle-hardened views were common in the ranks of the Parachute Regiment soldiers serving in Palestine. In another revealing instance it was thought that:

> On a Bn level no officer or other rank should ever be allowed to negotiate with a civilian on matters of security, other than through the medium of a bullet. This was probably one of the most important lessons learnt in Palestine.[119]

Pressure was now mounting to such an extent that the most senior General in the region, Sir John Crocker, resorted to issuing strong guidance to MacMillan, telling him that 'he must from now onwards display and use maximum strength everywhere where he wished to retain control' and that he 'must prescribe areas in which nobody will carry arms and shoot persons and even community leaders if the order is disobeyed. He *must* be master of his own house.'[120] Desperation was now setting in amongst the military hierarchy. More coercive use of force would serve to mark the order by which British forces withdrew inwards to the major towns and cities, before the last remaining troops finally departed Haifa. As a consequence, the spirit of impartiality quickly evaporated.

Aftermath

Britain's mandate over Palestine finally lapsed on 15 May 1948. However, that was not the end of the saga for those British troops still on the ground. While Sir Alan Cunningham was hastily evacuated on 14 May 1948, the GOC remained, assuming the role of military governor until the full withdrawal of British forces could be secured later in the summer. Authority for maintaining control of the tiny bridgehead areas continued to be delegated down through the chain of command to Divisional and Brigade commanders. It was under these arrangements that commanders in Haifa were given latitude to attempt to negotiate with local Arabs and Jews to ensure the safety of the men under their command. As the Chief of Staff wrote in his report on the evacuation:

> Thus, with dignity, with precision, without incident and entirely according to plan, ended thirty years of British occupation, and of British labours for Palestine.[121]

As orderly withdrawal continued, the Secretary of State for War sent a telegram to General MacMillan:

> The last British troops will leave Palestine to-day. I take this occasion to send you and all the officers and men who have served under you my congratulations on the completion of this hard task. We all appreciate how unpleasant it has often been to do your duty in the exceptional conditions before and after the end of the British Mandate, and we admire you for the good sense, steadiness and courage you have always shown. Good luck to you all.[122]

In total, some 20 British army officers and 203 other ranks lost their lives between 1945 and 1948, and some 77 officers and 536 soldiers had been wounded.[123] Strategically, civil–military relations on the ground and in Whitehall were strained. This had much to do with Labour's determination to relinquish control of Palestine at all costs. As Attlee later recalled:

> We'd held the Mandate and we couldn't get any agreement, and it was no good our holding the baby any longer with everybody gunning for us. The only thing was to pass the problem to the U.N. and agree to do

> what they said. It was one of those impossible situations for which there is no really good solution. One just had to cut the knot.[124]

Attlee was at pains to stress how, 'In dealing with the Palestine question we sought to hold a fair balance between the rival claimants to this little territory and, as usual, got small thanks from either side.'[125] The buck had now been passed on to the UN, who voted to appoint the Swedish diplomat Count Bernodette to mediate between the warring factions.[126] Bernodette's mission failed, and by the end of the summer the Stern Gang had eliminated him. Britain had handed responsibility to the whims of a divided population, which regarded force as the main currency for interacting with one another.

Dick Norman surveyed the ever-shrinking British base from his makeshift office overlooking the port of Haifa. He was restless and longed for action, though he was constrained by the imponderable fact that British forces were prostate, relying more on the goodwill of the Jewish and Arab belligerents to observe a tenuous détente as they completed the orderly business of withdrawal. In a letter home to his mother, Norman recalled how he was taken by surprise one day when General MacMillan dropped into his office to inform him that he had been awarded an OBE. Norman was ecstatic – telling his mother enthusiastically how he 'was the only soldier to get the OBE in the whole of Palestine'.[127] Awards shone brightly as the lights were slowly extinguished over the last vestiges of Britain's presence in the Middle East. For British officers who remained behind after the termination of the mandate on 15 May, boredom and idleness remained the order of the day. 'I've had a pretty dull week', Norman confided in yet another letter home. 'The HQ is getting smaller every day. All my officers and clerks have gone and by tomorrow we shall have only five people in the Mess. The only real work I've done is the Mess accounts, which were in a very bad state.'[128] Not to be intimidated by the prospect of humiliating defeat, a dizzying array of silver-service Mess dinners and cocktail parties kept the officers entertained as their last remaining troops were piped aboard troop transporters. Fortunately, British troops did not face concerted armed attacks from Jewish terrorists and insurgents, who 'were busy' according to Norman, turning their gun-sights on their Arab neighbours.

Now safely back in Warminster, the home of the British infantry, Norman had cause to reflect upon his irregular opponent in a course paper entitled *Terrorism in Palestine*. Norman's own estimation of the British role in Palestine was that 'the Mandatory administration had been heavily influenced by the anxiety felt in Whitehall'. In military terms he judged the failure of British efforts to defeat the Jewish groups especially to have been attributable to a lack of intelligence brought about because, usually, 'the Jews disliked the British more than they disliked the terrorists, and they shrank from betraying their own countrymen'. This was plainly important in the sense that most Jews, when they 'saw their young men and women defying the armed might of the greatest empire the world has ever seen, . . . could not help shewing [sic] a measure of sympathy, and often more than that'.[129] Without inside information on their opponent Britain could not sustain its small war in Palestine. As Sir Alan Cunningham boarded *HMS Euryalus*, one of his key opponents, Menachem Begin, observed how the 'demoralisation of impending evacuation spread overnight . . . The revolt was victorious.'[130] While Begin may have had the last word on the subject, his words were to be replaced by the opposition of an entire region's anger at what the Jews had done to the Arabs who had long considered Palestine their own. In Norman's words:

> It may be concluded, therefore, that terrorism may pay as a short term policy, but that eventually it is bound to affect adversely those who use it to attain their ends. Furthermore, those who are given the task of administering successfully a country in which terrorism thrives should not have their actions restricted either by outside political influence, or by the conventions of government and war. The fact is that the British will always be so influenced is unfortunately only too relevant.[131]

Following the evacuation of Haifa, Hughie Stockwell returned to England to take up the post of Commandant of the Royal Military Academy Sandhurst on 7 June 1948. One of the first tasks he set about was to pass on the lessons of the Army's involvement in Palestine.

Conclusion

Immediately after the termination of the Mandate, Arab forces invaded Palestine from Lebanon, Iraq, Egypt, Syrian and Transjordan. Their aim was to seize control of the territory vacated by Britain; but this was resisted by the Jewish community, thereby precipitating the second phase of the civil war. For their part, all the British could do was watch from the sidelines. Nonetheless, there is evidence that the Foreign Office wished to use the remaining troops as a bargaining chip to push British influence in the ensuing high-level meetings at the UN. Despite Bevin's assurances to Parliament in early May that 'there is no question of using our resources after 15 May to enforce any kind of settlement against the wishes of either party',[132] the Foreign Office sought to do just that. In a telegram to Middle East Command, Bevin's mandarins said that 'there might be considerable political advances in relations [sic] to the ARABS if we continue our occupation of the HAIFA enclave until 31 July as opposed to 30 June'.[133] MacMillan was unconvinced, maintaining that the consequences of doing so would be detrimental to the safety of his troops. 'If [the] JEWS . . . see evacuation clearly being slowed up', he cautioned his higher command, 'I consider we will expose British soldiers to further murderous attacks. JEWS will interpret delay as plot to remain in PALESTINE and extremists will exploit.'[134] MacMillan concluded that the evacuation was 'so far advanced that change of Plan would lead to serious difficulties, including the possible need for reinforcements and more supplies'. This might lead to 'violent local reactions'. Unsurprisingly, with British prestige at stake, the GOC got his way; the main threat to British soldiers came instead from terrible weather, cramped accommodation, poor-quality food and ghastly entertainment. Importantly, though, as some senior officers argued, 'high morale [remained] in spite of the fact that it had very few of the amenities sometimes considered prerequisites'.[135]

Despite the 'high morale' of the soldiers who served there, Palestine soon became a byword for Britain's strategic failure in the Middle East. Nonetheless, for senior British officers at Middle East Headquarters, a quiet defiance persisted, with incoming officers being briefed that they 'must not therefore regard the day we leave HAIFA as being the last day on which we will be interested in PALESTINE'.[136] Despite such morale-boosting chatter, the reality was that Britain's policy in Palestine had descended into chaos, humiliation and farce. Top-secret reports circulating in Middle East Command, bitterly concluded: 'We have evacuated PALESTINE, thereby greatly weakening our strategical hold of the MIDDLE EAST.'[137] By now, however, the strategic parameters of future policy had been set. General Crocker spoke for many under his command in a letter to the CIGS:

> There may now be a feeling amongst Ministers, and certainly in the minds of the British public, that we have attained our object so far as Palestine is concerned. In fact, of course, nothing of the sort has happened. We have been seen off and have suffered a great set back to our strategical interests.[138]

Whether this was through accident or design is a moot point, for future British governments, of whatever political complexion, would have to live with the decisions taken by their predecessors. On a related point, it was unlikely that such salutatory critique of Labour's handling of the Palestine issue would have endeared Attlee to Montgomery's suggestion that Crocker take his place when he moved on from the War Office.

In a highly political move, Attlee brought General Sir William Slim out of retirement to head up the Army.

What the Attlee administration put in train and then swiftly executed in Palestine had far-reaching consequences for future British policy in the Middle East. As one commentator somewhat apologetically noted, 'On Palestine, the Attlee-Bevin approach was much criticized but, arguably, these criticisms have lost much of their force in the light of history.'[139] The Parliamentary Labour Party report summed this up neatly when it noted how 'Britain had received little gratitude for the great part played in Palestine and would lay down responsibilities with relief.'[140] Palestine was a political disaster for the Labour government and would leave a lasting legacy for future British policy in the region. For instance, the troubles that soon sprang up in the greater Middle East in the 1950s and 1960s, from Egypt to Aden, could trace their antecedents to Britain's mishandling of the Palestinian issue. Of course the Suez crisis in 1956 was something that had been brewing much earlier, since the King dispensed with the assistance of British military mission,[141] and the country declared its independence in 1949. Egypt continued to cause problems for the British government, especially after a military coup in 1954 brought to power Gamal Abdul Nasser, 'the Soviet Union's first major Middle Eastern ally'.[142]

In a cutting analysis of Britain's strategic malaise in the immediate post-war years, Correlli Barnett compared the country to a stricken ocean liner: 'In summer 1950 this liner, having survived the great storm of the Second World War thanks to an American tow, was wallowing slowly ahead perilously overladen, more rusty than mighty.'[143] The overwhelming paranoia of the imminent Soviet encroachment of British interests was a spectre haunting Middle Eastern policy and filtered down from Whitehall to the military commanders on the spot.[144] It was thought that 'Any major threat to the security of the MIDDLE EAST must come from RUSSIA and would be part and parcel of a challenge to democracy.' The fact that the 'check and eventual overthrow of any such threat is beyond the UNITED KINGDOM'[145] necessitated drawing ever-closer into the special relationship with the United States, a view shared by Montgomery, who had by now moved on to become Deputy Commander of Supreme Allied Powers in Europe.[146]

The Anglo-American 'special relationship' would make a more indelible impression on British defence policy under the leadership of Winston Churchill, after the Conservatives were returned to power in 1951, as Labour were promptly consigned to opposition benches by a sceptical British public. Speaking to the Norwegian peace institute in Oslo, Harold Wilson, a former member of the Attlee Cabinet, thought that Britain should play a restraining influence on America in the future. He considered it only proper that 'we not only have the right but the duty as friends to speak frankly to one another'.[147] Wilson argued that Britain

> must use our strength, and our great moral power and leadership, to work within the United Nations for a peaceful solution of the world's difficulties, to convert that present form of hostile argument and counter-argument into a positive instrument for creating the conditions in which peace can be assured.[148]

Wilson's remarks came at a time when British power was being firmly eclipsed by the United States. In Paul Kennedy's words, though, 'it would remain an overextended but still powerful strategical entity, dependent upon the United States for security and yet also the country's most useful ally – and an important strategic collaborator – in a world dividing into two large power blocs'.[149] Cold War soon came to dominate the international context, as the Soviet Union moved to fill the vacuum left by Britain's retreat from the Middle East. Yet the retreat would remain incomplete, in that the UK continued to retain the formal colonies of Aden on the southern tip of the Southern Arabian Peninsular and in Kenya, East Africa, as well as sovereign bases on Cyprus in the Eastern Mediterranean. 'As late as 1949', noted Aldrich and Zametica, 'the Middle East still lay at the centre of Britain's strategic concept.'[150] Cyprus soon became the one strategic outpost Britain could not afford to squander. When an insurrection against British colonial rule was sparked off in the mid-1950s, it would be met with more grit and determination in civil–military relations than what had characterized Palestine. It was in this respect that military commanders looked around for new staging posts to retrench British power. The conclusion they drew was that: 'EAST AFRICA is the next best BRITISH area in which to locate the imperial garrison of the MIDDLE EAST. Our future policy should be to concentrate our troops there to the full extent that future commitments will permit.'[151]

Notes

1 Imperial War Museum (IWM), *Colonel C R W Norman Papers*, 87/57/2, Memorandum submitted to the United Nations Committee on Palestine by the Jewish Resistance Movement, dated 11 July 1947.

2 King's College London, Liddell Hart Centre for Military Archives (LHCMA), Papers of General Sir Hugh Stockwell, 6/26, Confidential: Lessons Learned in Palestine, report sent to Major-General Stockwell, dated 17 November 1948.

3 Law, Bernard, Viscount Montgomery of Alamein, *The Memoirs of Field-Marshal the Viscount Montgomery of Alamein, KG* (London: Collins, 1958), p. 466. Emphasis in original.
4 Tripp, Charles, *A History of Iraq*, third edition (Cambridge: Cambridge University Press, 2007), p. 51.
5 IWM, *MacMillan Papers*, DS/MISC/15, General Survey of His Majesty's Government's Policy in Palestine, in *Narrative of Events from February 1947 until withdrawal of all British Troops by Lieutenant General G.H.A. MacMillan.*
6 Fraser, T.G., *The Arab-Israeli Conflict*, third edition (Basingstoke: Palgrave Macmillan, 2007), p. 8.
7 Lawrence, T.E., *Revolt in the Desert* (London: Jonathan Cape, 1927), p. 255.
8 Morris, Benny, *1948: A History of the First Arab-Israeli War* (New Haven, CT: Yale University Press, 2008), p. 14.
9 Cesarani, David, *Major Farran's Hat: Murder, Scandal and Britain's War against Jewish Terrorism, 1945–1948* (London: Vintage Books, 2010), p. 13.
10 *The Times*, 23 March 1945.
11 Bullock, Alan, *Ernest Bevin: Foreign Secretary, 1945–1951* (London: William Heinemann, 1983), pp. 154–156.
12 *The Times*, 10 April 1945.
13 IWM, *Norman Papers*, 87/57/2, *The Palestine Problem*, dated October 1945.
14 LHCMA, *Pyman Papers*, 7/2/1, Top Secret: Middle East Strategy 1947, dated 11 March 1947.
15 Fraser, *The Arab-Israeli Conflict*, p. 6. Herzl's thoughts were contained in his 1896 book, *Der Judenstaat* ('The Jewish State').
16 Baron Rothschild was head of a well-known and respected Jewish family in England, many of whom had served in the ranks of the British Army.
17 Bodleian Library Special Collections (BLSC), *Attlee Papers*, MS. Attlee Dep. 20, fols 234–236, Correspondence from J.R.C. to J.M. Martin, 27 August 1945 and attached 'Memorandum on the Refugee Situation'.
18 BLSC, *Attlee Papers*, MS. Attlee Dep. 39, fols 89–90, A London Letter by Harold J. Laski, 12 July 1946'.
19 Morgan, Kenneth O., *Labour in Power, 1945–51* (Oxford: Oxford University Press, 1984), p. 211.
20 BLSC, *Attlee Papers*, MS. Attlee Dep. 41, fols 107–109, Speech by Clement Attlee to the Opening of the [Lancaster House] Palestine Conference, 10 September 1946.
21 IWM, *Norman Papers*, 87/57/2, Memorandum submitted to the United Nations Committee on Palestine by the Jewish Resistance Movement, dated 11 July 1947.
22 LHCMA, Private Papers of Major-General Charles Dunbar, 3/1–4, 'Some Experiences in 8 (Midland) Bn the Parachute Regiment by Major-General C W Dunbar CBE (n.d. 1972?).

23 Ibid.
24 Cesarini, *Major Farran's Hat*, p. 25. On this point, see also Begin, Menachem, *The Revolt*, revised edition, translated by Samuel Katz (London: W.H. Allen, 1983).
25 Grob-Fitzgibbon, Benjamin, *Imperial Endgame: Britain's Dirty Wars and the End of Empire* (Basingstoke: Palgrave Macmillan, 2011), p. 44.
26 Cesarini, *Major Farran's Hat*, p. 26.
27 Cited in IWM, *MacMillan Papers*, DS/MISC/15, Palestine: Narrative of Events from February 1947 until withdrawal of all British Troops by Lieutenant General G.H.A. MacMillan, p. 2.
28 Grob-Fitzgibbon, *Imperial Endgame*, p. 45.
29 LHCMA, Dunbar Papers, 3/1–4.
30 BLSC, *Attlee Papers*, MS. Attlee Dep. 37, fols 140, *Report of the National Executive Committee to the 45th Annual Conference to be held in the Pavilion, Bournemouth, 10–14 June 1946* (London: Transport House, 1946), p. 53.
31 Cesarini, *Major Farran's Hat*, p. 36.
32 The British regarded the Palmach as the frontline fighting force within the larger irregular Hagana (defence) movement. It was approximately the same size as an infantry brigade consisting of 5,000–6,000 irregular troops.
33 Begin, *The Revolt*, p. 217.
34 Cesarini, *Major Farran's Hat*, p. 40.
35 BLSC, *Attlee Papers*, MS. Attlee Dep. 39, fols 38–39, Private Letter from Winston Churchill to Clement Attlee, 2 July 1946.
36 Ibid.
37 BLSC, *Attlee Papers*, MS. Attlee Dep. 39, fols 5–8.
38 Ibid., fols 17–18.
39 IWM, *Norman Papers*, 87/57/2, Command Discussion Lecture No. 2, completed 18 July 1947.
40 IWM, Norman Papers, 87/57/2, lecture by Lieutenant Colonel Norman, dated 18 July 1947.
41 The King David Hotel death toll stood at 46 Arabs, 28 British and 18 Jews.
42 Grob-Fitzgibbon, *Imperial Endgame*, p. 51.
43 Hackett, General Sir John, *The Profession of Arms* (London: Sidgwick and Jackson, 1983), p. 227.
44 Montgomery, *Memoirs*, p. 466.
45 Hamilton, Nigel, *Monty: The Field Marshal, 1944–1976* (London: Hamish Hamilton, 1986), p. 635.
46 The National Archives, Kew, London (TNA), CO 967/100, Correspondence from Montgomery to Hall, dated 6 August 1946.
47 Herzog, Chaim, *The Arab-Israeli Wars: War and Peace in the Middle East* (Bath: Book Club Associates, 1982), p. 13.
48 *The Times*, 1 August 1946.
49 BLSC, *Attlee Papers*, MS. Attlee Dep. 48, fols 132–1334, Clement Attlee to the Marquess of Salisbury, 21 December 1946.

50 Crossman, Richard, *Palestine Mission: A Personal Record* (London: Hamish Hamilton, 1947), p. 64.
51 Bevin's attitude towards Palestine was not exactly helpful either. Although 'never anti-Semitic in the sense of having a racial hatred', observed Herbert Morrison, he had 'become anti-Jewish as regards the people living in Palestine'. He reserved particular anger for those who had visited 'a reign of terror against the British forces in the country'. Morrison, Lord Herbert, *Herbert Morrison: An Autobiography* (London: Odhams Press, 1960), p. 273. Another ministerial colleague, Emanuel Shinwell, thought that Bevin had 'underrated their fighting qualities, and this embittered him so that some of his utterances had the flavour of anti-semitism'. Shinwell, Emanuel, *Conflict Without Malice* (London: Odhams Press, 1955), p. 198.
52 TNA, KV 3/370, PIC Middle East, Top Secret: Russian Activities in the Middle East – quarter ending 31 July 1946, 1 August 1946.
53 TNA, KV 3/370, PIC Middle East, Top Secret: Russian Influence in the Levant, 31 August 1944.
54 Newsinger, John, *British Counterinsurgency: From Palestine to Northern Ireland* (Basingstoke: Palgrave Macmillan, 2002), p. 25.
55 House of Commons Debates (Hansard), 28 January 1947, Vol. 432, Col. 774.
56 London School of Economics (LSE) Archives, *Shore Papers*, 8/88, Parliamentary Labour Party Report, Session 1945–46, p. 62.
57 MacMillan replaced Barker on 12 February 1947.
58 IWM, *MacMillan Papers*, DS/MISC/15, Palestine: Narrative of Events from February 1947 until withdrawal of all British Troops by Lieutenant General G.H.A. MacMillan.
59 Ibid.
60 LHCMA, *Pyman Papers*, 7/1/8, Major General Pyman to Brigadier Kirkman, dated 23 August 1947.
61 LHCMA, *Pyman Papers*, 7/1/4, Diary of Pyman, dated 24 April 1947.
62 Cesarini, *Major Farran's Hat*, p. 83.
63 IWM, *MacMillan Papers*, DS/MISC/15, Palestine: Narrative of Events from February 1947 until withdrawal of all British Troops by Lieutenant General G.H.A. MacMillan. Farran had initially escaped to Syria and an order had been issued for his arrest on 14 June. He was arrested on 17 June but escaped from custody on 19 June. He surrendered on 30 June, was tried and then acquitted on 3 October 1947.
64 Cesarini, *Major Farran's Hat*, p. 208.
65 IWM, *Norman Papers*, 87/57/2, Memorandum submitted to UNSCOP by the Jewish Resistance Movement, dated 11 July 1947.
66 TNA, PREM 8/623, HD [Hugh Dalton], Treasury, to Prime Minister, 'Palestine', 11 August 1947.
67 Brown, George, *In My Way: The Political Memoirs of Lord George-Brown* (London: Victor Gollancz, 1971), pp. 50–51. Dalton's doubts over Attlee's leadership prompted him to place pressure on Bevin to initiate a

challenge against the embattled Prime Minister. The Foreign Secretary, however, was intensely loyal to Attlee and 'the movement to make Bevin PM had petered out'. Dalton later wrote that the 'seven months from mid-April to mid-November 1947 were the most unhappy of all my public life'. Dalton, Hugh, *High Tide and After: Memoirs, 1945–1960* (London: Frederick Muller, 1962), pp. 240, 254.

68 Dalton, *High Tide and After*, p. 254.
69 Ibid., p. 49.
70 Cited in ibid., p. 259.
71 Grob-Fitzgibbon, *Imperial Endgame*, p. 51.
72 IWM, *Norman Papers*, 87/57/2, Top Secret Appreciation written for the High Commissioner by Lieutenant-Colonel Norman, dated 10 July 1947.
73 IWM, *Norman Papers*, 87/57/2, Letter from Richard Norman to his mother, 5 October 1947.
74 Lieutenant-General G.H.A. MacMillan, 'The Evacuation of Palestine', *The Journal of the Royal United Services Institute*, Vol. 93, No. 571 (August 1948), p. 609.
75 TNA, CO 967/104, Cipher from GHQ, MELF, to Ministry of Defence, London, dated 10 January 1948.
76 MacMillan, 'The Evacuation of Palestine', p. 609.
77 TNA, CO 967/104, Letter from Alan Cunningham to J.M. Martin, dated 24 January 1948.
78 *The Times*, 2 January 1948.
79 TNA, DEFE 7/388, Withdrawal from Palestine: Administrative Implications, Top Secret: General Hollis to Minister of Defence, 14 January 1948.
80 LHCMA, *Stockwell Papers*, 6/9, Major-General Stockwell to Brigadier Colquhoun and Brigadier Rome, 11 January 1948.
81 LHCMA, *Stockwell Papers*, 6/9, Major-General Stockwell to A.H. Law, District Commissioner, Haifa, 19 February 1948.
82 LHCMA, *Stockwell Papers*, 6/9, Major-General Stockwell to Lieutenant-General MacMillan, 19 March 1948.
83 *The Times*,2 March 1948.
84 LHCMA, *Stockwell Papers*, 6/11, Message Out from Milpal.
85 LHCMA, *Stockwell Papers*, 6/9.
86 LHCMA, *Stockwell Papers*, 6/29/1, I.S. Lecture (n.d.).
87 Morris, *1948*, p. 77.
88 Ibid.
89 *The Times*, 5 January 1948.
90 *The Times*, 6 January 1948.
91 *The Palestine Post*, 7 January 1948.
92 *The Palestine Post*, 5 January 1948.
93 *The Times*, 10 January 1948.
94 *The Times*, 12 January 1948.
95 *The Times*, 15 January 1948.

96 *The Times*, 17 January 1948.
97 Ibid.
98 *The Times*, 21 January 1948.
99 Ibid.
100 Three British deserters were later found to have played an important role in the bombings.
101 *The Palestine Post*, 24 February 1948.
102 *The Times*, 24 February 1948.
103 *The Times*, 23 February 1948.
104 *The Times*, 1 March 1948.
105 The souring of relations between British army officers and politicians would come to a head twenty years later over another withdrawal, this time from Aden.
106 TNA, DEFE 7/388, Withdrawal from Palestine: Administrative Implications, Top Secret: General Hollis to Minister of Defence, 14 January 1948.
107 TNA, DEFE 7/388, Correspondence from Ernest Bevin to Clement Attlee, 21 January 1948.
108 TNA, CAB 128/12, 5 February 1948.
109 Ibid.
110 Williams, Francis, *A Prime Minister Remembers: The War and Post-War Memoirs of the Rt. Hon. Earl Attlee* (London: Heinemann, 1961), p. 178.
111 BLSC, *Attlee Papers*, MS. Attlee Dep. 77, fol. 151–152, Secret Memorandum on Palestine by the Secretary of State for Foreign Affairs, Ernest Bevin, to the Cabinet, 15 January 1949.
112 BLSC, *Attlee Papers*, MS. Attlee Dep. 77, fol. 158, Historical Memorandum on the Situation in Palestine since 1945.
113 TNA, CAB 158/3, JIC, Scale and Nature of a Russian Attack on the Middle East, Annex 1: Russian Operational Appreciation – Assumptions, 17 August 1948.
114 TNA, CAB 158/3, JIC, Memoranda, January–May 1948, Vol. 47, Nos. 1–44, Short Term Intentions of the Soviet Union in Palestine: Report by the Joint Intelligence Committee, 13 February 1948.
115 TNA, CAB 158/3, JIC, Chiefs of Staff Committee: Joint Intelligence Committee, Soviet Interests, Intentions and Capabilities, 26 January 1948, p. 59.
116 *The Palestine Post*, 3 March 1948.
117 LHCMA, *Stockwell Papers*, 6/29/2, I.S. Lecture Staff College, November 1950.
118 LHCMA, *Stockwell Papers*, 6/26, Confidential: Lessons Learned in Palestine, report sent to Major General Stockwell, signed JHMH/MRH and dated 17 November 1948.
119 Ibid.
120 LHCMA, *Pyman Papers*, 7/1/16, Diary entry for 2 May 1948.
121 IWM, *MacMillan Papers*, DS/MISC/15, The Planning of the Evacuation of Palestine: Notes by the Chief of Staff in Palestine: Narrative of Events

from February 1947 until withdrawal of all British Troops by Lieutenant General G.H.A. MacMillan.

122 Cited in *The Journal of the Royal United Service Institution*, Vol. 93, No. 571 (August 1948), p. 473.

123 Blaxland, Gregory, *The Regiments Depart: A History of the British Army, 1945–1970* (London: William Kimber, 1971), p. 506. General MacMillan's narrative of events reveals that between 1 January 1947 and the withdrawal of British troops, casualties stood at 50 officers and 543 other ranks, of which 13 officers and 161 other ranks were killed.

124 Williams, *A Prime Minister Remembers*, p. 182.

125 Attlee, Clement, *As it Happened* (London: William Heinemann, 1954), p. 175.

126 United Nations, Security Council Resolution 49 (1948), 22 May 1948. Archived: http://daccessdds.un.org/doc/RESOLUTION/GEN/NR0/047/74/IMG/NR004774.pdf?OpenElement. Accessed: 10 November 2008.

127 IWM, *Norman Papers*, 87/57/2, Letter from Richard Norman to his mother, 12 June 1948.

128 IWM, *Norman Papers*, 87/57/2, Letter from Richard Norman to his mother, 20 June 1948.

129 IWM, *Norman Papers*, 87/57/2, Terrorism in Palestine, dated 17 November 1948.

130 Begin, *The Revolt*, p. 331.

131 IWM, Norman Papers, 87/57/2, Terrorism in Palestine, dated 17 November 1948.

132 House of Commons Debates (Hansard), 4 May 1948, Vol. 450, Col. 1118–1119.

133 LHCMA, *Pyman Papers*, 7/1/17, Emergency Cipher Message from Chief of Staff MELF to GOC Palestine, COS/3260, dated 1 June 1948.

134 LHCMA, *Pyman Papers*, 7/1/17, Emergency Cipher Message from GOC Palestine to Chief of Staff MELF, dated 2 June 1948.

135 LHCMA, *Stockwell Papers*, 6/26, The High Morale of Troops in Palestine by Lieutenant Colonel P.G.F. Young, Oxf and Bucks L.I. (n.d.).

136 LHCMA, *Pyman Papers*, 7/1/16, Secret Briefing to new officers in GHQ Middle East Command (n.d.).

137 LHCMA, *Pyman Papers*, 7/2/3, Top Secret: Middle East Strategy 1947, dated 22 June 1948.

138 LHCMA, *Pyman Papers*, 7/1/17, Top Secret and Personal Communiqué entitled 'Palestine', sent from General Sir John Crocker to CIGS, Field Marshal the Viscount Montgomery, dated 24 June 1948.

139 Burridge, Trevor, *Clement Attlee: A Political Biography* (London: Jonathan Cape, 1986), p. 323.

140 LSE Archives, *Shore Papers*, 8/88, Parliamentary Labour Party Report, Session 1947–48, p. 66.

141 LHCMA, *Pyman Papers*, 7/1/4, Note for Oral Representation to King Farouk by HE, dated 11 April 1947. The brief stated that 'H.M.G.

cannot but think therefore that the action which the Egyptian Government are now contemplating to dispense with the services of the British Military Mission must have a deleterious effect on peace and security in the Middle East.' As history would show, it would also have a direct effect on Britain's national interests.

142 Andrew, Christopher and Vasili Mitrokhin, *The Mitrokhin Archive II: The KGB and the World* (London: Allen Lane, 2005), p. 141.

143 Barnett, Correlli, *The Lost Victory: British Dreams, British Realities, 1945–1950* (London: Macmillan, 1995), p. 397.

144 LHCMA, *Pyman Papers*, 7/1/4, Top Secret: Imperial Strategy – Deployment of British Troops in Middle East (n.d. 1947).

145 LHCMA, *Pyman Papers*, 7/1/16, Secret Briefing to new officers in GHQ Middle East Command (n.d.).

146 Kitchen, Martin, 'British Policy Towards the Soviet Union, 1945–1948' in Gorodetsky, Gabriel (ed.) *Soviet Foreign Policy, 1917–1991: A Retrospective* (London: Frank Cass, 1994), p. 130.

147 BLSC, *Harold Wilson Papers*, MS. Wilson C. 1106, fol. 330, 'Peace Through Rearmament?', Speech by Harold Wilson in Oslo, 10 May 1952.

148 BLSC, *Wilson Papers*, MS. Wilson C. 1106, fol. 325, 'Peace Through Rearmament?', Speech by Harold Wilson in Oslo, 10 May 1952.

149 Kennedy, Paul, *The Rise and Fall of the Great Powers: Economic Change and Military Conflict from 1500 to 2000* (London: Fontana Press, 1989), p. 474.

150 Aldrich, Richard J. and John Zametica, 'The Rise and Decline of a Strategic Concept: The Middle East, 1945–51' in Aldrich, Richard J. (ed.) *British Intelligence, Strategy and the Cold War, 1945–51* (London: Routledge, 1992), p. 265.

151 LHCMA, *Pyman Papers*, 7/1/4, Top Secret: Imperial Strategy – Deployment of British Troops in Middle East (n.d. 1947).

2

Winning 'hearts and minds'? From imperialism to independence in Malaya

> I think that it is now clear that 'the man' selected for Malaya must be the No. 1 Man, and one who will put things right as regards the top people who have to get on with the job.
>
> He must have full powers, civil and military.
>
> And he must be backed.
>
> He must arrive in Malaya with a bang and electrify the whole country.[1]

> The population represents this new ground. If the insurgent manages to dissociate the population from the counter-insurgent, to control it physically, to get its active support, he will win the war because, in the final analysis, the experience of political power depends on the tacit or explicit agreement of the population or, at worst, on its submissiveness.[2]

> Ideologies and politics can mutate and spread like a virus which counteracts every medical effort to pinpoint and eradicate it.[3]

Introduction

By the late 1940s Britain's turn towards decolonization was in full swing. India had been granted independence in 1947 and Palestine was jettisoned from the British outer empire a year later. The Labour government was anxious to keep the process moving, yet Prime Minister Clement Attlee was fully aware of the dangers posed by Communism. He told the House of Commons in a major debate on foreign affairs in January 1948 that the propaganda being spread by the Soviet Union was 'rather like the attitude of the early adherents of Islam. Every one outside it is an infidel.' Finding their message 'repugnant', he emphasized how the 'orders from Moscow are obeyed, not only by the satellite countries, but by Communist parties in other countries. There is just one party line; there is no room for thought or other views.' Britain would now be orientated to ridding the world of the 'Communist menace'.[4] This was somewhat half-hearted, given Attlee's earlier desire to avoid conflict with the Soviets in the East Mediterranean and the Middle East by urging a speedy withdrawal from Palestine.

For the Conservatives, under Leader of the Opposition Winston Churchill, Labour's lacklustre direction of British policy was insufficient; it was now time to 'bring matters to a head with the Soviet Government, and, by formal diplomatic processes, with all their privacy and gravity, to arrive at a lasting settlement'. If diplomacy failed to prevent war between East and West, then at the very least Britain might well secure the best possible terms of 'coming out of it alive'.[5] Churchill did not have to wait long for his stark warning of an iron curtain descending over Europe, as the Berlin airlift in 1948–49 was to prove. Liberal democracies, believing strongly in the rule of law and the perceived threat posed by the Soviet Union, formed the North Atlantic Treaty Organization in Washington on 5 April 1949. The Cold War had begun.

One of the most remarkable aspects of Britain's military experience in the 1950s was the number of simultaneous interventions it was undertaking. Apart from the major conventional war in Korea, in which Britain had deployed 12,000 troops by spring 1951, it was soon embroiled in counter-insurgency operations in Malaya, Kenya and Cyprus. The concept of overstretch loomed large in the minds of politicians and military chiefs in the early 1950s. The reasonable state of the defence budget and the re-introduction of conscription in 1948 were designed to meet the demands of this high-tempo post-war military environment. Yet Britain was not at peace, and the illusion that it was rang hollow as its armed forces struggled to maintain momentum in these simultaneous interventions, all the while attempting to balance resources for the main effort of opposing world Communism.

The Cold War provided the wider strategic backdrop for competition between the United States, Britain and the Soviet Union, as soldiers fought and died in small wars throughout Britain's ever-shrinking empire. Though, of course, as counter-insurgency expert Sir Robert Thompson had suggested, it was possible to 'wage a revolutionary war without direct Communist sponsorship or involvement',[6] Communist subversion posed a decisive and very real threat and was to be confronted wherever it reared its ugly head. Perhaps the best-known example of Communist penetration of British colonial interests was in Malaya. The formation of a Malayan Federation in 1948 immediately prompted the outbreak of an attempted armed insurrection by members of the ethnically Chinese Malayan Communist Party (MCP). The ensuing counter-insurgency campaign has since become celebrated for its success, though, in fact, failure was only narrowly averted after the colonial government responded with a new strategy to tackle the challenge posed by the MCP. It was only by reorganizing the civil and military leadership, encapsulated perhaps by the appointment of General Sir Gerald Templer as High Commissioner in 1952, which turned the tide on the MCP. Templer's mission, as he saw it, was to 'win the hearts and minds of the people' and work towards independence. While Korea was, perhaps, a clearer example of Britain's deployment of 'limited forces to achieve limited objectives'[7] in the vast confrontation between East and West, Malaya became a vital battleground in the Cold War.

Background to the Emergency

Rich in natural resources, Malaya was the centre for rubber plant and tin production, and a key staging post for Britain's projection of military power in South East Asia and beyond in the 1940s and 1950s. Covered in dense jungle, it was the home of the Malayan People's Anti-Japanese Army (MPAJA), which had fought gallantly against the Japanese forces during the Second World War. Indeed, one of its young leaders, Chin Peng, was personally decorated by Admiral Lord Louis Mountbatten, Supreme Allied Commander South East Asia, for his contribution to the war effort.[8] Shortly afterwards Peng was appointed to the Central Military Committee. Summoned to Kuala Lumpur to meet Lai Teck, Secretary General of the MCP, he 'intended to report that the party was ready to confront the British'.[9] By the time he replaced Lai Teck in 1947, Peng was openly advocating armed struggle against the colonial government.[10] Lai Teck had been the mastermind behind the MPAJA and MCP, single-handedly organizing wartime resistance against the Japanese. His 'inborn love of intrigue and aptitude for it', remarked Chin Peng, would be his undoing as he 'counselled patience' in the face of accusations about his wartime role and collaboration with perceived enemies.[11] For Peng, Lai Teck was 'surely one of Britain's greatest spying triumphs' – later eliminated on Peng's orders and 'unceremoniously dumped into the swift flowing waters of Bangkok's Chao Praya river'.[12] Peng later admitted that although he thought 'armed struggle' in Malaya 'inevitable', he had been hamstrung to do anything about it. Lai Teck had run down the MCP sufficiently enough to make this an inauspicious time for military action.[13] Events would soon change all of that.

The Federation of Malaya came into being on 1 February 1948. The exclusion of around one million Chinese from the political process immediately provoked further large-scale industrial unrest and subversion from within the ranks of the MCP. Interestingly, the news coincided with Peng's chance meeting with Lawrence Sharkey, Secretary General of the Australian Communist Party, at the Communist Asian Youth Congress in Calcutta. A dyed-in-the-wool Communist from New South Wales, Australia, Lance Sharkey had risen through the ranks of the party to become an elected member of the executive committee of the Cominform.[14] He had a reputation as a tough no-nonsense proponent of direct action and wasted little time in recommending to the Indian congress that strike-breakers be handled violently; 'we get rid of them', he bluntly told his audience. Sharkey's words 'sent a rush of reinforced fervour through our gathering', Peng later recalled. While Sharkey did not at any time urge those gathered 'to take up arms against the British', what he said 'was pivotal in its overall effect'.[15] Armed struggle had undoubtedly come more sharply into focus.[16] Peng thought Sharkey's words 'inspiring', and 'It was within this context and in this mood that we went on to accept we had no option now but to wage war for our principles'.[17] Sensing that the moment was ripe for action – and against the backdrop of Communist insurgencies in French Indo-China, Greece and China – the MCP 'saw no obvious reason why it should not be triumphant against the British-protected regime in Malaya and Singapore'.[18] Believing they were seizing the initiative, small groups of guerrillas escalated the violence in May and June 1948, though, as Stubbs puts it, they 'jumped the gun' and forced the government's hand in introducing emergency regulations following an outcry by the resident European community.[19]

While the government had been forewarned of the impending launch of an armed campaign, the colonial administration – and, in particular, the High Commissioner himself, Sir Edward Gent – underestimated the 'threat to law, order and good government, and failed to take sufficient steps to counter it'.[20] Furthermore, a question mark hung over the government's record, which made them structurally less effective, divided and lacking in legitimacy in the eyes of many Malays.[21] While the MCP may have misjudged the timing, the remarkable lack of foresight and imagination of the Malayan government in relation to the armed challenge created a political context for the unfolding armed actions.

The MCP was greatly influenced in its preparations for guerrilla warfare by the activities of other Communist groupings in Greece and French Indo-China. The achievements of Mao Tse-Tung's Red Army in China had the most far-reaching impact on the MCP's embryonic military doctrine. Peng sought to bring about a hasty British evacuation by attacking several important targets with small tight-knit groups of guerrillas, tactics similar to those he had used against the Japanese in the Second World War. Given that the strategy seemed to have worked earlier, Peng was reasonably convinced that it could be profitably applied to a new set of circumstances. The first attack, in which three European rubber plantation farmers were murdered in the Communist-dominated Perak district on 16 June 1948, sent a shock-wave through the European community. It prompted Gent to declare an Emergency in the north-western Perak district and in the southerly Johore district. He later extended the emergency legislation to cover the entire country. Gent's death in a plane crash near London on 4 July, however, robbed the administration of local strategic leadership at a 'critical time' and the pause 'probably saved the MPAJA'.[22]

The task of plugging the political-military gap until the appointment of a new High Commissioner now fell to Malcolm MacDonald, the Commissioner-General for South-East Asia, and Major-General C.H. Boucher, the General Officer Commanding (GOC) Malayan District, until a replacement for Gent could be found. In any event the appointee, Sir Henry Gurney, would not take up the position until 6 October 1948, thus leaving the Chief Secretary Sir Alexander T. Newboult as the interim head of government. The interregnum was marked by its clumsy and often very brutal military operations. 'Large-scale "sweeps", designed to locate and trap the guerrillas', writes historian Richard Stubbs, 'carried out by men trained on the wide-open flats of England's Salisbury Plain, were vigorously employed'.[23] Nor were the partially trained Gurkhas of the 17 Division as experienced as perhaps they ought to have been. These exaggerated manoeuvres simply gave guerrillas advanced warning that the security forces were closing in and they 'melted into the jungle or the troops were caught in an ambush'. 'Overall', Stubbs concludes, '[t]he success rate of these operations was low'.[24] Meanwhile in London the Colonial Secretary, Arthur Creech Jones, outlined the government's position to an increasingly alarmed House of Commons:

> I would say emphatically, particularly in view of the vilification of Britain – the wilful lies in regard to the Malayan situation which have been put across from Moscow – that we have not here at all the emergence of a nationalist movement which Britain is engaged in putting down. This is not a movement of the people in Malaya. It is the conduct of gangsters who are out to destroy the very foundations of human society – orderly life. We have no desire to create in Malaya a police state, nor are we doing so. What we are doing is to arm the necessary authorities with the requisite powers in order to cope with this situation of violence which has become too formidable a feature in the life of that territory.[25]

Creech Jones remained largely on the defensive throughout this lengthy debate, arguing that the colonial authorities had an obligation to 'defeat and destroy this menace'. Warning of a 'grave situation' developing, the Colonial Secretary further implied that the malign hand of Moscow might well be at work.[26] Much would now hinge upon Gurney's ability to transform the security situation.

Gurney, a long-time colonial administrator who had served in Kenya, Jamaica and the Gold Coast, had been Chief Secretary in Palestine prior to his appointment as High Commissioner of Malaya. In keeping with the Colonial Office's modus operandi of maintaining continuity between postings, and facilitated by the resignation of the current incumbent due to ill-health, Creech Jones appointed Colonel William Nicol Gray, the former Inspector-General of the Palestine Police, to the post of Police Commissioner. With the termination of the mandate in Palestine, the influx of colonial policemen enabled the Malayan administration to set about organizing, disciplining and training a new Special Constabulary.[27] Numbering 9,000 in June 1948, the police were rapidly expanded to 12,767 regular and 33,610 Special Constables by early 1949. However, as Richard Aldrich argues, the use of Palestine policemen to backfill vacant positions soon proved to be 'a major mistake' due largely to the fact that they were 'completely ignorant of local conditions', and 'the newly introduced police proved to be a liability and on a number of occasions they resorted to arbitrary behaviour'.[28] Matters were made worse by the plain fact that intelligence was 'a mess and would remain so until the arrival of General Sir Gerald Templer in early 1952'.[29] Both Gurney and Gray expected the Army to bridge the gap caused by institutional flux in the Malayan Special Branch. However, they failed to appreciate the Army's wider strategic responsibilities, most notably the defence of Singapore from Soviet and Chinese aggression, which it tended to regard as a higher priority at the time.[30] As the situation worsened, London increased the number of infantry battalions from 10 in June 1948 to 15 in January 1949. On the surface it appeared that the lessons learned in Palestine were being misapplied in a very different environment.

Responding to the need to rejuvenate Malaya's ailing security infrastructure, the Director General of the Security Service, MI5, Sir Percy Sillitoe, sent ahead the flamboyant agent Alex Kellar, who had been active against the Jewish resistance in Palestine, to assess the effectiveness of the intelligence structure. He promptly recommended the imposition of a new Special Branch.[31] Unfortunately it proved insufficient to turn the tide of events. Civil–military relations were at an all-time low, with the Director of Military Intelligence and the Chief of Police barely on speaking terms.[32] Senior MI5 officer, and Head of Security Intelligence Far East, Jack Morton later observed how there was 'nothing on the ground for the collection of intelligence, no facilities for interrogation, translation, document research, agent running or any of the other processes of counter-intelligence work'. 'In short,' Morton reported, 'the period was one of considerable muddle and ineptitude.'[33] It was little wonder that the Colonial Secretary in London could declare confidently at the time that there was 'no evidence that the bandits are receiving direct material assistance from the Communist Party in China or elsewhere' and that 'in spite of local setbacks, further steady progress' was being achieved.[34] It was an overly optimistic assessment of a dire situation; Creech-Jones' words would soon return to haunt him.

Recognizing the inability to co-ordinate an effective anti-terrorist response, Gurney recommended – and the British government agreed to – the appointment of Lieutenant-General Sir Harold Briggs as Director of Operations. Briggs had a long and distinguished career with the Indian Army, seeing action in France, Mesopotamia and Palestine; he served in the North-West Frontier during the inter-war period and commanded the 7th Indian (Infantry) Brigade in Eritrea, the Western Desert, Iraq and Burma during the Second World War. Briggs was 'given the task of devising a revised strategy to combat the Communist threat', and within two weeks of arriving in Malaya he produced a plan, in May 1950, which was supported by Gurney and approved by London.[35] The plan had several key objectives, including resettling all of the rural ethnic Chinese community in plantations or near tin mines, strengthening the civil administration, setting up more efficient co-ordination between the administration, police and army, extending the road infrastructure to harder to reach rural areas and finally to move the civilian-military authorities into cleared territories to dominate the ground and prevent insurgents from returning. It was an ambitious plan, envisaging a rapid timetable for completion of all objectives.[36] Despite its promising headline goals, it failed to produce the kind of short-term results some components of the security forces anticipated.

Most critical of the plan was the RAF, which complained bitterly about the 'fluid and indecisive operations', it thought had not, 'repeat not, achieved very significant results'; it was anxious to return to its main job of preparing for 'global hot war'. The RAF flew 403 sorties in the period July 1948 to March 1949, involving some 95 strike operations, and dropped 78 tonnes of bombs on targets. Between April 1949 and December 149, it flew 6,011 sorties, including 1,017 strike operations, and dropped a staggering 6,900 tonnes of ordnance.[37] As senior RAF officers privately admitted, 'air strikes appear to be an extremely expensive method of gaining such meagre results'. In congruence with Briggs' Plan, however, they conceded:

> It is increasingly felt here that a final and satisfactory solution of the Malayan problem will only be achieved as a result of political and economic action. This will inevitably take time and in the meanwhile military action will have to continue to hold the situation. But what we in Air Ministry want to know is whether the continuation of air action on the present scale is really vital or justifiable.[38]

While the theatre-level command agreed with many of the points raised, they duly informed London of a progress meeting with the Acting High Commissioner and General Briggs, which made 'quite clear that things are worsening rather than getting better'.[39] The lack of political direction from London, which had in any case been won over by the Gurney–Briggs partnership, irritated senior air force commanders, who were by now preoccupied with conflicts on a number of fronts. As secret correspondence made clear, 'The present difficulty is, of course, a typical example of the constantly recurring conflict between "hot" and "cold" war requirements', in Korea.[40]

A reality check was clearly needed, thus paving the way for a visit by the Minister of Defence, Emmanuel 'Manny' Shinwell. Arriving in the Federation in October 1950, he was greeted by turmoil. Reporting back to the Cabinet's Malaya Committee upon his return to London, Shinwell duly confirmed just how bad the situation had become. In contrast to an earlier meeting, in which Gurney remained optimistic that he could turn things around, Shinwell reported that the High Commissioner's early optimism of withdrawing troops by the end of 1951 was now 'hopelessly unrealistic', given the sharp decline in the security situation. 'Since then the position appears to have somewhat deteriorated', he told the Cabinet: 'According to recent reports the Johore authorities consider that the increased allocation of troops, expansion of the C.I.D., and the re-settlement programme are not likely to produce any marked improvement in the situation before the end of 1950.'[41] Patience was advised. Despite some reservations amongst the military, Briggs' plan, launched earlier in the year, was nonetheless still looked upon as the best opportunity to turn the tide before the end of the year. Privately, Shinwell himself remained cautious, even going as far as to view the present situation 'with grave anxiety' because of two principal reasons: first, that the nine British infantry battalions, eight Gurkha battalions, four Malay Battalions, in addition to 3 Commando Brigade and two Armoured car regiments, totalling some 40,000 men, could not be sustained; second, that the successful conclusion of operations in Malaya was part of a wider strategy of Cold War campaigning and had to be looked at in the wider strategic context of the clash with world Communism. For Shinwell:

> We have always maintained that the successful conclusion of operations against the guerrillas in Malaya is a vital step in the 'cold War' against Communism in the Far East. The Malayan campaign is not isolated, and must be considered in relation to the Far East theatre as a whole. The successes of the United Nations forces in Korea will lose a great deal of their value in the Far East if the position in Malaya is allowed to deteriorate.[42]

Shinwell appears to have remained convinced that the Briggs plan should have been given the necessary political space to operate. Clearing the areas of Communist terrorists (CTs) was seen as the first step in denying them their basis of support in the population. Nevertheless, a more sophisticated measure was soon being advocated. In the words of the Colonial Secretary, 'It was not possible to treat the squatters as criminals and simply bundle them into concentration camps'.[43] However, the evidence also points to the tough choices facing the War Office in London amidst the 'hot war' in Korea.[44] While the availability of Royal Australian Air Force Lincolns in Malaya gave adequate support, it was clear that further resources would not be forthcoming.

The obvious overstretch between the two theatres undoubtedly had a negative impact on Britain's strategic effectiveness to a certain degree. However, as far as the RAF was concerned, this was not an insurmountable obstacle. In an address to the Royal United Service Institute in March 1951, the Air Officer Commanding, Malaya, between May 1949 and January 1951, Air Vice-Marshal Sir Francis Mellersh, estimated that at the beginning of the Emergency there were 4–5,000 CTs, of which approximately 2,500 were 'hard core' members of armed groups. Their plan was three-fold: To create 'economic chaos throughout the country by a programme of assassination and terrorism designed to undermine the confidence of the British Administration'; to ' "liberate" certain isolated country areas'; and 'to link up "liberated areas", capture towns, and initiate a country-wide state of revolution'.[45] Interestingly, while it is often thought that the military initially failed because it did not perceive the conflict to be a political problem, in fact the opposite was true. As Mellersh revealed: 'I want now to make it clear that this campaign is not, in the strict sense of the term, a military operation. It is a problem for the Civil Administration and it is, first and foremost, a Police affair. Martial Law has not been declared.'[46] The burden placed on the Army at a tactical level was made worse by the lack of any formal training regime for newly arrived troops, many of whom were National Servicemen with little experience of soldiering. This was a classic example of how tactical-level shortcomings could have greater repercussions at the operational and strategic levels. It was not until a rigorous jungle warfare training school was established in Kota Tinggi that a more thorough programme of military operations could be advanced in correlation to efforts on the civil front.[47]

The colonial strategy now being pursued by authorities in Kuala Lumpur was nonetheless the best available at the time. That it was done in haste ought not to detract from the importance Malaya played in Britain's wider strategic calculus:

> Malaya is vital to the British Empire and Commonwealth, both strategically and economically. It may well be regarded as the frontier of Australia and a bulwark against the spread of Communism. Its products of rubber and tin are essential to our economy. The country *must* be held.[48]

Its focus on the politics of countering irregular adversaries 'hinged on the notion of separating the greater part of the colonial society from those involved in the insurgency'.[49] In general terms, the strategy sought to balance protecting the population with the pursuit of a ruthless military campaign against the insurgents. For the most part, senior civil and military officials in Kuala Lumpur and London remained optimistic, despite the fact that Briggs' plan 'was much more difficult to implement than its author had envisaged'.[50]

Around this time, Gurney penned a letter to his close personal friend General Sir John Harding, who was soon to relinquish his command of Far East Land Forces, which included the Army in Malaya and Hong Kong. 'Malaya will seem very far away but your work will long be remembered here', he lamented, 'certainly by all those who like myself have had the privilege of working with you.'[51] Harding had just replaced General Sir Charles Keightley as Commander of the British Army on the Rhine in a co-ordinated move that would eventually see him replace Field Marshal Sir William Slim as Chief of the Imperial General Staff (CIGS) within twelve months. In a letter congratulating Harding on his new appointment, the Commissioner-General in South East Asia (1948–55), Malcolm MacDonald, informed his close friend how:

> The Emergency proceeds much as you would expect. Very drastic steps to prevent food from reaching the terrorists have now been taken, and the Johore 'offensive' started about a week ago. Pugh says that he expects that this will cause a big improvement in the situation in the State before six months are out. I hope that he is right, for if we can break the back of the enemy in Johore we shall cripple him badly everywhere.[52]

Uncharacteristically, perhaps, Gurney was also sounding much more upbeat than he had been about the Briggs Plan. In a prophetic letter to Slim, he cautioned against reverting to the 'previous setup' in which 'the control of joint police and military operations was in effect in the hands of the Commissioner of Police'. He felt that perhaps a military man in civilian clothing would be the best way to move the plan forward:

> I have, of course, thought of the possibility of a military High Commissioner, but there is little advantage in putting on a military officer the sometimes arduous and generally unfamiliar responsibility of keeping the political waters smooth in addition to the responsibility for the direction of operations. Nevertheless it has been done in Indo-China, and there might conceivably be pressure for something similar here. In that event I should personally be very ready to accept it.[53]

Although Slim did 'not personally favour a Military High Commissioner', he did agree that the post should continue to be a civil one. Ironically, though, he recommended his old Indian Army comrade General Sir Rob Lockhart, who, he said, possessed 'the required character, temperament and experience' to succeed Briggs. Though lacking an appreciation of the nuances of a military commander in a civil role, Lockhart was nevertheless 'exceptionally fit and energetic', Slim continued. 'He is admirable at getting people of varied interests and services to co-operate and has always inspired confidence. In the sort of work that would be his in Malaya and in dealing with civil departments he has had considerable experience.' Although Lockhart had not held 'any high command in the field' in the Second World War, he was 'constantly in demand for other tasks'. Above all, Slim said, he had demonstrated 'in large measure the power of command and leadership' needed in Malaya.[54] Briggs' successor had all but been anointed.

It was now clear that MacDonald was coming under increasing flak for his mishandling of the overall strategy for the region. South-East Asia was a vital area in British imperial outlook. As MacDonald confided in another letter to Harding:

> You are much too kind in what you say about my efforts in this fascinating part of the world. As you know better than anyone, the making and implementing of policy here are done by a team of people, both civilian and Service chiefs. I was and am only one member of the team. Had it not been for the rest of the team, I would have made a great many mistakes![55]

Like all team-work, though, MacDonald's staff was only as good as its weak links, one of which now appeared to be Gurney. Interestingly, Gurney had already confided in Slim that '[t]hree years of this after eighteen months of Palestine can easily make one stale'.[56] The Malayan assignment was fast becoming an inconvenience and he was looking for a way out. 'None the less,' concludes A.J. Stockwell, 'his calm temperament and clear thinking, his experience of liaising with the military, his administrative skills and proven ability to plan for the long term' made him an exceptional High Commissioner.[57] In the immediate term Gurney would now have to seek a replacement for Briggs, who had requested a return from his continuous thirty-seven-year overseas service. Briggs was keen to make his successor aware of the constraints and also the possibilities of having to defend Malaya in the event of a global war.[58] As with Briggs' appointment, his replacement would occupy a civil post, 'responsible for the allocation of tasks to the various components of the security forces available for operations and for deciding, in consultation with the heads of police and fighting services, the priorities between these tasks and the general timing and sequence of their execution'.[59] Heavily reliant on personality for colonial success, Britain's policy in Malaya was in danger of unravelling.

The death of Henry Gurney

It was not long before the vast Whitehall apparatus creaked and groaned under the weight of decolonization. Gurney's old stomping grounds of Palestine and the Gold Coast were engulfed in flames as nationalist insurrection sought to overturn British colonial rule. It was a busy period for both the Colonial Office and Foreign Office, as they struggled to apply the scientific rigour of orderliness to a very fluid and chaotic post-war world. Yet, much of the strain fell disproportionately on the War Office as it too struggled to keep up the vigilant defence against the dangers of Communist subversion. Malaya and Singapore became Britain's final bulwark against the spread of Chinese Communism.

Within six months of corresponding with Slim, Gurney was dead. He was shot at point-blank range by up to three dozen MCP fighters who ambushed his car on Saturday 6 October 1951, three years to the day after he became High Commissioner. Gurney's wife and driver remained unhurt. It later transpired that a Malayan Races Liberation Army (MRLA) unit had ambushed his car near the town of Tras, a notorious Communist hotspot forty miles north of Kuala Lumpur.[60] While the MRLA argued that they were taking the fight to the enemy, all they really did in murdering the High Commissioner was to provoke anti-Chinese feeling amongst the non-Chinese communities. The new Colonial Secretary, Oliver Lyttelton, moved quickly to 'reaffirm the determination of His Majesty's Government to rid Malaya of terrorism'.[61]

Historians are divided about the repercussions of Gurney's murder. Anthony Short suggests that the 'government's Emergency policy appeared to have lost all direction by the end of 1951',[62] while Richard Stubbs contends that it 'was simply further evidence that the situation was getting worse and not, as the Government kept saying, better'.[63] Benjamin Grob-Fitzgibbon takes a more upbeat perspective, albeit one not supported by the evidence, suggesting that by October 1951, 'there were convincing signs that this [balanced] strategy was beginning to work'.[64]

The truth was that the situation was dire. The Briggs Plan was in its embryonic phase and needed considerable nurturing before it could gain traction. Even the outgoing government admitted that they were 'baffled by Malaya', with Oliver Lyttelton recalling his predecessor's remark that 'At this stage it has become a military problem to which we have not been able to find an answer'.[65] Again the breach had to be filled by the military, who were being asked to carry no less than the entire strategic project with the political backing to complete the job. Though the military were proving resolute and imaginative, the lack of a civilian lead was unsatisfactory. Before he visited Malaya, Lyttelton had made up his mind that:

> The campaign against Communist-inspired terrorism cannot be pursued by military action alone. I intend during my visit to Malaya to see as much as possible of the other counter-measures already in force and to discuss further measures with responsible officers on the spot.[66]

What he saw shocked him. 'The situation was far worse that I had imagined: it was appalling', he later confided in his memoirs.[67] Something had to be done, and fast.

As the situation in Malaya worsened Slim turned to his predecessor for advice. Not one to mince his words, Montgomery suggested that Slim push for MacDonald's sacking as South-East Asia Commissioner; there 'has also got to be a "clean out" of duds and unsuitable officers', including, he suggested, the Colonial Secretary in Singapore and the Commissioner of the Malayan Police, Colonel Nicol Gray, who, Montgomery noted, was 'a good Commando officer in the war', adding 'but that is no qualification for taking charge of a Police Force'.[68] In short, the Emergency needed a man 'whose very name will ensure that he is accepted, trusted and obeyed, and whose very presence in Malaya will at once inspire confidence and raise morale'. In typically alarmist fashion, Montgomery proposed that he should be 'a soldier' and that he must also have 'imagination'. 'We need "the spark". We must electrify Malaya', he said. This was interesting given his earlier correspondence with the Colonial Office on the Palestine issue, in which he advocated a civilian for the top job. Never one to let consistency get in the way of a firm recommendation for action, Montgomery admitted that the problem was both military and political, and needed an individual of the highest calibre to arrest the deterioration:

> I think that it is now clear that 'the man' selected for Malaya must be the No. 1 Man, and one who will put things right as regards the top people who have to get on with the job.
>
> He must have full powers, civil and military.
>
> And he must be backed.
>
> He must arrive in Malaya with a bang and electrify the whole country.[69]

Sensing a desperate vacuum developing, Montgomery thought that Communist China might use the insurgency in Malaya as a way of entrenching their influence in the region. Writing to Lyttelton, he expressed his concerns:

> In general, I am disturbed about the whole situation in our Colonial Empire. It has drifted downhill since the war, chiefly because of two useless Secretaries of State for the Colonies: Creech-Jones and Griffiths. Your advent seems to me to be exactly what is needed. You clearly are the man to put things right and you have the necessary courage to do so: which your predecessors did not.

Montgomery's comments found a sympathetic ear in Lyttelton, who complained in his own memoirs that his predecessor, Jim Griffiths, took an 'emotional approach to public affairs', which was 'to drive me first to boredom and finally exasperation'.[70]

Interestingly, upon his return from Malaya, Lyttelton received an invitation from Churchill to meet him at Chequers for lunch on 23 December 1951. That Malaya was to be the principal topic of discussion generated much press speculation, partly because the Prime Minister had forgotten that he had already invited Montgomery and partly because of Lyttelton's well-publicized comments while on his tour. Lyttelton later wrote that commentators 'understandably inferred that Montgomery was to be the new High Commissioner in Malaya, even that he wished keenly for the appointment himself'. The tendency of historians to overlook Montgomery's correspondence is curious given his reputation. Moreover, Lyttelton later claimed in his memoirs that the letter from Montgomery was 'the only one from him which I have ever received'. It read:

Dear Lyttelton,

Malaya

We must have a plan.

Secondly, we must have a man.

When we have a plan and a man, we

Shall succeed: not otherwise.

Yours sincerely,

(signed)

Montgomery (F.M.)[71]

In fact Lyttelton's recollection omits that he did, in fact, receive two further letters from Montgomery. Both are significant because they challenge Lyttelton's account that 'I may, perhaps with undue conceit, say that this had occurred to me' to appoint a military officer in civilian clothing.

Montgomery's correspondence with both Churchill and Lyttelton on a suitable replacement for Gurney is significant for another reason in that it demonstrates his direct interference in policy matters, which are often seen as the preserve of politicians and civil servants, rather than the military. The correspondence seems deliberately political in its tone and exposed Montgomery as the prying general that he had become. In his letter, he advocated nothing short of the complete overhaul of Britain's grand strategic architecture in South-East Asia in the contest between 'East and West, between Communism and Democracy, between evil and Christianity'.[72] Montgomery's second note to Lyttelton went further: 'We need one man to exercise overall direction of our interests and affairs in the Far East. He could be the same man as in 1 above: but not necessarily (personally, I consider he *should* be the same man) . . . In all this welter of trouble "the man" is what counts', he argued.[73] Dismissing MacDonald and Gurney, Montgomery lost no time in criticizing the latter for concentrating too much 'on the political problem' with the consequence that 'he never was able to handle the bandit problem; he did not understand how to keep law and order in the Federation, and he was unable to give clear guidance and direction'.[74] Coming to the point of his interjection, Montgomery told Lyttelton that it was 'doubtful if a first class civilian can be found with these qualities . . . It therefore seems that a first class soldier is necessary'.[75] There are multiple readings one could apply to Montgomery's correspondence, including that he may indeed have been setting himself up as a possible 'No. 1 man' responsible for the whole of the region. Whatever the explanation, the fact that the Army high command were closely consulted on these matters demonstrates how the government were moving towards a civil–military solution to the Malaya problem.

Electrifying Malaya

After short-listing several candidates for the job of High Commissioner, General Sir Gerald Templer was appointed by Prime Minister Winston Churchill in order to accomplish 'not only in the immediate task of defeating the terrorists but in the longer term objective of forging a united Malayan nation'.[76] Although he was the defacto civil and military supremo, he intimated to Churchill that 'I must therefore handle that aspect as a soldier, and with the operational set up which I consider necessary for the purpose'.[77] Templer had an impressive résumé of prior experience of civil–military affairs, when he served as Director of Civil Affairs and Military Government, presiding over parts of Germany and Belgium and Holland between May 1945 and April 1946. He later served as Director of Military Intelligence and then Vice-Chief of the Imperial General Staff. He was a workaholic, who did not suffer fools gladly and lost no time in sacking the most complacent and ineffectual administrators or soldiers under his command. As he himself put it, in an address to cadets commissioning from the Royal Military Academy Sandhurst, 'Never accept second-rate standards in any of these matters, from yourself or from anybody else – never'. On this occasion he advocated the time-honoured British military ethos of 'work hard, play hard', suggesting that apart from excelling at games and sports that cadets read literature, know the 'points of a horse', but also, 'what happens in a boys' club in the back streets, what are the problems of our great Colonial Empire where one day most of you will almost certainly serve'.[78] Templer spoke in direct language, Richard Stubbs informs us, his 'sharp, incisive voice, in a crisp forthright manner, echoing the traditions of the parade ground'.[79] Montgomery wrote to Churchill to express his delight at Templer's selection; 'I think the selection of Templer to go to Malaya as High Commissioner is excellent', he said, 'I have the very highest opinion of his qualities . . . He will do the job well in Malaya.'[80]

According to *Time Magazine*, which ran a cover story on Templer in December 1952, he was given 'such military and political powers in his kit bag as no British soldier had had since Cromwell'.[81] His powers were wide-ranging, though he had an explicit mission from Churchill, which read:

> Communist terrorism is retarding the political advancement and economic development of the country and the welfare of its peoples. Your primary task in Malaya must, therefore, be the restoration of law and order, so that this barrier to progress may be removed. Without victory and the state of law and order which it alone can bring, there can be no freedom from fear, which is the first human liberty.

This he was most comfortable with, especially since fulfilling the task of military governor of Berlin in the 1940s.[82] To assist him in uniting all civil and military instruments at his disposal, Churchill's directive also stated:

> In furtherance of your task, not only will you fulfil the normal functions of High Commissioner, but you will assume complete operational command over all armed forces assigned to operations in the Federation and will be empowered to issue operational orders to their commanders without reference to the Commanders-in-Chief, Far East. You should establish the consultation between yourself and the Commanders-in-Chief, Far East, in matters of common concern.[83]

In consultation with Templer, the incumbent CIGS, General Sir John Harding, wrote to General Brian Robertson, Commander-in-Chief of Middle East Land Forces, to inform him that Major-General Sir Hugh Stockwell would replace Major-General Roy Urquhart as military commander in Malaya on 11 June 1952. Harding informed Robertson that he had not taken the decision 'lightly', but due to developments in South Asia, 'it has become necessary to put an exceptional man in command of Malaya'.[84] Templer was '[d]elighted about Stockwell'.[85] Following a two-year term as Commander of 3 Infantry Division, Stockwell was promoted to Lieutenant-General and appointed GOC Malaya. A safe pair of hands, Stockwell's risky innovation of talking to armed groups in Haifa, while maintaining an uneasy peace in the dying days of the Mandate, marked him out as having a unique insight into civil–military relations. Thus, while Templer held overall operational control of the armed forces, his biographer makes perfectly clear how, 'Generally, Gerald left the actual conduct of operations to Hugh Stockwell and his other commanders'.[86] Stockwell served as GOC at a difficult time for British forces in Malaya. A close confident of Templer's, he believed whole-heartedly in winning the 'hearts and minds' of the Malayan people. And he had a very deliberate view on how this could best be done. In an essay entitled 'The part played by the Army in the Political Battle' Stockwell wrote:

> The Army's task can be a very potent factor in the cold war and it must give all the help to Government that it can, morally, physically and materially.

> By example – the spirit of a good Army must be exploited to the full and displayed to the people. The example set by officers and men is vitally important and their bearing must be exemplary.
>
> An Army must develop an awareness of the people and the country they live in and it must not be afraid to show itself to the people.[87]

Stockwell proved a most efficient commander in a war, 'which, by its very nature, had to be prosecuted by committee, and in which a great diversity of services and agencies were involved', wrote his biographer Jonathon Riley, and in which 'charm, tact and diplomacy were indispensible qualities'.[88]

Throughout his career Stockwell stuck rigidly to the Clausewitzian dictum that 'Policy is the guiding intelligence and war only the instrument, not vice versa. No other possibility exists, then, than to subordinate the military point of view to the political.'[89] A cerebral officer, who had read widely, he made frequent reference to Major-General Sir Charles Gwynn's influential book *Imperial Policing*, which became the Army's standard manual for fighting irregular opponents in the British Empire. In Gwynn's masterpiece, the minimum use of force, firm and timely action, and unity of control in civil–military relations, favouring civilian primacy, formed the triumvirate of Britain's guiding principles in small wars campaigning.[90] In Stockwell's seminal paper *The Army in the Cold War* he captured the essence of Gwynn's approach:

> You will see then at all levels the Army Officer is working with Police and Civil Authorities and that he is supported by Naval and Air Forces. Officers must know the organisation and function of the Civil Government and must approach all problems with patience. The officer who sees everything from the purely military angle will often conflict with a political or civil one and unless the officer understands the whole pattern he will feel frustrated, and may well upset the smooth running of operations in his area.[91]

Stockwell's understanding of the work of the Malayan civil service was impressive and he, more than any other military commander at the time or since, understood the tactical, operational and, ultimately, the strategic consequences of the Army's involvement in operations against the CTs. One of the main aspects of small-war campaigning that Stockwell sought to enhance in his time as GOC was one that bellied Gwynn's own thoughts on this type of warfare: the importance of the intelligence picture.

Intelligence

Intelligence about the enemy is essential in security forces operations against guerrillas and terrorists, most of whom are apt to exploit the human and physical terrain. While this was certainly recognized by military commanders on the ground, they had so far failed to 'get the intelligence organisation right' and it was not given the fullest attention until Templer 'grasped the point during a briefing in London'.[92] Upon arrival, Templer declared that the Emergency would 'only be won by our intelligence system – our Special Branch'. He immediately telegraphed London to ask Sir Dick White, a senior MI5 officer, to become his intelligence officer. 'Doubtless with one eye on the succession to [Sir Percy] Sillitoe, White refused', reveals Christopher Andrew. Templer turned to Jack Morton, Head of SIFE, to take up the post, which he accepted,[93] though with Templer's proviso that 'we've got to like each other. It won't work otherwise.'[94] As it happened, both men did work well together. For his part, Stockwell outlined the Army's contribution to the intelligence effort in his high-level report *The Army and the Cold War*, by emphasizing that the 'main source of tactical intelligence is the Special Branch'.[95]

It could be said that Stockwell was laying the specific foundations that were badly needed in building up the consent between the people and the Malayan authorities. The Army's assistance in welfare activities in 'new villages', training of the 'Home Guard', medical aid, and loan of transport and engineer equipment all helped to facilitate the flow of information between the local population and the security forces. Yet, he was at pains to stress:

> Don't let it be thought that, in Malaya, the State cannot and does not try to do all these things. The State does all it can, but everything cannot be done at once, though an awakening people will demand everything at once.[96]

In Stockwell's opinion, the Army 'must therefore do all it can to help'.[97] Between 1952 and 1954 the British Army was responsible for formalizing and disseminating the harsh lessons learned in the jungle; this took the form of the ATOM pamphlet, which proved an invaluable tool in defeating the long-running insurgency.[98] Stockwell later said that 'The enemies of the army are the C.Ts in the jungle. Our friends are the people and we like to think the army is the friend of the peoples'[99]

In the battle with CTs over the 'hearts and minds' of the Malayan people, it was unsurprising that Stockwell saw this small war as part of a much broader confrontation with Communism:

> In Malaya, the Communist rebellion cannot be considered as a local event determined by local circumstances, but as part of a wider South-East Asia plan of Soviet origin and design to drive the Western Powers from these economically rich areas. Conditioned by many years of conspiratorial activity, and inspired by a revolutionary association with World Communism, the Malayan Communist Party, its allies, and potential allies, constitute the main enemy, and the principal instrument of Soviet policy.[100]

Brigadier Dennis Talbot, who commanded 18 Infantry Brigade in the Pahang and Trengannu districts, and subsequently 99 Ghurkha Brigade, in Malaya, shared a similar view of communism as his GOC:

> The task of the Security Forces is clear. It is to defeat the aims of the MCP and restore law and order. It can and is being done in a variety of ways. By active operations to eliminate CTs and by isolating them from the rest of the community both physically and psychologically. The latter by capturing the hearts and minds of the people.[101]

Like Stockwell, Talbot considered Communism to be a virus or disease, against which societies such as Malaya had to be 'mentally inoculated'.[102] The way to combat it was through neutralizing the political message of the insurgent, which provided the lifeblood of the MCP's cause.[103] The great historian of Communism Robert Service has argued that 'ideologies and politics can mutate and spread like a virus which counteracts every medical effort to pinpoint and eradicate it'.[104] With Templer now in charge the MCP had a formidable opponent, who realized that, above all, the battle for 'Hearts and minds cannot be won by bribery alone'.[105]

The tide turns

Even though the RAF held firm to its reservations about the effect of its air operations, Templer continued to call upon aircraft to help turn the tide against the CTs. The RAF's offensive operations were three-pronged: they sought, first, to flush out the enemy into ambushes by ground forces; second, to 'soften up an area before our own ground forces go in'; and, third, to 'create a stop line by sustained air action in certain areas' by forcing the guerrillas into contact with ground troops. The use of heavy bombers would serve to split up guerrilla groups by attacking their command and control network. However, as late as June 1952, the RAF complained that there 'has been practically no reliable evidence to show how many of the enemy have been killed by air action', with only 118 enemy eliminated in the month of May despite the expenditure of £150,000–£200,000 a month in ammunition alone.[106]

After four years of conflict in the Federation, and with a new team in place only a matter of months, the Colonial Office commissioned a report entitled *Internal Security: Lessons of the Emergency in Malaya*. The report drew a core set of observations about how things might be done differently in future when faced with a similar challenge and set of circumstances. These included 'a regular and efficient system for information and intelligence', legislative powers to detain suspected terrorists (a total of 5,081 people had been detained for terrorist-related offences by July 1952),[107] properly trained colonial police forces, adequate timing when calling in military assistance, and the avoidance of martial law. Interestingly, the report urged caution when applying the 'lessons of experience' by observing that 'Malaya presents certain special features which are unlikely to be reproduced elsewhere'.[108]

That the CT threat remained resilient was unsurprising, as the history of revolutionary guerrilla movements elsewhere demonstrates. In the words of Marxist historian Eric Hobsbawn:

> Like the military resources of the bandit, those of the guerrilla are the obvious ones; elementary armaments reinforced by a detailed knowledge of difficult and inaccessible terrain, mobility, physical endurance superior to that of the pursuers, but above all a refusal to fight on the enemy's terms, in concentrated force, and face to face.[109]

Avoiding being drawn into the open seemed logical enough to those who had prior experience of this type of warfare. Templer and Stockwell were no exception and, unlike senior RAF officers, appreciated that the CTs would have to be confronted on their own terms in the jungle. While at a tactical and operational level lessons were applied from Greece and Palestine, these were wholly irrelevant in an environment where the physical terrain became a weapon just as much as the small arms the enemy used against the security forces. Nevertheless, with Templer's vision, especially in relation to the reorganization of intelligence and the structure of patrolling, apart from building up the intelligence, Templer had a difficult time in getting all of his subordinates 'to imbibe the spirit of the first directive: that the Emergency and ordinary government were inseparable'.[110] Templer improved communications from top to bottom, speaking personally to 'Civics Courses' and visiting the new villages. 'Touring the country was Gerald's real secret weapon', wrote John Cloak.[111]

From the moment Templer set foot in Malaya, it seemed that Montgomery's gut feeling that 'the man' could set Malaya ablaze had proven correct. 'For the first time', writes Stubbs, 'the Government was able to seize the overall initiative and force the guerrillas back on to the defensive'.[112] What undoubtedly helped the situation along was the good working relationship Templer enjoyed with the Malayan and South-East Asian authorities, as well as, crucially, the military and political hierarchy in London. 'I had only laid out the plan and chosen the instruments: the work and the skill and the success were Templer's', Lyttelton admitted in his memoirs.[113] The coincidence of Churchill's term as Prime Minister, Lyttelton's tenure as Colonial Secretary and Field-Marshal Harding's term as CIGS would give British strategy a continuity it badly needed amidst the upheaval now apparent across the empire.

In steadying the country's nerves, the Conservatives were returned for another term in office. By 1957, coinciding with the Sandys Review, the Chiefs of Staff agreed to cut the number of troops stationed in Malaya. This was sensitive for two reasons. First, Templer's replacement, Sir Donald McGillivray, moved to alleviate fears amongst the Malayan administration that the British were not seeking to prolong the Emergency after independence in 1957. Second, the government was anxious to head off Australian and New Zealand worries about security of Britain's territories in the Asia Pacific region.[114] That the Emergency was declared over left the way open for Britain to concentrate on new problems elsewhere, such as Kenya and Cyprus.

Conclusion

The insurgency in Malaya had been launched at an opportune moment for the CTs. What the MCP overlooked, however, was Mao's first rule of insurgency: that you must have the strength by which to inflict sustained losses on the enemy and fight a protracted insurgency.[115] The guerrillas may have struck at the right time, sensing weakness in the colonial administration, but their hope for a quick military victory did not materialize. As O'Balance points out, Peng 'saw that former great colonial empires were cracking and disintegrating, and that the British Empire in particular seemed to be falling apart'.[116] Yet, his forces were nowhere near the size that they ought to have been to sustain their campaign for the long haul. Where they could not gain consent themselves from within the ethnically Chinese community, MCP fighters often resorted to coercion as a means of prompting support from them. This was certainly wrongheaded and it ignored the timeless lessons of that great Prussian philosopher of war, Carl von Clausewitz, who so eloquently wrote, 'if policy is directed only toward minor objectives, the emotions of the masses will be little stirred and they will have to be stimulated rather than held back'.[117]

The turning of the tide against the insurgents in Malaya paid political dividends for the Conservative government. According to Lyttelton's own admission, they 'proposed to put a high premium on restoring the situation in Malaya through force of arms'. The truth was that neither Labour nor the Conservatives had 'a well-defined policy for Malaya' and both leant heavily upon the Army to bring about success.[118] It was not without some justification that the Tories could triumphantly claim in their election manifesto that the 'Commonwealth and Empire alone straddles the globe. For us isolationism is impossible'.[119]

By the closing months of 1955, the jungle war had all but been won. When high-ranking MCP delegates met with representatives of the Malayan and Singaporean administrations, Communist leader Ching Peng belatedly acknowledged that the 'British armed forces possess more modern equipment and therefore are still in a superior position'.[120] As one might have expected, Malayan government officials were at pains to stress that the surrender of the rebels was a prerequisite for an amnesty to be declared. However, the Federation Ministers went further in requesting the disbandment of the MCP, something Peng rejected outright. He, in turn, warned the officials that 'if this principle is insisted upon then we can only carry on with the struggle'.[121] Perhaps unsurprisingly the talks collapsed without agreement, and the MCP continued its increasingly moribund armed struggle. Anxious to prevent the impression that the surrender talks amounted to formal negotiations, MacGillivray moved swiftly to quash any such implications.[122] It was a last-ditch effort to secure a noble surrender for the MCP but it failed. The CTs were pursued vigorously until their political message became irrelevant. Peng and the rump of the MCP promptly absconded to Thailand.

Having cause to reflect on his two-year secondment to Malaya, Templer later wrote hauntingly of Britain being 'faced with a duel enemy – the immediate anti-British elements, of whatever origin, and the Russians in the background, seeking how best to exploit them'.[123] Before assuming his next command as CIGS, Templer was asked by Defence Minister Harold MacMillan to compile a report on colonial security and intelligence, which he submitted on 23 April 1955.[124] It was made public on the same day that he would succeed Harding as CIGS in November. One conflict identified by Templer in his report was Cyprus, ironically where Harding would now go in his retirement to serve as Governor. All eyes now turned to one of Britain's last remaining hubs of imperial power. Could the Templer model be applied under very different conditions? Only time would tell.

Notes

1 The National Archives, Kew, London (TNA), WO 216/394, Field-Marshal Viscount Montgomery of Alamein, Deputy Supreme Commander Allied Powers Europe, to Field-Marshal Sir William Slim, Chief of the Imperial General Staff (CIGS), 3 December 1951.
2 Galula, David, *Counter-insurgency Warfare: Theory and Practice* (London: Praeger Security International, 1964, 2006), p. 4.
3 Service, Robert, *Comrades: A World History of Communism* (London: Macmillan, 2007), p. 481.
4 House of Commons Debates (Hansard), 23 January 1948, Vol. 446, Col. 618.
5 Ibid., Col. 561.
6 Thompson, Robert, *Revolutionary War in World Strategy, 1945–1969* (London: Secker and Warburg, 1970), p. 2.
7 Hastings, Max, *The Korean War* (London: Michael Joseph, 1987), p. 419.
8 Peng, Chin, *My Side of History* (Singapore: Media Masters, 2003), p. 153. Richard Aldrich argues that this was part of a British attempt to 'encourage the MCP Politburo to entertain hopes of a negotiated place in the post-war government, forcing its members to tread water and lose momentum. Mountbatten kept up the charade.' See Aldrich, Richard, *The Hidden Hand: Britain, America and Cold War Secret Intelligence* (London: John Murray, 2001), p. 495.
9 Bayly, Christopher and Tim Harper *Forgotten Armies: The Fall of British Asia, 1941–1945* (London: Allen Lane, 2004), p. 462.
10 Peng, *My Side of History*, p. 182.
11 O'Balance, Edgar, *Malaya: The Communist Insurgent War, 1948–60* (London: Faber and Faber, 1966), pp. 59, 71.
12 Peng, *My Side of History*, p. 190.
13 Ibid., p. 193.
14 The Cominform was a Soviet-dominated organization aimed at co-ordinating actions between Communist parties around the world.
15 Peng, *My Side of History*, p. 204.
16 Stubbs, Richard, *Hearts and Minds in Guerrilla Warfare: The Malayan Emergency, 1948–1960* (Oxford: Oxford University Press, 1989), pp. 60, 246; O'Balance, *Malaya*, p. 76.
17 Peng, *My Side of History*, p. 205. Sharkey was later sentenced to three years' imprisonment for sedition.
18 O'Balance, *Malaya*, p. 19.
19 Stubbs, *Hearts and Minds in Guerrilla Warfare*, p. 247.
20 Carver, Michael, *Harding of Petherton: Field Marshal* (London: Weidenfeld and Nicolson, 1978), p. 162.
21 See Stubbs, *Hearts and Minds in Guerrilla Warfare*, pp. 36–38.
22 O'Balance, *Malaya*, p. 86.
23 Stubbs, *Hearts and Minds in Guerrilla Warfare*, p. 71.

24 Ibid. Stubbs suggests that Gent had been recalled to London for a disciplinary meeting when he was killed.
25 House of Commons Debates (Hansard), 8 July 1948, Vol. 453, Col. 603.
26 This view contrasted with the Cabinet's attitude towards the early stages of the Korean War, in which they had 'considerable doubts about the extent to which Peking and Moscow pursued a joint global strategy'. See Hastings, *The Korean War*, p. 71.
27 O'Balance, *Malaya*, p. 83. O'Balance puts the figure at 'several hundred'. However, the Colonial Secretary told the House of Commons that 44 were constables and sergeants and 103 acted as assistant or sub-inspectors. House of Commons Debates (Hansard), 16 December 1948, Vol. 459, Col. 207W.
28 Aldrich, *The Hidden Hand*, p. 497.
29 Ibid. See also Corum, James S., *Training Indigenous Forces in Counterinsurgency: A Tale of Two Insurgencies* (Carlisle, PA: Strategic Studies Institute, 2006).
30 Carver, *Harding of Petherton*, p. 164.
31 Andrew, Christopher, *The Defence of the Realm: The Authorised History of MI5* (London: Allen Lane, 2009), pp. 448–449.
32 Ibid., p. 449.
33 TNA, KV 4/408, Text of a lecture given by J.P. Morton, 'The Coordination of Intelligence in the Malayan Emergency' (n.d.).
34 House of Commons Debates (Hansard), 15 December 1949, Vol. 470, Col. 333W.
35 Stubbs, Richard, 'From Search and Destroy to Hearts and Minds: The Evolution of British Strategy in Malaya, 1948–60' in Marston, Daniel and Carter Malkasian (eds), *Counterinsurgency in Modern Warfare* (Oxford: Osprey, 2008), p. 118.
36 Ibid., pp. 118–119.
37 RAF, *The Malayan Emergency, 1948–1960* (London: MoD, June 1970), pp. 176–177.
38 TNA, AIR 8/1629, Message from the Air Ministry London to HQ, FEAF, dated 26 October 1950. The number fell from 6,011 sorties to 3,278 in 1951.
39 TNA, AIR 8/1629, Message from HQ, FEAF, to the Air Ministry, London, dated 8 November 1950.
40 TNA, AIR 8/1629, Correspondence between Deputy Chief of the Air Staff, Air Marshal Sir Arthur Sanders, and the Commander in Chief, Bomber Command, Air Marshal Sir Hugh Lloyd, dated 14 November 1950.
41 TNA, CAB 21/1682, Cabinet – Malaya Committee – Present Situation in Malaya: Memorandum by the Minister of Defence, dated 16 October 1950.
42 Ibid. See also RAF, *The Malayan Emergency*, p. 27.
43 TNA, CAB 21/1682, Cabinet – Malaya Committee – Present Situation in Malaya: Memorandum of a meeting of the committee held at the MoD on 17 October 1950.
44 TNA, AIR 8/1629, Cipher telegram from Ministry of Defence, London, to GHQ, Far East Land Forces, dated 3 January 1951. The telegram said

that 'Present conditions in Korea necessitate the use of all available resources and we cannot therefore withdraw a flying boat squadron to Malaya. We are reluctant to take these steps but unfortunately there is no alternative. Presume you will inform General Briggs.'

45 Mellersh, Air Vice-Marshal Sir Francis, 'The Campaign Against the Terrorists in Malaya', lecture delivered on 7 March 1951, *The Journal of the Royal United Service Institute*, Vol. 96, No. 583 (August 1951), p. 404.
46 Mellersh, 'The Campaign Against the Terrorists in Malaya', p. 404.
47 Cloak, John, *Templer, Tiger of Malaya: The Life of Field-Marshal Sir Gerald Templer* (London: Harrap, 1985), p. 242. Emphasis in original.
48 Mellersh, 'The Campaign Against the Terrorists in Malaya', p. 412.
49 Grob-Fitzgibbon, Benjamin, *Imperial Endgame: Britain's Dirty Wars and the End of Empire* (Basingstoke: Palgrave Macmillan, 2011), p. 171.
50 Stubbs, 'From Search and Destroy to Hearts and Minds', p. 120.
51 Imperial War Museum (IWM), *Harding Papers*, Letter from Henry Gurney to John Harding, 10 May 1951.
52 IWM, Private Papers of Field Marshall Lord Harding of Petherton, Malcolm MacDonald, Commissioner General for the UK in South-East Asia, to General Sir John Harding, 23 June 1951.
53 TNA, WO 216/394, Letter from Henry Gurney to Field Marshal Sir William Slim, dated 14 June 1951.
54 TNA, WO 216/394, Letter from Slim to Gurney, dated 24 July 1951.
55 IWM, Harding Papers, MacDonald to Harding, 23 June 1951.
56 TNA, WO 216/394, Letter from Gurney to Slim, dated 14 June 1951.
57 Stockwell, A.J., 'Gurney, Sir Henry Lovell Goldsworthy (1898–1951)', *Oxford Dictionary of National Biography* (Oxford: Oxford University Press, 2004).
58 TNA, WO 216/394, Letter from Lieutenant-General Sir Harold Briggs to Field Marshal Sir William Slim, dated 14 June 1951.
59 TNA, WO 216/394, Letter from Field Marshal Sir William Slim to General Sir Rob Lockhart, dated 14 July 1951.
60 O'Balance, *Malaya*, p. 114.
61 House of Commons Debates (Hansard), 14 November 1951, Vol. 493, Col. 43W.
62 Short, Anthony, *The Communist Insurrection in Malaya, 1948–1960* (London: Frederick Muller, 1975), p. 306.
63 Stubbs, *Hearts and Minds in Guerrilla Warfare*, p. 134.
64 Grob-Fitzgibbon, *Imperial Endgame*, p. 171.
65 Lyttelton, Oliver Viscount Chandos, *The Memoirs of Lord Chandos* (London: The Bodley Head, 1962), p. 362.
66 House of Commons Debates (Hansard), 21 November 1951, Vol. 494, Col. 55W.
67 Lyttelton, *Memoirs*, p. 366.
68 Short informs us that 'increasingly powerful and vehement representations by Malayan estate interests had been made both in London and Kuala

Lumpur to effect Gray's removal and within a few days of receiving a delegation in Kuala Lumpur which declared that they had lost confidence in the police, Lyttelton decided that Gray must go'. Short, *The Communist Insurrection in Malaya*, p. 306.

69 TNA, WO 216/394, Montgomery of Alamein, Deputy Supreme Commander Allied Powers Europe, to Field-Marshal Sir William Slim, CIGS, 3 December 1951.

70 Lyttelton, *Memoirs*, p. 346.

71 Ibid., p. 379.

72 TNA, WO 216/394, Montgomery to Lyttelton, 27 December 1951.

73 Ibid., 30 December 1951.

74 TNA, WO 216/394, Montgomery of Alamein 'Private and Top Secret: Success in Malaya, Note by Field Marshal Montgomery', dated 2 January 1952.

75 Ibid.

76 TNA, CO 1022/103, Directive to General Sir Gerald Walter Robert Templer, KCB, KBE, CMG, DSO, ADC, High Commissioner in and for the Federation of Malaya, by the Secretary of State for the Colonies on behalf of His Majesty's Government in the United Kingdom, 4 February 1952.

77 TNA, CO 1022/103, Note from Templer to Churchill, 12 January 1952.

78 'Speech of the Chief of the Imperial General Staff, Field Marshal Sir Gerald Templer at the Sovereign's Parade on 20th December 1956', *The Wishstream: Journal of the Royal Military Academy Sandhurst*, Vol. 11, No. 1 (February 1957), p. 6.

79 Stubbs, *Hearts and Minds in Guerrilla Warfare*, p. 144.

80 TNA, WO 216/394, Letter from Montgomery to Churchill, 4 January 1952.

81 'Battle of Malaya: Smiling Tiger', *Time Magazine*, 15 December 1952.

82 My thanks to Dr Ed Flint for reminding me of Templer's prior experience of civil–military affairs as Director of Civil Affairs and Military Government, 21 Army Group, in Germany between 1945 and 1946 and for correcting my thoughts about the 'good chats' shared between many civilian administrators and military commanders in a variety of theatres from the Second World War onwards.

83 TNA, CO 1022/103, Directive to General Sir Gerald Walter Robert Templer.

84 TNA, WO 216/630, Appointment of General Stockwell as GOC Malaya, Telegram from Harding to General Robertson, dated 12 March 1952.

85 TNA, WO 216/630, Appointment of General Stockwell as GOC Malaya, dated 13 March 1952.

86 Cloak, *Templer*, p. 243.

87 King's College London, Liddell Hart Centre for Military Archives (LHCMA), *Stockwell Papers*, 7/8/1–7.

88 Riley, Jonathon, *The Life and Campaigns of General Hughie Stockwell: From Normandy Through Burma to Suez* (Barnsley: Pen and Sword, 2006), p. 209.

89 Clausewitz, Carl Von, *On War*, edited and translated by Michael Howard and Peter Paret (Princeton, NJ: Princeton University Press, 1989), p. 607.
90 These principles were distilled in the work of the distinguished Irish-born soldier Charles Gwynn in his magisterial book *Imperial Policing* (London: Macmillan, 1934), pp. 13–14.
91 LHCMA, *Stockwell Papers*, 7/8/1–7, 'The Army and the Cold War'.
92 Cloak, *Templer*, p. 228.
93 Andrew, *The Defence of the Realm*, p. 449.
94 Cloak, *Templer*, p. 229.
95 LHCMA, *Stockwell Papers*, 7/8/1–7, 'The Army and the Cold War'.
96 Ibid.
97 LHCMA, *Stockwell Papers*, 7/9/1–13.
98 Marston, Daniel, 'Lost and Found in the Jungle: The Indian and British Army Jungle Warfare Doctrines for Burma, 1943–5, and the Malayan Emergency, 1948–60' in Strachan, Hew (ed.), *Big Wars and Small Wars: The British Army and the Lessons of War in the Twentieth Century* (London: Routledge, 2006), p. 105.
99 LHCMA, *Stockwell Papers*, 7/9/1–13, 'The Army and the People'.
100 LHCMA, Stockwell Papers, 7/8/1–7, Directive No. 5: The Organisation and Functions of Intelligence in the Federation of Malaya – Part 1: The Intelligence Organisation in Malaya (n.d.).
101 LHCMA, *Talbot Papers*, 3/7.
102 LHCMA, *Talbot Papers*, 3/7; *Stockwell Papers*, 7/8/1–7.
103 This was a view shared by one of the most prolific Malayan government officials to have written about his experiences, Sir Robert Thompson, in his books *Defeating Communist Insurgency: Lessons from Malaya and Vietnam* (London: Chatto and Windus, 1972), p. 28, and *Revolutionary War in World Strategy*.
104 Service, *Comrades*, p. 481.
105 Thompson, *Revolutionary War in World Strategy*, p. 69.
106 TNA, AIR 8/1629, Report by Air Vice-Marshal G.H. Mills, Air Officer Commanding, Malaya on the 'Effect of Air Action in Malaya', dated 18 June 1952.
107 Written answer from Oliver Lyttelton to Stanley Awbery, House of Commons Debates (Hansard), 31 July 1952, Vol. 504, Col. 188W.
108 TNA, DEFE 11/48, Defence of and Situation in Malaya, 15 May 1952–31 July 1952, 'Internal Security: Lessons of the Emergency in Malaya', dated 11 July 1952.
109 Hobsbawm, Eric, *Revolutionaries*, revised and updated edition (London: Abacus, 2007), pp. 224–225.
110 Cloak, *Templer*, p. 267.
111 Ibid., pp. 268–269.
112 Stubbs, *Hearts and Minds in Guerrilla Warfare*, p. 189.
113 Lyttelton, *Memoirs*, p. 383.

114 TNA, AIR 8/1924, Brief for the Secretary of State for Air and the Chief of the Air Staff: Reduction of the Army Garrison in Malaya, dated 2 October 1956.
115 Stubbs, *Hearts and Minds in Guerrilla Warfare*, p. 252.
116 O'Balance, *Malaya*, pp. 74–75.
117 Clausewitz, *On War*, p. 88.
118 Lyttelton, *Memoirs*, p. 326.
119 'United for Peace and Progress: The Conservative and Unionist Party's Policy – Conservative Manifesto 1955', in Craig, F.W.S. (ed.), *British General Election Manifestos, 1900–1974* (London: Macmillan, 1975), p. 187.
120 TNA, CO 1030/29, Record of the Baling Talks – First Day, December 1955, dated April 1956.
121 Ibid. Fourth Session, December 1955, dated April 1956.
122 TNA, CO 1030/29, Telegram from Sir Donald MacGillivray to the Secretary of State for the Colonies, dated 8 May 1956.
123 IWM, Erskine Papers, 75/134/4, Templer, General Sir Gerald Secret: Report on Colonial Security, 23 April 1955, p. 9.
124 Cloak, *Templer*, p. 331.

3

Quelling rebellion: countering the Mau Mau in Kenya

> Nationalist extremism is, after all, a political disease which has needed no more than the power of its own contagion to spread from Europe to the continent of Africa and beyond.[1]

> 'I do not believe bullets will finish the problem', he added, 'although forceful measures are necessary to obtain respect for law and order'. 'The problem was not military, and there was no military solution.'[2]

> [On] the first anniversary of the Emergency . . . [i]t was His Excellency who talked of the Government's determination and resolve of 'pressing the military campaign to its conclusion' and it was the General who declared, much to the chagrin of many tough guys in the Colony, that the ultimate solution of this really thorny problem would have to be along political lines. To many people it must have seemed an odd messing up of roles between the Governor and the Commander-in-Chief; for one would imagine that politics was the Governor's province and the military campaign the business of the General![3]

Introduction

On the evening of 24 January 1953 a quadruple murder took place in North Kinangop in Kenya's Central Province that would have immediate and far-reaching repercussions for life in the British colony. A gang of Kikuyu men, acting under the auspices of the anti-colonialist Mau Mau movement, entered the farm of Roger and Esme Ruck, which they shared with their young son, Michael. Mr and Mrs Ruck were lured separately out of their farmhouse by a ruse and promptly hacked to death in the garden with pangas (a type of machete), the Mau Mau's weapon of choice. One of the Ruck's servants, a young boy, was also cut to pieces in the frenzied attack. Having murdered Mr and Mrs Ruck, the gang then broke into the house and butchered the Rucks' son as he slept in his bed. All of the bodies were badly mutilated. After stealing a shotgun and pistol, as well as other household trophy items, the gang fled the scene. Pictures of the corpses clearly show the depravity to which the Mau Mau movement was prepared to sink in 1950s Kenya.[4]

The Ruck family murders, which took place about twenty miles north east of Lake Naivasha and forty miles north of Nairobi, 'sent a shock wave through the settler community'.[5] Shortly afterwards, 1,500 Europeans and a handful of Asians held a demonstration outside Government House in Nairobi. The assembled crowd had come to see the new Governor, Sir Evelyn Baring, but were prevented from advancing towards the building by a detachment of African *askaris* (armed policemen) who surrounded the building. Taking umbrage at having been met at the point of rifle bayonets, held by men they disparagingly referred to as 'dirty niggers', the protestors surged through the cordon and marched up the steps to the front entrance where they were again faced down, this time by more senior European officers.[6] Following a tense standoff, two spokesmen were begrudgingly received by Baring, who politely requested that they disperse peacefully. Following an address by the settler leader, Michael Blundell, the crowd broke up. Shortly after the demonstration, a top secret intelligence report noted how the Ruck murders 'have engendered a bitter hatred of the Kikuyu tribe as a whole, and determination to remove these people from the settled areas has gained immensely during the past week'.[7]

More than anything else, the murders personified a deep-rooted insecurity shared by many white settlers towards the local African population. Indeed, the 'symbolic weight which the Ruck family bore in the settlers' collective imagination' was far-reaching.[8] It fed not only demands on Baring's administration for further military assistance from Britain, which he readily conceded, but also some settlers' demands for 'a wholesale extermination of the Kikuyu population'.[9] Within hours of making Baring's request for additional troops to be dispatched to the colony, London promptly dispatched three more King's African Rifles (KAR) battalions to supplement the two existing battalions already in Kenya. They also appointed Major-General Robert 'Looney' Hinde as Director of Operations 'to jolly things along'.[10]

Britain's involvement in Kenya's Mau Mau rebellion has been the subject of several books and articles, almost all of which point to the coercive edge of military operations in the final days of British colonial Africa.[11] Indeed, 1950s Kenya is frequently eulogized as the poster-child for the punitive imperial approach to quelling rebellion in the British Empire. Authors like Caroline Elkins argue that Britain's Mau Mau Emergency represents the 'dark heart of colonial empire'.[12] This superficially attractive narrative continues to elicit controversy over half a century since the end of the Emergency.[13] Referred to at the time as 'the Kenyan safari' by anti-colonialist opponents of British military intervention, the involvement of British troops was touted as a doomed mission to prop up a beleaguered colonial government through the excessive use of force against native peoples.[14] Undeniably, the Emergency did lead to the imposition of some of the most draconian measures ever undertaken by a colonial administration, which included curfews, detention without trial, enforced migration, torture and restrictions on movement. However, the actual numbers affected continue to elude commentators, with some academics speculating that somewhere in the region of 160,000–320,000 people were detained during the Emergency, and intimating that the figure might be as high as 1.5 million.[15] Pushing her fragile methodology to the limit, Elkins further claims that between 130,000 and 300,000 Kikuyu remain unaccounted for in the 1961 population census.[16] What is often not in dispute though are the numbers killed; 10,000 Mau Mau rebels were killed by Security Forces and 1,086 were executed, mainly by hanging.[17] While there is an abundance of competing critiques on how force was employed, there continues to be a dearth of understanding about how strategic-level decisions guided the use of the military instrument during the Emergency.

The Mau Mau rebellion

Mau Mau emerged from the predominant Kikuyu tribe, who had expanded their numbers exponentially under British rule in the post-war period. The elite stratum of the Kikuyu were educated abroad; several returned to become loyal defenders of colonial rule, while still others went on to form the nucleus of the Mau Mau movement. The Mau Mau, or the self-styled 'Kenya Land Freedom Army' as they were also known, grew out of several socio-economic pressures, from a rising population and pressure on land, to the rapid increase in the number of squatters and 'enforced removal of surplus labour' which that provoked, to the ensuing discontent 'fuelled also by the low, bare subsistence-level wages paid to urban labour', particularly to those Kikuyu in Nairobi and lastly, and perhaps more importantly, to the 'internal Kikuyu conflict'.[18] Elkins sees the divisions within the Kikuyu tribe as something 'created by the colonial government and thus wholly illegitimate in the eyes of ordinary Kikuyu people'.[19] Her narrative barely considers the fate of loyalists; and in a sign of her crude anti-colonialist framework of sorts, the gruesome deaths inflicted by Kikuyu on fellow Kikuyu are attributed to a colonial blueprint followed by Britain, who 'sought out collaborators'.[20] Primitive Mau Mau rituals are explained away by Elkins' relativist standpoint, the reaction against them 'a reflection of both British imperial self-interest and a twisted sense of colonial paternalism'.[21] Moreover, flagging up the tiny body count for Europeans (only 32 European settlers and 63 European security forces were killed by Mau Mau) only serves to obscure the mass intra-ethnic conflict within the Kikuyu population in which approximately 25,000 Africans were killed.[22]

That the conflict was just as much about intra-tribal competition as it was about the stark battle of settler versus native or anti-colonialist versus imperial power has, thankfully, not been lost on those more attuned to appreciate its nuances.[23] Conflict was endemic in Kikuyu society and the Mau Mau's challenge to the established order only exacerbated the violence until it became a civil war.[24] The power of ethnic sentiment, deeply rooted in the rituals and symbolism of the Kukuya tribe, made the Mau Mau an implacable enemy for Kenya's colonial authorities. Its development, from a disparate body of gangs into a reasonably cohesive guerrilla movement, was fast. Although lacking in an ideology to bind together its followers, it did enforce severe discipline in its ranks, largely through its oathing ceremonies, which 'allowed Mau Mau to cultivate lines of intelligence and silence potential opponents'.[25] Although there was considerable unity of purpose within the Kikuyu, in terms of the political objectives of seeking the return of land, there was a sharp division between those who advocated physical force and those who sought to pursue a more constitutional path. The leader of the Kenya African Union (KAU), Jomo Kenyatta, urged his followers to adopt a political path, though this conciliatory strategy was rejected by those who resorted to terrorizing the Kikuyu 'with oaths and all the mumbo jumbo of tribal witchcraft'.[26] These extremists subsequently murdered a number of Africans loyal to the government in September and October 1952.[27] While not exactly a pre-meditated revolution, Kenya's volcanic mountains, deep ravines and awe-inspiring game reserves made it fertile ground for those who wished to launch an armed campaign against the colonial authorities. As Baring himself noted, 'there are plenty of hiding places among the wattles and in the patches of bananas. In short it is ideal country for a form of guerrilla warfare.'[28]

In response to the challenge now evident, Baring, who had only been in post for a few weeks, announced a state of emergency in a broadcast to the colony on 21 October 1952. Blaming the 'mounting lawlessness, violence and disorder', he said that the government had been forced to take 'drastic action to stop the spread of violence', 'not against men who hold any particular political views, but against those who have had recourse to violent measures'.[29] In response to questions on the matter, the Secretary of State for the Colonies, Oliver Lyttelton, told

Parliament that 'Anything in the present emergency which should result in the worsening of racial relations is, of course, to be highly deplored'.[30] The declaration of a state of emergency went hand-in-hand with the internment of known Mau Mau leaders in an operation code-named 'Jock Scott'. The swoops, which were carried out on the night of 20–21 October, led to 104 of the 138 Mau Mau suspects identified being arrested, including Kenyatta. However, as Baring candidly admitted in a telegram to the Colonial Office:

> I do not think that all members of the Kenya African Union are in the Mau Mau movement but I am sure that the leading members in the Mau Mau movement are for the most part prominent in the Kenya African Union.[31]

Kenyatta had been under surveillance by the British Security Service, MI5, for some time. They had flagged up his attendance at Moscow's Lenin Training School in 1933 and that he had allegedly joined the Moss Side Branch of the Communist Party in Manchester in 1944.[32] However, MI5 was able to confidently report after his arrest that '[w]e have seen nothing to suggest communist intervention in Mau Mau activities'.[33] Interestingly, Blundell took the same view, but for more explicitly paternalistic reasons. As he later wrote in his memoirs, 'we forget that Africa is a politically immature continent where the self-imposed frameworks of society are much less rigid than in more experienced countries'.[34] That Africans were less convinced by the prospects and promise of Communist modernity had been confirmed by Kenyatta's own writings. Since he was a leading political dissident, his book, *Facing Mount Kenya* (1938), drew the authorities to him like a magnet. In it he profiled the Kikuyu tribe in all of its splendid complexity. Articulating the case that the Kikuyu considered land tenure 'the most important factor in the social, political, religious and economic life of the tribe', Kenyatta made clear that for the Kikuyu 'the earth . . . [is] the "mother" of the tribe' and is the 'most sacred thing above all that dwell in or on it'.[35] It was the dispute over land, who it belonged to, and who had the right to cultivate it, which formed the political basis of the Mau Mau's campaign of terrorism.[36]

Given that Baring's predecessor, Sir Philip Mitchell, took a more pedestrian view of the problem brewing amongst the Kikuyu, the security forces were completely unprepared for the ensuing attacks.[37] What they did understand though was that force could only be met by force. As one Colonial Office minister, the Earl of Munster, explained:

> [T]his challenge of Mau Mau had to be met with a strong hand, for a body which will resort to murder, and to other brutal and inhuman crimes,

> as a means of securing its aim, is obviously challenging lawful authority; and no Government worthy of their name, whatever their complexion, could possibly allow the lives of a great number of law-abiding citizens, Africans, Europeans and Asians, to be placed in danger.[38]

A confused situation soon developed and Lyttelton, having the experience of Malaya in the forefront of his mind, lost no time in flying to Kenya to see for himself what was going on.[39] Returning to London, he informed Parliament that '[i]n effect, Mau Mau is the unholy union of dark and ancient superstitions with the apparatus of modern gangsterism'.[40] Although he was unwilling to estimate the proportions of the problem, there could be no hiding the fact that the security situation was deteriorating. The police were inadequately trained and the Special Branch was practically non-existent. In correspondence with Lyttelton, Baring made it clear that in order to counter the Mau Mau threat he needed the full co-operation of the Army:

> We should not delay in instituting the measures necessary to fight and to win a guerrilla war on however small a scale as distinct from a police operation. The main feature needed is unity of command. At the centre I think that our small committee functions all right and should continue in its existence . . . In brief I may need a Director of Operations and he should be a soldier with a rank senior to that of Brigadier. I think I would put him in charge of all operations in a scheduled area.[41]

Meanwhile, the violence spiked, as Mau Mau fighters went on the rampage. It was not long before the Mau Mau turned their attention to instilling fear amongst the local loyalists.[42] At Fort Hall a Mau Mau gang rampaged through the farm of Headman Dichon of Ichichi, killing twenty-eight of his sheep and burning down his house. When the tribal policeman guarding the farm opened fire on them, the gang ran off. Later that night a sixty-year-old man who was acting as a Crown witness at a Mau Mau trial was beaten to death by Mau Mau members armed with pangas. The gang later inflicted the same fate on a tribal sentry who dared to challenge them.[43] Early reports suggest that it was the same gang which had been responsible for the Ruck family murders. The violence soon worsened.[44]

When the Chief of the Imperial General Staff (CIGS), Sir John Harding, arrived for a visit at the end of February 1953 he 'did not like what he found, either on the military or the civil side'[45] and immediately ordered the deployment of 39 (Airportable) Brigade headquarters from Northern Ireland to increase the military resources available to Major-General Hinde. He also recommended 'the development of the Kikuyu Guard' to bolster the numbers of security forces on the ground.[46] Harding was abhorred by the poor state of security forces operations, noting that none of 'the lessons of Malaya seemed to have been learned, or indeed even been heard of'.[47] This was curious, given the rotation of units between each operational theatre. When he returned to London, the CIGS convinced the Cabinet of the need to appoint a new man to relieve Baring of his responsibilities as Commander-in-Chief. The man he had in mind was General Sir George Erskine: a personal friend and confidant of both Harding and, crucially, Prime Minister Winston Churchill.

General George 'Bobbie' Erskine was sent to Kenya with the explicit instructions to arrest the deteriorating security situation. From the moment he took up his post on 1 June 1953, Erskine faced an uphill struggle. On the one hand, he had been chosen because of his reputation in toughness and resolution in command; on the other, he had come to represent the tradition of solider-diplomat. In Huw Bennett's characterization of him, Erskine 'appreciated the political complexities involved and reoriented the campaign while imposing tighter discipline on the forces under his command'.[48] Born on 23 August 1899, Erskine had already earned a satisfactory reputation as a veteran of the 8th Army campaign in El Alamein in 1942, where his leadership and gallantry had won him the Distinguished Service Order. Despite his bravery, he had been judged 'unfit to command an Armd. Division in battle' and he was promptly removed from his command of 7 Armoured Division by Bernard Law Montgomery in August 1944.[49] In a report Montgomery wrote on him at the time, he mused that while he had 'a great liking for him, he needs a change of employment and outlook; he has been too long on the same line'. While a report from Montgomery could be fatal for an officer's career, Erskine nonetheless returned to a staff officer appointment and was later promoted to Lieutenant-General in December 1948. Yet, it was in his appointment as General Officer Commanding (GOC) British troops in Egypt and the Mediterranean Command from 1949 until April 1952, for which he is perhaps better remembered. His leadership during operations in the Suez Canal Zone in the winter of 1951–52, when he applied a firm hand against Egyptian forces, made him so successful at putting down the rebellion in Caro that an Egyptian newspaper offered a £1,000 bounty on his head.

Promoted to the local rank of General, Erskine assumed full control over all colonial auxiliary, police and security forces in Kenya.[50] Standing tall at 6′1″, Erskine's public school demeanour and stiff-upper-lip paternalism marked him out as an old-school imperial warrior. Erskine's predecessor, Lieutenant-General Sir Alexander Cameron, had proven ineffectual and was demoted to the role of deputy, and dealt with the remainder of the East Africa Command, leaving Erskine free to concentrate on gripping the situation in Kenya. The *Daily Telegraph* duly noted how Erskine's appointment was significant for two main reasons:

1. That the Mau Mau troubles have not yet abated
2. That the C-in-C, Middle East Land Forces, whose responsibilities have hitherto stretched from Malta to Ceylon, could not continue to handle so extended a command in the present difficult situation.[51]

During his tenure as GOC between 7 June 1953 and 2 May 1955 Erskine reported directly to Harding in London. He understood that it was his job to go on the offensive against the Mau Mau in order to re-establish law and order. In an early report to Harding, he said 'It is therefore most important that we should show without any shadow of doubt that we are determined to wipe out MAU MAU'.[52] The War Office itself had provided Erskine with a carefully crafted brief, which left few in any doubt about why he was being sent out to the colony:

> General Erskine is charged with the conduct of all military measures required to restore law and order in Kenya. For this purpose he will exercise full command over all colonial, auxiliary, police, and security forces in Kenya.[53]

Harding, however, was politically astute enough to realize that Erskine would not be assuming the same role as Templer had in Malaya:

> The Governor of Kenya will retain full responsibility for the government of and administration of the colony. He will give priority to such military and security measures as General Erskine may consider essential to the success of his plans for the restoration of law and order or for the security of the forces. These arrangements will be reviewed when the acute stage of the emergency in Kenya has passed.[54]

The appointment of a more established commander to combat the escalating Mau Mau threat had not been taken lightly. Indeed, it had been taken, as Lyttelton told MPs, to 'bring an end to the emergency as quickly as possible'.[55] The need to 'nip the rebellion in the bud' was made more urgent by events like those in the village of Lari in the Kiambu district. Lari had initially been afforded the protection of a KAR platoon, but the troops were withdrawn on 25 March, thereby triggering 'perhaps the most significant single event in the entire war'.[56] Six hundred Mau

Mau fighters attacked the village and hacked to death between 74 and 100 loyalists and their families.[57]

Not long after his arrival Erskine made a radio broadcast in which he informed his listeners that the police and auxiliary forces 'will come under my orders so that a fully co-ordinated effort can be made'. He said he was 'well aware of the need for the closest co-operation with His Excellency The Governor, the Government and all loyal citizens of KENYA. We will do this job together as a team. I will not be satisfied until every loyal citizen in KENYA can go about his work in peace, safety and security.'[58] Sticking rigidly to his initial brief, Erskine reminded those listening that 'Whilst I may have to take stern measures to restore respect for the law nobody need doubt that I believe in justice. I desire to see this country returned to a normal process of Government where justice and progress for all races and creeds can be developed in an atmosphere of peace.' Privately, Erskine placed much faith in wider public opinion in Kenya, noting how, within a week of his arrival, that 'as we discredit Mau Mau and make it unfashionable that public opinion will be able to express itself and will certainly do us a favour'.[59]

One of Erskine's major preoccupations was to limit the effects of military operations on the wider Kenyan population, and he continually raised the issue of proportionality in the use of force amongst his senior commanders:

> I realise that consideration must be given to protection of people, places and areas. It will be for you to judge the balance between aggressive action and protection bearing in mind that no troops should be purely protective but carry out some offensive role even if it is only local.[60]

He also left his commanders in little doubt about the priority they must give to the Army's notion of 'mission command', stating categorically that they should 'cultivate an offensive spirit against Mau Mau and encourage and help the establishment of KIKUYU Home Guard posts in the Reserve'.[61] In a letter to a friend in the British Embassy in Cairo, Erskine noted how he was 'fairly busy getting to work on the Mau Mau', in his first few weeks in Kenya. 'We seem to be having some success but it is extremely difficult to root it out quickly and completely', he said.[62] It was not long before Erskine had formulated a plan, the first signs of which came in a letter to the Military Secretary, Lieutenant-General Sir Euan Miller:

> It is very difficult to make a forecast but my own plans are to finish the military operations by October and break up the gangs by then. If this goes right we shall then enter a period in which the police will be taking

> the main initiative and the Army will be standing back a bit. There will be many criminals on the run and the Army may have to help from time to time. The length of this period, which I call civil consolidation, can only be a guess, but if the Police come up to scratch and are in a position to take over in October we should be on pretty good terms with the criminals in six months. It will be difficult to say exactly when the Emergency is over, but if the police are able to show adequate control over a period of six months I think one can regard the Emergency over as far as the Army is concerned. If I prove right in these forecasts, and it can't be more than a guess at the moment, a change over by Sandy in October would be about right. The new man would have about six months as Chief of Staff before taking over from me.[63]

Remarkably, Erskine informed Miller that he hoped to have anti-Mau Mau operations wrapped up within a matter of months, just in time for his carefully choreographed move to another command. Events, however, soon transpired against this most optimistic of assessments, as the Mau Mau proved more resilient to the limited operations Erskine's forces had mounted thus far. Nevertheless, Harding remained impressed by the direction of Erskine's campaign:

> I am also certain that your general policy of taking the offensive is the right one, and that you are justified in taking properly calculated risks to that end. We shall all be very interested to hear how your plans work out, and wish you every success.[64]

Opinions amongst the settlers were mixed, with Michael Blundell contending that, despite Erskine's arrival, 'little progress in the Emergency seemed to be made'.[65] Much would now hinge on Erskine's next move.

The 'Malaya Plan' and the turn to coercion

Cultivating an offensive spirit amongst his troops was one thing, but fighting a war by committee was quite another, as Erskine soon discovered. Harding's visit in February 1953 had identified the need for a complete overhaul of the civil–military command machinery along similar lines to what was already in operation in Malaya. The new Commander-in-Chief 'inherited an Emergency organisation of Provincial and District Emergency Committees where all aspects of the anti-terrorist campaign could be co-ordinated'.[66] However, the 'system as a whole tended to create friction between the military command and the local committees, particularly where these were under strong European influence'.[67] Unlike in Malaya, however, where Templer enjoyed overall responsibility for both the civil and the military spheres, no such central authority existed in Kenya. Moreover, Baring had little understanding, or appreciation, of the military operations needed to transform the situation. That did not prevent several newspapers eagerly anticipating the emergence of the same winning formula in some form of 'Malaya Plan'. Interestingly, Baring had earlier met Templer for talks on the 21 January 1953, after which he declared that no operation should begin which had not been agreed by the appropriate Civil–Military–Police Committee.[68] It was clear that Baring had taken away lessons from Malaya so that he could graft them onto the Kenyan Emergency, probably inevitable given Baring's previous colonial experience in South Africa and Southern Rhodesia. As the Malaya intelligence chief, Jack Morton, later recalled, Templer had also willingly 'passed on a lot of our experience to General Erskine in Kenya, where it was quickly applied'.[69]

That Erskine had consulted Templer about anti-Mau Mau operations was not immediately apparent, though there were signs. For example, Erskine's initial plan to clear the forest of insurgents had three main phases in its execution. In phase one, a brigade of infantry would probe deep into the forest areas, phase two would see the advance of a highly mobile force of armoured cars and infantry-based gunners, and in the final phase air assets would be called in to make prohibited areas 'unwholesome'. Once the area had been purged of Mau Mau fighters, the colonial administration could re-enter and establish Home Guard and police units to protect the districts from resurgent Mau Mau activity.[70] In tune with operations in Malaya, aggressive patrols would then be sent out to dominate the ground and ensure that these areas were held to prevent the insurgents from returning. Erskine impressed upon his men that:

> Mau Mau must be hunted. We must not be satisfied with a passive defensive outlook. It is no use waiting for these gangs to come and shoot up Home Guards or police stations. We have to go out and find these gangs and hunt them down.[71]

The first major operation against the Mau Mau – codenamed 'Operation Buttercup' – was conducted by 39 Brigade between 23 June and 8 July in the Fort Hall District. It was an all-out offensive operation designed to place the rebels on the back foot. The London-based *New Statesman* magazine, an influential left-wing publication, published a poem shortly afterwards, which captured the mood amongst anti-colonialists:

> Operation Buttercup!
> Soldiers on safari!
> Regiments are mopping-up,
> The ragged Kuke their quarry.

The game is tracked, the hunt's away,
The Fusiliers to the Devons say
'How many Kukes have bagged today?'
In Kenya on safari.
But the General cries as the bombers roar,
'Remember Britain's mission.
This isn't a full-scale, all-out war,
But a punitive expedition'.
One side has weapons and planes galore,
One side no ammunition,
And that's the difference between a war
And a punitive expedition.[72]

Buttercup was merely the opening salvo of Erskine's military campaign. He ordered 39 Brigade to keep unstinting pressure on the Mau Mau for the remainder of the year, especially in the Eastern Aberdares and the Fort Hall, South Nyeri and Thika Districts. In total, 241 insurgents were killed and 193 captured during the operation.[73] General Erskine said at a press conference that '[c]asualty figures were not the only, or even the best, criterion of success'. Despite having 'no detailed information as to the location, strength, armament, determination or method of maintenance of gangs', by the end of Operation Buttercup, Erskine himself reluctantly asserted that Mau Mau gangs were both 'numerous and aggressive'.[74] In a bid to maintain momentum, 39 Brigade, consisting of the 1st Battalion the Buffs and Devons, the Kenyan Regiment and the KAR, were now 'giving their full attention' to the Aberdares, while 70 Brigade operated in the Mount Kenya region.

It was not long before allegations of brutality during these operations surfaced in the mainstream press. In July 1953 two European members of the Security Forces were charged with manslaughter for allegedly having beaten up an African detainee. Even though Erskine had issued an order on 23 June making it clear how he 'would not tolerate breaches of discipline leading to unfair treatment of anybody' and that he 'strongly disapproved of beating up the inhabitants of this country',[75] rough treatment continued to be meted out. The General was undoubtedly right when he observed how 'in-discipline of this kind would do great damage to the reputation of the security forces and make our task of settling Mau Mau much more difficult'.[76] Where evidence of too punitive an approach could be found, therefore, Erskine moved quickly to stamp it out. On one such occasion, Brigadier Donald Cornah, the 46-year-old commander of the 70 East African Brigade, which consisted mainly of African troops, was relieved of his command in August 1953 because of his purported 'scorched earth' policy against the Mau Mau. Cornah had served as a regular officer with the old Indian Army, winning a Distinguished Service Order in Italy during the Second World War.[77] Press speculation claimed that he had been sacked because he failed to follow Erskine's new directives.[78] In another, perhaps better-known, case, a Kenyan settler, sadist and commissioned officer in the KAR, Captain Gerald Griffiths, was arrested and tried for the murder of a Kikuyu man. On 12 June 1953 Griffiths allegedly stopped three Kikuyu men to check their papers. When the men failed to comply with his search, Griffiths promptly shot two of them with a Bren gun. As he later disclosed in his court martial, 'I think I fired one burst – about six or eight rounds, possibly ten, not more – and they both fell to the ground wounded.' When he returned about 20 minutes later both men were still lying on the ground badly wounded. 'I was very upset', he said, drawing his pistol from his holster and firing two shots to 'put the men out of their misery'. 'My hand was very shaky and I missed the first time'.[79] Griffiths' Company Sergeant Major later told the court that when he asked what his orders were at a road block, 'the answer he got was that he could shoot anybody he liked, provided that they were black'.[80] As the allegations broke, the *Daily Mirror* called for a full and frank public inquiry:

> Keenness in combating terrorism is reasonable. Nobody can use kid gloves with savage terrorists. But this corpse counting is revolting. We demand that the whole conduct of the difficult operations in Kenya must be probed and laid bare.[81]

Similarly, the left-leaning *Daily Herald* noted how 'Suspected terrorists killed are outnumbering those wounded or taken prisoner by over two to one. The British people should be given an independent report on this profoundly disquieting situation.'[82] Erskine moved quickly to make an example of Griffiths but was thwarted by the latter's release on a technicality; the KAR officer was later convicted of torture and spent five years in an English gaol.[83]

Despite Bennett's argument that the law 'created a permissive environment for atrocities', or that the 'significance of the minimum force concept has been vastly overstated, and did not apply in insurrections or in the colonies',[84] there is certainly evidence to suggest Erskine was kept awake at night by the precarious legal position of British troops in Kenya. In a lecture he gave shortly after relinquishing the East Africa Command, he claimed that 'Officers and men must be quite clear about their duty and not feel that they are being invited to act against the law. In Kenya the rules were straightforward and simple.' Pursuing this line of enquiry further, Erskine re-iterated the legal point that the

Kenyan government had designated some areas 'prohibited' and 'special'. In the former, 'this gave the security forces full play for developing unhampered military operations' and in the latter it gave them 'the right to challenge and stop anybody and fire if they did not halt'.[85]

In his official report on the Emergency, Erskine admitted how his division of the country into different areas made it easier for troops to use force in a more discriminatory manner. In the Prohibited areas, the rules of engagement were so relaxed that 'troops were able to operate on a straight forward war basis knowing that anybody they met must be an enemy'.[86] This led to accusations that pattern bombing by the RAF was invariably killing innocent Africans caught up in these areas. Lyttelton remained nonplussed and confidently reminded Parliament that the Mau Mau 'have to be dealt with if we are to expect any great advance on the other fronts, but . . . there is no reason whatever to cancel the instructions to try to comb out these gangs from the forest'.[87] Stephen Chappell has even gone as far as to argue that senior military officers and members of the cabinet in London were attuned to the need to avoid civilian casualties.[88] In Special Areas, 'the action of the Security Forces was directed selectively against the Mau Mau terrorists and not against the general population whom we were protecting'.[89] In these circumstances Erskine was more precise in his understanding of the rules of engagement, arguing that there 'was an obligation under the Common Law to protect the inhabitants against a felony and in doing so to use the minimum force as judged by the Officer in Command to achieve his purpose'. In a directive from Erskine's Chief of Staff, Major-General Heyman, he made perfectly clear to subordinate commanders:

> The duties of military forces when engaging Mau Mau terrorists in special areas or in the reserve are simply those of troops employed in aid of the Civil Power to quell civil disturbance. The old principles applying to such duties are to use any degree or type of force or fire power which the commander on the spot considers the minimum necessary to achieve his military objective – no more and no less. If, in the course of the using of such force, troops are unfortunate enough to cause the death of an innocent person, or damage to property, the Law will regard this as an unavoidable accident.[90]

Realizing the weight of responsibility on his shoulders, Erskine had based his own orders on 'legal advice'. In words that would come to distinguish Britain's use of force in Kenya, Heyman signed off his General's orders with: 'Nothing in this instruction, of course, authorizes the indiscriminate use of force in an area occupied by innocent persons'.[91] What constituted an 'innocent person' was left deliberately loose.

There has been a tendency to overplay the indiscriminate nature of military operations in Kenya and to underplay Erskine's grip on command. In a brief he gave to troops before they deployed into the field, their Commander-in-Chief stressed the importance of adhering to the law in prosecuting their mission:

> Those who disagree with this selective policy should sit down and write out the disadvantages both short and long term of any indiscriminate assault on the Kikuyu tribe and the abolition of any legal process. I am convinced such a policy would be mass action against Kikuyu tribe as a whole [and] is NOT Govt policy. The Army must direct its action against the bad and only the bad men.[92]

Nevertheless, Erskine appreciated how his orders might well have caused some consternation; after all they demanded difficult decisions by soldiers fighting in difficult circumstances:

> This selective process treatment makes our task particularly difficult because we are always up against the problem of gaining contact with people who can easily hide themselves.[93]

While few would doubt the willingness of the disciplined military forces to adhere to Erskine's strict rules of engagement, a question mark continued to hang over the quality of the Kikuyu Home Guard. Erskine was perfectly right to assume that these laws 'in fact gave security forces sufficient scope to use force in a sensible, reasonable, and controlled manner'. However, he was wrong to conclude that he 'never had any trouble with the application of these rules once the position had been made clear to everyone' as the Cornah and Griffiths cases clearly demonstrate.[94]

Negotiating with the enemy

After unleashing some devastating firepower on the Mau Mau gangs, a new scheme was hatched by the authorities to bring the Emergency to a swift conclusion.[95] In late August, Governor Baring flew back from a visit to Mombasa on the coast 'to initiate, in conjunction with General Erskine, a policy, based on that already put into operation in Malaya, of persuading terrorists to surrender'.[96] Although Erskine would later claim that the option had been on the table since his arrival, he had been more concerned with 'trying to make the life of the gangs in the mountains as unpleasant as possible'. Nonetheless, he was prepared to concede that 'when the alternative is the gallows you can understand the reason for their resistance'.[97] In all likelihood the surrender option had come through a gradual process of osmosis in correspondence with

Templer, where it had been tried in Malaya, with some success. However, in Kenya it was a different story. The Mau Mau lacked the same centralized leadership that made the Malayan Communist Party (MCP) cadres so resilient[98] and, consequently, it had no firm control over its large number of fighters. Many ethnic Chinese joined the MCP for ideological reasons, as well as ethnic ones, and were perhaps less prone to local dynamics. In Kenya, the Mau Mau press-ganged many villagers into their ranks, with illegal oathings visited on them against their will. Put simply, the MCP enticed its supporters into its ranks, while the Mau Mau compelled their supporters through threats, intimidation and physical violence into taking the oath of loyalty to the organization. The surrender option, therefore, could only have limited effect.

Within a few weeks, therefore, Erskine decided to apply further pressure on the Mau Mau from another angle. He recalled the 1st Battalion, Royal Inniskilling Fusiliers from their base-camp in the Rift Valley, 100 miles south to Nairobi, as a means of re-establishing law and order in a 'sharply deteriorated' situation in the Kenyan capital.[99] The Iniskilling's commander, Lieutenant-Colonel Robert Grimshaw, a Dubliner, was 'given a free hand' by Erskine to mount a major joint operation with the police. Marching out of their tented headquarters at Nairobi Racecourse with bayonets fixed, the soldiers assisted police in their checking of identity documents and work permits. The operation was designed to reassure the city's citizens and would be co-ordinated under Timmerman, a Canadian who had come to Kenya in 1951 to reorganize the Criminal Investigation Department.[100]

While the operation saw British troops 'flying the flag', it had little long-term effect on the Mau Mau. Nairobi, the nerve centre and logistical support-base for all their military operations, remained in place. Erskine began to express his doubts about the direction of his campaign in letters to his wife:

> I don't feel in anyway optimistic on the long term policy. I am sure I can put down the gangs in a reasonable time but I can't do much to alter the outlook of the Kikuyu as C-in-C except to knock them on the head when they are troublesome – and that is the answer to the real problem although it is an essential for democracy.[101]

It was perhaps with a touch of irony that the former Mayor of Nairobi invited the deputy leader of the Labour Party, George Brown, to Kenya in October 1953 to see for himself the progress that was being made on the security front. Although Brown admitted to encountering 'high praise' for the troops, he found only 'cause for complaint' in relation to the Kenya police reserve and Kikuyu Home Guard.[102] The levels of crime in the city and the surrounding Eastlands district soon spiralled out of control. Mau Mau was resurgent.

By now relations between Erskine and Baring had become strained. Confiding in his wife, Erskine noted, with derision, how, with the Governor, 'I always have to make up his mind for him – that may not be quite fair but that is what it feels like'.[103] The General's gloomy mood was only lifted when he spoke of the tallies of Mau Mau eliminated:

> The battle with Mau Mau is going reasonably well. We are killing them 100 a week and slowly but surely breaking them up – My difficulties with the local government and settlers is now ending. I am fed up with them all – particularly the latter. I can't tell them exactly what is happening because if I did so I would also be telling Mau Mau. So I have to grin and bear it.[104]

As this letter implies, Erskine was becoming increasingly paranoid. This was somewhat unavoidable given the amount of pressure he was under, especially from those who wanted him to take ever more drastic measures. Rather sheepishly, he told his wife:

> The most difficult thing is to keep my temper. There are times when I boil with rage at the attitude of the locals. But it would be fatal to lose my temper and I have to smile and be amiable![105]

Sensing a repetitiveness in military operations, Baring took an initiative of his own, informing the Legislative Council that the Commissioner for Community Development had been put in charge of a 'special rehabilitation department', the object of which was to 'win back where possible Africans in prisons, in detention camps, or in the African Land Units, whose minds have been polluted by Mau Mau propaganda'. In establishing this department the Commissioner visited Malaya, 'and from the work of this nature done there learnt many useful lessons'.[106]

Meanwhile, in London, debates raged inside and outside Parliament about the effectiveness of Erskine's heavy-handed strategy. Labour politicians were concerned that the use of 'pattern bombing' on what the government and military regarded as 'hard core' terrorists represented nothing less than 'a policy of extermination of innocent people'.[107] Even the *Daily Mail* was cautious in its pronouncements:

> The British soldier is no fiend in human shape, nor is the 'black brother' an angel without wings. There has been dire provocation in Kenya – though we agree that reprisal is not the answer to savagery.[108]

Erskine blamed the hostile press attention on the lack of progress among the local civil representatives. In a letter to his wife he relayed a picture of chaos:

> The whole thing is a proper muddle – I am doing pretty well with my military operation[s] and everyone knows it. But we are not getting to the end of it . . . because the Colonial Government are without any policy – I have always liked Baring but I can't get him and his people into top gear or anything approaching it. The big question is: – can I finish this thing alone or does it require Government action – I am certain it requires Government action and it would be a sheer fluke if I am able to finish it by myself.[109]

By now Erskine's frustrations were palpable. On the one hand, the settlers were eager for more heavy-handed actions on the military front, and, on the other, there was was the indecision encapsulated in the civilian who had overall authority for the campaign:

> We are getting a bit bogged down here – although the military operations have gone pretty well and we kill off about 80 Mau Mau a week it will take years to finish the thing this way. I need to take a good many more drastic measures to finish the thing.[110]

Erskine was not alone in thinking negatively about the calibre of the civilian 'man on the spot'. In a copy of a Parliamentary report quietly passed to Erskine from the Secretary of State for War, Anthony Head, the Minister made several frank admissions, including that there was 'a lot of dead wood in the administration', that the 'Emergency Committee is too big and is not run on businesslike lines', and that 'intelligence was poor' across the piste. 'Without adequate intelligence', he maintained, 'they might as well be at home because looking for Mau Mau in that area . . . is like looking for a needle in a haystack.'[111] Other criticisms of the administration included the Government's agricultural policy, which Head thought needed a new minister with 'drive and energy' to replace the current 'charming member of the old guard'. It was suggested that a change of Governor was not needed but that a smaller 'War Council', comprising Baring, Erskine, Blundell and one other would greatly improve the direction of the campaign. Head concluded by thwarting Erskine's ambitions for assuming overall control by stating categorically: '[w]ith regard to a solution I think it would be quite impractical and most unwise to consider that General Erskine should do the same kind of job as Templer'.[112] The risk of following too heavy-handed a military approach was overtaken by the practicalities of a War Office increasingly overwhelmed by overseas commitments.

On operational grounds Erskine bought fully into the War Council idea. His lengthy colonial policing experience told him that a command structure combining civil, military and police representatives in a committee-based system – at all levels – was a winning formula. At the apex of the structure sat the War Cabinet, which replaced two cumbersome committees known as the Colony Emergency Committee and the Director of Operations Committee. The War Cabinet consisted of the Governor, Deputy Governor, Commander-in-Chief East Africa Command and the Minister without Portfolio. An Emergency Joint Staff secretariat was also established, made up of civil, military and police representatives; permitted in the War Cabinet, in Erskine's view, 'to concentrate on broad policy and decisions'.[113]

Military operations in the six months prior to the establishment of the War Council in March 1954 had centred on the predominantly Kikuyu districts of Fort Hall and Nyeri. Erskine admitted that 'elsewhere I used the minimum troops to hold the situation while the Police were building up their strength'.[114] Yet, despite the fact that the 'Mau Mau had had hard knocks which were evident to all', their 'militant wing was still in the field' and 'there was no falling off in the support terrorism was receiving from the passive element'. Importantly, he complained, 'there still was a lack of forward planning on a joint and overall basis'.[115] Erskine set about wiring in African locations to give the Security Forces 'better control of the African population'.[116] However, the failure of his earlier operation to have any strategic effect on the Mau Mau led him to duly authorize operations in April 1954 aimed at tackling the insurgency at its source. In developing his plan for capturing Nairobi 'once and for all',[117] Erskine moved increasingly closer to initiating a major operation in the city. Yet he struggled to find a suitable precedent. For this he turned to military history for answers:

> I could find no precedent for an operation of this nature except the Tel Aviv clean up in Palestine. There, approximately three divisions had been employed for a smaller problem and the operation had lasted only 48 hours.[118]

Adapting a similar plan for the much larger city of Nairobi, Erskine arrived upon the codename 'anvil', an indication perhaps of the aggressive actions it would involve.[119] He planned to erect screens around different sectors and move Security Forces systematically through each one questioning, arresting, detaining and subsequently segregating those 'who had no apparent reason for being in Nairobi, whose passes were not in order or were in other ways suspicious characters'.[120] However, it very quickly dawned on him that a lack of resources (in this case detention facilities to hold, screen and process detainees) was not going to be ready in time to handle a 'clean sweep'. He therefore modified his plan and, instead, ordered 'a selective pick up of Kikuyu,

Embu and Meru'. As Erskine later admitted, planned detention camps for about 50,000 never materialized and they had only accommodation for half of that number, a factor that led to the longer duration of Operation Anvil.[121] As he remarked in his official report, 'in operations of this sort the means to detain those apprehended will always prove the limiting factor and not the ability of the Security Forces to arrest'.[122]

The failure of coercion, the success of deterrence?

Running parallel to Erskine's military operations was a vast bureaucratic process of villagization and detention. One district level officer who was responsible for setting up and running of these facilities later noted how 'an enormous amount of villagisation was put in hand' so that vulnerable Kikuyu could be 'guarded and controlled'. It had some success and led to the expansion of Home Guard units across the Central Province. Nonetheless, there were signs that this vast enterprise was running up against problems:

> Although the new villages brought a feeling of security to the majority of the occupants the hard-core hated them, doing their best to upset things. Frequent reports of oathing parties came to our hearing and not a few murders took place within the new confines. The gangs still got support. However the water dripping on the proverbial stone was having its effect.[123]

Reflecting back on his time as a colonial administrator, Thompson opined how 'If the battle for Kikuyu hearts was to be won there was no alternative but to make use of the Emergency Powers of Detention without trial'. Unfortunately, as would become plain almost two decades later in another British territory, '[a]lmost all of these detainees were the muscle men of the movement. The top-brass political brains were either in hiding or out of the country.'[124] Nevertheless, the ill-treatment, not to mention the primitive conditions in which detainees were housed, and the public 'purging' of the oath, made the rehabilitation process arguably less effective in the longer term.

Indeed, show trials, collective punishments, internment without trial, small-scale reprisals, and the routine bombardment of Mau Mau positions by the RAF's heavy bombers were commonplace in the first two years of the Emergency. Even though there is no firm evidence to suggest the existence of harsh techniques – Elkins' alleged 'dark heart' of imperialism – military operations during this period nevertheless raise important questions about the ethics of waging 'small wars', especially against an irregular enemy.

Many of the military operations at this time were being augmented by the information passed on to the colonial authorities at a strategic level by General China, a captured insurgent leader who 'was prepared to attempt to arrange the surrender of the Mau Mau gangs which had formerly been under his command in the Mt. Kenya area'.[125] In the third directive to his subordinate commanders on 8 March 1954, Erskine moved to allay fears about his motives, arguing that he was 'making use of "China" to bring about a surrender of terrorists'. Erskine continued: 'Already we have obtained more information of a very useful kind in the course of a few weeks than we could ever have expected to have obtained by normal methods over a much longer period.'[126] In any event, Erskine had discussed the exploitation of China with Baring directly and had his plan (codenamed 'Wedgewood') rubberstamped by Lyttelton and Harding when they visited Kenya in Easter 1954.

By now Baring was on sick leave, battling his long-term problem of amoebic dysentery, something which precluded him from working in more harsher climes.[127] Again, Erskine privately criticized him for his indecisiveness: 'It is pathetic to see him faced with a problem and quite incapable of saying Yes or No. In this particular problem I do not think it much matters whether you say Yes or No. The fatal thing is to say nothing and have everybody in doubt.'[128] Erskine's complaints about Baring intensified as it became clear that the Governor was too sick to return to his post:

> it is difficult to say how this will go but Oliver Lyttelton is a very powerful personality and does not care a damn for anybody. I must say I was much impressed by his approach to the whole problem. I don't think he intends to alter the set up here – i.e. Baring and myself. But Baring may be too sick to return. There has been talk of a High Commissioner I am glad to say![129]

There is evidence to suggest that Erskine's suspicions about colonial officials meant that he was less candid with Baring than he was with the generals in Whitehall. As he admitted to Harding in a letter requesting more troops, 'I have not shown this letter to H.E. as I do not want to advertise to him my thoughts to you'. It was a difficult relationship, a personification perhaps of the tense civilian–military relations pertaining at the time.[130]

Indeed, Erskine's feelings about the strategic goals of the campaign were not shared by everyone. In a handwritten minute, dated 31 July, a Colonial Office official wrote:

> In the long run the greater effort is required on the civil side – Police and Administration – to break down support and supplies. Intelligence is the

> key to effective action. Politically – in UK and internationally – reinforcement by a new brigade would get bad publicity – strengthen the contention that this is suppression of national movement.[131]

As it soon became apparent, Baring also had friends in the Colonial Office. Not only was he an experienced 'man on the spot', whatever Erskine thought in private, but he was also someone who was highly regarded by the Legislative Council. The settlers liked him and more than once petitioned Lyttelton, and his successor Alan Lennox-Boyd, for an extension to his term in office. While the Governor was conspicuous by his absence, Erskine was left to face the press about the coercive edge to his anti-Mau Mau operations.[132] Lyttelton admired his resilience, sending him a letter of commendation for having 'revolutionised the military situation in Kenya. I only hope that the war will now enable you to get some leave and that you will soon be adding a baton to your stars.'[133]

Yet, much remained to be done. The prowess of Britain's fighting units was not in doubt, though questions were soon asked about the effectiveness of the police. The task of building up an effective police force in Kenya was given a necessary fillip by the arrival of Colonel Arthur Young, a trouble-shooter for colonial hotspots. Appointed City of London Police Commissioner in 1950, he was twice seconded for colonial policing tasks in the Gold Coast (1951) and in Malaya (1952–53). Young was sent to Kenya in February 1954 to replace outgoing Commissioner Colonel Michael O'Rourke, who had come in for criticism from both settlers and Kikuyu loyalists. In a letter to Erskine, Bishop Leonard of Mombasa complained, 'Surely O'Rourke must go, and with him the men who have failed to clean up this business . . . I remain unshaken in my belief that it's the Police, by and large, who are making your job impossible and prolonging the whole campaign.'[134] Acts of brutality had not yet been stamped out in some of the police and Home Guard units and, although rare, were a constant headache for Erskine. Enforcing discipline in Army ranks was relatively straight-forward; however, colonial forces did not conform to the same ethical standards. At the time, Erskine was enthusiastic at the prospect of Young's arrival:

> I am very glad we have this chap Arthur Young coming out as Commissioner of Police. It will make all the difference. We also have a first class deputy who is coming from Malaya and he will be able to take over from Young in a year's time. So the future of the police looks a great deal more rosy.[135]

In the re-organization of the police priority was given to improving the operational capabilities of the Special Branch, which Erskine judged to be 'practically non-existent'[136] at the outset of the Emergency. Erskine thought that 1954 'had been a year of real progress' and that Operation Anvil had 'proved to be the turning point in the Emergency'. At long last the Security Forces could 'take the offensive after the long period of holding the situation in 1953'. European representation in the higher echelons of the Kikuyu Home Guard units had risen and 'terrorist initiative and morale had shown a marked decline' with more and more arms being recovered and Mau Mau rebels killed.

Erskine viewed the role of an effective intelligence-gathering and exploitation system as vital to the success of military operations in Kenya. In a lecture to police recruits he highlighted the importance of Special Branch, which 'will give you a line on many characters together who are undesirable and trouble makers'. Special Branch would be able to 'link these characters together and show a pattern of organization'. 'The S.B. with its tentacles all over the territory should be your most important and reliable source of information'.

> I have found that in addition you need a Field Intelligence Organization probably built up by the soldiers and police whose object it is to find the gangs and take immediate action against them. The S.B. can't do this because they will prejudice their sources of information if they take immediate action – they are looking for long-term steady intelligence. The Field Intelligence is looking for immediate targets. Hence our pseudo-gangs in Kenya.[137]

In internal security operations of this nature, Erskine argued, intelligence is vital and the creation of a good machine ought to take first priority.

Young's development of the police intensified over the summer months of 1954, but he soon encountered friction from the civilian authorities. In a letter to Erskine, Lyttelton said that Young 'went out of his way to say how helpful the military have been to him especially in the last month or two, and mentioned that the Commander-in-Chief had helped him enormously in building up the Police'.[138]

Military operations in Kenya during 1954 were marked by the increasing ramping up of coercive measures. Operation Anvil in April 1954 and Operation Hammer, a follow-up mission in January 1955, illustrate this well. Before deploying on the latter, Erskine praised his men for doing a 'good job' in Nairobi, but announced that now 'the main battle must be won':

> You will have a chance of showing what you can do in the forests in Hammer. These operations are very important. You must go in determined to kill or capture every gangster in your area. I know it is not

> going to be easy but you must make a supreme effort. You must wipe the floor with Mau Mau. The more successful you are the easier our tasks later.[139]

In the run up to Operation Hammer, intelligence suggested that there were approximately 1,700 Mau Mau in the Aberdare forests.[140]

The RAF had been softening the area up for some time, conducting around 150 aircraft sorties per month in 1954.[141] There was a belief in the local Air Command that 'It has taken us a long time to build up the momentum of our air operations in Kenya and we are now meeting with success. Ideally of course we should reinforce this success by increasing our pressure where it has been proved to be hurting.'[142] No further cuts to the Lincoln force were recommended, and by late summer 1954 requests were being made for the importation of 4,000lb bombs from Aden. As a senior official in the Air Ministry commented, 'Personally I think the dropping of a few [4,000lb HC bombs] would be of good morale value against the terrorists'.[143] However, neither the Governor, nor Erskine, had requested them, and were said to be 'both strongly opposed to use of 4,000lb bombs'. On average some 200 tonnes of bombs were being dropped per month in anti-Mau Mau operations, all of which, argued one RAF officer, were 'making a positive contribution to the effort of the security forces'.[144]

To complement the effectiveness of the RAF's air strikes, Erskine set about reorganizing Army units into Forest Operating Companies and Tracker/Combat Teams. It was anticipated that, although battalion commanders might be wary of the scheme, unit cohesion would not be affected. Erskine hoped that these units would be trained and equipped by Easter 1955, which, indeed, proved to be the case. Erskine also set in train an acclimatization programme and 'forest warfare school' for all incoming units, building on the Malaya model, to which all junior leaders could be sent once they arrived in theatre. Another one of Erskine's innovations was the issue of a field manual, Anti-Mau Mau Operations, which drew its inspiration from Templer's ATOM, and the formation of what he called 'Trojan Teams'. These were small, highly mobile 'detachments', comprising a Swahili-speaking team leader, an NCO, five other ranks and an interpreter, who could be tasked by local commanders for operations in their tactical area of responsibility (TAOR). Erskine said:

> The men selected must be those who show an aptitude for 'commando' type of operations. They must have a high sense of discipline. Their task is to kill or capture terrorists who have been identified by intelligence. They are bound by the same rules as all security forces. TROJAN teams

> must be most careful that they actions never become irresponsible or indiscriminate. There is no objection to the Administration, after consultation with Special Branch, forming TROJAN teams from Tribal Police to assist MIOs and FIOs in the Reserves.[145]

Intelligence became more and more vital to the success of operations in Kenya. Looking back on his service with the Trojan Force, one former commander of the teams recalled how it was 'an "ill wind" that brought us Mau Mau' but that he could 'at last see an end to this futile rebellion'. As he concluded ominously, 'it pleases me to know that my little band of Trojans is out and about knowing now how to get under the enemies skin!!' I will miss them terribly, but one day I will write of all their exploits, which have never been recorded and are known to only one or two of us.'[146] In any event, it would take a military intelligence officer, Major (later General Sir) Frank Kitson, to exploit the idea further in a more covert manner.

Surveying the year's operations, Erskine noted that he

> did not expect spectacular terrorist casualties, nor were they achieved, since the terrorist always avoid combat and in the dense forest escape is very easy. The invariable reaction of gangs when bumped was to splinter and lie low until the patrol had moved on.[147]

Despite Mike Dewar's labelling of Erskine's campaign as 'a war of attrition', there was undoubtedly a shift in emphasis towards building up the colony's policing capabilities and further developing the potential of its Special Branch. Moreover, as Erskine came to conclude, it was necessary for the Army to develop its own intelligence gathering and exploitation process; the Trojan Teams and, later, the counter-gangs allowed them to do just that. As outlined above, while Erskine was not beyond engaging in less coercive measures, he liked to keep his options open:

> It was obvious that the leaders would not surrender if their inevitable fate would be a trial in Court followed by a death sentence. The surrender offer, if it were to prove successful, would have to leave the irreconcilables with their lives at least. The difficulty, of course, was to decide when this card should be played and it would have to be offered from strength and not from weakness.[148]

Nevertheless, Erskine still remained fixated on the use of brute force in the 'Prohibited Areas'. He reported how military operations in the high Aberdare ridge-lines 'were better than I anticipated' and that [p]urely statistically they raised the average monthly killing rate in the forest in 1955 to sixty six as against a figure of thirty nine in 1953 and forty nine in 1954'. While the body count was certainly piling up, Erskine claimed that he 'never visualised that these operations would finish the Emergency', although he thought that 'they have dealt the terrorist a blow, the severity of which is comparable with Anvil'.[149] Despite the flexibility in his strategic thinking, Erskine's position was hardened by the overly coercive measures preferred by the settlers, the view of bringing about a swift victory by politicians in London and an increasingly beleaguered colonial administration with an indecisive governor. A new strategic impetus was needed.

On 21 April 1955 Erskine received official confirmation that he would be relieved by General Sir Patrick Lathbury.[150] As Blundell observed, appreciatively, the outgoing Commander-in-Chief had done 'a good job for us'. The 'fact remains', he wrote, 'that we were on the offensive and the military end was in sight when Lathbury took over'.[151] Such was the mood now prevalent in the colony that Lathbury decided, almost immediately upon arrival, to cut the number of battalions by three and dispense with the RAF bombers that had made such a definite impact on operations the forested areas. Consequently, the brigade headquarters were reduced from three to two, prompted by the breaking up of the larger Mau Mau gangs into smaller gangs. Nevertheless, Baring remained cautiously optimistic, informing the Legislative Assembly:

> Any further reductions will be considered very carefully in the light of changing conditions, but there can be no doubt that the struggle against Mau Mau is still a military operations requiring military command.[152]

By now the back of the Mau Mau rebellion had been broken. In Blundell's words, although the rebels had created 'high-sounding organizations', including 'Grand Councils, high parliaments, field-marshals, presidents and generals', who 'all debated . . . the latest turn of events', in the end, he argued, apart from the 'bloody work of the panga and the stealthy tread of the oath administrator, the actual outcome was more a caricature of war than war itself'.[153]

The intelligence war

Lathbury's arrival in Kenya coincided with Erskine's reorganization of the colonial security and intelligence machinery. Entrepreneurial schemes by Special Branch officers, such as Ian Henderson, designed to entice the gangs to surrender, were now rolled out across Central Province. Baring's administration moved to decisively neutralize the threat posed by the gangs. Indeed, the British approach to imperial intelligence had been given something of a fillip when Templer's Report on Colonial Security and Intelligence was published in April 1955. It recommended that all senior members of the Colonial Police Services (Heads of Special Branch, Commissioners and Deputy Commissioners) be trained by MI5 on techniques and processes for collating, managing and utilizing intelligence.[154] The idea was endorsed by the new Colonial Secretary, Allan Lennox-Boyd, and a course was immediately convened in London. Visiting the course on its closing day, Lennox-Boyd impressed upon its students how:

> The holding of these courses for senior Police Officers is a reflection of the importance to be attached to an organised and systematic approach to intelligence, as an essential part of governmental machinery in modern conditions.[155]

It would later emerge that MI5's Director-General Roger Hollis was more than willing to play the role of midwife to Templer's plan to restructure the colonial security apparatus. In large part this was attributable to the fact that Hollis arguably 'found security in colonies and British-administered territories of greater concern than security in Britain itself'.[156] In his speech, Lennox-Boyd also made the point that intelligence serves a two-fold purpose: to secure the Colonial government and to serve the Secretary of State in carrying out his responsibilities.

> the close and vital bearing which information on events and trends both in the 'security' and 'political' fields may have on major policy decisions to be taken either by the Secretary of State himself or in consultation with his colleagues, in such matters as constitutional advancement or in the handling of serious security situations (such as Cyprus) in which political and security considerations are inextricably linked.[157]

This made all the difference, he said, in 'government defence commitments throughout the world, and to international problems in a shrinking world'. In retrospect, it could be said that military and civilian intelligence capabilities eventually worked seamlessly in Kenya. In one report it was noted:

> Relations with military intelligence have been very good throughout the Emergency; and for the last year and a half the military and Special Branch intelligence organisations have been completely integrated, an experiment that has been extremely successful.[158]

Moving to further entrench the professionalism of the security forces machinery, Lennox-Boyd decreed that the membership of the Local Intelligence Committee should be confined to 'permanent Government servants, and ordinarily to representatives of the Administration, the Police and Special Branch, the Armed Forces and the United Kingdom Security Service (i.e. the Security Liaison Officer)'.[159]

After a couple of months in charge, Lathbury wrote to Erskine to inform his predecessor how he was 'finding [his] new job intensely interesting but rather exacting!'[160] One of the problems he faced was in getting the RAF high command to work with the Security Forces to a common unifying plan. It is certainly apparent from the evidence available that the RAF were keen to 'make use of everything we have to exert maximum pressure' on the Mau Mau as they debated the surrender process in 1955. The Air Force Commander in Aden said, 'I personally fear General Lathbury may have been swayed by the anti-air element who were kept in place by General Erskine. Also he may not have had time to appreciate the limitations of the soldier in the forests'.[161] Yet within weeks the RAF had accepted Lathbury's assessment,

> that Terrorists in Kenya are now reduced in number and activity and hide in small gangs which seldom present worthwhile targets for heavy bombers or large scale Army operations. He is planning to employ most of the Army in small tracker teams which will spend most of their time in the forests and will cover the whole area. It will be difficult in these circumstances to employ heavy bombers with safety even when they [are] likely to be effective.[162]

The heavy bombers were, therefore, withdrawn on operational and financial grounds.[163] Though somewhat reluctant to withdraw the aircraft, RAF command in the Middle East respected Lathbury's decision. The War Council finally approved the order to withdrawal bomber support on 19 July 1955.

With the rebellion quelled and the Emergency declared over, the Mau Mau was militarily defeated. Over 10,000 militant Mau Mau were killed during the Emergency, with a further 3,000 surrendering and more than 2,500 being captured. Between October 1952 and the end of February 1957, 1,070 Africans were executed for Mau Mau offences; some 326 were hanged for murder.[164] Even though intelligence reports were still being received by London in 1957 which highlighted the fact that oathing was still taking place, it remained a small-scale affair linked to criminality.[165] A more potentially serious outbreak of oathing occurred in September 1957, but again was swiftly put down.[166] The Security Forces moved quickly to apprehend those responsible and, on 3 February 1958, 111 Meru appeared before a Magistrate's Court in Meru District, charged with sedition. A week later another 100 men appeared before a judge. To all intents and purposes, however, the Mau Mau rebellion had died out and, in the move towards Kenyan independence, Britain would preside over its corpse.

Conclusion

One of the most remarkable aspects of the Emergency in Kenya was the cross-fertilization of colonial policing techniques from one context to another. The extent to which this permitted the application of 'lessons learned' at the tactical or operational levels has not been the main concern of this chapter, though it was undoubtedly a common feature for the Security Forces in their operations against the Mau Mau. Despite the 'softening up' of targets by heavy bombers and the constant harrying from ground troops, the Mau Mau continued to dominate the higher ground in the Central Province for most of the Emergency, holing up in the thick jungles and cavernous ravines of the Aberdares and Mount Kenya. The Security Forces, under Erskine's command, operated against an enemy that capitalized on its ability to blend into the Kenya's unique terrain. Erskine often used strong language to drive home the need for forces under his command to obliterate the movement's military capacity. In this, he was largely successful. However, by breaking up the larger gangs he drove the movement further underground and made its subversion relatively difficult to defeat. The disease had been pushed to another part of the body. Nevertheless, the re-imposition of law and order was to be based on firm evidence against suspects. 'It is no use capturing a terrorist and handing him over to the Police if you produce against him no evidence of terrorism or atrocity', emphasized one report; 'the police merely have to release him, and everyone's time is wasted'.[167]

Erskine recognized early on that he needed the local population to support the Security Forces in their task of rooting out and defeating Mau Mau. However, there were places, like Nairobi, which he regarded as a 'gangster town'; he argued that only by separating the people from the Mau Mau could they hope to win the campaign. 'It is not a question of rough treatment', he later said, 'but a question of civil organisation which has got badly out of hand'. Erskine did not shirk from what he saw as his responsibility to return law and order to Kenya. 'The population must not only be controlled but also protected', he said. The tough measures he approved, he maintained, 'must not be regarded as oppressive but as temporary and necessary'.[168]

Erskine had always anticipated a short stay in Kenya. Within a few months, however, it dawned on him that he would be there for another year. He hated the posting and, by the end of 1953, was sinking deeper into prolonged fits of paranoia. In a letter to his wife he claimed that he was a 'No. 1 target'. Fearing that she too would become a target, he dissuaded her from coming out to Kenya. In any event, he concluded, she might 'find the local population as unpleasant as I do – I hate the guts of them all – they are all . . . middle class sluts'.[169] In a separate letter to Harding, Erskine elaborated further: '[m]any of them are excellent stout hearted chaps, some are absentee Landlords and a few are just plain mad'.[170] Nevertheless, Erskine won the respect of the settler community for his tough actions. Michael Blundell noted how 'I'm afraid it has been at times a thankless task but looking back on it all, it seems to me that your planning and operations have all fallen into place and achieved their objectives'.[171] Alan Lennox-Boyd, who had replaced Lyttelton in 1955, sent a personal note of praise to Erskine to thank him for his adept handling of the situation. 'When I compare the present hopeful outlook with that in 1953 when you went to Kenya, I realise what tremendous progress has been made and how much of it is due to your military skill and to the wise and co-operative part you have played in the life of the Colony.'[172] There was a general feeling both in Nairobi and London that Erskine had performed admirably in enormously difficult circumstances during his time as Commander-in-Chief. In a hastily scribbled note passed onto Erskine after his departure, the Governor Evelyn Baring wrote,

> I could not be more grateful to you for the way in which we have worked together. I am sure that very close military/civil cooperation is the only way to deal with a messy situation like this in Kenya and it is one which is liable to occur again elsewhere. But thanks to the combination of your great drive on the Mau Mau with your appreciation of the civil side of the picture things have worked.[173]

Despite the stresses and strains which these types of operations had on civil–military relations, they were extremely important learning experiences for commanders and colonial officials alike. Field-Marshal Harding, who had presided over colonial policing strategies in both Malaya and Kenya, now hoped to apply the same approach on his next appointment as Governor of Cyprus.

Notes

1 The National Archives, Kew, London (TNA), CO 1035/30, J.V.W. Shaw to T.S. Tull, 23 December 1952.
2 Comments by General Sir George Erskine at a press conference on anti-Mau Mau military operations, cited in *The Times*, 22 October 1953.
3 *The Daily Chronicle*, 2 July 1954.
4 TNA, CO 1066/2, 'Photographs – Ruck Family Murder by Mau Mau Movement, 24 January 1953'.

5 Carruthers, Susan L., *Winning Hearts and Minds: British Governments, the Media and Colonial Counter-Insurgency 1944–1960* (London: Leicester University Press, 1995), p. 136.
6 Douglas-Home, Charles, *Evelyn Baring: The Last Proconsul* (London: Collins, 1978), p. 237.
7 TNA, CO 822/377, Political Intelligence Kenya, 'Top Secret: Kenya Colony Political Intelligence Summary for Period Ending 31 January 1953'.
8 Carruthers, *Winning Hearts and Minds*, p. 136.
9 Elkins, Caroline, *Britain's Gulag: The Brutal End of Empire in Kenya* (London: Jonathan Cape, 2005), p. 43.
10 Clayton, Anthony, *Counter-Insurgency in Kenya, 1952–60* (New York: Sunflower University Press, [1976] 1984), p. 5.
11 For an outline of the literature see Bennett, Huw, 'The Mau Mau Emergency as Part of the British Army's Post-War Counter-Insurgency Experience', *Defense & Security Analysis*, Vol. 23, No. 2 (2007), pp. 143–163.
12 Elkins, *Britain's Gulag*, p. 366.
13 See Bowcott, Owen, 'Kenyans Sue UK for Alleged Colonial Human Rights Abuses', *The Guardian*, 5 April 2011.
14 Bennett, 'The Mau Mau Emergency', pp. 143–163. Bennett (p. 158) argues that 'intimidation of the population, summary executions, torture and unrestrained violence were prevalent for at least eight months'.
15 Elkins, *Britain's Gulag*, pp. x, xii.
16 Ibid., p. 366.
17 Clayton, *Counter-Insurgency in Kenya*, p. 53. I wish to record my sincere thanks here to Dr Clayton for talking to me about some of the broader scholarly issues surrounding these figures from his own unique perspective of having been involved in many of the events which are detailed in this chapter.
18 Clayton, Anthony, *Frontiersmen: Warfare in Africa since 1950* (London: UCL Press, 1999), p. 12.
19 Elkins, *Britain's Gulag*, p. 19.
20 Ibid., p. 18.
21 Ibid., p. 21.
22 Branch, Daniel, *Defeating Mau Mau, Creating Kenya: Counterinsurgency, Civil War, and Decolonization* (Cambridge: Cambridge University Press, 2009), p. 5.
23 See Daniel Branch's excellent book on the Kikuyu loyalists, *Defeating Mau Mau*.
24 Clayton, *Counter-Insurgency in Kenya*. See also Branch, *Defeating Mau Mau*.
25 Branch, *Defeating Mau Mau*, p. 23.
26 Blundell, Sir Michael, *So Rough the Wind: The Kenya Memoirs of Sir Michael Blundell* (London: Weidenfeld and Nicolson, 1964), p. 88.
27 Clayton, *Counter-Insurgency in Kenya*, p. 5.

28 TNA, CO 822/547, CO 822/450, 'Correspondence from Evelyn Baring to W.L. Gorell Barnes, 27 October 1952'.
29 Imperial War Museum (IWM), *Erskine Papers*, 75/134/4, *The Kenya Picture* (Nairobi: GHQ East Africa, 5 January 1954), transcript of the governor's broadcast.
30 House of Commons Debates (Hansard), 21 October 1952, Vol. 505, Col. 866.
31 TNA, CO 822/547, CO 822/450, 'Correspondence from Evelyn Baring to W.L. Gorell Barnes, 27 October 1952'.
32 TNA, KV 2/1788, MI5 File on Johnstone Kenyetta [sic]. Secret Source Report, dated 4 November 1952.
33 TNA, KV 2/1788, MI5 File on Johnstone Kenyetta [sic]. Secret and Personal report from MI5 to C.J.J.T. Barton at the Colonial Office, 22 November 1952.
34 Blundell, *So Rough the Wind*, p. 107.
35 Kenyatta, Jomo, *Facing Mount Kenya: The Tribal Life of the Gikuyu* (London: Secker and Warburg, [1938] 1953), p. 21.
36 Clayton, *Frontiersmen*, p. 25.
37 Clayton, *Counter-Insurgency in Kenya*, p. 5.
38 House of Lords Debates (Hansard), 29 October 1952, Vol. 178, Col. 1134.
39 Grob-Fitzgibbon, Benjamin, *Imperial Endgame: Britain's Dirty Wars and the End of Empire* (Basingstoke: Palgrave Macmillan, 2011), p. 234.
40 House of Commons Debates, 7 November 1952, Vol. 507, Col. 459.
41 TNA, CO 822/547, CO 822/450, Correspondence with Sir Evelyn Baring concerning the situation in Kenya, 'Correspondence from Evelyn Baring to Oliver Lyttelton, 24 November 1952'.
42 TNA, CO 822/377, Political Intelligence Kenya, 'Top Secret: Kenya Colony Political Intelligence Summary for Period Ending 31 January 1953'.
43 The Home Guard were raised amongst the loyal members of the Kikuyu tribe.
44 TNA, CO 1035/30, Barton to Hall and Rogers, 7 January 1953.
45 Carver, Michael, *Harding of Petherton: Field Marshal* (London: Weidenfeld and Nicolson, 1978), p. 181.
46 IWM, *Erskine Papers*, 'Notes for British Units Coming to Kenya'.
47 Carver, *Harding of Petherton*, p. 181.
48 Huw Bennett, 'Erskine, Sir George Watkin Eben James (1899–1965)', *Oxford Dictionary of National Biography* (Oxford: Oxford University Press, 2008); online edn, January 2011. Archived: www.oxforddnb.com/view/article/97289. Accessed on 21 June 2011.
49 IWM, *Erskine Papers*, 75/134/1, 'Report on Major-Gen. Erskine' by B.L. Montgomery, Commander-in-Chief, 21 Army Group, 3 August 1944.
50 *The Times*, 30 May 1953.
51 *Daily Telegraph*, 30 May 1953.

52 TNA, CO 822/693, Personal Reports by General Sir George Erskine on the Situation in Kenya, 'Top Secret Report from General Erskine to the CIGS, Field-Marshal Harding, dated 14 June 1953'.
53 *The Times*, 30 May 1953.
54 Ibid.
55 House of Commons Debates (Hansard), 11 June 1953, Vol. 516, Col. 454.
56 Branch, *Defeating Mau Mau*, p. 56.
57 Ibid., p. 57.
58 IWM, *Erskine Papers*, 'Broadcast by C-in-C – about 24 hrs after arrival in evening at about 9pm after BBC News'.
59 IWM, *Erskine Papers*, 75/134/4, General Erskine to Lord Latham, 16 June 1953.
60 TNA, WO 276/526, War Diary, June–December 1953, GHQ East Africa Op Directive No 1, Erskine to Cornah, Commander 70 Infantry Brigade, dated 16 June 1953.
61 TNA, WO 276/526, War Diary, June–December 1953, GHQ East Africa Op Directive No 1.
62 IWM, *Erskine Papers*, 75/134/4, General Erskine to John Hamilton Esq, British Embassy, Cairo, 7 July 1953.
63 IWM, *Erskine Papers*, General Sir George Erskine to Euan Miller, 14 July 1953.
64 TNA, CO 822/693, Personal Reports by General Sir George Erskine on the Situation in Kenya, 'Reply from the CIGS, Field-Marshal Harding, to General Erskine, dated June 1953'.
65 Blundell, *So Rough the Wind*, p. 148.
66 IWM, *Erskine Papers*, 'Erskine – The Kenya Emergency'.
67 Clayton, *Counter-Insurgency in Kenya*, pp. 8–9. See also Blundell, *So Rough the Wind*, pp. 129–130.
68 IWM, *Erskine Papers*, The Kenya Picture.
69 TNA, KV 4/408, Text of a lecture given by J.P. Morton, 'The Coordination of Intelligence in the Malayan Emergency' (n.d.).
70 *The Times*, 20 June 1953.
71 *Daily Telegraph*, 20 June 1953.
72 *New Statesman*, 16 July 1953.
73 *Daily Telegraph*, 8 July 1953.
74 IWM, *Erskine Papers*, 'Erskine – The Emergency in Kenya'.
75 *The Star*, 3 July 1953.
76 Ibid.
77 *Daily Express*, 22 August 1953.
78 *Sussex Daily News*, 22 August 1953.
79 Griffiths' account is taken directly from the *Daily Mirror*, 28 November 1953.
80 *Daily Mirror*, 26 November 1953.
81 Ibid.
82 *Daily Herald*, 23 July 1953.

83 Anderson, David, *Histories of the Hanged: Britain's Dirty War in Kenya* (London: Phoenix, 2006), p. 259.
84 Bennett, 'The Mau Mau Emergency', p. 143.
85 IWM, *Erskine Papers, Kenya – Mau Mau*, lecture given by General Sir George Erskine on Wednesday 23 November 1955 at 3pm.
86 IWM, *Erskine Papers*, 'Erskine – The Kenya Emergency'.
87 House of Lords Debates (Hansard), 18 November 1953, Vol. 520, Col. 1723.
88 Chappell, Stephen 'Air Power in the Mau Mau Conflict: The Government's Chief Weapon', *The RUSI Journal*, Vol. 156, No. 1 (February/March 2011), p. 66.
89 IWM, *Erskine Papers*, 'Erskine – The Kenya Emergency'.
90 IWM, *Erskine Papers*, 75/134/4, 'Confidential: Operations in Special Areas and in the Reserve', signed by Major-General Heyman, CoS, dated 7 January 1954.
91 Ibid.
92 IWM, *Erskine Papers*, 75/134/4, Handwritten notes for a lecture entitled Emergency (n.d.)
93 Ibid.
94 IWM, *Erskine Papers, Kenya – Mau Mau*, lecture given by General Sir George Erskine on Wednesday 23 November 1955 at 3pm.
95 *East Anglian Daily Times*, 24 August 1953.
96 Leader, *The Times*, 24 August 1953.
97 TNA, CO 822/693, Personal Reports by General Sir George Erskine on the Situation in Kenya, 'Top Secret Report from General Erskine to the CIGS, Field Marshal Harding, dated 7 July 1953'.
98 The lack of a central leadership was noted by Erskine in his submissions to the CIGS, Field-Marshal Sir John Harding in 1953. 'My impression is that MAU MAU direction from any central point does not exist'. See TNA, CO 822/693, Personal Reports by General Sir George Erskine on the Situation in Kenya, 'Top Secret Report from General Erskine to the CIGS, Field Marshal Harding, dated 7 July 1953'.
99 *Daily Express*, 1 October 1953.
100 *The Times*, 2 October 1953.
101 IWM, *Erskine Papers*, 75/134/10, General Sir George Erskine to Lady Erskine, 30 September 1953.
102 Brown, George, 'Guns Alone Won't End Mau Mau', *Daily Herald*, 19 October 1953.
103 IWM, *Erskine Papers*, 75/134/1, General Erskine to Lady Erskine, 9 October 1953.
104 Ibid., 27 October 1953.
105 Ibid.
106 TNA, CO 822/547, The Governor of Kenya's Speech to the Legislative Council on 20 October 1953.
107 Comments made by Mr Hale, Labour MP for Oldham West, *The Times*, 19 November 1953.

108 'Comment/Leader: Cloud over Africa', *Daily Mail*, 1 December 1953.
109 IWM, *Erskine Papers*, 75/134/1, General Erskine to Lady Erskine, 17 January 1954.
110 IWM, Erskine Papers, 75/134/1, General Erskine to Philip Erskine, 29 January 1954.
111 IWM, *Erskine Papers*, 75/134/1, Anthony Head to General Erskine, 28 January 1954. Minute dated 20 January 1954.
112 Ibid.
113 IWM, *Erskine Papers*, 75/134/3, *Kenya – Mau Mau*.
114 Ibid.
115 IWM, *Erskine Papers*, 'Erskine – The Kenya Emergency'.
116 Ibid.
117 Elkins, *Britain's Gulag*, p. 124.
118 IWM, *Erskine Papers*, 'Erskine – The Kenya Emergency'.
119 Elkins, *Britain's Gulag*, p. 123.
120 IWM, *Erskine Papers*, 'Erskine – The Kenya Emergency'.
121 Ibid.
122 Ibid.
123 IWM, 89/13/1, *Papers of W H Thompson*, *Only the Foothills* (dated 13 January 1987), p. 95.
124 Ibid., p. 97.
125 IWM, *Erskine Papers*, 'Erskine – The Kenya Emergency'.
126 IWM, *Erskine Papers*, Commander-in-Chief's Directive No. 3, dated 8 March 1954.
127 TNA, CO 967/325, Sir Evelyn Baring, 'Liesching to Sir Thomas Lloyd, 2 January 1951'.
128 IWM, *Erskine Papers*, 75/134/1, Letter from General Erskine to Lady Erskine, 21 February 1954.
129 IWM, *Erskine Papers*, 75/134/1, General Erskine to Lady Erskine, 3 March 1954.
130 TNA, CO 822/693, Top Secret Report from General Erskine to the CIGS, dated 23 July 1953.
131 Ibid.
132 IWM, *Erskine Papers*, 75/134/15, Letter from Robert Erskine to his father, 6 March 1954.
133 IWM, *Erskine Papers*, 75/134/10, Rt Hon Oliver Lyttelton MP to General Erskine, 11 August 1954.
134 IWM, *Erskine Papers*, 75/134/10, Leonard Mombasa to General Erskine, 16 February 1954.
135 IWM, *Erskine Papers*, 75/134/1, General Erskine to Lady Erskine, 23 February 1954.
136 IWM, *Erskine Papers*, 'Erskine – The Kenya Emergency'.
137 IWM, *Erskine Papers*, 75/134/4, 'Lecture to Police College: Army Aid to the Civil Power in Colonial and Protected Territories by General Sir George Erskine, GCB, KBE, DSO'.
138 IWM, *Erskine Papers*, 75/134/10, Lyttelton to Erskine, 16 July 1954.

139 IWM, *Erskine Papers*, 75/134/1, 'Commander-in-Chief's Directive', dated 10 December 1954.
140 IWM, *Erskine Papers*, 'Erskine – The Emergency in Kenya'.
141 TNA, AIR 8/1886, Message from HQ MEAF Ismailia to Air Ministry, London, 18 September 1954.
142 TNA, AIR 8/1886, Minute sheet, dated 18 September 1954.
143 Ibid.
144 TNA, AIR 8/1886, Loose Minute: Air Operations against Terrorists in Kenya, signed by Air Commodore H.R. Graham and dated 3 November 1954.
145 IWM, *Erskine Papers*, Secret: Emergency Directive No. 14: Operations after Hammer, dated 6 December 1954.
146 IWM, *Erskine Papers*, 75/134/10, 'Francis', 'O'Coy, The Kenya Regiment (TF) to General Erskine, 24 January 1955.
147 Ibid.
148 Ibid.
149 IWM, *Erskine Papers*, 'Erskine – The Emergency in Kenya'.
150 IWM, *Erskine Papers*, 75/134/4, Priority Cipher Message to GHQ East Africa, 21 April 1955.
151 Blundell, *So Rough a Wind*, p. 194.
152 IWM, *Erskine Papers*, 75/134/4, 'His Excellency the Governor's Communication from the Chair to the Legislative Council on the 18th October 1955'.
153 Blundell, *So Rough a Wind*, p. 197.
154 IWM, *Erskine Papers*, 75/134/4, Templer, General Sir Gerald Secret: Report on Colonial Security, 23 April 1955.
155 TNA, CO 1035/55, Secret: Security Service Training Course for Senior Overseas Police Officers, 1956, Visit by the Secretary of State during the final session on Thursday 5 July.
156 Andrew, Christopher, *The Defence of the Realm: The Authorized History of MI5* (London: Allen Lane, 2009), p. 462.
157 TNA, CO 1035/55, Secret: Security Service Training Course for Senior Overseas Police Officers, 1956, Visit by the Secretary of State during the final session on Thursday 5 July.
158 TNA, CO 1035/30, Sir Evelyn Baring to Rt. Hon. A. T. Lennox-Boyd, MP, Secretary of State for the Colonies, 19 September 1956.
159 TNA, CO 1035/55, Top Secret Circular by Lennox-Boyd on the Organisation of Intelligence, 28 April 1956.
160 IWM, *Erskine Papers*, 75/134/10, Patrick Lathbury to Erskine, 13 June 1955.
161 TNA, AIR 8/1886, Message from AOC, HQ British Forces Aden, to SASO, HQ, MELF, dated 4 June 1955.
162 TNA, AIR 8/1886, Message from HQ, MEAF, to Air Ministry, London, 11 July 1955.
163 Ibid.

164 TNA, CO822/1220, Note on the History of the Emergency in Kenya (n.d.: May 1957?)
165 TNA, CO 822/1254, Report on Mau Mau Oathing in Meru District by the Director of Intelligence and Security, Nairobi, 24 January 1958.
166 Ibid.
167 TNA, WO 276/526, War Diary, June–December 1953, Police HQ, Nairobi, Notes for Military and Police personnel on possible offences committed by terrorists, dated 17 August 1953.
168 IWM, *Erskine Papers*, 75/134/4, General Erskine notes on the Emergency, dated 16 October 1953.
169 IWM, *Erskine Papers*, 75/134/1, General Erskine to Lady Erskine, 17 January 1954.
170 TNA, CO 822/693, Top Secret Report from General Erskine to the CIGS, dated 7 July 1953.
171 IWM, *Erskine Papers*, 75/134/10, Michael Blundell to General Erskine, 28 April 1955.
172 IWM, *Erskine Papers*, 75/134/10, Lennox-Boyd to General Erskine, 3 May 1955.
173 IWM, *Erskine Papers*, 75/134/10, 13 May 1955.

4

Securing the base: fighting EOKA terrorists in Cyprus

> This is the place where we have decided to erect a base which is to be the key to the Eastern Mediterranean, and on which the defence policy not only of the United Kingdom but of the West hinges.[1]

> But for us, the British, Cyprus is directly concerned with all our military effort in the Middle East. It is the nerve centre of our whole Middle East military organization.[2]

> [I]n the Second World War . . . 30,000 Cypriots were induced to join the British army by assurances that they were fighting 'for Greece and freedom'. Like every other Cypriot, I believed that we were also fighting for the freedom of Cyprus . . . As the empty post-war years went by I was forced to realise that only in one way would the island win the freedom which it had sought so long: by fighting for it.[3]

Introduction

The former Chief of the Defence Staff (CDS), General Sir Michael Carver, once remarked that 'it was fortunate for Britain that her colonial conflicts followed in succession. If they had all struck her simultaneously, she would have been hard put to cope with them.'[4] While the battle of wills between Britain and her irregular challengers were weighted heavily in favour of the colonial authorities in both Malaya and Kenya by the beginning of 1955, a question still remained over whether Britain could sustain its already high level of military activity across the world. National Service had dramatically increased the Army's manpower cycle: 400,000 men from Britain and several hundred thousand more from the colonies gave the military an over-inflated strength of approximately 1 million.[5] Despite the massive numbers involved, however, the size of the armed forces was proving financially unsustainable by the mid-1950s and the government was poised to declare an end to conscription.[6] The drawdown in manpower was something that would later be confirmed in Duncan Sandys' Defence Review, eventually published in 1957,[7] which favoured a reliance on nuclear weapons as the ultimate strategic deterrent. For the time being though Britain vowed not to compromise on its overseas commitments. If nothing else, the incomplete and uneven nature of decolonisation and the growing threat posed by Communism made it difficult for her to do so. The incoming Chief of the Imperial General Staff (CIGS), Sir Gerald Templer, was in no doubt where the security challenges were now emanating from: 'we are faced with a dual enemy – the immediate anti-British elements, of whatever origin, and the Russians in the background, seeking how best to exploit them'.[8] One of the British Empire's weak spots identified by Templer in his influential *Report on Colonial Security* was Cyprus, the gateway to the Middle East and Britain's 'nerve centre' for military operations in the region.[9]

British military intervention in Cyprus reached a crescendo in the major counter-insurgency campaign fought by the island's Security Forces between 1955 and 1959. The terrorist group National Organisation of Cypriot Combatants (EOKA), led by Colonel George Grivas, a Greek Cypriot and retired army officer, immediately embarked on *enosis* (union with Greece) through an armed campaign. He was backed politically by Archbishop Makarios III, leader of the Cyprus Orthodox Church, who, while not taking an active part in the terrorist campaign himself, 'hinted that the Church would not shrink from violence if necessary'.[10] Makarios had been making inflammatory anti-British speeches in public for some time, which were designed to push the issue of British occupation to the forefront of public attention in Cyprus and across the world. Thus, Grivas' aim was 'not to expel or to defeat the British, but to draw the attention of international public opinion by harassing them'.[11] The whole idea was to feed into Makarios' plan – with the backing of Greece – to lobby hard on the world stage for the liberation of Cyprus by forcing the United Nations to apply pressure on Britain to withdraw.[12] After the Emergency was called off in 1959, Britain retreated to its Sovereign Base Areas, where it was to remain after Cyprus became an independent state in 1960. It had always been a priority of British defence, foreign and security policy that the sovereign military bases would be retained, even in the event of a settlement between the two rival Cypriot groups. Indeed, it was the outspoken comments of a junior Colonial Office minister, Henry Hopkinson, confirming this, which led to the heightening of tensions on the island.[13]

The failure of EOKA to gain ground through violence can be directly attributable to the security plan designed and implemented by Field-Marshal Sir John Harding, the former CIGS, which stressed 'alertness, readiness and observation as an aid both to efficient counter-terrorism and security and to intelligence' and who brought the full weight of British power to bear on Grivas' group between 1955 and 1957. It was Harding's tough, no-nonsense approach, allied with his diplomatic overtures to both the Greek and Turkish Cypriot communities, which drove Britain's Cyprus policy in the mid-1950s. Moreover, it was the failure of the colonial authorities to resolve the matter which had initially led to the Conservative government taking 'the easy way out' in turning to 'the military to apply a simple solution to a problem whose complexities otherwise eluded them'.[14] Ironically, the military no more succeeded than the politicians, despite the fanfare surrounding the campaigns in Malaya and Kenya. Revisiting Harding's 'duel' with Grivas offers us considerable insight into how Britain's small wars campaigning could so easily come unstuck when its 'winning formula' was applied in a very different colonial setting.

The 'shooting war' begins

Hostilities began on 1 April 1955 when a series of explosions rocked the island. Operations by EOKA were directed mainly at sabotaging key installations, such as the Cyprus Broadcasting Corporation transmitter, police stations and government offices.[15] Sensing trouble afoot the government arranged for the dispatch of General Sir Gerald Templer to the island to essentially 'ginger up . . . what is patently an inadequate security force'.[16] What he found shocked him. The police were poorly trained and equipped and lacked proper leadership. In 1954 the police force numbered only 1,386 men, over 37 per cent of whom were drawn from the minority Turkish Cypriot community.[17] Grivas' organisation had little trouble in dissuading Greek Cypriots from joining, or, indeed, from eliciting information from those sympathetic to *enosis*. It was mess. Templer recommended the immediate expansion in numbers and the formation of a Special Branch. As he later concluded in his *Report on Colonial Security*:

> Prior to the emergency, it was reported by the Security Intelligence Adviser to the Colonial Office, Mr MacDonald, the Special Branch in Cyprus was 'in an embryonic stage . . . it is at present inadequate in strength, completely lacking in training and short of funds'.[18]

With more pressing financial concerns elsewhere, Templer's warnings fell on deaf ears. Not for the first time was it to take the declaration of an emergency 'to bring about an increase in police establishment and the force's subsequent reform'.[19] This was unfortunate, argues Robert Holland, given that the 'key battle-ground at this stage of the incipient rebellion was the Police'.[20] The security situation rapidly deteriorated. Explosions became much more frequent as the weeks passed by and an attempt was even made on the life of the Governor, Sir Robert Armitage, at the end of May.[21]

Sensing weakness amongst the colonial authorities, Grivas launched a second offensive in June, which was aimed at 'terrorisation of the police' and it was not long before EOKA managed to murder a member of the Security Forces: a Greek Cypriot policeman, Constable Poullis, was shot dead on 19 August in the old town of Nicosia. The attack, although relatively unsophisticated, did more than anything else to expose the chinks in the rusting security armour. The response was typically lacklustre, largely because of a lack of resources. Special Branch was poorly staffed and trained and, above all, was devoid of effective leadership. The Cyprus Police Commissioner, George Robins, had only recently been appointed and he 'feared that morale was too low to retaliate against Grivas's full-scale attacks, designed to terrorise the police and kill as many as possible'.[22] Fortunately, the visit to Cyprus by the CIGS, Field-Marshal Sir John Harding, in mid-July put in motion the recommendation to London that further reinforcements be sent to the island to beef up the Security Force presence. Soon after his return, the War Office promised to bolster the garrison by sending out two Royal Marine Commando units and two infantry battalions, but they would not arrive until later in the year. In the short term, it was not enough. Operationally, the security forces were losing momentum, in large part because of the almost total lack of intelligence on the enemy they faced. Armitage, unwisely perhaps, rejected Harding's recourse to analogy with other colonial conflicts and suggested instead that an alterative model be used to handle the subversion. Unfortunately, argues Holland, the Governor's 'warnings were overshadowed by the necessities of the moment'.[23]

Politically, Armitage was on borrowed time. The week prior to the London conference on Cyprus and a few days before Constable Poullis' murder, Harold Macmillan wrote to Prime Minister Anthony Eden to recommend a change at Government House in Nicosia.[24] Macmillan had grown tired of the indecision on Cyprus and was determined to rectify the problem once and for all. 'At different times the task of finding a solution to the problem had oscillated', Holland has written, 'like a game of "pass the parcel" – between the administration in Nicosia, the Colonial Office, the Foreign Office, the British Embassy in Athens, and 10 Downing Street'.[25] In keeping with the Tories' penchant for resolute military direction in their small wars campaigning, Downing Street opted, once again, to send in a military supremo in civilian clothing to solve the problem. A search for Armitage's successor began in earnest, with the leading contender appearing to be Harding, whose term as CIGS was coming to an end, and who had impressed the Cabinet and other British officials with his views on the issue. The Governor of Hong Kong, Sir Alexander Grantham, wrote to his old friend General Sir George Erskine to express his disappointment at Harding's impending retirement:

> John Harding passed through here not so long ago and it was nice to see him again. It does seem a shame that he is retiring, but he was quite firm that even if he were asked to stay on he would not do so. I only hope that he gets some important job where his undoubted talents can be used to the best advantage. He should, however, have a bit of a rest before taking on anything else.[26]

Harding's rest was to be short-lived; as Michael Carver revealed in his biography of the Field-Marshal, he 'accepted with considerable misgiving' Eden's request to assume overall responsibility for Cyprus on 3 October 1955. Harding had been looking forward to the stability of family life in retirement, but 'it was not to be: duty came first and brought with it an invigorating challenge'.[27] Eden's letter to Harding made clear that Downing Street was eager to have someone in Nicosia who could inspire confidence in the colonial administration, the security forces and Cypriot community as well as the government and public at home. In Eden's words 'after a brilliant military career there is nothing to be gained, and may be something to be lost, in undertaking such responsibilities, but equally I know how little you allow matters of that kind to weigh in the scale where the national interest is concerned'. Eden then elaborated:

> I have been profoundly unhappy about Cyprus for some time past. I do not think that we could have avoided this situation. Papagos was headed for it and attempts to stop him only created resentment. On the other hand, for the Turks Cyprus is the last of the off-shore islands. What we must now hope to do is to show the Cypriots steadily and firmly rather than harshly that we mean to carry out our responsibility and that the offers we have made still stand. The sooner these last can be discussed again the better will it be for all those concerned.[28]

Having a military man in charge, especially one who could whip the island's security apparatus into shape at short notice, had considerable gravitational pull amongst the top echelons of the Conservative government. Eden found the Colonial Secretary 'understanding of my concern and ready to agree to the appointment I had in mind';[29] after all, who better to find a 'solution to the Cyprus problem' than the man who had overall responsibility for turning the tide in Malaya and Kenya? 'All acknowledged that he had been an exceptionally successful CIGS, as good as a leader of the army, then engaged in operations all over the world, as he had been in Whitehall', wrote Carver.[30] That Harding could work with government departments outside the War Office was not lost on senior politicians and Whitehall mandarins either.

Shortly after his arrival in Nicosia, Harding sought to reassure the Cypriot people that he meant business. In his first broadcast on 9 October 1955, he promised to 'eliminate terrorism and intimidation so that men and women everywhere can go about their daily business without fear or favour'. Ending violence, he urged, 'would bring peace' and 'peace brings prosperity'. Rounding off his remarks, he promised that they would be able to elect their own representatives, albeit it on internal political matters.[31] Earlier, as a goodwill gesture, Harding had departed from the ways of his predecessor, by meeting with Archbishop Makarios the day after his arrival. His 'patient and ingenious efforts to reach a basis of co-operations with the Archbishop',[32] however, ended without agreement. Harding was disappointed that the Greek Cypriots rejected what he regarded as 'reasonable and practical' proposals. Yet the Field-Marshal consoled himself in his first duty to 'maintain law and order' and issued firm orders to the police and troops to bring the terrorists to justice, all while exercising 'proper restraint'.[33] Harding was not in the post long before he began to bear the brunt of Greek propaganda. Athens Radio, the main organ by which the Greek government 'provided moral support to the insurgents',[34] was remarkably anti-British, leading Harding to request that the Foreign Office 'should seriously consider taking more forcible steps by diplomatic or other means to put an end to the lying abuse'[35] being transmitted from Greece. Public opinion was vital to the success of his plan.[36]

Harding was to continue to press other parts of the Whitehall machinery to do their bit in helping to bring the campaign of terrorism to heel. Indeed, he saw it as essential that all 'activities of government were to be knitted together to act under his direction', observed Carver. 'The methods which Templer had used with such success in Malaya were to be immediately applied in Cyprus'.[37] Almost from the outset the cross-fertilisation of lessons was felt across the strategic, operational and tactical levels of civil–military machinery in Cyprus. As Harding confided in a letter to his old friend Bobbie Erskine:

> I only hope I can make as much impression on the problems here as you did in Kenya. I am most grateful to you for the loyal support and

> good comradeship you have always extended to me whenever we served together, and particularly during the time you were Commander-in-Chief Kenya and I was C.I.G.S.[38]

However, in the haste to combat the growing EOKA campaign, Harding moved too quickly in some respects and not in enough in others. For instance, in terms of the former, he lacked experience of colonial policing,[39] leading him to neglect Sir Arthur Young's model in Malaya of building up a cadre of professional local leaders when pushing through an accelerated recruitment and training programme for the police.[40] Moreover, his appeals to the Greek Cypriot community to join the police fell flat. On the latter, though, he understood his chief opponent, EOKA leader George Grivas, and was 'stubbornly' prepared to stand firm against him. The guerrillas had met their match in Harding.[41]

Fighting EOKA on the cheap

From the early days of the Cold War, Cyprus had continually formed a vital piece of the wider strategic jigsaw for successive British governments. One Joint Intelligence Committee Report, written in the summer of 1948, ranked Cyprus and Libya as Britain's two main strategic assets in the Mediterranean.[42] At a time when public intellectuals, such as historian and Middle East expert Arnold Toynbee, were declaring that '[t]oday, Britain's relations with the Arab world are worse than those of any other Western country',[43] London was aiming to maintain a foothold overlooking its interests in the Middle East and South Asia: Cyprus, more than any other British territory, permitted the securing of imperial interests east of Suez. It was being severely challenged by the outbreak of EOKA terrorism.

While the outbreak of hostilities pointed to serious shortcomings in EOKA's military operations, including, crucially, the lack of widespread support amongst the Greek Cypriot community, it did not deter recruits from volunteering for the cause.[44] That they nurtured a 'concept of revolution [which] was apt to be naïve', however, did not dampen their 'enthusiasm and ideas'.[45] Grivas ran his terrorism campaign from remote spots on the island's mountains. He relied on the effectiveness of a courier system to facilitate his elaborate command and control structure.[46] Yet, in keeping with irregular groups more generically, Grivas was able to call upon the support of Greek Cypriot communities to harbour his EOKA fighters, while at the same time striking fear into the hearts of those who might engage in loose talk of EOKA operations. Consequently, information about the terrorist's plans was hard to come by and insight into the organisation was only really ascertained after Grivas' diaries were discovered by British soldiers in a rummage of some disused farm buildings.[47] Major Charles Dunbar, a staff officer with 19 Parachute Brigade Group, who arrived in Cyprus in the spring of 1956, observed how:

> Intelligence was almost non existent, EOKA, the Cypriot terrorist group, having terrorised or killed the local Special Branch to a man. Raids, bombings and murders were frequent, although nearly always conducted in a pretty cowardly fashion.[48]

Having previously served in Palestine in the mid-1940s, Dunbar had much experience of internal security operations, yet he immediately sensed a difference between the Jewish resistance and the Greek Cypriots: 'EOKA terrorists were neither so brave nor so cunning as the Jews but they were well led and organised and very difficult to find', he said. 'Although some were thugs, many believed in their cause.'[49]

Meanwhile, George Grivas was in little doubt that his small bands of fighters were the latest in a long line of Hellenic warriors. 'All war is cruel', he later wrote, 'and the only way to win against superior forces is by ruse and trickery; you can no more afford to make a difference between striking in front or from behind than you can between employing rifles and howitzers.'[50] By the beginning of 1956 Grivas had constructed an island-wide resistance movement that sought to challenge the British head on. He estimated that he had a total strength of 273 fighters and 100 guns, as well as 750 villagers armed with shotguns, at his disposal vis-à-vis his opponents, who had 20,000 members of the armed forces and 5,000 police ranging against him. They were favourable odds for Harding's forces, yet, to Grivas, more troops equalled more opportunity: a 'cumbersome body [which] provided a wealth of targets', and favoured a 'bolder strategy'.[51]

Harding was up for the challenge laid down by his arch-rival. He later recalled that 'as the summer wore on, the true, sinister character of the terrorist adventure had become clear'. They had begun to target innocent Greek Cypriots and British nationals in a campaign of terror and intimidation. Noting the EOKA slogan, which claimed that '[t]he police were out of the fight', Harding moved quickly to stiffen the resolve of the Security Forces. He noted 'the inadequately staffed Special Branch' and the unreliability amongst some sections of the police force.[52]

The moves to improve the quality of the police took place against the backdrop of Harding's continuing negotiations with Archbishop Makarios. Harding reminded the domestic audience at home that the strategic utility of Cyprus remained unaffected by the growing terrorism engulfing the island. Behind-the-scenes correspondence between Colonial Office officials revealed a sneering disregard for Harding's military understanding of what were essentially political issues. 'Although strategic and political are mixed up', wrote William Morris to Hilary Young, 'it does not necessarily follow that relations on the political plane are fully described by reference to strategic considerations'.[53] That they mattered to Harding, though, served to colour his appreciation of the broader international scene and the place of Cyprus in Britain's colonial empire. As he told a reporter from the London *Times*:

> But for us, the British, Cyprus is directly concerned with all out military effort in the Middle East. It is the nerve centre of our whole Middle East military organization.[54]

This was echoed unreservedly by Colonial secretary Alan Lennox-Boyd in the House of Commons, in response to questions from the opposition benches,

> that sometimes there are worse things than a breakdown from the point of view of safeguarding vital interests, but throughout we have been conscious of the vital importance of Cyprus to Middle East defence.[55]

The government saw the best way forward to lie in a negotiated settlement, but any agreement that emerged had to take place alongside a cessation of violence by EOKA. Inevitably negotiations broke down, with Makarios continuing to fall back on the sponsorship of Athens. The British Ambassador in the capital, Sir Charles Peake, reported that the Greek Foreign Minister thought Makarios ought to claim success, 'since this would make it easier for the Greek Government to support him and would forestall the inevitable and bitter criticism which would be forthcoming from the opposition both right and left'. Interestingly, Peake reported, '[t]he right were opposed to an agreement for "capitalist" reasons and the left because Soviet Russia did not want it'. Peake nonetheless informed Athens that, 'if agreement could be reached, I did not think either the Governor or my own Government would be greatly concerned to whom the credit should be attributed'.[56] Interestingly, one Foreign Office official in London remarked how 'I do not for a moment suppose they will use their influence with the Archbishop unless they think there might be some electoral advantage'.[57]

In any case, negotiations duly stalled because of deadlock in the positions taken by both Makarios and Harding. The truth of the matter was that Harding was not prepared to cede ground, either on the internal law-and-order question or on the strategic front. On the latter point he was backed up by Eden's government in London, who were eager to 'find a solution which would meet Western defence needs in the eastern Mediterranean'.[58] As far as Harding was concerned, four cardinal principles should 'govern our handling of the situation from now on'. First, he advocated refraining from discussing constitutional matters with anyone who refused to 'declare themselves publicly against violence and disorder'. Second, he felt that private behind-the-scenes discussions should be replaced by those held in public and 'on a wide basis representative of all sections of the community and shades of opinion'. Third, he recommended that the British government host a 'consultative conference'. Finally, Harding suggested postponing elections until the prevailing conditions were established which would 'permit really "free" elections'.[59] A Foreign Office official scribbled on his notes that, while '[t]hese are sound principles . . . [they would be represented publicly] 'as an unwarranted hardening of our position' with several being 'acceptable to the Turks'.[60] Yet, time and again, whenever Harding met with the Turkish Cypriots, he emphasised his view that he 'had no intention of bringing constitutional government into being until law and order had been restored'.[61]

Westminster debates on Cyprus at the time were notable for their restraint. The self-determination issues at stake, naturally, had exercised senior members of the Parliamentary Labour Party, which included Francis Noel-Baker, Kenneth Robinson, Jim Griffiths and Barbara Castle. A friend of Makarios, though a firm opponent of Grivas and EOKA, Noel-Baker campaigned regularly on the issue of *enosis*. He acted as a mediator between Harding and Makarios as the 'shooting war' entered its second year.[62] Noel-Baker remained convinced that a breakdown in the talks and continuing violence would have 'disastrous repercussions throughout the area, and in particular the disastrous damage to British prestige throughout the Middle East and throughout the Arab countries' and he lost few opportunities in reminding the Commons of this fact on a regular basis.[63]

Following the breakdown of the Makarios–Harding talks in the spring, Harding moved swiftly to clamp down on EOKA activities. On 9 March 1956 he ordered the deportation of Archbishop Makarios, which led to the outbreak of large-scale rioting throughout the island. Makarios was sent to the salubrious Seychelles, where he was to remain 'unless he renounces violence, and that, in any event, he should not be allowed back in Cyprus until the new constitution is working and the first Cypriot Government is well in the saddle'.[64] The Archbishop remained in exile for the next year; although he did not return to Cyprus until after the Emergency had ended in 1959.

Towards the 'final duel'

The Prussian philosopher of warfare Carl von Clausewitz reminds us that, in the clash of wills between belligerents, 'war is nothing but a duel on a larger scale'.[65] Although Harding's biographer, Michael Carver, gives us little insight into Harding's thinking about the design and execution of security force operations, it is clear from his rival's memoirs that as 1956 drew to a close the two leaders had 'plunged into a final, bitter duel'.[66] Harding's determination to face down EOKA terrorism almost cost him his life on one occasion, when a young EOKA sympathiser placed a bomb under his bed on 21 March 1956. He later remarked how on that night he had never slept better.[67] Such was the steely resolve of the man whose battle of wills with Grivas now approached its endgame. When he went on a visit home to London in May 1956, officials in the Colonial Office felt that there must 'be a risk, albeit slight, of an attack on Harding while he is in England in reprisal for the two executions which are to be carried out on Thursday, 10th May'.[68] The threat of EOKA agents assassinating the Governor was taken very seriously indeed and he was afforded 'special protection' by the Metropolitan Police. Four plain-clothes detectives accompanied Harding's entourage throughout the visit and even went to the extent of vetting all 80 members of staff at the Naval and Military Club, while posting a uniformed officer outside.[69]

Knowing the personal risks to his own life did not deter Harding from pressing ahead with the death sentences of Michael Karaolis and Andreas Demetriou, two 23-year-old EOKA suspects, who had been found guilty of killing a police officer and wounding a businessman. Harding found 'no grounds for exercising Royal Prerogative of Mercy' in commuting their sentences; both men were promptly hanged.[70] The hangings sparked off the worst street violence in Cyprus since the Second World War. It was not long before EOKA retaliated, claiming that it had kidnapped and hanged two British soldiers on the 10 May in reprisal for the colonial government's hanging of two Greek Cypriots. Lance Corporal Gordon Hill had gone missing on 19 December 1955 and Private Ronnie Shilton had been last seen on 17 April 1956. Such was the confusion over what had happened that the Secretary of State for Defence, Anthony Head, could not report conclusively about the fate of the two soldiers.[71]

By now Harding's firmness was winning him few friends in the Labour Party, yet he continued to enjoy the support of the Conservative government. Francis Noel-Baker found Harding somewhat difficult to get on with, as he told Lady Harding in correspondence, since 'it [is] easier to write these things than to say them':

> No doubt you still think I was all wrong during the negotiations with the Archbishop. I quite see that it is no good going back over that now. But personally I am firmly convinced that the fundamental trouble was that *no-one* in authority, either in Nicosia or London, ever really understood the point of view and aims of the Archbishop or the feelings of most of the Greek Cypriots. To do that we must *know* the people concerned.
>
> I am equally convinced that we shall never see a complete end of the violence until we make a new political move of some sort and that no representative moderate Cypriots will work with us until the Archbishop agrees.[72]

Harding nonetheless pressed ahead with his plan, though there were few positive signs that it was having a strategic effect on EOKA's capacity to wage its guerrilla war.

Shortly after the hangings of Karaolis and Demetriou, soldiers on a cordon and search operation closed in on Grivas' hiding place. The Colonel, sensing impending capture, had fled, leaving his coffee pot still brewing. Vital intelligence was uncovered which gave the impression that EOKA was on its knees. In a letter to one of his commanders, Grivas had written: 'Taking into consideration the great numerical strength of our opponent we shall not be able to impose a solution by force. Accordingly we are obliged to exploit politically the excellent results of our dynamic activity up to now and all our efforts should be directed to this end.'[73] As the document also revealed, EOKA was being sustained, both financially and logistically, by contacts Grivas had built up in Athens, who smuggled arms principally through the Cypriot postal system. Grivas remained deeply cautious about his sponsors, however, stating: 'God forbid that the Greek Government learn about it now. The English would know at once. Only those officials who can help us will be informed.' EOKA began internal housekeeping to alter its failing strategy:

> EOKA must seek to ensure that the Intelligence Organisation does not get on top whatever its composition. Earlier, EOKA would appear to have been deterred from attacking Turkish Cypriot police officers as such and at one time pleaded that it regarded Turkish Cypriots as brothers. That fiction has since been abandoned and fears of retaliation by the Turkish Cypriot community are less, or perhaps encouraged with a view to creating another distraction for the Security Forces.[74]

Inevitably, EOKA's shift towards targeting Turkish Cypriots would inflame intercommunal emotions, and Grivas risked opening up another front on his organisation.

In order to keep pressure on Grivas, the British launched 'Operation Pepperpot', a major sweep of the mountainous Troodos area aimed at capturing key EOKA leaders. Troops flooded Troodos, at one stage almost snaring Grivas in a trap. Counter-insurgency expert Julian Paget claims that the operation was a 'definite success' for the security forces, which 'forced Grivas thereafter to resort to terrorism, with guerrilla warfare in a secondary role'.[75] Most immediately, it constrained EOKA's options and led them to make their first offer of a truce in the middle of August, a magnanimous gesture promptly rejected by Harding, who thought he had his enemy on the back foot. Grivas was nonplussed and the sound of gunfire and explosions once again rang out across the island. In the particularly violent month of September, thirteen people were killed and another twenty-five injured; EOKA's murder of two servicemen and two policemen in Nicosia's Old Town led to the imposition of collective punishment measures in the form of a nine-day curfew.

Back in London, Noel-Baker continued to urge the government to return to the negotiating table with Makarios. In a lengthy debate on Cyprus in the House of Commons on 14 September 1956, he said that although he abhorred 'the bloodshed which E.O.K.A. started' including 'the death and wounding of British soldiers, many of them National Service men', it was right to restart dialogue. Yet, he was terribly worried about the strategic implications of a more protracted conflict, which threatened the stability of the NATO alliance and posed 'the long-term danger of popular hostility to a British base, the bitter feeling between nations which have been, and should be, the closest friends'. In emphasising how Britain had negotiated with those they regarded as terrorists before, Noel-Baker drew MPs' attention to the Government's handling of Anglo-Irish hostilities earlier in the Twentieth Century, which led to the Treaty of 1922:

> What the Government of 1921 did for Ireland, we ask our Government to do for Cyprus now. Do not wait for E.O.K.A. Propose the truce yourselves. Do not wait for new, more moderate leaders who do not appear. Bring Makarios and his colleagues here to London. [HON. MEMBERS: 'Oh.'] Restart negotiations on the basis of the documents which had been exchanged when the Colonial Secretary broke off negotiations six months ago.[76]

Despite political pressure now mounting from Labour benches, Harding stood firm and was backed by the Government.

In a bid to confound his critics, Harding adopted an even-handed approach on the constitutional front. He was keen to gain support amongst the Turkish Cypriot minority, who were concerned about the prospects of partition. Sir Peter Ramsbotham, who served on the UK's Permanent Mission to the UN, reported that rumours were now rife that partition was under active discussion.[77] While partition may have had its appeal for some British ministers, it had few supporters at the UN. In their determination to seek reconciliation between Greek and Turkish Cypriots within the broader framework of an independent Cyprus amiable to NATO aims, they had now implanted the idea in Ankara.[78] At the same time, Harding managed to get agreement in a meeting with Colonial Office Ministers that, in order for the aim of British policy to be achieved in Cyprus, 'E.O.K.A. as an organisation must be liquidated', and that 'an agreement must be reached between the United Kingdom, Greece and Turkey on the future international status of the island'. Without this, they concluded, 'no lasting settlement of the problem of Cyprus can be achieved'.[79] Lord Radcliffe, the Chairman of the Constitutional Commission for Cyprus, had been sent to Cyprus in May 1956 to work up constitutional proposals. The omens were not good. Nearly a decade earlier, Radcliffe had presided over the partition of India and Pakistan in 1947, and his report on Cyprus, when it was later published in December 1956, was roundly rejected.

By the autumn, events elsewhere in the region would profoundly shift world attention, albeit temporarily, away from Cyprus and onto another more pressing issue. President Nasser, who seized power in Egypt some years earlier, moved to nationalise the Suez Canal in the summer of 1956. His decision soon precipitated the raising and deployment of a tripartite intervention force, consisting of troops from Britain, France and Israel. The United States, which had been working against Britain's Cyprus policy at the UN, immediately opposed the expedition. Major Charles Dunbar, whose Parachute Brigade formed part of the Army's strategic reserve on Cyprus, was dispatched to the Canal Zone to reinforce the main intervention force. Dunbar candidly complained that 'one of the main problems during this time was the frequency with which HMG changed the political aim', making 'military planning very difficult indeed'.[80] As Dunbar and many other soldiers came to realise, Suez had exposed an even deeper, and recurring, structural problem in Britain's defence posture: the lack of money. It was 'in the bank of England that the Empire was effectively lost', wrote Niall Ferguson; as 'the Bank's gold and dollar reserves dwindled during the crisis, Harold Macmillan (then Chancellor of the Exchequer) had to choose between devaluating the pound . . . or asking for massive American aid'.[81] Only when Eden agreed to withdraw from the Canal Zone did Eisenhower agree to a bail-out deal for Britain. It was humiliating. That it had led to the re-direction of forces involved in anti-EOKA operations gave Grivas the necessary breathing space in order to exploit yet another opportunity; during November EOKA carried out 416 attacks, the highest monthly figure of the whole Emergency. Forty people were killed, RAF aircraft were blown up and sabotage became widespread across the island.[82] Britain's strategic distraction in Port Said had proven costly in both blood and treasure.

Amidst the upsurge in terrorism, Lennox-Boyd stood firm on the course the Conservatives had charted for themselves on the Cyprus issue:

> Meanwhile, our first task must remain to bring terrorism to an end. Security forces have been maintaining relentless pressure on Grivas and his gangs. To those forces and to Sir John Harding and his administration I should like to express the sincere thanks of the Government. In recent weeks operations have been carried out in the Kyrenia hills and in the mountain ranges. They have had good results and have brought nearer the day of the destruction of E.O.K.A. and the day when the people of Cyprus can turn away from the nightmare of E.O.K.A. and set their eyes towards a brighter future of orderly political development. Then Cyprus will take her place in the natural progress of all British Colonial Territories towards self-government.[83]

The lost momentum occasioned by the Suez operation had been regained by the New Year. In the opening months of 1957, sixteen EOKA fighters, including several prominent leaders, were killed and a further sixty captured.[84] As a sign perhaps of the desperation now gripping the terrorist group, targets were being increasingly chosen at random; many of its victims included civilians, which EOKA tried to distance themselves from, or claimed were 'traitors'. With the return of British forces from Egypt, 'towards the end of the winter', argues Crawshaw, 'EOKA's defeat seemed imminent'.[85] This was disputed by Grivas, who maintained that EOKA were now taking 'the full force of Britain's power in a steady series of blows and we were shaken, but very far from crushed'.[86] Whatever the perception of Grivas' situation, the reality was somewhat different, with British policy caught between the proverbial 'rock and a hard place'. While Harding and Lennox-Boyd both agreed that the security situation had improved and that a fresh political process should be tried, most notably by releasing Makarios from exile, other high-ranking members of the government, like Lord Salisbury, roundly disagreed. They argued that 'a close and confident relationship with Turkey' should be the basis of British policy at the time.[87] Nonetheless, the decision to release Makarios was, however reluctantly, taken, despite his refusal to condemn EOKA violence. The Greek Cypriots were afforded tremendous propaganda value by the

Archbishop's release; it was duly claimed in EOKA's 'smear campaign' and via Athens Radio that pressure from the guerrillas had led to the concession.[88]

Although the British had failed to seize the political initiative with Makarios' release, this single conciliatory action had led to a fillip in Anglo-Greek relations. Pressure from Athens eased and, eventually, Grivas decided to call another ceasefire. Harding, perhaps unsurprisingly, remained less flexible. Nevertheless, by the summer, Britain's strategic outlook had again altered, largely due to the Suez debacle, though it had much more to do with Duncan Sandys' Defence White Paper, which called into question Britain's sprawling military footprint east of Suez. The reduction of military manpower (and supporting civilian staff) by the abolition of conscription had been mooted for some time, but it was the government's decision to cut overseas bases that caused heated debates in the domestic political arena in the wake of Suez. Sandys told MPs that the government would not be 'maintaining garrisons and other forces overseas on the scale that we have been doing hitherto'. Though he did acknowledge Britain's need to maintain her standing commitments with strategically vital anti-Communist alliances, such as NATO and the Baghdad Pact, he remained steadfast on his fundamental theme of exploiting new technologies ahead of more traditional methods of power projection:

> We must, of course, keep an adequate number of troops in those places where there is a threat of local attack or where there is some special internal security problem. In planning the size and distribution of our garrisons, however, we must take full advantage of the greatly increased size and range of modern transport aircraft, which now make it possible to dispatch reinforcements rapidly to any place where trouble occurs.[89]

Meanwhile, the hitherto frosty diplomatic relations between Greece and Turkey had also begun to thaw, thanks in part to Britain's diplomatic overtures at the UN. Although Britain failed in its bid to organise a tripartite conference, all parties now accepted the need to get agreement. By the autumn, the 'question of British sovereignty was no longer an insurable obstacle'.[90]

'Passing the buck'

As the year drew to a close so too did Harding's tenure as Governor. Before he left Nicosia, he drafted a chunky report on British policy in Cyprus during his term in office. It was submitted on 3 November 1957 and sought to 'provide a consecutive account of the efforts, as seen from here, that have been made over the past two years to bring about a settlement of the Island's political problems'.[91] Harding hoped his report would be 'useful to others who in future may be concerned in this most intractable of political problems'.[92] Perhaps unsurprisingly, the Colonial Office kept a tight leash on the distribution of the report, arguing that there 'was no question of the Governor's memorandum being published', although it did ensure copies were sent to both the Foreign Office and Ministry of Defence. There was undoubtedly a sneering feeling within the Colonial Office regarding 'the lack of faith which he had come to have (perhaps because he had not had any of the tradition of development of self-governments which the normal colonial Governor enjoys) in the creation of a "vested interest in a self-governing Cyprus"'.[93] Colonial Office mandarins' critiques of Harding's report may have been limited to churlish annotated remarks that this was the 'first compliment to the Secretary of State and the Colonial Office', or the odd jibe about a 'soldierly comment or two', but there can be no question that Harding had successfully crossed Whitehall's tribal lines. In many respects, his appointment, moreover, served to expose how far the 'buck had been passed'.[94] It was little wonder that Colonial officials balked as it was finally passed back.

Although he had long since resigned as Prime Minister, Eden wrote to Harding to thank him personally for 'the wonderful service you have given the Nation of Cyprus', stating that 'I cannot forget the generosity with which you undertook this thankless task in a critical hour: yours was indeed a selfless action'.[95] In appointing Harding, Eden's government had acted for purely strategic reasons. 'In geography and tactical considerations', Eden later wrote in his memoirs, 'the Turks have the stronger claim to Cyprus; in race and language, the Greeks; in strategy, the British, so long as their industrial life depends on oil supply from the Persian Gulf'.[96] There was no great mystery in any of this, although by the end of the decade even Macmillan was prepared to make concessions by rowing back from the insistence on retaining the whole of Cyprus as a base. For Eden, the value in any future compromise depended 'upon the spirit in which it is worked and upon acceptable arrangements for our military bases'.[97] Macmillan was also duly impressed, telling Harding:

> During the whole of your tenure of office Cyprus has been at the centre of bitter political and international controversies. This has made your task doubly hard but you have steered your course with such courage, fairness and skill that I feel no doubt that your Governorship will long be remembered with pride even by those who have not agreed with your policies.[98]

Even Grivas was not without admiration for the Field-Marshal, later passing on the ultimate compliment by admitting how he held 'Harding the soldier in regard'. The EOKA leader added one insightful caveat: 'in the military field he was lord and master', he opined, 'politically he was in the hands of the old colonial officials'.[99] While perhaps a little unfair, Grivas' critique exposed the nub of the problem: that there was a lack of synchronisation in policy between Nicosia and London, which, invited a military stop-gap and ultimately left EOKA decisively undefeated.

Although Harding had formally resigned on 22 October and departed on 4 November, senior officials in Government House were concerned that his successor, Sir Hugh Foot, who had 'the more challenging and less comfortable task'[100] of succeeding Harding, might not come to command the same respect as his distinguished predecessor. In order to prepare the ground, George Sinclair, Harding's able deputy, remained in a caretaker role until Foot's arrival. Sinclair continued to seek regular direction from Harding, keeping him updated, especially on the security situation on the island. It could be argued that during this 'interregnum', in between Harding's resignation and Foot's arrival, officials in Nicosia became over-dependent on the Field-Marshal's address book. Sinclair himself revealed:

> I know that the acceptance of our policy and actions here and of our advice to H.M.G. will depend largely on the confidence that the incoming Governor can build up among Ministers at home in his leadership and judgement. Nobody could do as much as you can to see that Sir High Foot starts off at the right level and with the greatest possible degree of support in London.[101]

Although Sinclair later earned 'a golden reputation both in his handling of Harding and subsequently his relationship with Hugh Foot',[102] he was somewhat impulsive and became ever more anxious about the precarious security situation. In correspondence with Harding, he admitted how, 'I do not believe that we can allow EOKA's campaign of violence to develop much further without us challenging it with effective counter-measures'.[103] The colonial government was deeply worried that EOKA's increasingly bitter attacks would lead to 'a loss in confidence of the Turkish community and leave them little alternative but to take the law into their own hands'.[104] Lennox-Boyd followed up with a reassuring letter to Sinclair:

> I am afraid that you have had a most trying period as Acting Governor, with a sharp intensification of the campaign of 'creeping terrorism' coming at a time when the needs of the wider political situation imposed such frustrating limitations on your freedom of action.[105]

Nevertheless, Harding continued to ride to Sinclair's rescue by making continuing representations to the government at the time. He even took the unusual step of lobbying hardnosed US President Dwight D. Eisenhower via his old friend and comrade Field-Marshal Sir Bernard Law Montgomery:

> Ike was very glad to get my letter about Cyprus – written as from me but really yours! He agrees. He is going to tell the Greeks and Turks – this week in Paris – that they must make the sort of concessions that are needed. He is ready to do whatever is needed to end the quarrel.[106]

Consequently, the military situation now facing the Acting Governor was grave. Grivas was using the opportunity to carry out acts of sabotage, scoring some successes with the destruction of five fighter jets and by damaging the merchant ship the *African Prince*, which was anchored off Karavostasi.

Foot arrived into the affray and promptly set off on a tour of the island, despite considerable risk to his own personal safety. It was a well-worn tactic that had helped him enormously on his previous assignment during the Arab rebellion in Palestine and it worked, immediately endearing him to the Greek Cypriots. Grivas was less convinced, replying wryly how the new Governor 'would have our support if he sincerely intended to work for peace; otherwise our fight for freedom – our "violence" – would go on'.[107]

By the New Year, Foot had embarked on a renewed political course, returning to London armed with a new plan where he made representations to the Cabinet. Lennox-Boyd informed his colleagues that 'a new initiative by the Government was necessary if the situation in Cyprus was not seriously to deteriorate once again'. He suggested self-determination seven years after the ending of the Emergency, with in-built assurances to the Turkish Cypriot community.[108] Although the Cabinet were anxious to maintain bi-partisan support for any settlement at Westminster, they thought it desirable to avoid 'any suggestion that we might be prepared to abandon our sovereignty over the Island would be politically damaging and might provoke the Turkish Government to renew intercommunal strife in the hope of forcing the issue of partition without further delay'.[109]

Meanwhile, the island's General Officer Commanding (GOC), Douglas Kendrew, wrote to Harding to tell him of the difficulties now facing the security forces:

> We are having an awkward time – trying to keep up the SB [Special Branch] side and having to do nothing to upset HE's [His Excellency's] policy . . . The boys are working hard, but I believe find life very hard. We are

> having 100% support, but to play this game both ways is not easy. We are bending over backwards not to 'upset the Greeks' yet there are the continuing threats being made on the mobile Reserve and our chaps. Anyway H.E., I believe, does realise that if this thing goes bad again we will be there and trying to help him in any way he wants us to.[110]

In a revealing letter to Lennox-Boyd, Sinclair displayed an impressive grasp of what had been achieved on the island:

> All of us have realised, throughout the last two years, that this problem could not be solved merely by internal security operations; these were designed always to give greater scope for a political initiative. The understanding and collaboration which had been established over the last two years between the civil administration, the police and the armed services greatly reduced the risk of loss of confidence by the Security Forces.[111]

Reflecting back over Harding's two years in charge, Sinclair said that it was his own belief that 'a high degree of co-ordination and unified direction was achieved in the mounting and maintenance of our campaigns against Eoka' and that, by their teamwork, were 'able to make the biggest improvement is in the development of the Intelligence organisation'.[112]

Conclusion

Historian Nancy Crawshaw argues that, by the time he had resigned as Governor, the 'main object of his mission, the restoration of law and order, had been achieved'. Yet, she admits that the fact that 'the security forces had been halted at the height of their successful drive against EOKA was due to political factors beyond his control'.[113] Robert Holland is a little more circumspect, arguing that 'Harding's achievement was much more ambiguous'. His 'honest but doomed integrity'[114] placed him at a disadvantage, especially as he clumsily put in place a template designed more for Asian and African climes than more urbane Mediterranean sensibilities. Since the end of the Emergency in 1959, successive British governments have arrived at the conclusion that retention of the Sovereign Base Areas (SBAs) is vital to Britain's projection of power in the world. A year after stepping down as Governor of Cyprus, Lord Harding (as he had now become) was at pains to stress that the real military value of the island, since the British agreed to administer it on behalf of the Ottoman Empire in 1878, had to be assessed 'in the context of this general world-wide struggle between what is generally called the free world and international Communism'.[115] The Deputy Governor suggested that Britain ought to continue to shoulder its responsibilities as a Sovereign Power and that they continue to strive by all possible means to achieve a settlement between Greek and Turkish Cypriots, which would command the confidence of both Athens and Ankara. This had been the rationale underpinning Harding's views during his time as Governor. Above all, they were aimed at preserving the island's strategic importance, allowing Britain to fulfil its commitments to NATO and the Central Treaty Organization (CENTO), also known as the Baghdad Pact. Harding thought that this type of policy would 'have all the better chance of success if it would be put on to a bipartisan basis in this country and if it could be given the full and active support of the American administration'.[116] On the last point, he was thwarted as the US put national interests above its close friendship with Britain. It was not the first time, nor would it be the last. In the end Harding claimed victory in Cyprus, while others told a very different story: preferring to see it as a 'draw' at best and as a 'defeat' at worst.

However, if anything, EOKA's armed campaign against the British was only a pyrrhic victory. Grivas' group had lost several high-ranking commanders, yet it could not beat the British, at least not in a military sense. In this respect, parallels can be drawn with the Kenya campaign. However, in terms of the failure to adapt the Templer Plan to Cyprus, there were also echoes with British policy in the last days of the Palestine Mandate. Thus, while military operations – such as the evacuation of troops and equipment – were planned with great precision and care, the political structures for maintaining an uneasy peace between Arab and Jew had been woefully abandoned. A decade later, in Cyprus, Britain's damage limitation exercise was limited to what this would mean for NATO's Turkish flank. It had, nonetheless, set a dangerous precedent for those who wished to oppose Britain's colonial outposts by force of arms, as Aden would soon prove.

Notes

1 Imperial War Museum Department of Documents (IWM), *General Sir George Erskine Papers*, 75/134/4, Templer, General Sir Gerald *Secret: Report on Colonial Security, 23 April 1955*, p. 52.
2 Comments by Field Marshal Sir John Harding in *The Times*, 24 January 1956.
3 Grivas, George, *The Memoirs of General Grivas*, edited by Charles Foley (London: Longmans, 1964), p. 43.
4 Carver, Michael, *War since 1945* (London: Weidenfeld and Nicolson, 1980), p. 44.

5 Dockrill, Michael, *British Defence Since 1945* (Oxford: Blackwell, 1989), p. 57.
6 Ibid., p. 51. Dockrill points out that out of its $11\frac{1}{3}$ Divisions, $10\frac{1}{2}$ were based overseas: 4 in Germany, $2\frac{1}{2}$ in the Middle East, 2 in Malaya and the remainder in Trieste, Hong Kong and Kenya.
7 Sandys served as Secretary of State for Defence between January 1957 and October 1959.
8 IWM, Templer, *Report on Colonial Security*, p. 9.
9 Britain announced in June 1954 that Headquarters Middle East Command would move from the Canal Zone to Cyprus.
10 Carruthers, Susan L., *Winning Hearts and Minds: British Governments, the Media and Colonial Counter-Insurgency, 1944–1960* (London: Leicester University Press, 1995), p. 196.
11 Carver, *War since 1945*, p. 46.
12 Grivas, *Memoirs*, p. 204.
13 Carruthers, *Winning Hearts and Minds*, p. 195. Hopkinson was later sacked.
14 Holland, Robert, *Britain and the Revolt in Cyprus, 1954–1959* (Oxford: Clarendon Press, 1998), p. 82.
15 Paget, Julian, *Counter-Insurgency Campaigning* (London: Faber, 1967), p. 120.
16 The National Archives, Kew, London (TNA), FO 371/117629, Nutting to Eden, 1 April 1955.
17 Corum, James S., *Training Indigenous Forces in Counterinsurgency: A Tale of Two Insurgencies* (Carlisle, PA: Strategic Studies Institute, March 2006), p. 31.
18 IWM, *Erskine Papers*, 75/134/4, Templer, *Report on Colonial Security*, p. 53.
19 Sinclair, Georgina, *At the End of the Line: Colonial Policing and the Imperial Endgame, 1945–80* (Manchester: Manchester University Press, 2006), p. 118.
20 Holland, *Britain and the Revolt in Cyprus*, p. 59.
21 Crawshaw, Nancy, *The Cyprus Revolt: An Account of the Struggle for Union with Greece* (London: George Allen and Unwin, 1978), p. 121.
22 Sinclair, *At the End of the Line*, p. 118.
23 Holland, *Britain and the Revolt in Cyprus*, p. 70.
24 Ibid., p. 71.
25 Ibid., p. 82.
26 IWM, *Erskine Papers*, 75/134/10, Sir Alexander Grantham to General Erskine, 17 June 1955. Erskine had been Commander of British Forces in Hong Kong in 1947–48 when Harding was Commander-in-Chief Far East Land Forces. Grantham was appointed Governor of Hong Kong in 1947, a post he held for over a decade.
27 Carver, Michael, *Harding of Petherton: Field Marshal* (London: Weidenfeld and Nicolson, 1978), p. 196.

28 IWM, *Private Papers of Harding of Petherton*, Anthony Eden to Sir John Harding, 24 September 1955. Field-Marshal Papagos was Greek Prime Minister at the time.
29 Eden, Anthony, *The Memoirs of Sir Anthony Eden: Full Circle* (London: Cassell and Company, 1960), p. 402.
30 Carver, *Harding of Petherton*, p. 196.
31 TNA, CO 926/2084, Field-Marshal Sir John Harding, Cyprus Policy, October 1955 to October 1957: Appendix 1: Broadcast by Governor of Cyprus, 9 October 1955.
32 Eden, *Memoirs*, p. 402
33 TNA, CO 926/2084, Broadcast by Governor of Cyprus, 9 October 1955.
34 Carruthers, *Winning Hearts and Minds*, p. 196.
35 TNA, CO 926/386, Telegram from Field Marshal Sir John Harding to the Secretary of State for the Colonies, dated 20 October 1955.
36 Carruthers, *Winning Hearts and Minds*, Chapter 4.
37 Carver, *Harding of Petherton*, p. 204.
38 IWM, *Erskine Papers*, 75/134/10, Sir John Harding to Sir George Erskine, 6 October 1955.
39 Sinclair, *At the End of the Line*, p. 120.
40 Corum, *Training Indigenous Forces in Counterinsurgency*, p. 31.
41 Grivas, *Memoirs*, p. 126.
42 TNA, CAB 158/3, JIC, Middle East Defence Policy – Potentialities and Scale and Direction of Attack – 1950: Report by the Joint Intelligence Committee, 7 June 1948.
43 Toynbee, Arnold, 'Britain and the Arabs: The Need for a New Start', *International Affairs*, Vol. 40, No. 4 (October 1964), p. 638.
44 Crawshaw, *The Cyprus Revolt*, p. 115.
45 Ibid., p. 119.
46 Grivas, *Memoirs*, pp. 28, 58.
47 Ibid., p. 126.
48 King's College London, Liddell Hart Centre for Military Archives (LHCMA), Dunbar Papers, 3/3, 'Cyprus', transcript of a draft recording for the Airborne Museum (n.d. 1973?).
49 Ibid.
50 Grivas, *Memoirs*, p. 43.
51 Ibid., p. 67.
52 TNA, CO 926/2084, Harding, Cyprus Policy, October 1955 to October 1957, dated 3 November 1957.
53 TNA, FO 371/123867, Top Secret Correspondence from W.A. Morris to W.H. Young, 18 January 1956.
54 *The Times*, 24 January 1956.
55 House of Commons Debates (Hansard), 26 January 1956, Vol. 548, Col. 379.
56 TNA, FO 371/123867, Secret Cypher from Athens to Foreign Office, dated 1 February 1956.

57 TNA, FO 371/123867, Annotated notes on Secret Cypher from Athens to Foreign Office, dated 2 February 1956.
58 Eden, *Memoirs*, p. 404.
59 TNA, FO 371/123867, Telegram from Harding to Colonial Secretary, dated 31 January 1956.
60 Ibid. Notes dated 4 February 1956.
61 TNA, FO 371/123867, Secret telegram from Governor to Secretary of State for the Colonies, dated 31 January 1956.
62 Dalyell, Tam, 'Francis Noel-Baker: Labour Politician who Clashed with the Party over Cyprus and Helped Create Amnesty International', *The Independent*, 30 September 2009. See also Noel-Baker's obituary in the *Daily Telegraph*, 28 September 2009.
63 House of Commons Debates (Hansard), 26 January 1956, Vol. 548, Col. 378.
64 TNA, FO 371/123932, 'The Future of Cyprus', aide-memoire of discussions held at Government House, Nicosia, during the visit of the Minister of State for Colonial Affairs, from 10 to 12 October 1956.
65 Clausewitz, Carl Von, *On War*, edited and translated by Michael Howard and Peter Paret (Princeton, NJ: Princeton University Press, 1989), p. 75.
66 Grivas, *Memoirs*, p. 106.
67 Carver, *Harding of Petherton*, p. 218.
68 TNA, CO 926/386, Correspondence between T.I.K. Lloyd and Sir Frank Newsam, dated 8 May 1956. Newsam was Permanent Under Secretary of the Home Office between 1948 and 1957.
69 TNA, CO 926/386, 'Security arrangements for Sir John Harding's Visit, June 1956', dated 30 May 1956. Personal security provisions continued to be made each time Harding returned to London.
70 'Cyprus: Deepening Tragedy', *Time Magazine*, 21 May 1956.
71 House of Commons Debates (Hansard), 5 June 1956, Vol. 553, Col. 857.
72 IWM, *Harding Papers*, Francis Noel-Baker to Lady Harding, 29 May 1956.
73 TNA, FO 371/123897, Telegram from Nicosia to London detailing contents of capture documents, dated 13 June 1956. The captured documents were discovered on 10 June. They included Grivas' diary, sleeping bag, shaving kit, spectacles and brown beret. Diary entries ran from 16 May until 9 June.
74 TNA, FO 371/123897, Telegram from Cyprus to London detailing intelligence on EOKA, dated 10 June 1956.
75 Paget, *Counter-insurgency Campaigning*, p. 133.
76 House of Commons Debates (Hansard), 14 September 1956, Vol. 558, Col. 364.
77 TNA, FO 371/123932, Peter Ramsbotham to Hilary Young, dated 20 October 1956.
78 TNA, FO 371/123932, Ankara to Foreign, dated 25 October 1956.

79 TNA, FO 371/123932, 'The Future of Cyprus', aide-memoire of discussions held at Government House, Nicosia, during the visit of the Minister of State for Colonial Affairs, from 10 to 12 October 1956.
80 LHCMA, *Dunbar Papers*, 3/4, 'Suez', restricted transcript of a draft recording for the Airborne Museum (7 April 1973) and 'Suez Operation – D Inf's Recollections', dated 7 May 1973.
81 Ferguson, Niall, *Empire: How Britain Made the Modern World* (London: Penguin, 2003), pp. 355–356.
82 Paget, *Counter-Insurgency Campaigning*, p. 135.
83 House of Commons Debates (Hansard), 13 November 1956, Vol. 560, Col. 755.
84 Paget, *Counter-Insurgency Campaigning*, p. 135.
85 Crawshaw, *The Cyprus Revolt*, p. 234.
86 Grivas, *Memoirs*, p. 107.
87 Ibid., p. 236.
88 For more on the 'smear technique' see Carruthers, *Winning Hearts and Minds*, p. 201.
89 House of Commons Debates (Hansard), 16 April 1957, Vol. 568, Col. 1769.
90 Crawshaw, *The Cyprus Revolt*, p. 262.
91 TNA, CO 926/859, Memorandum by Sir John Harding entitled 'Cyprus Policy, October, 1955 to October, 1957', dated 4 December 1957.
92 TNA, CO 926/859, Top Secret letter from Harding to Alan Lennox-Boyd, dated 3 November 1957.
93 TNA, CO 926/859, Top Secret note on Harding's Memorandum entitled 'Cyprus Policy'.
94 TNA, CO 926/860, Statements and Speeches by Governor of Cyprus, W. McLean, Minute, 27 November 1957, cited in Holland, *Britain and the Revolt in Cyprus*, p. 213.
95 IWM, *Harding Papers*, Eden to Harding, 8 November 1957.
96 Eden, *Memoirs*, p. 415.
97 Eden, *The Memoirs of Sir Anthony Eden*, p. 415.
98 IWM, *Harding Papers*, Macmillan to Harding, 17 October 1957.
99 Grivas, *Memoirs*, p. 126.
100 'Lord Caradon – Obituary', *The Times*, 6 September 1990.
101 IWM, Harding Papers, George Sinclair, Deputy Governor, Government House, to Harding 12 November 1957. Sinclair signed off with the postscript 'This leaves only one record copy and that [sic] in my safe. It is intended only for your eyes and then the furnace.'
102 Dalyell, Tam, 'Sir George Sinclair: Deputy Governor of Cyprus and Tory MP', *The Independent*, 30 September 2005.
103 IWM, *Harding Papers*, Sinclair to Harding 12 November 1957.
104 Ibid., 23 November 1957.
105 IWM, *Harding Papers*, Rt Hon. Alan Lennox-Boyd, MP to Sinclair, 6 December 1957.

106 IWM, *Harding Papers*, Montgomery to Harding, 16 December 1957.
107 Grivas, *Memoirs*, p. 129.
108 TNA, CAB/128/32, Cabinet Meeting, 6 January 1958.
109 Ibid.
110 IWM, *Harding Papers*, GOC Cyprus Douglas Kendrew to Harding, 28 December 1957.
111 IWM, *Harding Papers*, Sinclair to Rt Hon. Alan Lennox-Boyd, MP, 17 December 1957.
112 IWM, *Harding Papers*, Sinclair to Harding, 25 April 1959.
113 Crawshaw, *The Cyprus Revolt*, p. 234.
114 Holland, *Britain and the Revolt in Cyprus*, p. 212.
115 Harding, Field-Marshal Lord, 'The Cyprus Problem in Relation to the Middle East', *International Affairs*, Vol. 34, No. 3 (July 1958), p. 292.
116 Ibid., p. 296.

5

Holding the thin red line: retreat from Aden

> You British! We will expel you as you were expelled by the nations of Asia and Africa . . . We, the women, shall be at the front until the last drop of our blood. We are not afraid of death. We are not afraid of . . . your aeroplanes, your armoured cars, your tanks . . . We will fight you by word and deed . . . We shall take our freedom by force and faith. Oh, Arab nation . . . We all know Britain. We have known it in Port Said, Cyprus, Malta, Kenya. So why are we afraid. Death comes once. Why should we not die, if our death will erase shame, defend the country and will raise the flag of Arab nationalism.[1]

> It was not as if direct colonial rule was proving effective. The colonial government could neither hear nor see. British soldiers who knew nothing about Aden and who had no means of understanding of communicating with one Arab in a thousand . . . In these foreseeable circumstances an alien soldiery were bound to excite the fiercest Arab xenophobia against themselves and against the regime which they represented. It was not long before the colonial regime in Aden was friendless. Without friends, no regime can survive for long.[2]

> Lessons were learned in Aden especially towards the end, but none of them were new; merely a variation of emphasis, a new slant, or a different priority.[3]

Introduction

For Colonel George Wigg, Labour MP for Dudley, 'Suez, like Cuba, was a supreme example of half-witted, half-baked failure. The moral of all this will, I am afraid, be drawn in Baghdad, Peking, Moscow, not to mention numerous other spots on the world map, and it augurs ill for the West and for those who use the United Nations as an instrument of National policy.'[4] The Labour party remained split on the issue of Suez, with some, like Wigg, arguing that 'a new balance of power had made the Middle East as dangerous and explosive a cauldron for our children as Germany was for us and for the fathers of our generation'.[5] Many within the Labour Party opposed the Suez intervention, remaining convinced afterwards, 'essentially on pragmatic grounds of the damage caused to Britain's standing as a world power'.[6] For these individuals a repeat of the 'Suez fiasco', as Labour's 1964 election manifesto referred to it, was to be avoided at all costs. On the one hand, writes Mark Phythian, it reinforced in many Labour MPs 'a strict restrictionist approach to the use of military force'.[7] However, on the other hand, Wigg, who had served out most of his army career in the region, led calls by other opposition MPs for the steadying of government nerves. The Conservatives, having presided over the decolonization of empire since 1951, entered the early 1960s with no clear strategic vision for furthering British power. For Wigg[8] and those British politicians who shared his realist view of international relations (albeit combined with firm anti-Communism), retrenchment was a welcome remedy; alas, Britain's opponents in the Soviet sphere of influence would take advantage of its dithering on the world stage.[9] One of the main battlegrounds of the Cold War in the Middle East, especially in the 1960s, was the colonial port of Aden. It would come at once to represent both the impoverishment of British strategy-making and the tensions now inherent in civil–military relations.

Aden had been a key strategic staging post for the British military in the Middle East for generations. Situated at the heel of the South Arabian peninsula, with easy access to the East African port town of Mombasa in Kenya, it provided a hub for military operations from the Eastern Mediterranean, to the Red Sea and beyond, to the Indian Ocean and South Asia. The port had been first colonized in 1839; Britain's involvement in Aden is downplayed in the literature on post-war history, in large part because of the failure of the counter-insurgency campaign, which, according to historian Spencer Mawby, became 'increasingly brutal and indiscriminate' in its nature.[10] The 'pervasive neglect of the Aden episode in imperial history', Mawby has written, 'is such that it is possible to write a popular history of Britain's role in the Middle East during the twentieth century, while self-consciously excluding any mention of it'.[11] Later, the British withdrawal in 1967, which was 'neither properly planned nor particularly dignified',[12] came in the wake of a bitterly protracted insurgency, waged with the objective of overthrowing British colonial rule. Moreover, it came as a direct result of the Wilson government's decision in the 1966 Defence Review – what his Defence Secretary Denis Healey referred to in the Commons 'essentially an exercise in political and military realism'[13] – to terminate support for its allies in the Federation of South Arabia.[14]

Britain's withdrawal from Aden was premised on the Federal Administration, along with the South Arabian Army (SAA), taking over internal security from British forces; their competency was seen as key to an orderly transition. In a secret memorandum to the Foreign Office in the days leading up to withdrawal, the High Commissioner Sir Humphrey Trevelyan hoped that the SAA, which he recognized as being 'more closely aligned with the NLF than with FLOSY', could occupy the rebellious Crater district and seize control 'with or without the collusion of some of the Sultans and/or more of the Opposition parties'.[15] The notion of colluding with local moderates was a recurrent theme in Britain's small wars, as too was the often contradictory (and utterly clandestine) moves towards negotiating with extremist insurgents and terrorists. The colony promptly descended into chaos in the wake of Britain's ignominious departure. 'The oldest traditional ruler of all, anarchy', remarked its penultimate British representative, Kennedy Trevaskis, 'was back on his throne'.[16]

Like British policy in Palestine, the announcement in 1966 of withdrawal placed the British Army and their allies in Aden's Security Forces at a disadvantage. Because of the bloody and protracted nature of the resistance launched by the National Liberation Front (NLF) and Front for the Liberation of Occupied South Yemen (FLOSY), it was highly likely the armed groups would simply bide their time until the British departed. The NLF's armed struggle against 'British imperialism' and the 'Sultanic forces of reaction' was unflinching and it spiked in the aftermath of the announcement. Perhaps unsurprisingly the political constraints on the use of force in Aden triggered disquiet in the ranks of the British regiments that had been tasked with maintaining an orderly withdrawal. This was to culminate in 1967, when Lieutenant-Colonel Colin 'Mad Mitch' Mitchell, the commanding officer of the 1st Battalion, the Argyll and Sutherland Highlanders, led his troops into the dissident stronghold of Crater to regain control for the colonial authorities. Mitchell's actions – played out largely under an intense media spotlight – were to invite much incredulity amongst his immediate military superiors, colonial officials and politicians in Westminster. In hindsight, the whole episode was symptomatic of the breakdown in joint civil–military relations at a strategic and operational level,[17] which would precipitate Britain's inglorious retreat from South Arabia. Moreover, the bitter entanglement of policy and force precipitated disaster in Aden and had significant consequences for Britain's involvement closer to home in Northern Ireland at the end of the decade.

The end of 'gunboat romanticism'

The Conservative government's determination to hold onto Aden, regarded as 'Britain's Guantanamo' by one *Spectator* journalist,[18] had 'unintended consequences' according to Mawby, who detailed the circumstances under which British policy-makers were 'motivated not by a simple calculation of material interests but by a desire to maintain their prestige and influence in the Middle East'.[19] Maintaining a major base in Aden provided a crucial means by which to service that strategic goal, but like other aspects of Britain's security outlook in the 1960s it suffered from acute under-investment and an increasingly resilient opponent in the form of militant Arab nationalism. The armed groups ranging against Britain's presence in South Arabia included the NLF, a Marxist-inspired terrorist group that specialized in targeted assassination and lobbing grenades in the general direction of anything symbolic of colonial authority, and FLOSY, a broad-fronted organization with links to the Aden Trades Union Council (ATUC) and a predilection for mass demonstrations. Both groups led interdependent campaigns of subversion, intimidation and terrorism against the colonial administration and their allies in the Federation.

Against the backdrop of hostility towards British colonial rule was the structural problem of gathering intelligence on the terrorists. Two visits by Sir Percy Sillitoe, the head of Britain's Security Service, MI5, in September 1954 and November 1955 had pointed to the need to develop better indigenous intelligence machinery. The War Office (subsequently the Ministry of Defence), in particular, had levelled charges at the Colonial Office's door,[20] and there was a groundswell of resentment from within the ranks of the colonial civil service, who tended to believe in the supremacy of 'political intelligence'. This particular intelligence product gave ministers a wider account of the political and strategic context within which potential dissidents operated. As one report concluded:

> There is obviously a serious gap in our intelligence coverage of the Middle East as a whole, despite the course of recent events and their importance to the United Kingdom's position. There has been no study at all, for example, of the extent to which modern Arab 'nationalism' is cutting across traditional religious and dynastic divisions in the Arab world. Yet the J.I.C., while joining in the recent chorus of criticism about intelligence in Aden, has taken no initiative at all on the wider front.[21]

Christopher Andrew's careful trawling of MI5's vast archives confirmed the incoherence of Aden's intelligence machinery. The failure of the Security Service to learn the lessons of the Malaya

Emergency, Andrew observed, meant that their role in Aden was downgraded to the point where it was 'not asked to play a role which approached the significance of its participation in previous counter-insurgencies in Malaya, Kenya and Cyprus'.[22]

Despite Aden's vulnerability, occasioned by the rising tide of Arab nationalism, Britain continued in its mission to transform the colony from a transitional colonial outpost into a major base for military operations in the Middle East and East Africa. The establishment of Middle East Command in 1960 signalled Britain's intent to carry out these proposals and a brigade-strength strategic reserve was soon garrisoned there. An indication of Aden's importance to Britain's military and defence outlook can be discerned from a letter sent by Foreign Secretary, Alec Douglas-Home, to the incumbent Governor, Sir Charles Johnston, in which the future Prime Minister emphasized how:

> Aden and this Headquarters will play an increasingly important part in all defence matters concerning not only the Arabian Peninsula and the Persian Gulf but also the Horn of Africa.[23]

In another respect, Johnston's appointment exposed the friction building over Aden between the Colonial Office, War Office and Foreign Office. Douglas-Home supported the move to appoint

> one of our own people in Aden, more especially at a time when events in Africa moving fast and when it may become increasingly difficult for us to maintain our position in the Persian Gulf and Middle East generally.[24]

Around this time, Oxford historian Stephen Howe reminds us, the anti-colonialist movement in Britain was beginning to pay more attention to the last vestiges of British rule.[25] The London-based *Daily Worker* was first to offer its prosaic analysis:

> British imperialism has been chased out of her base in Suez. She has found things uncomfortable in Cyprus. And only recently Jomo Kenyatta reiterated Kenya's opposition to the British military base there . . . The people are firmly against an imperialist-sponsored federation dominated by a handful of unrepresentative sultans . . . The smell of oil seems to drive British imperialism desperate. It must not be allowed to cause a new explosion in the Middle East.[26]

It is certainly true that Western European states were the largest importers of crude oil in the 1960s and that Aden was by now responsible, along with Bahrain, Kuwait and Saudi Arabia, for over 82 per cent of the total output of refined oil products.[27] Indeed, its former Governor, Sir Charles Johnston, even referred to it as 'the citadel of the oil burning age'.[28] Yet it must also be noted that, by the closing months of 1964, the British government estimated that the cost of maintaining the base in Aden was fast approaching £20 million per annum.[29] Therefore, the cost to the British tax-payer of protecting the base from internal and external enemies would have tightened the noose on defence expenditure at a time when a financial crisis was brewing. Moreover, with the arrival of a new Labour government in 1964, with very different ideas about how to safeguard Britain's national interests, the writing soon appeared on the wall for Britain's long-standing colonial foothold in the Middle East.[30]

Indeed, all eyes were on internal challenges as civil disorder began to hold Aden in a vice-like grip from the early 1960s. The pace of dissident activity had been slowly building from the late 1950s and culminated in large-scale strikes and demonstrations against the proposals to lead Aden into the Federation in 1962. In a letter to a colleague, Permanent Under Secretary of the Colonies, Sir (Arthur) Hilton Poynton was uncharacteristically pragmatic:

> We have little doubt of our ability in terms of force to contain and handle such disturbances, but their reverberations might continue for a period, lasting well until the end of the year.[31]

Officials in the Protectorate administration pinpointed the cause of the trouble to two main sources: from Yemeni forces and dissidents crossing the border into Aden and from internal dissidents. It was thought that the latter group would stir up trouble by playing up the grievances of local migrant workers. As one assessment of Aden's internal security noted, all this took place

> at a time when the extreme nationalist element, stirred up in particular by Nasser, might well feel that they had both the occasion and the opportunity to stir up serious internal disturbances.[32]

By the end of September events had taken a turn for the worst. The revolution in Yemen, initiated by a coup undertaken by republican forces resentful of British colonialism, became, in Mawby's view, 'perhaps the most significant event in the twentieth century history of southwest Arabia'.[33] It fanned the flames of Arab nationalism in the colony, with many Yemeni labourers taking to the streets to protest. Police were promptly dispatched, opening fire on a mob that had attempted to burn down a shop in the Crater district. One man was killed and several wounded in the unfolding chaos. Arrests were also made in Maala, when a mob set fire to the Immigration Department.[34] Anticipating trouble, the Federal government had even issued a warning against people taking part in unauthorized processions, meetings and assemblies.

Despite the order from Colonial authorities, over 3,000 people turned out to register their grievances in the streets. Riots and internal disturbances ensued, and the police responded by discharging tear gas at the crowd as a way of dispersing them. The colonial governor, who had responsibility for dealing with internal security matters,[35] stubbornly refused to be moved by these disturbances; shortly after midday, three platoons of British troops were deployed in aid of the civil power.[36] Britain's 'attempt to impose a British-designed federation scheme on Aden', reported the *New Statesman*, 'was bound to produce bloodshed'.[37]

Those involved in fomenting civil disturbances soon graduated to bombings and shootings, which served to draw the dissident factions closer into direct conflict with the federal government. Trouble was brewing for the Federation's ministers, many of whom were downhearted, and morale was generally low in the wake of the demonstrations. Some ministers, like the founder of the moderate nationalist United National Party (UNP), Hassan Bayoomi, thought that the police had not taken enough action, a claim disputed by the British Governor at the time.[38] Their main concern was that the police had been unable to protect the UNP Headquarters and the *Al Kifah* newspaper from attacks by the mob. Local Adeni ministers viewed these actions as an affront to their position and authority, and considered that the passive response of the police merely reinforced this view, widespread amongst the dissident factions. The British, for their part, saw things differently and were at pains to persuade their Arab colleagues that 'they must not look on these events from a narrow Aden point of view but must consider the effect on the British Parliament and on world opinion'.[39]

As a means of building up a broad consensus among 'friendly governments both in the Arab world and elsewhere', Sir Charles Johnston wrote a letter to King Hussein of Jordan, suggesting that [s]upport from any Arab Government would of course be particularly valuable to us'.[40] The King replied personally to inform the Governor that he had 'brought the matter of the support you need in the United Nations to my Government, and I am hopeful that our decision on the subject would be a positive and constructive one'.[41] That Britain could call upon generous support from Jordan and other 'friendly Arab governments' would enable the issue to be carefully managed by the British at the UN.

Although 'concerned by the continuous howling of the Arab nationalist gale', the local moderate parties 'had little else in common'.[42] Bayoomi's UNP was the second largest political group in Aden after the ATUC and his colleagues held key positions in the administration.[43] Naturally, ministers representing the UNP remained dogged in pressing the Governor to declare a state of emergency and to take firmer action against protestors, something he was unwilling to do on the grounds that it would 'be politically unwise except in response to violence from the PSP side'. In typically clear-sighted fashion, the Governor went on to state:

> Without violence however in my view declarations of a state of emergency would be interpreted – rightly – as designed mainly to lock up our opponents and as suggesting that conditions here are worse that they at present are. It would also I imagine make it more difficult for you to justify London proposals before Parliament.[44]

Despite refusing to authorize such a course of action, preparations were nonetheless made to declare a state of emergency should it be warranted.

Moreover, and further to the claims made by some Colony Ministers, when the loyalty of the police was questioned, a visit by N.G. Morris CMG, Deputy Inspector General of Police at the Colonial Office, to check the reliability of the police, gave the organization a clean bill of health. As the report concluded, whatever the private concerns of officers and rank-and-file men on federation, 'this would not affect them in carrying out their duty to preserve law and order and to suppress rioting'.[45] Nonetheless, within a matter of days he had changed his mind, even going as far as to send a telegram to London with the caveat that there still existed the potential for morale and efficiency to deteriorate. One of the main concerns seemed to be the prominence of ex-pat officers commanding Arab men. As Morris noted:

> Deep resentment among local officers over the slowness of Adenisation in the ranks of Superintendent and above is alarming and with the serious security threat which will continue in the foreseeable future it is vital that Police morale be sustained.[46]

That the local security forces continued to be commanded by British officers, however, formed only one part of the local Arab dilemma over wearing the uniform of the Federation. They could not remain immune from rabble-rousing speeches from influential figures on the ground in places like Crater, who made much of the need to oppose British interference. In time this would prove to be an explosive mix.

What alarmed colonial officials most though was the tendency of even moderate parties to adopt the rhetoric of hard-line nationalist groups. This clearly had much more of an impact after the Yemen Revolution in late September 1962. In many ways this was a response to the infighting between the various nationalist factions. The President of the People's Socialist Party (PSP) and General Secretary of the

ATUC, Abdulla Abulmajeed al-Asnaq, gave a speech at which he praised the Yemeni revolution as providing the dynamic that would lead to the 'eventual merger of the whole of South Arabia' under an independent sovereign banner. While Al-Asnaq publicly criticized British and American colonialism, he reserved most of his disparaging remarks for King Saud of the Saudi Royal family and King Hussein of Jordan. He remained undeterred by warnings from the colonial authorities:

> All these threats shall not make us deviate from our path, shall not make us forget our duty. We shall march in spite of these threats. We shall march over these threats to realise our principles in expelling colonialism and achieving the unity of Yemen, North and South.[47]

As a direct response to his rabble-rousing speeches, Al-Asnaq was arrested and charged with sedition several weeks later, accused of fomenting further industrial unrest. 'Nationalist emotion', recalled Johnston, 'was on the rampage.'[48]

In response to the growing crisis Johnston created the post of Director of Security, into which Nigel Morris stepped, and appointed Bayoomi Ministerial Adviser on Security; Johnston immediately set about coordinating the colonial government's response. The main tactics available to the authorities for dealing with subversion included arrests for sedition, detention without trial, and even deportation. Between 1945 and the beginning of December 1962, for instance, a total of 7,398 people were deported, mainly to Yemen but also to Somalia.[49] Against the backdrop of these repressive measures, the ATUC grew in power. Writing to the Colonial Secretary, Duncan Sandys, Governor Johnston privately admitted that

> the Aden TUC has succeeded in consolidating its organisation and is now a strong political power which commands the respect and support of an increasing number of even the most moderate Adenis.[50]

After a visit to Aden, Sandys recommended harsher methods for tackling the growing subversion, including the prosecution of teachers encouraging school children to engage in intimidation and the deportation of Yemenis stirring up trouble and engaging in strike action.[51] Sandys' resolution that firmer measures should be taken came amidst claims from the anti-colonialist left that 'British rule is being enforced by methods such as the beating of nine hunger strikers in jail'. The *Daily Herald* even went as far as to note in its leader how:

> We are in danger of repeating the wretched folly of Cyprus. The lesson that in the long run a base cannot be held against the will of the people who live there has not been learned.[52]

Exasperation with the Tory policy of retrenchment in South Arabia even led Labour's Denis Healey to observe how Sandys provided 'the extraordinary spectacle of seeing a dinosaur, living and breathing before our eyes'.[53]

Aden's admittance to the British-backed Federation of South Arabia in January 1963 proved to be the catalyst for further violence as Britain set about 'making another Cyprus out of Aden'.[54] Unsurprisingly, the outlook on the security front was dire, with a Joint Intelligence Committee weekly summary concluding: 'Dissidents from Yafa, Aulaqi States and Baida are said to be undergoing training in the use of time bombs and grenades in camps of the Yemeni National Guard'.[55] By July two people had been killed at the office of the Arabian News Agency and intimidation and civil disturbance remained rife. By December 1963, however, 'a turning point occurred' when the new High Commissioner, Sir Kennedy Trevaskis, had a bomb lobbed at him. Although he escaped unharmed, the explosion killed two people, including his trusted political officer George Henderson, who later earned a posthumous second bar to his George Medal for saving Trevaskis' life. The ferocity of the attack, during which over fifty-one other people were wounded, weighed heavily on Trevaskis' mind; he declared a state of emergency shortly afterwards. The serious deterioration in internal security meant that by '1964, amid the towering peaks and fertile wadis of the Radfan, British troops once more embarked on what was to be the last of this type of "small war"'.[56]

The military in South Arabia

The deployment of British troops onto the streets of Aden between 1964 and 1967 is a forgotten episode in the literature on decolonization. Yet the intensity of this campaign in the South Arabian peninsula should not be underestimated. Islamist extremism has a long history in Aden in particular and in Yemen more generally. Mosques were hotbeds for militancy in the 1960s and often served as observation posts for rebels in many Adenese districts, such as Maala, Crater, Mansura and Sheikh Othman. British soldiers serving in Aden at the time recalled how 'we were there to keep the peace' and, for ordinary squaddies, 'most troops on the ground had no concept of the bigger picture'. The one abiding memory of their tour was that 'it was so hot, all you wanted to do was sit and sweat'.[57]

Politically, an agreement between the UK and the Federation copper-fastened British sovereignty over the colony. It was also agreed:

> The Federation shall permit Her Majesty's Forces to be based in and to move freely within and to and from the Federation together with their equipment and stores and to fly their aircraft over the Federation and to carry out other operations that may be necessary. The Federation shall grant any Forces that may be in the Federation in pursuance of this Section such facilities and take such other steps to assist them as may be necessary.[58]

Harold Wilson's Labour government had conceded its claim of sovereignty over Aden following the Federal South Arabian Conference in June/July 1964, 'subject to the continued exercise of the British Government of such powers as may be necessary for the defence of the Federation and the fulfilment of Britain's worldwide responsibilities'. Yet ministers and military remained divided over whether to maintain sovereign base areas, given the intent to withdraw. In a brief prepared for the Colonial Secretary it was suggested that:

> Since it would not reduce the Base's dependence on local goodwill, but would serve to arouse opposition to our presence, the formation of Sovereign Base Areas is not therefore viewed as serving our best interests.[59]

Covering some 12,000 acres and housing approximately 25,000 service personnel and their families in a colony of over 220,000 people,[60] the base served to project British power in the region. In a secret assessment of the costs and benefits of its continued retention it was revealed how the base offered four key advantages: protection of the Federation and unfederated states; support for military forces in the Gulf in servicing treaty obligations; support for peace-keeping operations in Commonwealth countries in Eastern and Southern Africa; and finally potential staging facilities for our forces in South East Asia and the Far East.[61]

The costs included the political ammunition that continued retention of the base generated for the spread of President Nasser's rampant brand of Arab nationalism. For Labour's Defence Secretary between 1964 and 1970, Denis Healey, 'in some areas [like Aden] the presence of British troops was becoming an irritant rather than a stabilising factor'.[62] Indeed, it probably did not help matters that there was an indemnity clause for members of the British forces in respect of 'tortuous acts committed whilst performing IS [Internal Security] duties and other duties in aid of civil authorities'.[63] Indeed the alleged torture of detainees during the conflict was used by the insurgents and their sponsors in Cairo as a stick with which to beat the British. In an interview with an NLF spokesperson on Radio Cairo, the terrorist group called 'on all popular organisations and bodies in Aden, the Arab homeland and the world to proclaim their protest against the imperialist authorities because of the ill-treatment of the detainees' and invited the Red Cross and the Red Crescent to 'send delegations to investigate the condition of the detainees and prisoners in the prison of terrorism in the occupied South'.[64] Subsequent broadcasts said that the NLF (or *fediyeen*, as they called themselves) had issued a warning to those 'traitors' who collaborated with imperialism 'that it will not be merciful to those who had abandoned their people and become tools of imperialism to be used against the people's cause'.[65] Attacks against British forces soon escalated.

It was not long before Special Forces were deployed in intelligence operations. The SAS had a distinguished war-time reputation but was disbanded at the end of the Second World War, only to be reconstituted for use in the jungles of Malaya in the 1950s. It had proven itself in Malaya and Oman and was now tasked by Headquarters Middle East on a two-fold mission in Aden and the wider protectorate; to establish 'cleverly-concealed forward observation posts from which they could direct artillery fire and air strikes on parties of the enemy' and the 'interception of arms and supplies being sent to the Aden city revolutionaries'.[66] In Aden state Special Forces duties were somewhat different. The SAS worked closely with Special Branch to augment the security forces' intelligence capability.[67]

Meanwhile, on the political front, elections were looming and were scheduled to take place on 16 October. There were forty-eight candidates nominated for sixteen seats and they included big businessmen and property owners, professional politicians, small shopkeepers and traders, former government officials, white-collar workers and unemployed. The PSP, which was linked to the NLF, boycotted the elections and called upon the people of Aden to do so too.[68] On the eve of the election they issued a warning on Radio Sanna to Aden electors 'that they would be traitors if they voted and saying that the NLF intended, if necessary by the use of grenades and firearms, to ensure that the election failed'.[69] Even the more moderate newspaper *The Recorder* went as far as to state:

> As a matter of fact, no matter who comes to power, the forthcoming elections will go down in Aden's history as the biggest farce perpetrated on a gullible public. Without the solemnly promised Citizenship Act coming through, South Arabians who have lived in Aden all their lives, married here, brought up families here and have earned a living here have been deprived of the vote, let alone their being allowed to contest the elections. The effrontery of the Government is indeed shocking. With less than a third of Aden's population voting the powers that be have the cheek to call what has yet to happen a popular election.[70]

Serious doubts hung over the proceedings, with the newspaper claiming that the British government was 'anxious to have certain men in power and it is going to have them come hell or high water'. There is certainly proof that this was indeed the case and the archival sources inform us that the British government representatives judged candidates on the basis of those 'whose election would seem best to suit our interests'. Typically the favoured candidate was one who had a 'moderate nature of views and capacity to co-operate with Baharoon, attitude towards Federation . . . , previous experience of Legislative Council (the devil one knows being better than the devil one does not), general susceptibility to influence etc'.[71] Despite the threatened violence from the NLF, the polls remained open and, although the PSP did not officially contest the poll, candidates 'known to enjoy their patronage' were elected. It was a close-run thing, with both Bayoomi and Khalifa claiming victory.[72]

Changing British interests and strategic priorities

In the 1960s, British interests rested on two assumptions: that oil would become increasingly important and that Arab nationalism would grow in intensity to oppose Britain's involvement in the Middle East. The establishment of a major base in Aden by the early 1960s signalled to Arab nationalists in the Middle East that Britain would not be bullied. Nevertheless, Britain had moved its strategic reserve out of necessity, following the protracted campaign against the Mau Mau in Kenya, which culminated in the release of imprisoned nationalist leader Jomo Kenyatta and the move towards independence. Earlier forecasts by the Foreign Office's Long Term Study Group, undertaken in 1964, speculated that Britain would be 'virtually forced to give up its use of Aden' by 1970. This view was premised on Britain's presence becoming a primary target for the wrath of President Nasser, who had been actively sponsoring subversion in the Arabian Peninsula since the Suez intervention in 1956.[73] That neither Aden nor Singapore, for that matter, could be held in the face of local opposition was a view shared by much of the Parliamentary Labour Party and meant that 'as soon as the new government began its term of office [in 1964], withdrawal from east of Suez was a definite option, even if no timetable for it could be set'.[74]

However, broader economic realities meant that Wilson's government had to tread carefully. While committed to scaling back Britain's commitments East of Suez, they were also faced with a dilemma, brought about by the harsh reality that two-thirds of Britain's overseas investment and trade were located in this part of the world. Labour's decision to place a ceiling on defence expenditure at £2 billion for the period 1966–67 necessitated the dual-edged policy of downsizing its peace-keeping activities overseas while maintaining a foothold in a limited number of places, such as Singapore and Hong Kong. However, Defence Secretary Denis Healey subsequently revealed in his memoirs that the harsh cuts in expenditure could not be avoided and that, in the end, 'I had to reduce defence spending from over seven per cent of the nation's output to five per cent [making a] total saving over the period . . . [of] £5,000 million'.[75] The severity of the cuts envisaged by Healey's Defence Review in 1966 prompted the resignation of the First Sea Lord, Admiral Sir David Luce, and the Ministry of Defence's Permanent Under Secretary (responsible for the Royal Navy), Christopher Mayhew, who could not support the efficiency savings proposed, especially when they necessitated the cancellation of a new carrier for the Royal Navy. In his resignation statement to Parliament, Mayhew noted how:

> The basic mistake of the Defence Review has been the classic crime of peacetime British Governments of giving the Armed Forces too large tasks and too few resources. The overseas Departments have laid down a proud defence role for Britain, the Treasury has laid down a humble defence budget for Britain, and the Service men 'carry the can'.[76]

Healey later conceded that historians might judge his six years as Defence Secretary to have been responsible for 'the liquidation of Britain's military role outside Europe, an anachronism which was essentially a legacy of our nineteenth-century empire'.[77] In this, however, he believed strongly that the 'temptation to oversimplify for political or intellectual convenience should be resisted'.[78]

While the Labour government had given a commitment to contain terrorism in Aden, it lacked the stomach for a fight and, in strategic terms, it no longer possessed the economic resources to sustain a robust policy either. It was unfortunate for Aden's Federation that the forthcoming Westminster election coincided with Healey's Defence Review, the stated purpose of which was to 'relate expenditure on defence to the nation's resources'. As the party's own internal papers reveal, Labour was continuing with a policy previously initiated by the Attlee government in the immediate post-war period:

> In the past Britain has attempted too much. As a result we have wasted fantastic sums and scarce resources on unrealistic projects, our economy has been subjected to an increasingly unbearable strain and in the past some of our forces, performing key roles in Britain's peace keeping and Commonwealth commitments, were left undermanned and underequipped.[79]

Almost every administration criticizes the last one. And Labour's policy in the mid-1960s was no different, in laying the blame for the poor health of the defence budget squarely at the door of the previous Conservative government.

This was reaffirmed by Wilson in Prime Minister's Questions several months later, when he responded to a Conservative charge that the British Government was now abandoning its Federation allies. The Prime Minister told the House, 'we simply cannot go on a basis of accepting these unilateral military commitments which are far beyond the economic, military and financial capacity of this country'.[80] Yet this was done in such a way as to expose the vulnerabilities placed on those who he had previously bought British assurances that they would maintain a base in Aden for its own protection, even after independence.[81] Nevertheless, it *was* the reality. As the former Governor made perfectly clear in his memoirs, 'the safest way of determining our aims in South Arabia will be by a hard-headed calculation of the two interests involved – those of Britain, and of the indigenous inhabitants'.[82] Imperial self-interests, principally, what was good for the Metropolis, would always trump local sentiment.

It is often said that British colonial strategy was a unique admixture of 'divide and rule' and there is certainly much evidence of this outlook in the Middle East, as one top secret report concluded: 'The more the Arab countries are divided among themselves the less difficulty we shall have in maintaining our positions in Arabia.'[83] Mawby would, of course, disagree with this view. In his scholarly opinion, British policy in the Middle East was 'not governed by a narrow notion of self interest but by a broader conception of Britain's proper role in the world'.[84] The disagreements between the 'man on the spot' and the political hierarchy in London would soon intensify and, ultimately, lead to Trevaskis being moved on.[85]

Worryingly, the number of violent incidents continued in intensity, with the first quarter of 1967 recording over 300 armed actions, mostly involving grenade attacks.[86] The effect on British service families was highlighted in a briefing for the Chief of the General Staff by Major-General Charles Dunbar, who told his boss that '[w]e may ultimately have to choose between our efforts to leave stability behind and our need to protect Brit [sic] servicemen and civilians'. He concluded with the words, 'If this seems gloomy it is not meant to be – merely realistic.'[87] Attacks against the police had been ongoing for some time, and a co-ordinated assassination campaign soon removed key figures in the CID and Special Branch. The militants even claimed as their victim the mild-mannered Speaker of the Aden Legislative Council, Sir Arthur Charles.[88]

Writing to the Permanent Under Secretary at the Foreign Office in 1967, Aden's former Governor, Sir Charles Johnston, recorded his distress at developments in the colony. Reassuring the Permanent Under Secretary of State at the Foreign Office, Sir Paul Gore-Booth, that he was 'not questioning our decision to get out' (in large part because he did not think the British would be in Aden after the late 1960s), he nonetheless pointed out his 'worry' about 'the more general point that we seem to be heading for the sort of departure which will leave bloodshed behind us'.[89] In calling for more wholehearted support for the federation, he said that the British authorities 'can be certain that after our departure the Arabs will work out their own solution'. Unfortunately, the restraint urged upon the people of Aden fell on deaf ears. There was also a question over the loyalty of some elements of Aden's Security Forces, especially the police, who maintained close associations with the terrorists.

The NLF and other extremist nationalist groups preferred to invest in armed struggle to bring down the federation and precipitate the withdrawal of British forces. Despite heavy losses, the NLF and FLOSY remained resolute, demonstrating their brazen disregard for British imperialism by taunting the colonial authorities with statements celebrating the lives of 'insurgent struggling martyr[s]' who died always having performed 'unique acts of heroism'.[90] As one NLF communiqué read:

> In the cause of purging the imperialist presence, the sultans, agents and reactionaries until this presence is eliminated, it is inevitable that the armed revolution must continue with increased violence and even more hard blows struck against the enemy positions until they tremble with fear and grant the people their full rights. The N.L.F., its heroic Liberation Army and its brave commandos have made a vow to all the people that they will bear arms until victory is achieved and the banner of freedom flutters over the soil of the homeland.[91]

Appealing to the people of Aden, the political detainees in Al-Mansura Central Prison gave their blessing and support for the NLF's call for Wednesday 10 May to be a day of national unity. However, violence was never very far away and they also appealed 'to every bearer of arms who realises his responsibilities to direct his fire at the enemy of the people, imperialism and reaction'.[92] Strikes drew large numbers of people onto the streets to agitate for political concessions from the Federation. They were rarely peaceful and instead led frequently to riots, the burning of shops and sniping at British soldiers.

Amidst this undercurrent of subversion, the NLF stepped up its co-ordinated assassination campaign against Arab and British colonial officials. Amongst the casualties was the wife of the Security Services

Liaison Officer, Sandy Stuart, who had been blown up with her husband and friends when the NLF exploded a bomb in their flat. As Jonathan Walker reminds us, these terrorist attacks were followed in the period between April and June 1967 by 'an even sharper rise in both terrorist inter-factional fighting and attacks on British troops'.[93] Over 1,000 incidents were recorded in the run-up to a disastrous visit by a three-man United Nations commission on 2 April 1967. In the immediate aftermath the Wilson government authorized talks with FLOSY, undertaken by the 'highly promiscuous and reckless homosexual' Tom Driberg, MP for Barking, whose left-wing credentials and 'links with guerrilla and nationalist movements in old colonial territories, including FLOSY and the ATUC' had 'made him a useful instrument for HMG [Her Majesty's Government]'.[94] The talks amounted to nothing and attacks continued, with the NLF informing its supporters that '[t]hese actions and events are the testimony and the touchstone of the way to escalate the armed battle until victory or death'.[95] A collision course with the remnants of the pro-Federation Arabs, their colonial sponsors, and the British Army had been set.

Black Tuesday

Just after Midday on 20 June 1967, reports were received at British military headquarters that a British Army reconnaissance patrol had been ambushed near a petrol station in Crater. It soon became clear that militants armed with assault rifles and blindicide rockets had attacked two Landrovers carrying soldiers from the Royal Northumberland Fusiliers and the Argyll and Sutherland Highlanders. Added to the murder of 9 British soldiers returning from rifle-range practice near Champion Lines earlier that morning, the incident in Crater brought the death toll to 22 soldiers and over 200 Arabs.[96] One British soldier later surrendered after holing up in an apartment block overlooking the ambush site. He was immediately taken prisoner by the Police and handed over to a group of locals who had witnessed the battle.[97] Ironically, the Fusiliers were at the end of their six-month tour. The incident added to an already ever-extending casualty list of 35 officers and men, who had been wounded in previous incidents.[98]

As the picture became clearer, it emerged that the troops were actually attacked by disgruntled Police officers that had taken umbrage at the sacking of three Arab colonels and mutinied. Seeing an opportunity to attack a lightly armed patrol, several hundred NLF fighters in the local area joined in, firing wildly in the intensely built-up area. It was a callous act that would shake the colony to its very foundations.

Interestingly, an NLF statement issued earlier on the morning of 20 June encouraged the SAA to 'refuse to take over internal security in the country' and to be aware of the 'dirty imperialist plot' which was unfolding:

> The revolution is on the road to victory. It will no doubt be victorious and imperialism will try to protect its sons from the blows and the daring of the free commandos in their attempt to cause conflict among the people of the area. Let us be alert and frustrate them.
>
> O free officers and men,
>
> You are the sons of this heroic people. You are the sons of the wretched toiling people. The revolution came to remove tyranny and exploitation from the back of every citizen. Hold the Occupation Forces and the imperialist authorities responsible for the internal security until the end, their inevitable speedy end.[99]

It was not long before other armed groups joined in the affray, eager to exploit the propaganda opportunity. A slightly different approach from the NLF's was adopted by FLOSY, who chose to lambast the British for their reliance on 'psychological, moral or humanitarian support to give backing to their imperialist movement'. The Popular Organization of Revolutionary Forces (PORF), FLOSY's military wing, 'with its military and popular organisation', gave its full backing to those who had taken up 'weapons in the face of British imperialism and its supporters'. They called upon those who had engaged in armed actions against the British to '[s]tand resolutely and strike violently. This is your day: do not retreat. All classes of people support you and victory us your ally.'[100]

As sunset fast approached the terrorists had turned Crater into a 'no-go' area. The NLF flag was hoisted aloft the district and fluttered defiantly in the light summer breeze. Issuing a triumphant communiqué, the NLF gloated, claiming that the ambush

> was a natural outcome of the imperialist policy of exploitation and contempt for fellow human beings, and its concentration on the traditional reactionary forces which thereby guarantees its interests and political influence in the area and their (the forces) being bound up with imperialism and colonialism.[101]

As the defence correspondence at *The Times* speculated, 'it is probably fair to say that the shooting and its aftermath were more a spontaneous combustion than a premeditated time-fused explosion'.[102]

The deaths of the British soldiers on that day sickened one newly arrived officer, Lieutenant-Colonel Colin Mitchell, the Argylls Commanding Officer, who had just deployed to Aden with his advance party.

Shortly after the ambush, he boarded a helicopter in order to survey its aftermath:

> From two thousand feet I looked down into the Crater of a volcano. Only in the geographical sense was it extinct, because the scene I watched through binoculars from the circling helicopter was one of fire and violence.[103]

Though he was not yet in command at that time, Mitchell lost no time in planning a counter-action, which was to eventually lead to the occupation of Crater. As he hovered above Crater on the afternoon of 20 June, he reached the conclusion that:

> What had just happened there – and what I was witnessing at that very moment – was the culminating disgrace of British policy in Aden, the horrifying point when political expediency has so influenced military judgment that needless sacrifice is made.[104]

He found himself in an impossible position; matters were not helped much by a determined enemy ready to exploit the lack of reaction from the British. 'In tribal eyes', wrote the former High Commissioner, 'this was a humiliating defeat for the British and an even more humiliating one for the Federation.' In many ways, it was 'the final nail in the coffin' for the British-backed experiment in self-government.[105]

Sensing that the British were about to close in on their positions, the NLF continued to issue defiant communiqués to its supporters, in which it warned that 'British troops . . . have been amassed and positioned on the hills and coastal areas . . . for an entry into Crater by means of force'. The statement continued:

> NLF, in the face of these hireling methods and imperialist-sultanic provocations announces quite clearly to one and all that the revolution will continue and will sweep away these forces. This is because NLF relies on the broad popular masses in its popular resistance and it will be able to annihilate the tyrannical imperialist presence and will be able to burn down and blow up all imperialist-sultanic establishments and interests and all who have any contact with this vile presence.[106]

By now the NLF had whipped its supporters into a frenzy. They were unshakable in their determination to defend the territory they had captured from the British. Keeping up the pace of revolutionary zeal, they reminded their supporters how the 'great event' was the 'accumulation of persecution, tyranny, exploitation and human degradation brought about by reactionary, imperialist establishments, organisations and mentality'.[107] In the face of such steely resolve, however, the British lacked decisive action. There was a high degree of apprehension amongst the colonial hierarchy about the consequences of retaking Crater, with senior officials urging 'restraint, arguing that military action would be politically wrong and militarily dangerous'.[108] A tense standoff between Mitchell and his superior officers was only resolved when, in the absence of the GOC, Major-General Phillip Tower, his deputy Brigadier Charles Dunbar agreed to a limited reconnaissance mission into Crater.[109]

Imposing 'Argyll Law'

The Argylls were piped into Crater on the night of 3–4 July 1967 to the tune of their Regimental charge 'Monymusk', despite threats from the NLF that it would become 'a graveyard for the British'.[110] In reality, they faced little opposition, including from the Police, many of whom were actively collaborating with the NLF. The battalion's aim was '[t]o kill genuine terrorists while conducting a military occupation of Crater aimed at establishing good relations between 1 A & SH and the local nationals'.[111] In the break-in phase of the operation, one Arab was killed and six wounded when the troops returned fire on militant positions. By dawn 'Argyll law' had been imposed. In a letter to Lord Chalfont, a Minister of State at the Foreign Office, Mitchell's Second-in-Command, Major Nigel Crowe, complained how:

> For three nights we sent in recce patrols and we listened in silence to the counsel of gloom and pessimism eminating [sic] from HQ Middle East Command and from the Intelligence Agencies.[112]

Crowe, an Arabist, who had served with 22 SAS in Malaya and was later Mentioned in Dispatches for Distinguished Conduct in Aden, said of the prolonged non-responsiveness of the political and military hierarchy, 'I fear we are now never going to see anyone brought to justice for the massacre, and this will only be taken as a sign of weakness by the Arabs'.[113] His observation soon proved correct: no one was brought to justice for the killings in large part because of the inertia displayed by the Adenese Police.[114]

One officer subsequently noted in a report for the regiment's magazine, *The Thin Red Line*, how the Argylls were 'paying a high price indeed for maintaining law and order in the one square mile district of Aden that we control', given the 'vigorous smear campaign' launched against British troops at the time. Describing the battalion's Tactical Area of Responsibility in the following way, he said:

> We live in Crater cheek-by-jowl with the local population. A Company hold the Northern part of Crater, from a line just north of the Chartered Bank Building. B Company hold the Western and Southern part, including the main residential area alongside Holkat Bay, and the line south of

> Aidrus Road. Their section now includes the Aidrus Mosque, a source of trouble on several occasions which was until recently D Company's task. D Company dominates the very heart of Crater.[115]

Sub-units took up position in fixed positions overlooking the main trouble-spots:

> Platoons and Sections live in a variety of buildings which dominate each particular area of responsibility. Occupied buildings vary from schools to the Treasury Building, from the clinic to ordinary private flats. Each position is chosen for its ability to dominate its particular area, and the Argylls are masters of the rooftops. Foot, mobile, and armoured car patrols police the streets at frequent and varying intervals.[116]

Often to be found in the thick of it, either challenging locals about their movements or standing aloft high-rise buildings relating his maps to the ground, Mitchell was extremely frustrated by the lack of firm direction from his superiors. He made no secret of the fact that he thought that British prestige was badly damaged by the murder of the soldiers and the imposition of terrorist rule over the Crater district on 'Black Tuesday'. Yet he could do little about it. As Mitchell later noted in his memoirs, he 'had spent long enough in Whitehall to know the stultifying effects of rule by committee'.[117] His position was clear. 'I was not prepared', he said, 'to see my men killed by being forbidden to defend themselves simply to avoid upsetting Arab leaders of politicians remote from the fighting back home'.[118]

To make matters worse, the Chief Justice's inquiry into the circumstances of the British Army deaths in Crater on 20 June 1967 blamed the outbreak of violence not on the natural consequence of tribal dynamics, split loyalties or criminality, but as a 'spur of the moment decision' taken in the heady atmosphere generated by the Arab-Israeli Six-Day War.[119] According to the report, rumours were rife that the British were going to abandon their allies – inevitably, discipline within the ranks of the Police quickly broke down. An ensuing gun battle broke out and, according to the report, things just 'got out of hand'. As the Chief Justice observed:

> It is noted that the behaviour of the Armed Police on 20 of June was entirely out of character, that it is a force which has enjoyed the highest reputation in the past, that throughout the emergency it has proved its worth time and again in the control of disturbances of all kinds, and that it clearly has a vital role to play in the future.[120]

In fact, the ambush had been triggered by an earlier clash between the Police and the SAA at a police station near Champion Lines, where troops from 1 Para and the Lancashire Regiment, together with a detachment of the King's Own Borderers, were stationed. The troops were ordered in to secure the armoury, storming the building amidst stiff resistance.

Rumours spread like wildfire in Crater that the British were imposing their will on the police force. In what became known to the troops as 'Black Tuesday', it was reported that 'Radfan camp will never be the same again after the 20 June. [T]here is a sense of alertness which is apparent every time firing is heard on the range.'[121] Despite the uncertain circumstances surrounding the attack, the report nevertheless made the following recommendations:

(i) The cause of the differences in the South Arabian Army and South Arabian Police should be immediately removed. The Aden Armed Police are closely connected with those forces.
(ii) Certain changes should be made in the senior command of the Armed Police.
(iii) Every effort should be made to bring the ringleaders to justice. However, this poses no easy task and, under the present conditions prevailing in Aden, it may well prove impossible of fulfilment.[122]

In terms of political expediency, the report provided some mild relief for the Labour government, who saw the violence as an atavistic throwback. The constant media attention, now centring on Mitchell, also complicated matters by highlighting the government's steely resolve to withdraw from Aden come what may.

By the end of the summer – and despite the tough imposition of 'Argyll law' in Crater – the violence continued unabated. Daily reports were received of terrorists opening fire on British patrols with Kalashnikov rifles and the lobbing of grenades, an NLF specialism. One situation report noted how there were over 41 armed incidents in one 24 hour period, ranging from heavy machine gun fire on patrols to mortar attacks on piquets.[123] Despite soldiers returning fire in self-defence, setting up snap vehicle checkpoints and deploying Ferret armoured cars to dominate the ground, the enemy remained undeterred. Ironically, the NLF even stepped up its terrorist attacks, largely because of the ongoing Crater occupation. A statement issued to its rank-and-file urged NLF fighters to violently oppose the British:

> The entry of British troops into the town of Crater after the siege cannot be considered an act for regaining a lost dignity, but a foolish act. Our bullets and grenades will continue to cause fear in the hearts of the Scottish 'red rats'. When will Britain understand that the solution does not lie in continuing along the wrong path but in correcting the mistakes . . . When will Britain learn this?[124]

Interestingly, the NLF was now convinced that 'the use of force and violence, [will] achieve what political methods have failed to achieve'. In a sign of things to come, it reminded its supporters: 'Victory is always for the people who struggle for the sake of freedom, unity and socialism.'[125]

Shootings and bomb attacks now became more frequent as British troops began to withdraw from the colony. Nonetheless, up until the bitter end, British troops continued to live amongst the people in order to at least create the impression of order. The truth was that Internal Security operations in Aden were chaotic. While still clinging to somewhat nominal control over the rebellious Crater district in the summer months, Britain followed no overall strategic-level plan. Although the focus had now switched to ensuring that withdrawal took place in an orderly fashion, the politicians now turned to the soldiers to shoulder the burden. Mad Mitch had other ideas and, in his interviews with the media, alleged that the events of 20 June personified a 'national malaise', precipitated locally just as 'the British civil and military authorities thrust their ostrich necks deeper and deeper into the Arabian sands in the hope that, by pretending there was no emergency, this wish could become fact'.[126]

Meanwhile, soldiers had been following Internal Security doctrine, which emphasized the use of CS gas to curtail rioting,[127] internment, vehicle checkpoints, house raids, cordon and search, and the use of lethal force when an individual commander's judgement deemed necessary.[128] Many of those who tried to run away, for example, were shot in the back, their deaths owing in some cases to the nervousness of those who wanted to survive the intensity of the tour. Other Arab civilians who failed to stop at checkpoints were simply fired upon, as the following incident report revealed:

> At 2032 hrs, a foot patrol stopped an LN car in the area of block 5, GR 97732151. When the patrol commander began to talk to the driver, the car accelerated away. A burst of fire from a GPMG [general-purpose machine gun] was directed at the car, which came to a halt. There were two women, three children and one man in it. One woman was seriously injured, and the other woman and the man received minor wounds. The three children suffered from shock. All six persons were evacuated to QEH. A search of the car was made but nothing was found.[129]

Attacks like this did little to endear the soldiers to the local population. Foot patrols were sent out to dominate the ground, though they were susceptible to blindicide rockets, mine strikes, bursts of gunfire from Kalashnikovs, mortar fire, and the lobbing of grenades. The hectic sounds of anarchy, rather than order, rang out in the enclosed streets of Crater as the British troops grappled to contain the sheer volume of attacks mounted against their defensive positions. Indeed, in and around the Mansura detention centre, one military piquet came under 43 separate contacts in a 24-hour period.[130]

Undoubtedly, there was a palpable disconnection in civil–military relations. Almost from the outset of their deployment for military aid to the civil power (MACP), the military had encountered a lack of will amongst the civilian authorities. Furthermore, mutual distrust had built up between the military and the police, with one Army commander observing how there is 'still good material to build on in the police force but this will not last long under the present leadership'.[131] In an interview he gave to a London-based newspaper after his retirement from the Army, Mitchell disclosed how:

> I had already displeased my superiors when, on arrival, a few days before, I was interviewed for Aden Forces Radio and, when asked what I thought of the security situation, had replied that Aden was 'the least buttoned-up place I had ever known'.[132]

Recognizing how he had over-stepped the mark, Mitchell lost no time in explaining his rationale for these cutting remarks:

> This was tactless, but true. I knew what I was talking about. Unlike both General Tower and Brigadier Jeffries I had constantly been on active service since the end of the Second World War and, of the six campaigns in which I had taken part, those in Palestine, Cyprus, East Africa, and Borneo had involved counter-terrorism or internal security work or both.[133]

Politicians gave a mixed reception to Mitchell's military operations in Crater. The occupation was perceived to have come about because of a contravention of orders. Moreover, Mitchell's continual courting of the media irked some Labour backbenchers, such as MP for West Lothian Tam Dalyell, the 35-year-old Eton-educated former Scots Greys trooper. Mitchell later dismissed the criticism, stating: 'Mr Dalyell was not in Aden and has extremely limited military experience. He is a professional politician. I am a professional soldier in a professional regiment.'[134]

Nevertheless, Dalyell continued his criticism of the Argylls' conduct in Crater, saying of Mitchell that he was 'not my kind of hero'. In a parliamentary debate on the future of the Scottish Regiments, Dalyell made great play out of Mad Mitch's media profile:

> I ask my hon. Friend, is it or is it not true that Colonel Mitchell disobeyed administrative and operational orders in Aden given by his

> Brigade Commander, Brigadier Jefferies, and the Army Commander, Major-General Tower? Secondly, if Colonel Mitchell disobeyed orders, what was the reaction of the Commander-in-Chief? Did the Commander-in-Chief raise this matter with the Secretary of State for Defence? If Colonel Mitchell disobeyed orders, why was he not relieved of his command?

Probing further, he alleged that the Argylls had in fact disobeyed an order from the GOC, Phillip Tower, a charge if true that would have led to a severe disciplinary offence under the Army Act (1955). Dalyell asked:

> What exactly happened in the progress into Crater? That was a tricky political operation. Is it true that the Colonel of the Argyll and Sutherland Highlanders disobeyed the time schedule of his orders? I had better be very blunt about it. Is it not true that the Argylls in Aden, far from being the superbly disciplined force which they were claimed to be by the British Press, in fact suffered from a lack of discipline? Is not that the actual truth of what happened?[135]

Defence Secretary Denis Healey, who had no truck with harsh military tactics, nonetheless felt compelled to defend the Argylls by informing MPs how there was 'no evidence that Lieutenant-Colonel Mitchell disobeyed administrative and operational orders', and he remained 'assured that although they were tough and spirited, they were also extremely well led and well disciplined'.[136]

Writing to General Sir Geoffrey Baker, Lieutenant-General Sir John Mogg felt that Mitchell had become 'very much the victim of the Press' and warned that he was coming 'under severe pressure from Regimental and political factions in Scotland who have sought to exploit the public image of Mitchell and his Battalion for their own particular purposes'.

> In short, while Mitchell may be in part to blame for the trouble in which he now finds himself, I have a great deal of sympathy for him and, as he is one of my commanders and his Battalion is one of my units, I want to do all I can to see that Mitchell's interests are safeguarded and that the Battalion can return as soon as possible to a more settled and less excitable condition.[137]

Journalist Chapman Pincher, renowned for his exposure of the so-called 'Profumo Affair', was a fierce critic of the Labour government and immediately set about writing on the political interference which had led to Mitchell being denied the Distinguished Service Order. The Argylls Commanding Officer had over-stepped the mark and would pay the price of all those before and since who chose to break ranks and express a political opinion. Mitchell soon left the Army, opting instead for a career as a Conservative politician. He was elected to the seat of West Aberdeenshire in the 1970 Westminster Election. On the occasion of his maiden speech Mitchell began by welcoming Britain's continuing role east of Suez,[138] highlighting especially the strategic dangers of evacuating the Persian Gulf at a time of Cold War confrontation. Referring to the Soviet Union he said, 'They will not fight, but if, as in Aden, we get out of the Persian Gulf, they will automatically fill the vacuum because there is no one else to go there'.[139]

It later transpired that Mitchell had not, in fact, disobeyed orders. He was made a scapegoat for something altogether more sinister. Prior to the occupation of Crater secret negotiations had been taking place involving the Chief of Staff, Middle East Command, Brigadier Charles Dunbar, the Commissioner of the Police, Peter Owen, and the NLF, which would have paved the way for British forces to re-enter Crater peacefully.[140] Indeed, evidence suggests that civil and military representatives were talking with Abdul Hadi, who was 'favourable to the NLF', and 'he almost certainly knew that we knew this'. But 'our people were negotiating with the senior Arab officer in the police on the spot and as far as I know we were not negotiating with the NLF as such'.[141] Cleverly twisting the facts to meet a more benign interpretation, an explosive document detailing the extent of negotiations between the British and the insurgents[142] points to the duplicity of the British approach in Aden. When taken together with the presence of corruption, divided loyalties and ineffectual leadership[143] in the Adenese police, it is little wonder that British forces died at the hands of those they had thought of as allies. The dilemma posed by intervening forces working in conjunction with unreliable indigenous police officers would be faced again, forty years later, in other parts of the Middle East.

For some time the Labour government had been investing a disproportionate amount of diplomatic resources in seeking out indigenous leaders to whom they could hand over the mantle of power. In November 1967, Wilson's government authorized a delegation, led by Lord Shackleton, to meet NLF leaders in Geneva, Switzerland. The Foreign Secretary, George Brown, informed the House of Commons in confident mood in mid-November:

> I believe that when the dust has died down, not only this country, not only Arabia and the Middle East, but also hon. Members opposite, will realise that, given the situation from which we started, we have done a tremendous job in getting it sorted out.[144]

It was a difficult speech for Brown, who had to contend with a number of MPs shouting him down with calls of 'absolutely disgraceful'. While Labour's suspicion of power politics, its anti-colonial impulse, and the use of force as a last resort may well have loomed large in the minds of Labour ministers, it was nonetheless the commitment to their 1966 electoral manifesto that dominated much of their decision-making at this time.[145]

Conclusion

'There can be no compromise with violent extremists', wrote the fervent anti-Communist and 'Spy-Master General', George Wigg; 'one must either fight them or submit to them'.[146] In the wider political context of the Cold War the loss of Aden, the 'fulcrum of British power in the Arabian Peninsula',[147] was a self-inflicted wound for the British. It had been made possible largely by the malign interference of external actors – ranging from the Soviet Union, Yemen and Egypt – not to mention a complete dearth of strategic thinking.[148] The Aden debacle also came at a time when Western military power was being worn down by anti-colonial movements in Vietnam and South Africa, amongst other places. For Julian Amery, Conservative MP for Preston North and former Parliamentary Under Secretary at the Colonial Office, Britain's decision to withdraw from Aden would 'create a vacuum, and Nasser and the Soviets will fill it'. In many respects Amery was proved right, insofar as the United States chose to avoid any diminution in its own self-interests in the region and continued to play a key role in propping up Israel while giving assurances to the oil-rich Arabs.

Britain may have been in decline since the Suez debacle a decade earlier, but it was sent into freefall by the inglorious retreat from Aden. After Suez, wrote Dean Acheson, Middle Eastern states 'discovered that their bargaining power with their European customers was enhanced, since no matter what they did to the property or rights of others, they would not be restrained by force'.[149] This should not have come as a surprise, as Paul Kennedy has reminded us in his *tour de force*, *The Rise and Fall of the Great Powers*, for '[t]he agenda of world politics was no longer exclusively in the hands of those powers possessing the greatest military and economic muscle'.[150]

Giving up its foothold in the Middle East, and instead placing disproportionate reliance on treaties, rather than sovereign bases, made Britain's defence posture East of Suez increasingly untenable. Nevertheless, the small war in Aden also uncovered something altogether more interesting about British colonial and foreign policy: that, 'while

Conservative governments (1951–64) resorted to force more often, Labour governments (1945–51, 1964–70) also appealed to arms an average of once a year'.[151] Britain's main reason for intervening militarily in its colonial outposts was often explained away as being necessary for good order or stability. In reality, it was the product of increasing political bankruptcy. In Aden, the cost in blood and treasure was judged unworthy of an extended campaign. A total of 33 soldiers had been killed and 274 wounded in over 1,861 incidents between 1964 and July 1967.[152] Casualties elsewhere in the protectorate stood much higher. In actual fact, while most interventions under Conservative governments were prompted by feelings of obligation under the treaties they signed with allies and partners across the world, Labour shifted its policy to 'one that sought to protect British interests through a military withdrawal'.[153] Underpinning all of this was a severe economic deficit, which had an interminable bearing on almost all of Wilson's decisions, the Prime Minister even reminding his critics that '[t]here is no military strength whether for Britain or for our alliances except on the basis of economic strength; and it is on this basis that we best ensure the security of this country'.[154] Furthermore, devaluation of the pound in 1967 provided more of a catalyst for the liquidation of empire, 'but the economic crisis gave the impression, then and forever after, of precipitating a scuttle'.[155] The truth was somewhat different though depending on the context. Aden was a microcosm for a broader conflagration in the Middle East, which exposed the 'risk of a growing dichotomy . . . between the administrators and the conspirators', between the 'people who know how to use power' but 'don't know how to defend it against modern arms'.[156]

In terms of civil–military relations, Aden was an unmitigated failure. The security apparatus lacked a Director of Operations, and the Police Commissioner was lacking in professional competence. Moreover, the idea of 'mission command', in which commanders are given a degree of autonomy, had been fatally compromised and soldiers constantly felt they needed to justify their actions. The lack of actionable intelligence to guide soldiers in their IS operations reinforced the structural weakness of the security forces war against the terrorists, typified perhaps by Mitchell's unwitting interruption of an undercover SAS mission as the Argylls moved in to retake Crater. As a consequence, the Jocks, and other troops, compensated by administering blunt force trauma in a bid to fight an enemy that blended seamlessly into the local population. Some of these problems had been encountered before, of course – in Palestine, Malaya, Kenya and Cyprus – yet the lessons were either not applied or, worse still, misapplied. By following too closely the military doctrine produced amidst the Cyprus Emergency, the British Army simply permitted failure to beget failure. Presiding over all of this was a coterie of officials in the colony and in London who just did not understand the threat they faced and, moreover, lacked the compunction to do anything about it. All this took place in the context of pending withdrawal and the woeful abandonment of Britain's Federation allies, culminating in the events of 'Black Tuesday'.

In dodging the bullet in Aden, Britain chose instead to come to terms with its relative power in the world, and embarked on a course of action that would lay the foundations of its new defence posture, which, significantly, was to be firmly rooted in Western Europe. Imperial hubris became a reality. It was nevertheless to be a short-lived respite, as ethnic conflict and a groundswell of anti-colonial feeling threatened to suck Britain into an intervention closer to home in Ireland, often regarded as its first colony.

Notes

1 The National Archives, Kew, London (TNA), CO 1015/2596, 'Speech made by female dissident Ruqayya Umar, 20 October 1962', cited in Correspondence between Governor's Deputy to Secretary of State for the Colonies, 20 October 1962.

2 Trevaskis, Sir Kennedy *Shades of Amber: A South Arabia Episode* (London: Hutchinson, 1968), p. 239.

3 King's College London, Liddell Hart Centre for Military Archives (LHCMA), *Papers of Major-General Dunbar, 2/1*, 'Restricted: Brief Lessons from Aden' [Royal Marines-centric document] (n.d. 1968?).

4 London School of Economics and Political Science, Special Collections (LSE), George Wigg Papers, 3/39, Letter from George Wigg to James Chuter-Ede, 4 January 1962.

5 Wigg, Lord George, *George Wigg* (London: Michael Joseph, 1972), p. 186.

6 Howe, Stephen, *Anticolonialism in British Politics: The Left and the End of Empire 1918–1964* (Oxford: Clarendon Press, 1993), p. 272.

7 Phythian, Mark, *The Labour Party, War and International Relations, 1945–2006* (Abingdon: Routledge, 2007), p. 58.

8 Wigg was appointed to the office of 'Paymaster General' in 1964, fulfilling the somewhat vague role of 'linkman' between the Wilson government and the Security Services. He was nicknamed the Spy-Master General' by those suspicious of his motives. See Young, John W., 'George Wigg, the Wilson Government and the 1966 Report into Security in the Diplomatic Service and GCHQ', *Intelligence and National Security*, Vol. 14, No. 3 (1999), pp. 198–208.

9 Wigg later wrote in his memoirs that 'Under Eden's flabby guidance the country was slithering towards the drama of Suez and the tragedy of the end of Britain as a first-class power'. Wigg, *George Wigg*, p. 204. Eden,

who took full responsibility for the Suez adventure, confided in his memoirs how 'I thought and think that failure to act would have brought the worst of consequences, just as I think the world would have suffered less if Hitler had been resisted on the Rhine, in Austria or in Czechoslovakia, rather than in Poland. This will be for history to determine.' Eden, Anthony, *The Memoirs of Sir Anthony Eden: Full Circle* (London: Cassell and Company, 1960), p. 559.

10 Mawby, Spencer, *British Policy in Aden and the Protectorates 1955–67: Last Outpost of a Middle East Empire* (London: Routledge, 2005), p. 167.

11 Ibid., p. 189.

12 Holt, Maria, 'Memories of Arabia and Empire: An Oral History of the British in Aden', *Contemporary British History*, Vol. 18, No. 4 (2004), p. 94.

13 Speech by the Secretary of State for Defence, Denis Healey, House of Commons Debates (Hansard), 22 February 1966, Vol. 725, Col. 240.

14 Trevaskis, *Shades of Amber*, p. 237. Reflecting back on the episode, the former High Commissioner thought that 'Our actions seemed to me both dishonourable and cynical'.

15 TNA, DEFE 24/1896, Priority Cypher (marked secret) from Humphrey Trevelyan to Foreign Office, dated 13 August 1967.

16 Ibid., p. 248.

17 LHCMA, Dunbar Papers, 2/4, 'Staff in Confidence – some random facts about the South Arabian Army and Arab Police Mutiny 20 June 1967'. Dunbar observed in the aftermath of the incident on 20 June 1967, how 'You will realise that intelligence is virtually non-existent'.

18 Beichman, Arnold, 'Britain's Guantanamo', *The Spectator*, 26 July 1963, p. 102. The analogy was of course a false one insofar as the American hold over Guantanamo was judged by Beichman as 'invulnerable to large-scale sabotage'.

19 Mawby, *British Policy in Aden and the Protectorates*, p. 3.

20 TNA, CO 1035/1, Templer Report: Intelligence and Security Aspects, Committee on Security in the Colonies: Brief on Membership of the Joint Intelligence Staff, 1956.

21 TNA, CO 1035/1, Committee on Security in the Colonies: Brief on Membership of the Joint Intelligence Staff, 1956.

22 Andrew, Christopher, *The Defence of the Realm: The Authorized History of MI5* (London: Allen Lane, 2009), p. 474.

23 LHCMA, *Papers of Sir Charles Johnston*, 2/25, Letter from Alec Douglas-Home to Sir Charles Johnston, 7 March 1960.

24 Ibid.

25 Howe, *Anticolonialism in British Politics*, p. 272.

26 *Daily Worker*, 27 July 1962.

27 Source: UN, Economic Developments in the Middle East, 1961–63 (New York: UN, 1964), pp. 47–48. Archived: www.un.org/en/development/desa/policy/wess/wess_archive/1963_1961wes_middleeast.pdf. Accessed: 6 June 2011.

28 Johnston, Charles Hepburn, *The View from Steamer Point: Being an Account of Three Years in Aden* (London: Collins, 1964), p. 198.
29 House of Commons Debates (Hansard), Written Answer, 30 November 1964, Vol. 703, Col. 1W.
30 For more on this point see Trevaskis, *Shades of Amber*, pp. 224–225.
31 TNA, CO 1015/2596, Letter from A.H. Poynton to Sir Richard May, 16 April 1962.
32 Ibid.
33 Mawby, *British Policy in Aden and the Protectorates*, p. 90.
34 TNA, CO 1015/2596, Telegram from Sir C. Johnston to the Secretary of State for the Colonies, 24 and 25 September 1962.
35 Under the Treaty between the UK and Federation, Britain promised to 'take such steps as may at any time in the opinion of the United Kingdom be necessary or desirable for the defence of the Federation and after consultation with the Federation for its internal security'. Interestingly the Treaty also called for the maintenance of a Federal Army under the command of 'a person appointed by the Federation with the agreement of the United Kingdom'. See Her Majesty's Government (HMG), *Treaty of Friendship and Protection between the United Kingdom of Great Britain and Northern Ireland and the Federation of South Arabia and Supplementary Treaty Providing for the Accession of Aden to the Federation, September 1964* (London: HMSO, 1964), Cmnd. 2451. The title of the Federation of Arab Amirates of the South was changed to the Federation of South Arabia on 3 May 1962.
36 Johnston, *The View from Steamer Point*, p. 192.
37 *The New Statesman*, 28 September 1962.
38 TNA, CO 1015/2596, Sir C. Johnston to the Secretary of State for the Colonies, 29 September 1962.
39 Ibid.
40 LHCMA, *Johnston Papers*, 2/30, Letter from Sir Charles Johnston to His Majesty King Hussein of Jordan, 7 September 1962. Johnston had been Her Majesty's Ambassador to Amman prior to taking up his appointment as Governor of Aden.
41 LHCMA, *Johnston Papers*, 2/30, Letter from King Hussein of Jordan to Sir Charles Johnston, 25 September 1962.
42 Mawby, *British Policy in Aden and the Protectorates*, p. 91.
43 Johnston, *The View from Steamer Point*, p. 118.
44 TNA, CO 1015/2596, Sir C. Johnston to the Secretary of State for the Colonies, 4 October 1962. Johnston recognized perfectly well how, in security matters, the Governor 'is thus squeezed in a painful dilemma between the local requirement for summary action if order and stability are to be maintained, and the need of the British Government to justify its policies in Parliament'. Johnston, *The View from Steamer Point*, p. 201.
45 TNA, CO 1015/2596, Secret Telegram from Sir C. Johnston to the Secretary of State for the Colonies, 14 October 1962.

46 Ibid., 20 October 1962.
47 Cited in TNA, CO 1015/2596, Telegram from the Governor's Deputy to the Secret of State for the Colonies, 20 October 1962.
48 Johnston, *The View from Steamer Point*, p. 126.
49 TNA, CO 1015/2596, Sir Charles Johnston to Secretary of State for the Colonies, 4 December 1962.
50 Ibid.
51 TNA, CO 1015/2596, Visit of Secretary of State for the Colonies to Aden – December 1962, Notes on a meeting in Government House at 0930hrs and 1100hrs, 2 December 1962.
52 *The Daily Herald*, 15 November 1962. Johnston claimed in his memoirs that he 'personally thought at the time it was carried out, it was already backed by a majority of Adenese'. Johnston, *The View from Steamer Point*, p. 196.
53 *The Observer*, 18 November 1962.
54 *The Daily Worker*, 6 February 1963.
55 TNA, CAB 191/5, JIC Middle East Weekly Intelligence Review No. 12, 22 March 1963.
56 Barthorp, Michael, *Crater to the Creggan: A History of the Royal Anglian Regiment, 1964–1974* (London: Leo Cooper, 1976), p. 34.
57 Interview with David Ullah, 20 December 2010.
58 HMG, *Treaty of Friendship and Protection.*
59 TNA, CO 968/734, Secret: South Arabia, Secretary of State's Visit to Aden – Supplementary Brief: Aden Base – Tenure, prepared by the Aden Department, 26 November 1964.
60 Aden Colony had a total population of 100,000 in 1950; by 1960 that figure had risen to 155,000 and by 1962 it had increased again to 220,000. Source: *UN, Economic Developments in the Middle East, 1961–63*, p. 145.
61 TNA, CO 968/734, Secret: The Aden Base, assessment by the Aden Department, 6 May 1965.
62 Healey, Denis, *The Time of My Life* (London: Penguin, 1990), p. 280.
63 TNA, CO 968/734, 'Safeguards for British Interests in Aden after Relinquishing Sovereignty, 23 February 1965.
64 TNA, CO 1055/33, Transcript of Radio Cairo broadcast entitled 'Voice of the Arabs' on the Occupied South Programme, 21 September 1964.
65 Ibid.
66 Seymour, William, *British Special Forces*, with a foreword by David Stirling (London: Sidgwick and Jackson, 1985), pp. 293–294.
67 Ibid.
68 *Al Kifah*, 23 September 1964.
69 TNA, CO 1055/33, Telegram from Sir K. Trevaskis to the Secretary of State for the Colonies, 15 October 1964.
70 *The Recorder*, 20 September 1964.

71 TNA, CO 1055/33, Telegram from Acting High Commissioner to Secretary of State for the Colonies, 28 September 1964.
72 Trevaskis, *Shades of Amber*, pp. 221–223 Khalifa contested the election from his prison cell, where he was languishing for the murder of George Henderson.
73 TNA, CAB 148/8, Defence and Overseas Policy (Official) Committee Long-term Study Group – range of circumstances leading to the relinquishment of Aden by 1970 and 1975, Memorandum by the Foreign Office, 18 June 1964. The Group was set up by Cabinet Secretary Sir Burke Trend to examine alternatives to Britain's overseas commitments.
74 Young, John W., *The Labour Governments 1964–70*, Volume 2: *International Policy* (Manchester: Manchester University Press, 2003), p. 36.
75 Healey, *The Time of My Life*, p. 271.
76 Statement by Christopher Mayhew, House of Commons Debates (Hansard), 22 February 1966, Vol. 725, Col. 264–265.
77 Healey, *The Time of My Life*, p. 277.
78 Ibid., p. 232.
79 LSE, *Peter Shore Papers*, 5/97, Papers on Foreign Affairs, Labour Research Department, accompanying letter dated 10 February 1966.
80 House of Commons Debates (Hansard), 10 May 1966, Vol. 728, Col. 219.
81 See comments by Duncan Sandys, Minister for Commonwealth Relations and the Colonies, House of Commons Debates (Hansard), 7 July 1964, Vol. 698, Col. 216; and those made by Denis Healey, Defence Minister, in House of Commons Debates (Hansard), 27 October 1967, Vol. 751, Col. 576; see also Mawby, *British Policy in Aden and the Protectorates*, p. 152, for commentary on Labour's retreat on these assurances.
82 Johnston, *The View from Steamer Point*, p. 194.
83 TNA, CAB 148/8, Defence and Overseas Policy (Official) Committee Long-term Study Group – range of circumstances leading to the relinquishment of Aden by 1970 and 1975, Memorandum by the Foreign Office, 18 June 1964.
84 Mawby, *British Policy in Aden and the Protectorates*.
85 Trevaskis, *Shades of Amber*, p. 229.
86 Walker, Jonathan, *Aden Insurgency: The Savage War in South Arabia* (Staplehurst: Spellmount, 2005), p. 219.
87 LHCMA, *Dunbar Papers*, 2/4, 'CGS Briefing – 1 February 1967: Summary of Main Problems'.
88 Trevaskis, *Shades of Amber*, p. 235.
89 TNA, CO 1015/2596, Letter from Sir Charles Johnston to Sir Paul Gore-Booth, 11 April 1967.
90 LHCMA, *Dunbar Papers*, 2/3, Important Statement from FLOSY, dated 15 June 1967.
91 LHCMA, *Dunbar Papers*, 2/3, NLF – Victory for us and death to the imperialists: Military Communiqué, 26 April 1967.

92 LHCMA, *Dunbar Papers*, 2/3, Appeal by the Political detainees (98 Detainees), Al Mansura Central Prison, 9 May 1967.
93 Walker, *Aden Insurgency*, p. 221.
94 Ibid., p. 225. Stephen Howe writes that in the 1940s Driberg 'became in effect a one-man solidarity campaign with the Burmese cause' and that his 'efforts to educate British Labour about Burmese nationalism undoubtedly contributed to the outcome'. Howe, *Anticolonialism in British Politics*, pp. 155, 156.
95 LHCMA, *Dunbar Papers*, 2/3, NLF Military Communiqué, 5 June 1967.
96 Casualties included 1 soldier from the Lancashire Rifles, 9 soldiers from the Royal Northumberland Fusiliers, 8 soldiers from the Royal Corps of Transport, 1 soldier from the King's Own Borders and 3 soldiers from the Argyll and Sutherland Highlanders, giving a total of 22 killed; there were also 31 wounded.
97 LHCMA, *Dunbar Papers*, 2/3, NLF Military Communiqué: The Battle of Main Pass, 22 June 1967.
98 LHCMA, *Dunbar Papers*, 2/1, Extracts from *St George's Gazette*, Vol. 85, 30 June 1967. Giving a flavour of the intensity of contacts during their tour, the Fusiliers reported 212 grenade incidents, 308 shootings and 24 rocket attacks.
99 NLF, Important statement from NLF on the attempt by Britain to hand over responsibility for security to the Arab Army, 20 June 1967.
100 LHCMA, *Dunbar Papers*, 2/3, Statement from PORF, FLOSY, 22 June 1967.
101 LHCMA, *Dunbar Papers*, 2/3, NLF, Important statement from NLF on the events of the immortal 20 June, dated 21 June 1967.
102 Douglas-Home, Charles, 'A Mistaken Policy in Aden: The Case for Union with the Yemen', *The Round Table*, Vol. 58, No. 229 (January 1968), p. 22.
103 Mitchell, Lieutenant-Colonel Colin, 'The truth about Aden by the one man who can tell it . . . MAD MITCH', *Sunday Express*, 13 October 1968, p. 8.
104 Ibid.
105 Trevaskis, *Shades of Amber*, p. 247.
106 LHCMA, *Dunbar Papers*, 2/3, 'The Blazing Hills' Daily Bulletin published by the NLF in Crater, No. 3, 4 July 1967.
107 LHCMA, *Dunbar Papers*, 2/3, Important statement from NLF on the events of the immortal 20 June, dated 21 June 1967.
108 'Obituary: Major-General Phillip Tower', *The Independent*, 8 July 2007.
109 'Obituary: Lt-Col C C "Mad Mitch" Mitchell', *Daily Telegraph*, 24 July 1996.
110 LHCMA, *Dunbar Papers*, 2/3, NLF, 'The Blazing Hills' Daily Bulletin published by the NLF in Crater, No. 2, 3 July 1967.
111 LHCMA, *Dunbar Papers*, 2/1, Extract from *The Thin Red Line: The Regimental Magazine of the Argyll and Sutherland Highlanders*, September 1967.

112 LSE, *Wigg Papers*, 3/45, Letter from Major N.D.L. Crowe, 13 July 1967.
113 Ibid.
114 See the comments of Brigadier Dunbar in LHCMA, *Dunbar Papers*, 2/4, 'Staff in Confidence: Commissioner of Police – P.G. Owen, Esq, CMG, document written by Dunbar examining the shortcomings of the Commissioner, dated 8 March 1967.
115 LHCMA, *Dunbar Papers*, 2/1, Extract from *The Thin Red Line: The Regimental Magazine of the The Argyll and Sutherland Highlanders*, September 1967.
116 Ibid.
117 Mitchell, Lieutenant-Colonel Colin, *Having Been a Soldier* (London: Hamish Hamilton, 1969), p. 169.
118 *Daily Express*, 17 July 1968.
119 Trevaskis knew differently, arguing that 'The crisis came like a thunder storm in June out of the sultry atmosphere of injured Arab pride which had followed Israel's victory in the Six Day War. Tribalism reacted according to its own rules and, for all their British parade-ground look, some of the sympathisers with the aggrieved did what any indigo-daubed warrior would have done. They shot down the first group of British soldiers to come within range of their weapons.' Trevaskis, *Shades of Amber*, p. 247.
120 TNA, DEFE 24/1793, Summary of the Chief Justice's Report on the events of 20 June in Crater, 14 August 1967.
121 LHCMA, *Dunbar Papers*, 2/1, *1 Para in Aden*, newsletter (n.d. Marked 25th July 1967).
122 TNA, DEFE 24/1793, Summary of the Chief Justice's Report on the events of 20 June in Crater, 14 August 1967.
123 LHCMA, *Dunbar Papers*, 2/2, HQ Aden Brigade Sitrep as at 120700, 12 August 1967.
124 LHCMA, *Dunbar Papers*, 2/3, 'The Blazing Hills', No. 4, 5 July 1967.
125 Ibid.
126 Mitchell, 'The Truth about Aden'.
127 Interestingly, Denis Healey boasted in the House of Commons that the use of CS gas was in many ways 'more humane' than the employment of lethal force. 'I think that on reflection my hon. Friend would agree that it was far more humane for British forces and police to be able to use this gas in the Hong Kong riots last year and in some of the civil disturbances in Aden than to be confined to the use of, for example, rifles and machine guns, as was the case at Amritsar, for example.' House of Commons Debates (Hansard), 17 July 1968, Vol. 768, Col. 1420.
128 See War Office (WO), *Keeping the Peace: Part 1 – Doctrine*, WO Code No. 9800 (London: The War Office, 7 January 1963); WO, *Keeping the Peace: Part 2 – Tactics and Training*, WO Code No. 9801 (London: The War Office, 16 January 1963).
129 LHCMA, *Dunbar Papers*, 2/1, 1 Lan R (PWV), Radfan Camp, SITREP AS AT 150700 C, 15 July 1967.

130 LHCMA, *Dunbar Papers*, 2/1, SIT REP, 11–12 August 1967.
131 LHCMA, *Dunbar Papers*, 2/4, 'Staff in Confidence: Commissioner of Police – P.G. Owen'.
132 *Sunday Express*, 13 October 1968.
133 Ibid.
134 *Daily Express*, 17 July 1968.
135 House of Commons Debates (Hansard), 15 July 1968, Vol. 768, Col. 1087.
136 House of Commons Debates (Hansard), 24 July 1968, Vol. 769, Col. 139–140W.
137 TNA, DEFE 24/1793, Lieutenant-General Sir John Mogg to General Sir Geoffrey Baker on Lieutenant Colonel C.C. Mitchell, 19 July 1968.
138 Dalyell, Tam, 'Colin Campbell Mitchell, 1925–1996', *Oxford Dictionary of National Biography* (Oxford: Oxford University Press, 2004).
139 House of Commons Debates (Hansard), 19 November 1970, Vol. 806, Col. 1487.
140 TNA, DEFE 24/1793, JE Pestell to Private Secretary of Minister, 'Crater Incident', 15 July 1968. Ironically, Dalyell and Mitchell later became firm friends, particularly after the latter entered the House of Commons as MP for West Aberdeenshire in 1970.
141 TNA, DEFE 24/1793, B L Crowe, FCO, to JE Pestell, MoD, 17 July 1968.
142 Ibid.
143 LHCMA, *Dunbar Papers*, 2/4, 'Staff in Confidence: Commissioner of Police – P.G. Owen, Esq, CMG, document written by Dunbar examining the shortcomings of the Commissioner, dated 8 March 1967. His assessment found Owen to be 'untruthful', 'evasive and extremely plausible', 'lazy and totally lacking in drive', 'either timid or disinterested', lacking in organisational and administrative ability', 'completely in the hands of his subordinates' and 'a weak and obstructive character'.
144 House of Commons Debates (Hansard), 14 November 1967, Vol. 754, Col. 231.
145 Labour's manifesto claimed that 'Britain's security and influence in the world depend no less on the strength of her economy than on her military power. Excessive and mis-directed defence expenditure by Conservative Governments has weakened our economy without providing forces sufficient to carry out the tasks imposed on them without dangerous over-strain.' The 1966 Defence Review therefore had three objectives: to bring the runaway growth in defence expenditure under control, to decide on military objectives according to the limits of resources and to carry out these tasks with 'the full range of weapons needed for the job'. Labour Party Manifesto: Time for Decision (1966).
146 LSE, Wigg Papers, Wigg 4/30, 'Political Extremism' (n.d.).
147 Amery, Julian, 'East of Suez up for Grabs', *The Reporter Magazine*, 1 December 1966.
148 For a similar point see Mawby, *British Policy in Aden and the Protectorates*, p. 188.

149 Acheson, Dean, *Power and Diplomacy: The William L. Clayton Lectures on International Economic Affairs and Foreign Policy* (Cambridge, MA: Harvard University Press, 1958), p. 114.
150 Kennedy, Paul, *The Rise and Fall of the Great Powers: Economic Change and Military Conflict from 1500 to 2000* (London: Fontana Press, 1989), p. 507.
151 Wingen, John Van and Herbert K. Tillema, 'British Military Intervention after World War II: Militance in a Second-Rank Power', *Journal of Peace Research*, Vol. 17, No. 4 (1980), p. 293.
152 Dunbar Papers, 2/4, Casualties and Incidents – Aden State – 1964 – 1967 (July).
153 Young, *The Labour Governments*, p. 108.
154 LSE, *Wigg Papers*, 4/9, Public Expenditure in 1968–69 and 1969–70, presented by Harold Wilson, Cmnd 3515, p. 5.
155 Louis, William Roger, 'The Dissolution of the British Empire in the Era of Vietnam', *The American Historical Review*, Vol. 107, No. 1 (February 2002), p. 5.
156 Johnston, *The View from Steamer Point*, pp. 197–198.

6

Soldiering the peace: combating terrorism in Northern Ireland

> When military force falls into disrepute, it does not necessarily follow that it has lost its utility; what is much more likely is that it has been misapplied.[1]

> No one ever likes the internal security task. It imposes a very severe strain on all troops from the highest commander down to the N.C.O.s and private soldiers manning a checkpoint. But add to all this the fact that their task is to keep apart warring factions of their fellow countrymen and the strain on each individual is immeasurably increased. If one is doing internal security overseas one cannot understand the insults hurled in Chinese, or Greek, or Turkish, but it is a very different matter when they are hurled by one's countrymen.[2]

> It was a credit to the military that soldiers were not trained as policemen, yet they were able to adapt, conform and constrain themselves to meet policing objectives.[3]

Introduction

That the Army found itself deployed on the streets of the United Kingdom, after having spent most of the post-war period securing orderly withdrawal from empire, was not an irony lost on Secretary of State for Defence Denis Healey. Returning from the summer recess to a somewhat heated parliamentary debate on the violence now gripping Northern Ireland, Healey took the opportunity to 'remind the House and the British public that the forces have been displaying these sorts of qualities in many situations all over the world for the last 20 years'.[4] In line with the thinking now pervading the top echelons of the Ministry of Defence (MoD), Healey urged his fellow MPs to 'see this as a long-term problem – perhaps years rather than months'.[5] He later recalled how he had warned his cabinet colleagues 'from the beginning that, once we committed the army to keeping law and order in Northern Ireland, we would find it difficult to end, or even limit, our commitment'.[6]

In line with the government's chosen policy, however, Healey 'could see no alternative' to the Army's deployment in August 1969. Nevertheless, the Labour government took the view that military aid to the civil power (MACP) was of limited utility for what were ultimately deep-rooted and complex circumstances. 'It has been said that one can do anything with bayonets except sit on them', quipped Healey, as he reminded MPs how '[f]orces can gain time for a solution but they cannot provide the solution themselves'.[7] In a strategic sense, of course, Healey was right: the means should never be confused with the ways or indeed the ends. Much would now depend on the politicians to work out what that policy ought to be.

In lieu of the preconditions for an immediate end to the crisis, and in the haste to combat a growing Irish Republican Army (IRA) insurgency that had emerged from intercommunal violence between Protestant unionists and Catholic nationalists, the Army, in Thomas Mockaitis' view, soon came to 'both repeat every mistake and finally apply every lesson learned in campaigns' since 1945.[8] Despite the lack of a cohesive political strategy to combat the IRA's armed campaign in the early 1970s, civilian officials came to rely heavily on skills and drills that the Army had tried and tested in colonial policing settings. At this time, the influence of Internal Security operations in Kenya, Cyprus and Aden loomed large in the minds of British military personnel. The one unifying feature, asserted the *Army Quarterly*, 'that all of these experiences have in common, and it would be well to mark it in the Northern Ireland context, is the length of time that it takes to eradicate terrorism once it has gained a footing in any community'.[9] For the most part, these quick-fix military solutions were only designed to 'hold the ring' temporarily until the political vacuum could be filled with a more durable permanent settlement. However, a solution was not to come for many years.

The Army later complained in its retrospective lessons-learned pamphlet, *Military Operations in Northern Ireland*, how no campaign authority had ever been in place throughout the conflict. Operation Banner was instead guided by a number of directives handed down from the British government via the Northern Ireland Office (NIO) to the Security Forces on the ground. In many respects this was a sore point for an Army that did not, until relatively recently, acknowledge the existence of the operational level of warfare. While on one level these comments demonstrate a rather avuncular way of reading the history of military operations during the 'troubles', they also betray a much more nuanced account of military adaptation in the face of intense terrorist violence. On the one hand, they downplay the harsh lessons learned by the military, and, on the other, they completely disregard the tremendous advances made in harmonizing civil–military relations in Northern Ireland. Furthermore, the *Military Operations* pamphlet failed to emphasize just how operations – involving the NIO, Royal Ulster Constabularly (RUC) and Army – had become synergized, preferring to hide behind the tautological point that there was 'little evidence of a strategic vision and no long-term plan'.[10] One crucial point that was identified, though, and which is worth exploring in more detail, is the claim that '[b]y 1980 almost all the military structures which eventually defeated PIRA [the Provisional IRA] were in place'.[11] This chapter pieces together the story of just how these civil–military co-ordinating structures were assembled at the operational level and how this eventually laid the foundations for future strategic success against the Provisional IRA.[12]

Britain and the Ulster crisis

The British Army was initially deployed on the streets of Northern Ireland on 14 August 1969 in a peacekeeping role, in the main to protect the Catholic minority from orchestrated attacks by militant loyalists.[13] While conventional wisdom suggests that little consideration was given to formulating a coherent strategy beyond providing short-term assistance to the local Unionist government, the Home Secretary James Callaghan did ask the MoD to draw up contingency plans for MACP over the Christmas leave period of 1968. Moreover, up until December 1968, it was being reported by the Whitehall-based Director of Military Operations how, in his talks with the General Officer Commanding (GOC) Northern Ireland and Inspector-General of the RUC, neither man professed to 'look upon the use of troops in aid of the Civil Power for the maintenance of law and order as anything more than a remote possibility'.[14] Indeed, so unprepared for the eventuality was the Army, that the influx of new troops was to be hastily absorbed by pre-existing force structures, provided by 39 (Airportable) Brigade, which had only two infantry battalions and an armoured car regiment at its disposal.[15] Nonetheless, it was decided at a Chiefs' of Staff Committee meeting as early as January 1969 that the GOC 'should have operational control over all forces of the three Services for the purposes of internal security covering aid to the civil power and ground defence'.[16] With the Army now committed to restore law and order amidst growing sectarian conflict, the GOC, Sir Ian Freeland, emerged to 'spell out that his soldiers were under military control and that there was no question of the police giving them orders'.[17]

Admittedly, the initial decision to request Army support was a torturous one, reached by the Stormont government in a last-ditch effort to calm tempers amongst those who had now taken to the streets in protest. Given that the RUC was overstretched and its part-time auxiliary force, the Ulster Special Constabulary (known popularly as the 'B Specials'), had proven wholly inadequate in applying urban-based riot-control drills and techniques, the Army was constitutionally obliged to provide MACP.[18] With an upsurge in sectarian violence, the government appointed Lord Hunt to advise on the policing issue. Hunt and his colleagues made forty-seven recommendations, including the disbandment of the B Specials, the setting-up of a police authority and federation, the end of paramilitary style duties for the RUC, the routine disarmament of the force, and the change of uniform from green to blue.[19] Apart from being strongly opposed by the majority unionist community, the Hunt Report demonstrated a lack of understanding of the emerging conflict and did little to clarify the role of the military.[20] Consequently, the Army was left without political direction and caught between 'two masters' amidst the ongoing political wrangling between Belfast and London over the direction of security policy.

The Labour government remained undaunted by the prospect of a collapse in law and order. As a direct result of the Hunt Report, James Callaghan invited Colonel Sir Arthur Young to become the last Inspector-General and first Chief Constable of the RUC in November 1969. Having been a policeman for forty-four of his sixty-two years, Young was a trouble-shooter for successive British governments. First deployed to work with the military government in Italy in 1943, he was quickly made director of public safety, responsible for the restoration of the *carabinieri*. On his return to Britain, Young was appointed Chief Constable of Hertfordshire and later Assistant Commissioner of the Metropolitan Police. Young subsequently served as Met Commissioner from 1950 to 1971, being seconded to remodel colonial policing structures in the Gold Coast (1951), Malaya (1952–53) and Kenya (1954).[21] By the time he came to Northern Ireland, he had a reputation for imperial policing that was second to none. One former Special Branch officer, who encountered him in Newry RUC station in 1970, remembered that Young had three main policies: his mantra of 'softly, softly', the improvement of feeding arrangements in station canteens (Young liked to style himself as the 'policeman's policeman'), and the need to persuade the RUC to don bottle-blue uniforms like those worn by bobbies on the beat in London.[22] However unorthodox Young's methods, Martin Jones has argued that he was 'a hard worker and he had pushed through all the Hunt proposals'.[23] He also got results, claimed

Jones, and was instrumental in liberating the RUC from executive interference from Stormont and the Army.[24]

While, at long last, it now seemed that the police had effective leadership, the Army continued to lack strategic direction from its political masters in London about how best to contain growing civil disobedience and with the mounting problem of increasing sectarian polarization. Somewhat predictably, the Army drew on its huge intellectual reservoir of colonial experience for a quick-fix 'one-size-fits-all' solution to the problem of violence. By now, however, it was too late and the two communities began to direct their anger towards the troops and police, who struggled to keep the peace. The *Army Quarterly* moved to reassure its readership that, though the Army 'is well versed in the arts of counter-insurgency . . . usually it has had a freer hand in exercising them than it can expect to be given, or than it would wish to take, in a home environment'. In highlighting the military's long experience of colonial policing, it informed its readers that, 'in taking on the British Army the I.R.A. Provisionals are tackling the most expert restorers of peace in the world'.[25] However, it neglected the long history associated with Britain's involvement in Ireland.[26] Incredibly, and despite the purported reservoir of Internal Security and counter-insurgency knowledge, the Army was woefully unprepared for operations in Northern Ireland.[27] At a purely tactical level, London had placed a huge amount of responsibility on the shoulders of the most junior of commanders without providing them with the adequate training for such intense close-quarter fighting.[28] Had the Army actually learned the lessons of their small wars campaigning in the post-war period, they would not have come to a position where they were about to repeat illadvised actions.[29]

With hindsight it might be claimed that politicians and military commanders had not been warned about the gathering storm of internal conflict; the truth was that they had been, on multiple occasions. One of the best known, albeit controversial, soldiers who had come to epitomize the disconnection between strategic direction from London and the tactical and operational-level realities of small-wars soldiering was Lieutenant-Colonel Colin 'Mad Mitch' Mitchell. As Commanding Officer of the 1st Battalion, the Argyll and Sutherland Highlanders, Mitchell had participated in the evacuation from Aden in 1967. Having retired from the Army in 1968, he became Conservative MP for Aberdeenshire between 1970 and 1974. Known for his staunch views on defence matters, Mitchell's maiden speech to Parliament in November 1970, served as a Cassandra-like warning against Britain's strategic drift. Concerned that the time was fast approaching when 'the British Army, particularly, will be concerned with counter-subversion on the ground in this country', Mitchell pointed to where '[i]t is already doing it, in Ireland'. In words one might think uncharacteristic of the man, he proposed that Parliament, and the MoD particularly, 'would be well advised publicly to discuss some of the techniques which they will require, because they are tough techniques. They are difficult to put into operation and require good commanders and leaders.' In words that echoed around the debating chamber, he urged, 'Let us now, for once, think ahead to something which is coming our way'.[30] As events in Northern Ireland over the closing weeks of 1970 would soon prove, Mitchell's words had fallen on deaf ears.

One officer who perhaps had more colonial soldiering experience than Mitchell and was in a position to have an effect on military operations was Brigadier (later General Sir) Frank Kitson, who had been sent to take command of 39 Brigade on 18 September 1970. It was, perhaps, with more than a touch of irony that 39 Brigade should have been stationed in Northern Ireland at the outbreak of the troubles and that Kitson would find himself as its commander as violence escalated. Both had seen action in Kenya during the Mau Mau Emergency in the 1950s. A decade later, 39 Brigade's Headquarters, then under Field-Marshal Sir Gerald Templer's former Military Assistant, Brigadier (later General Sir) Cecil Hugh 'Monkey' Blacker, deployed on counter-insurgency operations to Aden. In many ways, it was Kitson's early experience of working alongside the brigade in Kenya that would leave a lasting impression on Northern Ireland.

A notable authority on counter-insurgency, Kitson believed the process was 'a sort of game based on intense mental activity allied to a determination to find things out and an ability to regard everything on its merits without regard to customs, doctrine or drill'.[31] Though articulating a highly sophisticated understanding of intelligence-led operations, it was his penchant for applying covert techniques from Britain's 'dirty wars' in the Middle East, Africa and Asia that soon ran him into trouble. Fresh from Britain's small wars in Kenya and Malaya, Kitson had acted as a trouble-shooter for the Army, advising in areas such as military intelligence, covert operations and propaganda. In 1958 he was sent to Oman by the War Office Planning Branch where he met the Commanding Officer of 22 Special Air Service (SAS) Regiment, Lieutenant-Colonel Anthony Deane-Drummond.[32] The SAS were on the verge of being deployed on operations against insurgents in Oman, and Kitson had been sent ahead with a plan involving similar deception tactics that he had successfully employed in Kenya. However, as Deane-Drummond soon discovered when he saw the ground, Kitson's plan was flawed.[33] Writing to Deane-Drummond in the 1980s, a long-serving Intelligence Officer with the Sultan's Armed Forces, Major Malcolm Dennison, explained why:

> Yes, I met Frank Kitson when he came with you to Nizwa to explore his idea for defeating the rebels on the Jebel Akhdhar. I was the officer who took him to meet Sayyid Tarik. On the way down to Nizwa in my Land Rover he expounded his scheme. I poured cold water on it. To me it smacked too much of fighting the Mau Mau to which he made frequent reference – jungle squads, turned-round rebels, disguised British officers. He was insufficiently aware of local conditions – scant cover, very little water, no British officers who pass off as Omanis. I could see he regarded me as pretty negative, another case of what you call Jebelitis. But he impressed me nonetheless. Here was a man with a logical mind.[34]

Despite his warning that those engaging in counter-insurgency should 'regard everything on its merits without regard to customs, doctrine or drill',[35] the blueprint Kitson expounded was not easily applied in other contexts. Nevertheless, it is one thing to critique Kitson for ignoring his own advice; it is quite another to level the charge that he initiated a plan for covert operations that led to the introduction of 'death squads' onto the streets.[36] The special covert unit he was alleged to have created in Northern Ireland, known as the Military Reconnaissance Force (MRF), had limited success and 'this quiet but self-assured soldier' was soon moved on because he had become 'a liability'.[37] One former CID detective, who had knowledge of MRF operations, recalled that Kitson was 'very hands on', believing that '[t]he only way to beat the terrorist was to terrorise them'. Although 'originally the concept [of the MRF] was good', admitted the RUC officer, it soon ran into difficulties when the police discovered the extent of the unit's activities, which had bordered on the illegal.[38] In another respect, one might also argue that Kitson's inflated reputation in the eyes of the British media and Irish republicans, then and now, is somewhat misplaced. If nothing else, the indelible mark he left only served to expose the Army's misapplication of force, a microcosm perhaps of London's broader political failure at the time.

While schemes like Kitson's may have gleaned only limited intelligence, there was unmistakably a view in the higher echelons of the Army that they were, in some respects, 'forgetting the lessons' from the past. General Sir Roger Wheeler, who later became GOC Northern Ireland and Chief of the General Staff (CGS), remembered how, when he was Assistant Military Assistant to the CGS in 1970,

> over the next two or three years – and probably to around 8–10 years – there was a generation of people who said, 'why haven't we remembered

> the lessons of Malaya?' Because it seemed that, with the passing of the primacy from the RUC to the Army, that what we had forgotten was [just] that . . . And what people were saying . . . Colonels and Brigadiers . . . [was that] Templer was the one who pioneered having the politics, the social policy, the economic policy, the security policy and the place of the military all run together. And . . . there was quite a strong feeling amongst the middle to senior people that it took us quite a long time to organise ourselves in dealing with the problem in Northern Ireland in such a way as all those strands were drawing together.[39]

The Army undoubtedly continued to harbour this opinion for the remainder of Operation Banner, as the *Military Operations* pamphlet makes clear. In the meantime, the politicians looked to the military to stablize the situation.

The Permanent Under Secretary at the Northern Ireland Office, Sir Frank Cooper, was a consummate Whitehall mandarin. In his view, the 'Government and Army knew nothing about Northern Ireland', and their '[a]ttitudes and actions [only really] related to previous experience'.[40] Britain's reluctance to acknowledge the presence of an endemic problem in Northern Ireland extended to its belief that the Unionist-dominated region could be reformed from within. With the advent of the Civil Rights movement[41] in the late 1960s this view very quickly lost ground to more militant calls for the prorogation of the Stormont regime and the extension of Direct Rule from London. Nevertheless, Harold Wilson's government lacked a failure of nerve in its dealings with the Unionist government, shirking its responsibility to wrest control from the Unionists once the crisis broke.[42] Even the election of a new Conservative government under Edward Heath failed to provide the necessary impetus to transform the security situation. For Heath, there was an urgency to find a lasting political solution, but that, firstly, in his view, 'Security in the province needed to be increased and our intelligence operation had to be vastly improved.'[43] This was a demand of the Unionist hierarchy, especially James Chichester-Clark, who had been coming under fire from those in the right wing of his party. Despite repeated requests for more troops, Heath's small concessions for further troop numbers was met with a chilly reception by the Chiefs of Staff. The Chiefs remained 'adamant that no amount of military force could bring lasting peace. Force could only contain the problem pro tem.'[44]

In a bid to arrest the violence, Brian Faulkner's newly formed Unionist government persuaded Heath to consider authorizing internment. On 3 August 1971 Heath asked the cabinet for approval, which was forthcoming, and the next day Faulkner flew to London with a 'tense but decisive' meeting at Downing Street, involving the GOC (Sir Harry Tuzo), RUC Chief Constable (Graham Shillington), Home Secretary (Reginald Maulding), Foreign Secretary (Alec Douglas-Home), Defence Secretary (Peter Carrington) and the CGS (Sir Michael Carver).[45] The British had already made contingency plans by approving the construction of a building for detainees at Long Kesh, outside Lisburn. Though the GOC 'expressed doubts about whether internment could be militarily effective in the long run', he nonetheless 'conceded that there were compelling reasons for it'.[46] In private, the military preferred to hedge their bets.

In the days running up to internment, those at the very top of the MoD, including the GOC and CGS, took the view 'that internment should not at present be recommended on military grounds'. As with almost all of the Army's actions, however, it was emphasized that the 'Ministry of Defence entirely accepts that the final decision must rest with Ministers who will have to take into account both military and political considerations'.[47] By carrying out operations such as internment and the earlier Falls Road Curfew of July 1970, however, the Army 'was soon seen to become primarily engaged against armed groups within the Catholic nationalist community'.[48] This had far-reaching consequences for the military, not least in that it failed to detain the IRA's senior members, some of whom fled across the border, while others, including Joe Cahill and Gerry Adams, stayed to organize a defiant press conference in the heart of Ballymurphy Estate.[49] The swoops were 'based on an old intelligence picture',[50] which handed the IRA a public relations victory of sorts, and in the longer run it prompted the complete drying-up of intelligence.[51] While it was a political disaster, internment (codenamed Operation Demetrius) gave the Army a chance to test the security machinery in a major operation and provided the RUC's fledgling Special Branch with 'breathing space to rebuild and get themselves back into nationalist areas'.[52]

The failure of counter-insurgency strategy

The alienation of the minority Catholic population across Northern Ireland was secured when soldiers from the 1st Battalion, the Parachute Regiment, opened fire on civil rights marchers in Londonderry on 30 January 1972. Here intelligence machinery was partly to blame. The Joint Security Committee reported on 27 January 1972 that 'intelligence reports indicate that the IRA are determined to produce a major confrontation by one means or another during the march'.[53] Moreover, the troops were operating in a high-intensity threat environment, whereby, in the week running up to the march, one soldier and two policemen had been shot dead and scores injured.[54] Nevertheless, by the afternoon of what later became known as 'Bloody Sunday', twenty-seven people had been shot – fourteen fatally. The military immediately responded by suggesting that those killed had been IRA gunmen and bombers, an assertion later exposed as untrue. Betraying a more nuanced appreciation of events, the Army concluded that 'few people are concerned any more with the truth, only with enjoying an orgy of self righteous condemnation'.[55] The shootings were the final nail in the coffin for Unionist rule at Stormont.

The prorogation of Stormont in March 1972 signalled the British government's long-awaited intent to find a political solution to the Northern Ireland 'problem'. Unionists, however, feared the interference of the Republic of Ireland in the resuscitation of a local arrangement. While Heath ruled out the involvement of the Republic in the future constitutional affairs of the United Kingdom, he had done much to encourage closer co-operation between the Belfast and Dublin governments towards the end of 1971 in 'a variety of economic, social and cultural projects'.[56] As Heath told journalist W.D. Flackes, his experience of meeting Khrushchev in Moscow and other leaders in trouble spots across the world, 'who may disagree with people violently' convinced him of the need to 'go and talk to them in an attempt to solve our problems'.[57] By overlooking the power of ethnic sentiment and national identity, Heath was courting further entrenchment and inviting local parties to respond to the British intervention in a way that increased polarization.[58]

What made matters worse was that the RUC had also been relegated to a subordinate position by the Army, who themselves were receiving little guidance from the London-based government. Policemen observed how, critically, with the growth of so-called 'no-go' areas, their military colleagues 'gave the village headman an inflated sense of importance'.[59] But there were deeper issues for the RUC. Incredibly, the Army, who were firmly in the driving seat and 'jealously guarded their intelligence', prevented the police from getting into nationalist areas. The lack of intelligence-sharing was so bad that Special Branch 'did not even have pictures of these people'.[60]

Many of the difficulties in police–Army co-operation had not just been engendered by the latter's experience of colonial policing. Army training was also to blame. For instance, the training model being taught to Officer Cadets attending the Army's prestigious Royal Military Academy Sandhurst at the time[61] attempted to inculcate an understanding of doctrine on well-worn Internal Security procedures from colonial experiences in the 1950s, 1960s and 1970s.[62] However, it was the misapplication of these techniques on the streets of Londonderry and Belfast in the 1970s that saw the military sleepwalk towards disaster. A former Cheshire Regiment officer recalled being taught these drills in the early 1970s:

> We started our training immediately, but we did not know what to do. We watched parts 1 and 2 of the film, 'Keeping the Peace', which was made by my battalion in the 1950s. We were being trained to go into Northern Ireland as though we were going into somewhere like Singapore, Palestine or Amritsar. It was dreadful. We did not know what we were doing. We practised dealing with riots at Weeton camp in Lancashire using formations that the British Army had so often used in the past. In the formation, we had snipers, cameramen, diarists and banner-men, and the banner that I was issued said, on one side 'Anyone crossing the white line is liable to be shot' and on the other, 'Disperse or we fire'. We took that banner to Londonderry, but what was farcical was that the second language on it was Arabic.[63]

While young officers fresh out of Sandhurst remained sceptical about the doctrinal pronouncements on the type of Internal Security missions they were likely to encounter, those officers promoted from the ranks – the 'old and bold' – were just as sceptical. One Parachute Regiment officer, for example, questioned the utility of what he was doing in 1973:

> They've been bullshitting us again with crap about how we're winning the war. The new C.O. is running around like a chicken with his head cut off, and I'm standing here on the street doing the interminable census.
>
> 'Get to know your local community'. Bullshit.
>
> Hearts and minds, comes the never-ending cry from the politicians. Get a fucking rifle in your hand and get out here, comes the never-ending reply from the toms on the streets.[64]

David Benest, who served with the 2nd Battalion of the Parachute Regiment, in Northern Ireland on multiple tours, later wrote that the emphasis on winning 'hearts and minds' was perhaps more 'wishful thinking than reality'[65] in a society so evidently segregated along ethnic lines.

While troops did in fact take the lead in operations, they were not completely ignorant of the role of the police, nor were they without the expertise of local members of the security forces. The formation of the Ulster Defence Regiment (UDR) to replace the 'B Specials' did allow the Army to tap into a vast reservoir of local knowledge. Throughout the 1970s and 1980s 'the UDR grew from being a part-time, bunch of colonials into a more professional organisation'.[66] It eventually grew in size to several full-time and part-time battalions, supplementing the numbers of regular Army units in the Province and eventually taking up most of the burden of soldiering in Northern Ireland.[67]

Paul Dixon has cautioned against a view that sees a clear shift in strategy from 'a colonial counter-insurgency approach to an internal security strategy'. Rather, he argues, rightly, that 'police primacy was an integral part of British counter-insurgency strategy and it was the objective of British security strategy from the moment the troops were deployed on the streets of Northern Ireland in August 1969'.[68] While this is certainly true, Dixon overlooks the fact that counter-insurgency is, firstly, at its very core, a political activity, and, secondly, does not adequately address the issue as to why the Army had forgotten its own experience in a haste to combat a growing IRA insurgency. Moreover, he seems to downplay the reasons behind why the Army only reluctantly ceded control over the security situation to the RUC after 1976–77. At its heart, this was a strategic problem that grew out of the reluctance on the part of the politicians to take decisive action in finding a political solution.

One of the lessons Rees believed he had learnt seven months into his time at the NIO was 'that if it were not for the British troops in the Province, there would be civil war'.[69] The aim of British policy at this time seemed to be to use the Army to 'bathe the wounds and put on a new skin' and was very much guided by a '[p]olicy of damage limitation'.[70] However, the Labour government was running out of patience and set about formulating a plan to restore law and order in the province.[71] The foundations were being laid by the NIO during the paramilitary ceasefires of 1975. At an NIO/Army conference on 29 May 1975, the policy aim was summed up as follows: 'To bring about a situation where there is a local legislative and Government in Northern Ireland and to develop an effective and fair system of administration which does not require Army support.'[72]

By the mid-1970s mandarins like Sir Frank Cooper were noting how the conflict was changing and, although it was likely that the IRA truce declared on 9 February 1975 would not remain indefinitely, it 'may take a different form' given that the IRA was 'too much [on the] surface'. By 'encouraging dialogue' Cooper thought that a solution could be found. The trouble with this hopelessly optimistic view was that, despite the ceasefires called by loyalist and republican paramilitaries, 1975, in fact, represented the high-water mark of sectarian murder. It was a dismal situation. The 'prisons were crammed to bursting point', wrote Cooper, as the contagion of violence spilled over onto the mainland, leaving 'political and public opinion in GB' exercised by the prospect of settlement or withdrawal.[73] For its part, the government began a policy of conciliation towards the various paramilitary factions. The IRA and the Ulster Volunteer Force (UVF) were de-proscribed in order to encourage them to pursue political paths out of violence. For the moment though the government stood firm on anti-terrorist legislation. As Rees told broadcaster RTE at the time:

> As long as there are killings, as long as there is a need for the Army, we will have to have the Emergency Provisions Act . . . The time one could end the Emergency Provisions Act would be when there is a permanent and genuine cessation of violence.[74]

Rees' comments came at a time of great disquiet within the Provisional IRA. Many volunteers viewed the ceasefire as 'an irrelevance'.[75] In a note written by Cooper, he admitted:

> The Provisional Sinn Fein is in an ambivalent situation. Leadership takes the view that road to violence has taken them as far as it is likely to do for the moment but their options are open and their followers [are, however] eager to return to the fray. [They] know they cannot beat [the] Army but believe [the] Army cannot beat them.[76]

The strategic dilemma facing the Provisionals became something of a moot point, as the explosion of bombs rang out in several towns across Northern Ireland on 22 September 1975, exposing the truce as a façade.[77] While the truce may have been a strategic miscalculation for the Provisionals, its leadership in Belfast, including Gerry Adams, believed they had 'collapsed because of British duplicity and bad faith'.[78] There was little appetite for any further exploratory dialogue and shortly afterwards the Provisionals' Belfast-based leadership opted to settle into its so-called 'long-war' strategy.

Within eighteen months of his appointment as Secretary of State, Rees had prepared the ground for a shift in British security policy which would see police primacy re-established.[79] In July 1976 he laid down the terms of reference for the Ministerial Committee he himself convened to examine law and order in the Province, which would

> examine the action and resources required for the next few years to maintain law and order in Northern Ireland, including how best to achieve the primacy of the Police; the size and role of locally recruited forces; and the progressive reduction of the Army as soon as is practicable.[80]

The Bourne Committee Report, as it became known, had arrived at the conclusion that the Army's role ought to be scaled back to provide military assistance to the police as and when required. Despite Rees' 'encouraging words on the publication of the security report', however, 'relations between the army and the police were now deteriorating'. Rees later admitted that 'while the army agreed in principle with police primacy, it was difficult for them to accept it in practice'.[81] Nonetheless, Ulsterization, the policy of handing over security to local security forces, was now in train.

A cabinet reshuffle in September 1976, under new Prime Minister James Callaghan, saw Rees succeeded at the NIO by the former Defence Secretary Roy Mason, a tough-talking former miner who had no truck with terrorists and sat firmly on the right of the party. Mason was given the task of implementing the Committee's 'Way Ahead' report. He shared the view of his predecessor by arguing that it was important 'to create a political framework that would restore peace and stability to the province, thus making it possible for the British government to downscale its commitment to Northern Ireland'. Yet, where he parted company with Rees was that he 'did not believe that an institutional accommodation between the two communities was necessary to achieve this'.[82]

The shift in British security policy in Ulster had the immediate effect of integrating the Army's command structure into a Security Policy Committee, over which the Secretary of State presided. In addition, the Chief Constable and GOC continued to meet on a weekly basis to decide operational matters. In a directive issued in the summer of 1977, the GOC's formal title changed from Director of Operations to Director of Military Operations. It emphasized how:

> The Secretary of State for Northern Ireland is responsible for deciding the security policy to be followed in Northern Ireland. In your capacity as Director of Military Operations, you will:
>
> a. Advise him (or, where appropriate, his senior representative in Northern Ireland) on the military aspects of his responsibilities for security policy.
> b. Consult him (or, where appropriate, his senior representative in Northern Ireland) on all policy matters concerning the operations of the Armed Forces, and act in agreement with him on such matters.
>
> Should you disagree on military grounds with the views of the Secretary of State for Northern Ireland (or, where appropriate, his senior representative in Northern Ireland), you are to refer the matter to the Chief of the General Staff, who in turn will refer it if necessary to the Chief of the Defence Staff and the Secretary of State for Defence before a final decision is made.[83]

The directive demonstrated how far the pendulum had swung back in favour of civilian control of British security policy in the province. It signalled a new departure that heralded a far-reaching shift from counter-insurgency to counter-terrorism, with the law-enforcement agencies taking the lead and the Army in support.[84] The government had now settled on a policing-led strategy, where the aim was 'to achieve the restoration of the rule of law by isolating the terrorists from their support in the community and prosecuting them as criminals through the courts'.[85]

That the implementation of a new security policy should coincide with the appointment of a new GOC was not an accident. When he arrived in November 1977, according to Colonel Mike Dewar, Lieutenant-General Sir Timothy Creasey was tasked with overseeing 'the "Way Ahead" policy and in particular the gradual handing back of responsibility for security to the RUC'.[86] Earlier in his career, Creasey had served with 39 (Airportable) Brigade in anti-Mau Mau operations in Kenya, returning with the brigade to conduct operations against the IRA in 1956, and led his own battalion, 1 Royal Anglian Regiment, in Aden during the height of the Emergency. 'Essentially a soldiers' soldier', it was said that Creasey 'was in temperament more like his political master in the province, Mr Roy Mason. Both believed in speaking their minds, and they got on well together.' Yet Creasey had earned his spurs as 'a tough, operational commander, used to the ultimate responsibility of running a war in a remote part of the Persian Gulf'.[87] Creasey's colonial experience did not endear him to RUC Chief Constable Sir Kenneth Newman, who had, by now, become a strong advocate of the Ulsterization policy. A collision course between the Army and RUC was set.

A shift in security policy

The employment of a purely military strategy to defeat the IRA was effectively ruled out with Labour's acceptance of the Bourne Commission's Report on Policing. Yet the switch from counter-insurgency to counter-terrorism would have profound repercussions at the operational level. For instance, the military's heavy-handed approach was jettisoned in favour of prosecuting terrorists like any other criminals, relying on building a case using primarily forensics, which saw the police increasingly take the lead in the fight against the IRA.[88] That Mason had been moved from the MoD to the NIO, however, meant that the policy was only half-heartedly implemented. Unlike his predecessors, Mason took a much firmer attitude towards violence. He was enthusiastic about the utility of Special Forces and lobbied Wilson for the deployment of the Special Air Service (SAS), something confirmed in 1976 when a squadron was sent to South Armagh. Mason also wrote to his Cabinet colleague, Defence Secretary Fred Mulley, to gain his support for a further bolstering of the military's covert capabilities:

> We have been aware for some time of the tremendous and lasting boost for public morale which followed the posting of an SAS Squadron to South Armagh sixteen months ago. It says a great deal for the SAS Regiment's reputation for professional skill in the counter-terrorist role that ever since their arrival, there have been calls for their operations to be extended and their number increased.[89]

Noting the success of the Army's role in the covert war in Ulster, Mason asked Mulley 'whether more could be done' to ensure 'a better success rate' and 'to give extra credence to our claim that the Army's expertise in dealing with terrorists continues to grow'. Mason's correspondence with Mulley on covert operations demonstrates the government's understanding of the changing character of the terrorist threat. In Mason's words: '[T]he problem has ceased to be one of large confrontations with rioters and is one of identifying and tracing and finding evidence against small groups of terrorists.'[90] To that end Mason became a reliable supporter of the need for further covert action; it was unsurprising perhaps that the military were receiving mixed signals about the importance of their role.

The collapse of James Callaghan's government precipitated the return to office of the Conservatives under a new Prime Minister, Margaret Thatcher, in May 1979. Prior to her arrival in Downing Street, almost all of Thatcher's speeches seemed to suggest that she would adopt a much more hard-line approach to the security situation. The murder of her long-time friend and confidant Airey Neave by the Irish National Liberation Army in April 1978 certainly entrenched her steely resolve. On her first day as Prime Minister, Margaret Thatcher received a briefing on Northern Ireland from the Cabinet Secretary, Sir John Hunt, who impressed upon her the need to make progress by appointing someone as Secretary of State who could be 'firm on law and order' but sufficiently 'open-minded' to try new ideas.[91] Thatcher chose Humphrey Atkins, an experienced Conservative MP whom the Reverend Ian Paisley greeted as being someone who was indeed firm on law and order. Atkins arrived at the NIO to several highly sensitive problems, ranging from a hostile US administration to a brewing crisis in counter-terrorist strategy. In his maiden speech as Northern Ireland Secretary, Atkins set the parameters of the government's security policy:

> The objective of all of us must be to bring about a state of affairs where the policing of the Province is done by policemen as opposed to soldiers, as in the rest of the United Kingdom. It will be my objective to do this.

> I am sorry that it is not possible at this stage to say that the presence of the Army is unnecessary.[92]

This was in keeping with Thatcher's own thoughts on security, which centred on two main questions: 'how were we to improve the direction and co-ordination of our security operations in the Province? And how were we to get more co-operation in security matters from the Irish Republic?'[93] In answer to both questions, Thatcher very quickly arrived at a solution: in the short term, at least, she would maintain the course as set by her predecessors.

In a letter to Defence Secretary Francis Pym, Atkins announced that he intended to place his meetings with the Chief Constable and GOC on a more regular footing, by holding a 'formal meeting, with agenda and papers, to consider issues of policy and any disagreements which have arisen on the implementation of the policy. My concern throughout will be to ensure that the most effective policy is followed on the ground.'[94] What is interesting about Atkins correspondence is that he candidly admits the limitations of the powers of his office over security, despite the 'Way Ahead' reforms. 'I do not have executive authority over the police, or indeed over the army, and I would not think it right that we should seek Parliamentary authority for me or a NIO Minister to exercise such authority.' What he was seeking, however, was to 'produce in effect the most integrated arrangements that are practicable for our security operations even though we cannot in form have a single executive authority'.[95]

Indeed, there is further evidence to suggest that the internal views of the NIO and MoD were at odds and that this was having a negative impact on the security situation. The MoD were worried that the shift in patterns of violence indicated that the Provisional IRA had restructured its organization, making it more difficult to combat the threat. Consequently, a number of ideas flooded the MoD and Headquarters Northern Ireland about how to deal with this change in strategy, which included the appointment of 'a supremo-type figure who could co-ordinate police, civil and Army operations'.[96] Reports suggested that the Chiefs of Staff 'liked the idea', giving it traction at the top of the MoD. Sir John Hunt duly reported to Mrs Thatcher that 'Some people in the MoD would also like to see the appointment of a Resident Minister in Belfast and a Director of Operations. The NIO, on the other hand, tended to see these suggestions as undeserved criticism from soldiers who would like to be let off the leash.'[97] Hunt urged caution that ultimately chimed with Thatcher's own thinking on the matter: 'The appointment of a Director of Operations would raise great difficulties vis-à-vis the RUC and would be a major reversal of the present policy of giving "primacy to the police".'[98]

In any case, it was historically inaccurate to take the view, as successive military commanders in Northern Ireland did, that a military supremo should be appointed. In all of the contexts in which a General was appointed – namely Cunningham in Palestine, Templer in Malaya and Harding in Cyprus – the post remained, ultimately, a civilian one. The War Office simply provided men with considerable experience in civil–military relations, who could make all components pull in the same direction. Moreover, Thatcher's robustness in the face of military disquiet is perhaps the starkest illustration that the Conservative government would not be bullied by the Army into reversing its policy. Had they done so it is likely that the security situation would have degenerated further, not only because of the lack of intelligence on the terrorists but also as it would have hastened a breakdown in civil–military relations.[99] Nevertheless, Creasey continued 'to press for a military solution, a stance which put him at loggerheads with his opposite number in the RUC, Sir Kenneth Newman'. It was not long before their 'disagreements came to a head in 1979 with the general demanding that the Army take over responsibility for policing'.[100]

Relations between Creasey and Newman sunk to an all-time low following the Provisional IRA murder of Lord Mountbatten, the former Chief of the Defence Staff and cousin of the Queen, in the Republic of Ireland. Later that day a twin bomb attack on an Army convoy in Warrenpoint, County Down, which saw the deaths of 18 British soldiers and the wounding of many others, only served to strengthen Thatcher's resolve. Speaking to the media shortly afterwards, Thatcher lost no time in condemning the perpetrators, stating categorically that 'The people of the United Kingdom will wage the war against terrorism with relentless determination until it is won'.[101] Nevertheless, she refused to allow the military a free hand to deal with the terrorists; Creasey had failed in his attempt to 'roll back police primacy'.[102] It was becoming clear that the Chiefs of Staff were becoming increasingly 'concerned about the present arrangements for command and control of these operations', and these high-profile killings gave the military the opportunity to push their case further.

As a means of reorganizing the security machinery, and again to take the sting out of the criticism now mounting inside the MoD, Thatcher appointed Sir Maurice Oldfield, the former Director General (or 'C') of the Secret Intelligence Service between 1973 and 1978, to the position of Security Co-ordinator to further harmonize civil–military relations. Unsurprisingly, Sir Frank Cooper, now Permanent Under Secretary at the MoD, was anxious that the Security Co-ordinator should operate on behalf of the Northern Ireland Secretary and 'have no powers of Command'.[103] As Whitehall stressed in a communiqué to the British Embassy in Dublin, 'The Security Forces naturally depend heavily on intelligence dealing with terrorism. The more they have the better. But this is not the reason for the appointment.'[104] Oldfield's appointment did little to placate some Unionist politicians, who criticized the Prime Minister's decision not to permit the Army 'a free hand'. Despite the criticism, the government remained undeterred with its commitment to police primacy:

> The essence of the policy is that the RUC, with the Army in support where necessary, should bring terrorists to justice before the courts. But there are many ways in which the security forces frustrate the evil designs of the terrorist.[105]

That Atkins had reshuffled his top team in 1979 undoubtedly eased pressure on the government; out went Creasey and in came Lieutenant-General Sir Richard Lawson. After four years as head of the RUC, Newman, who had served as a Special Branch detective in the last days of the Palestine Mandate, was soon moved on to become HM Inspector of Constabulary. He subsequently followed in Arthur Young's footsteps to become Met Commissioner. Newman was replaced by his able deputy, John Hermon, who had been the only RUC officer appointed to the Labour government's 'Way Ahead Committee', which reshaped security policy and led to the police taking the lead in counter-terrorist operations.[106] Six months later, Atkins moved to reassure MPs that he had no reason to doubt the new GOC's assurances that 'the Chief Constable's and my mind work as one'.[107] He later reiterated the government's conviction that it should press on with the policy 'started by the previous Labour Government'.[108]

The consistency with which Thatcher's Northern Ireland Ministers succeeded in subordinating the military instrument to civilian control became a winning formula in the management of the British state's response to loyalist and republican terrorism. It was certainly true that the Army recalled its much celebrated experience in battling irregular opponents, but what it casually overlooked was that the military always remained an instrument to be utilized by the civilian authorities. That Northern Ireland was part of the United Kingdom, a long-respected liberal democracy, made it doubly important to the British Government that civilians should oversee security policy. As British strategist J.F.C. Fuller argued:

> The maintenance of law and order requires two forces, one mobile and one stable. The mobile force is represented by the police, who do not so

> much enforce the law as, through their uniforms, express it. They move everywhere, and, though little is said, they endow peace-lovers with a confidence in security and peace-haters with a fear of punishment. The stable force is the army, which, quite rightly, is little seen in public; nevertheless, silently it stands behind the police ever ready to enforce the law when persuasion not to break it fails to impress the lawless.[109]

It was rather ironic that it would take a violent domestic conflict for the British Army to rediscover the operational level of warfare.[110]

Rediscovering the operational level

By the early 1980s the RUC and Army were well on their way to harmonious working relations. In his first speech as Chief Constable in February 1980, Jack Hermon told his audience 'We will be more professional. We will be more determined. We will be more vigorous.'[111] Hermon brought a fresh approach to the handling of policing-led operations and he was firmly committed to taking up the challenge thrown down by the Thatcher Government. A sign perhaps of his desire to build up the RUC's own organic counter-terrorist capability, Hermon was personally responsible for forming an elite group of 'uniformed Special Branch' officers who would be trained by the SAS in Hereford.[112] These police officers were soon working closely with the Army's Special Forces operators on joint operations, often operating in plain clothes and specializing in close target reconnaissance and house assaults. They also served as the linchpin between RUC Special Branch, E4A (the RUC's covert surveillance team) and the Army. As one founding member remarked, 'our advantage was that we knew the law [better than our] military colleagues'.[113]

Special Forces operators were experts at surveillance, intelligence-gathering, and effecting arrests, convictions and pre-emptive actions against terrorists. In the broader strategic context, Colin S. Gray argues that Special Forces 'provide a unique capability to apply pressure when no other class of military action is politically feasible'.[114] Security force successes in compromising terrorist operations from the late 1980s, not to mention 'counter-ambush' drills practised by undercover Special Forces units, 'brought IRA activity in some of the group's most active areas to a virtual standstill', according to Peter Neumann.[115] Looking back over the IRA's armed campaign, one of its most active volunteers, Tommy Gorman, noted:

> You see people think you turned it on and off . . . but the IRA was always at full pelt. Now and again they scored and they didn't score. They call

> them spectaculars. It was just that sometimes they came off and sometimes they didn't.[116]

The journalist and broadcaster Malachi O'Doherty has gone further by suggesting how '[t]he knowledge that the SAS were so ruthless, and would be excused their excesses, would deter further IRA missions a lot more effectively than any suggestion that the SAS were thinking, considerate people who would tailor each ambush to the conditions of the time'.[117]

The fear of ambush by the SAS weighed heavily in the minds of many IRA volunteers in the late 1980s and early 1990s. However, what is rarely appreciated is that the use of aggressive Special Forces operations had been done 'with the acquiescence of politicians and senior officers, who knew little of the operational detail, and who in any case were more easily convinced than their predecessors had been of the political benefits'.[118] Nevertheless, the law needed to be observed. Surprisingly, the use of Special Forces as a means of attaining wider goals has always coloured military thinking. For Frank Kitson:

> As an insurgency de-escalates from heavy rioting and a high level of violence, it is often helpful to pass as much of the offensive operations as possible to special forces as their activities tend to be less obvious and provide less opportunities for enemy propaganda.[119]

Despite the shaky start to civil–military relations in the early 1970s, it could be said that, with the bedding down of police primacy, the Security Forces were well on their way to forming an effective partnership.

Intelligence operations 'come of age'

One Special Branch officer recalled how the breaking down of paramilitary structures only became possible once 'intelligence came of age'.[120] It could be argued that, from the early 1980s, Northern Ireland became more of an 'intelligence-led war', a point later recognized by the higher echelons of the RUC Special Branch.[121] Looking back over the 'troubles', many senior officers expressed the view that 'it was only when all intelligence agencies worked together that we beat the IRA and pushed them to the table'.[122] By 1992, MI5 was taking over lead responsibility for countering IRA terrorism from the Metropolitan Police Special Branch on a national basis.[123] At the time there was press speculation that a secret deal had been drawn up between security officials in the province in the summer of 1993, which would see a draw-down in army patrols in nationalist areas and less intrusive searches of republican prisoners. A rumour had even arisen that a 'peace party' was developing within the Provisionals led by Adams and McGuinness.[124] Leaked details of the plan were condemned by Unionist politicians, such as Ken Maginnis, who stated that, 'All our experience shows the only way we can deal with the IRA is to first win a decisive military advantage over them. The government should settle down to the task of defeating the terrorists and leave aside risky plans like this'.[125] The operational reality was somewhat different, however.

General Sir Roger Wheeler recalls that when he was appointed GOC in late January 1993, 'other than the fact that Paddy Mayhew made his speech in Coleraine . . . that there was no sign of any kind of peace process on the surface'. On an operational basis soldiers and police officers continued to apply themselves to the government's policy of defeating terrorism. At a higher level there had been such a dramatic improvement in co-operation between the security forces that 'there wasn't really a cigarette paper between the police and the army'.[126] As General Wheeler recalled:

> By then we really had sorted out the proper coordinated direction. And starting at the top in terms of the committee meetings that reflected the need to have military, police, civil, economic, financial policy, etc, drawn together. The Security Policy Meeting (or SPM) was chaired by the Secretary of State [and] included the . . . Director of Intelligence, the Chief Constable, the GOC, the Permanent Under Secretary, the Head of the Civil Service, really looking at the strategic plan and immediately below that . . . [was the Province Executive Committee (ProExComm)].

The ProExComm was formed to ensure that counter-terrorist operations ran seamlessly at the strategic-operational-tactical interface:

> It only actually started on 16 December 1992 . . . I remember some months after I arrived, Blair Wallace, who was the ACC Ops, who sat on the Province Executive Committee jointly chairing it was the Commander Land Forces and a reflection of bits of the police and bits of the Headquarters [NI], and bits of the Northern Ireland Office, sitting round the table . . . But I remember Blair saying that we as a result of the formation of the Province Executive Committee got to the stage where, at the operational level, as distinct from the strategic level, there was an organisation which was proof against personality difficulties, of which there had been some over the past and there was some GOCs and some Chief Constables who hardly spoke to each other, which didn't help much really. And I think the Province Executive Committee idea grew to an extent out of that.

Meanwhile, the close co-operation of civil–military relations was being driven forward by the formation of the Tasking and Co-ordination

Groups (TCGs), which brought together RUC and military operations in the same command centres. As General Wheeler explained:

> as a reflection of the joined up nature and direction of the campaign, the real key, organizationally, in carrying out the tactical battle, was the co-terminable boundaries. So that 3 Brigade, 39 Brigade and 8 Brigade matched Southern Region, Belfast Region and Northern Region. And below them the Battalion TAORs matched the RUC Divisions and below that the company patrol bases matched the RUC Sub-Divisions. I think the other aspect, which happened a little bit before I got there – it certainly grew in those couple of years '93, '94 was the operational direction and exploitation of intelligence through the TCGs.[127]

TCGs ultimately served to enhance response times to incidents, improve communications between security forces and meet the Government's aim of defeating terrorism. They were run by Special Branch officers of Chief Superintendent rank, who worked in close proximity with Special Forces.[128] For the Army, the ProExComm was modelled on the successful district-led approach utilized by the British and colonial authorities in Malaya.[129] It was this fusion of intelligence which helped constrain the Provisional IRA's options and pushed it to the negotiating table. At the same time, the more sparing application of brute force by the state did present a dilemma for the Provisionals. On the one hand, republicans could exploit incidents like Gibraltar, when three unarmed IRA volunteers were killed by the SAS, for propaganda purposes. On the other, however, the Provisionals clearly had to take on board the deterrent effect which the archetypal SAS ambush had on the minds of their volunteers.

Just as civil–military relations entered a new phase, disaster struck the heart of police–army counter-terrorism operations in May 1994 in the most unexpected of ways. An RAF Chinook helicopter ferrying senior intelligence officials, including the head of MI5 in Northern Ireland, the deputy Military Intelligence officer at HQNI and the head of RUC Special Branch, crashed in bad weather on the Mull of Kintyre. They had been travelling to a recreational event in the Scottish highlands. Arguably, the impact of the deaths on intelligence operations was only mitigated by the recall to service of Chief Superintendent Frank Murray, who quickly assembled a dedicated team around him. Though rumoured to have been on the ill-fated flight in 1994, Murray pulled out at the last minute because of an ongoing security operation in Belfast. The bridge provided by Murray and other seasoned members of the RUC Special Branch – and the impressive relations he had built up with the Army's Special Forces – accounts for the damage limitation that it was to have on British security-force operations in Northern Ireland.[130] That the security forces kept pressure on the Provisional IRA long after the Mull of Kintyre tragedy was testament of how far relations had come.

By the 1990s, some British politicians far removed from the day-to-day tempo of security force operations were convinced that the IRA could not be defeated. The longevity of its 'armed struggle' had proven that it had the potential to continue. For the Provisional IRA's figurehead and principal strategist Gerry Adams, all evidence suggested that 'the IRA could not be defeated by the use of tactics which could clearly have been counter-productive for the London government'. In his opinion, 'British policy instead aimed more and more towards containment, though this strategy was exposed as being inadequate'. As a result, he argued, there was 'a military and political stalemate'.[131] There has been an unfortunate tendency in the academic literature to swallow this interpretation wholesale, without much circumspection. For example, McAuley *et al.* have argued that

> the development of the peace process highlighted a growing perception by both state and non-state actors that stalemate had emerged, and that military victory or defeat for either side did not seem probable.[132]

This interpretation is indicative of an old-fashioned way of conceptualizing asymmetric conflicts that runs against the grain of advances in the international relations literature. Rarely have any conflicts ever been as clear cut as this, perhaps explaining why the terms 'victory' and 'defeat' seem to have been jettisoned from the contemporary lexicon on asymmetric conflict.[133]

Meanwhile, for the vast majority of those involved, the 'long war' continued much as it had done before. There were few signs that it was coming to an end. As one officer recalled, the security environment was 'very dynamic' and 'much more fast-moving' in the Greater Belfast area. There was a 'real threat, essentially based on bombs rather than mortars'. Yet, underpinning all of this, he recalled, was the 'interesting relationship with the RUC', which was above all 'a very positive one'. While much of this could be attributed to the new breed of military commander in the Province – Brigade Commanders like Mike Jackson and Alastair Irwin – who had served most of their careers in the province, there was much more compelling evidence that they were 'forming a very good link' with the RUC.[134]

That the Provisional IRA ceasefire was declared in late August 1994, therefore, took everyone by surprise, even those volunteers who had been invited to seminars on the issue at republican headquarters in

Conway Mill.[135] For senior republicans, like the Publicity Director Danny Morrison, the ceasefire was brought about because

> we have to deal with practicalities and pragmatics and the fact of the matter is that the armed struggle went a certain distance, and I would argue, as far as it could go without deteriorating into something unseemly and impossible to end. Ironically, in the 1990s the IRA was probably better armed than ever as a result of the delivery of the weapons from Libya – the ones that got through before the capture of the Eksund – and, for all we know, with other weapons that got through from other places.[136]

The sense that the IRA was an unbroken army and could have opted to continue with the campaign informed Sinn Fein's rhetoric that a 'stalemate' had developed.[137]

Shortly after the IRA ceasefire broke down in February 1996 Army patrols once again returned to the streets. One Army officer, serving in West Belfast at the time, noted some important changes in the methodology by which the troops were now operating:

> We had to think long and hard about the message we were sending on the street when we went back out because so much had improved. And what we had to do was pitch it right. So, for instance, we didn't go out in our helmets, we went out in our Glengarries. And of course . . . a Scottish Battalion is always going to 'get the vibe' better than an English Battalion . . . It's the Celtic connection . . . We made decisions about what we were wearing, how we were patrolling, the depth to which we were patrolling, the frequency to which we were patrolling.[138]

By now the security forces had constrained the IRA's room for manoeuvre. Counter-terrorism operations were so efficient that weapons and explosives were being seized on a frequent basis. As one senior Special Branch officer observed, the British state's intelligence-led war had become 'a Rolls Royce of an operation' by the 1990s.[139]

Meanwhile, the long-running 'peace process' soon bore fruit when the all-party Belfast Agreement was signed on 10 April 1998. The stop–start implementation of the Agreement presented its own problems. Military assistance to the police would only be called out if absolutely necessary. Apart from the major police-led operation in containing the Holy Cross dispute between Protestant and Catholic residents in Glenbryn, Upper Ardoyne, in 2001–02, the military continued with routine framework patrols. Politically, however, the Army had become firmly subordinated to New Labour's peace strategy. Lieutenant-General Sir Philip Trousdell, who served as GOC in 2003–06, explained how this worked:

> I flew back to London to see the Chief of the General Staff – one [Sir] Mike Jackson – to tell him what I was going to do in Northern Ireland, which is what his invitation to me had been when I took up the post. And I said to him, 'well my job, as I see it, is to get the army out of Northern Ireland and to reduce it to the garrison that you would find in Hampshire or Yorkshire'. 'There will still be soldiers in Northern Ireland but they will be nothing to do with Northern Ireland. They will be ready to fly off at the nation's behest to somewhere or other.' And he said that 'you will find that really difficult to do'. And I said, 'well, it is my strategic aim'. And he then said 'I will fight your Whitehall battles for you', which meant that he had accepted what my thinking was. And I remember, just as I left his office, that sort of 'door handle moment' he said, 'any soldiers you can spare me for Iraq will be hugely welcome'. And so I had the higher commander's intent in place, I think.[140]

The long-drawn-out implementation of the Belfast Agreement's terms and the commitment of the parties to see a lasting peace created the conditions for the Provisional IRA's eventual disarmament in the summer of 2005. These years saw a carefully choreographed plan followed by Downing Street, which led to the Army's eventual drawdown, first from the streets, and, finally in the termination of Operation Banner in July 2007.

In his oral evidence to the House of Commons Select Committee on Defence, Professor Lawrence Freedman reminded MPs how the UK had 'many years' experience of dealing with terrorism' insofar as 'the Armed Forces have been deployed, in support of the civil power, to Northern Ireland'. In his opinion they should 'not neglect that experience, particularly in the field of intelligence'.[141] The role of intelligence in shaping the government's security strategy has not been adequately covered in the academic literature on the Northern Ireland 'troubles', despite its importance in counter-terrorism operations, from the collation of intelligence at the tactical level of the green army, prodigiously writing up and submitting intelligence summaries for ministers, to the covert 'top secret' intelligence on individual terrorists and organizations. Without sufficient co-operation between the police and army at all levels, it is almost certain that success against the IRA and loyalists would never have been realised.

Conclusion

A considerable amount of myth and misunderstanding has grown up around security force operations in the 'troubles'. This chapter has identified three, although there are undoubtedly others. The first is that lessons drawn from previous colonial experience were effortlessly applied by the security forces; the second is that the success of security force operations can be traced back to Frank Kitson, of whom Mike Jackson said that he was 'the sun around which the planets revolved, and he very much set the tone for the operational style';[142] and the third is that the Army undertook counter-insurgency operations throughout the entire duration of Operation Banner. As this chapter has shown, like all good myths, these ones lack firm foundation in empirical fact. The misapplication of colonial policing techniques had led inexorably to the alienation of the Catholic population in the early 1970s. That Kitson transmuted his vast wealth of knowledge on colonial policing to his troops when he was Commander of 39 Infantry Brigade was a moot point because, in Northern Ireland at least, the lessons from Malaya, Kenya, Cyprus and Aden were irrelevant.[143] Indeed, only in the case of Malaya did the concept of a co-ordinating approach become firmly embedded in counter-terrorism operations. Importantly, while the formation of the MRF counter-gang, which happened under Kitson's watch, was a military and political disaster, it did lead to a slow improvement in the Army's intelligence-gathering capabilities. Finally, the Army's counter-insurgency campaign lasted for only five years between 1971 and 1976. Thereafter, the military instrument was firmly subordinated to a civilian-led policing strategy, which ultimately paved the way for the defeat of terrorism in Northern Ireland. As this chapter has shown, it was by no means certain that the advent of 'police primacy' would herald results for the British government. Margaret Thatcher risked much politically by continuing with a policy concocted by her Labour government predecessors.

The course of military operations in Northern Ireland certainly chimed with Major-General Sir Charles Callwell's dictum that 'tactics favour the regular troops while strategy favours the enemy'. The problem for the military, as Callwell saw it, was 'to fight not to maneuver, to meet the hostile forces in open battle not to compel them to give way by having recourse to strategy'.[144] That was easier said than done, of course, as the Provisionals moved from a guerrilla organization towards a cellular terrorist structure from the late 1970s onwards. As one of the early GOCs, Lieutenant-General Sir Harry Tuzo, put it, '[t]he hard fact is that in guerrilla war the enemy holds the initiative for large parts of the time and information is the key to his defeat'.[145] Without the support of key sections of the population, the flow of information soon dried up. As a result, the co-ordination of security policy became of even more strategic importance.[146] While the regular army was at a disadvantage compared with the irregular adversary, concluded Callwell, this was 'by no means an invariable rule'.[147] The development of the ProExComm became an exception to the rule and ultimately gave Britain the strategic edge to win the campaign. Without the improvement in civil–military co-operation between the RUC and British Army, there is every likelihood that the 'troubles' would have taken longer to subside after the signing of the 1998 Belfast Agreement.

Notes

1 Fuller, J.F.C., *The Dragon's Teeth: A Study of War and Peace* (London: Constable, 1932), pp. 304–305.

2 Denis Healey speaking in the first House of Commons debate after the outbreak of the Northern Ireland 'troubles' in 1969. House of Commons Debates (Hansard), 13 October 1969, Vol. 788, Col. 154.

3 Interview with a former Head of RUC Special Branch, Belfast, 4 April 2011.

4 House of Commons Debates (Hansard), 13 October 1969, Vol. 788, Col. 156.

5 Ibid., Col. 157.

6 Healey, Denis, *The Time of My Life* (London: Penguin, 1990), p. 343.

7 House of Commons Debates (Hansard), 13 October 1969, Vol. 788, Col. 164.

8 Mockaitis, Thomas R., *British Counter-Insurgency in the Post-Imperial Era* (Manchester: Manchester University Press, 1995), p. 96.

9 'Editorial', *The Army Quarterly and Defence Journal*, Vol. 100, No. 1 (April 1970), p. 4.

10 Ministry of Defence (MoD), *Operation Banner: An Analysis of Military Operations in Northern Ireland* (July 2006, Army Code 71842), paragraph 812.

11 Ibid.

12 Bass, Christopher and M.L.R. Smith, 'The Dynamic of Irwin's Forgotten Army: A Strategic Understanding of the British Army's Role in Northern Ireland after 1998', *Small Wars and Insurgencies*, Vol. 15, No. 3 (2004), pp. 1–24.

13 The following section on the Army in the 1970s draws upon: Edwards, Aaron, 'Misapplying Lessons Learned? Analysing the Utility of British Counter-Insurgency Strategy in Northern Ireland, 1971–76', *Small Wars and Insurgencies*, Vol. 21, No. 2 (June 2010), pp. 303–330. For an extended analysis of the 'troubles' see Edwards, Aaron *The Northern Ireland Troubles: Operation Banner, 1969–2007* (Oxford: Osprey, 2011).

14 The National Archives, Kew, London (TNA), DEFE 25/257, Northern Ireland Political and General – IRA Activity, Secret: Notes by DMO on a Visit to Northern Ireland – 11/12 Dec. 68, 16 December 1968.

15 TNA, DEFE 25/257, Northern Ireland Political and General – IRA Activity, Top Secret: Note of a Meeting held at 10.30am on Tuesday 28th January 1969 at the Home Office on Northern Ireland. Ironically, this was exactly the same number of troops available in Kenya at the outbreak of the Mau Mau Emergency in 1952.

16 TNA, DEFE 25/257, Secret: Chiefs of Staff Committee, Northern Ireland – Internal Security Higher Chain of Command – Draft Note by the Defence Operations Staff, 15 January 1969.

17 Hamill, Desmond, *Pig in the Middle: The Army in Northern Ireland, 1969–1984* (London: Methuen, 1985), p. 21.

18 See Deakin, Stephen, 'Security Policy and the Use of the Military: Military Aid to the Civil Power, Northern Ireland 1969', *Small Wars and Insurgencies*, Vol. 4, No. 2 (autumn 1993), pp. 211–227.

19 Ryder, Chris, *The RUC: A Force Under Fire* (London: Methuen, 1989), p. 115. My thanks to Chris Ryder for corresponding with me on the development of RUC–Army co-operation.

20 Edwards, Aaron, *A History of the Northern Ireland Labour Party: Democratic Socialism and Sectarianism* (Manchester: Manchester University Press, 2009), p. 168.

21 Jones, Martin D.W., 'Young, Sir Arthur Edwin (1907–1979)', *Oxford Dictionary of National Biography* (Oxford: Oxford University Press, 2004), pp. 875–877.

22 Interview with a former Senior Special Branch Officer, Belfast, 25 October 2010.

23 Ryder, *The RUC*, p. 119.

24 Jones, 'Young'.

25 'Editorial', *The Army Quarterly and Defence Journal*, Vol. C, No. 1 (April 1970), p. 4.

26 Strachan, Hew, *The Politics of the British Army* (Oxford: Oxford University Press, 1997), pp. 181–182.

27 Tuck, Christopher, 'Northern Ireland and the British Approach to Counter-Insurgency', *Defense and Security Analysis*, Vol. 23, No. 2 (June 2007), 165–183.

28 King's College London, Liddell-Hart Centre for Military Archives (LHCMA), MoD, *Land Operations: Volume III – Counter Revolutionary Operations, Part 2 – Internal Security* (London: MoD: 1969), p. 1.

29 See the arguments developed in Mockaitis, *British Counter-Insurgency in the Post-Imperial Era*, p. 134. See also Smith, Rupert, *The Utility of Force: The Art of War in the Modern World* (London: Penguin, 2005).

30 House of Commons Debates (Hansard), 19 November 1970, Vol. 806, Col. 1489.

31 Kitson, Frank, *Low Intensity Operations: Subversion, Insurgency, Peacekeeping* (London: Faber, 1971), p. 131.

32 Peterson, J.E., *Oman's Insurgencies: The Sultanate's Struggle for Supremacy* (London: SAQI, 2007), pp. 117–118.

33 Kitson later claimed that he 'had come to realise that the plan in its original form would have to be adapted to the fact that the right officers to run it were obviously not going to turn up in time'. Kitson, Frank, *Bunch of Five* (London: Faber, 1977), p. 174. Interestingly, Kitson (p. 197), also candidly said 'It is difficult to say whether the original idea would have worked had the right people and the money been made available. Admittedly when I first made the plan I had no first-hand knowledge of Oman.'
34 LHCMA, Major-General Anthony Deane-Drummond Papers, Malcolm G. Dennison to Tony Deane-Drummond, 29 January 1989.
35 Kitson, *Low Intensity Operations*, p. 131.
36 Adams, Gerry, 'Third Damien Walsh Memorial Lecture', 10 August 2000, St Mary's College, Falls Road, Belfast. Archived: www.victimsandsurvivorstrust.com/TellingTheirStory/3rdDWMLectrue/default.htm. Accessed: 16 January 2009.
37 Dillon, Martin, *The Dirty War* (London: Arrow Books, 1991), p. 28.
38 Interview with a former CID detective, Belfast, 25 October 2010.
39 Interview with General Sir Roger Wheeler, Warminster, 28 January 2011.
40 LHCMA, Sir Frank Cooper Papers, Cooper 5/1/3, 'Talk at Wilton Park, 18 July 1975'.
41 The Civil Rights Movement in Northern Ireland demanded an end to discrimination in jobs, housing and the electoral franchise. The tragedy of the movement was that while it initially attracted both Protestants and Catholics to its cause, its insistence in confrontational tactics soon became a cushion for the more malign ambitions of the IRA. See Purdie, Bob, *Politics in the Streets: The Origins of the Civil Rights Movement in Northern Ireland* (Belfast: Blackstaff Press, 1990).
42 See Edwards, Aaron, '"Unionist Derry is Ulster's Panama": The Northern Ireland Labour Party and the Civil Rights Issue', *Irish Political Studies*, Vol. 23, No. 3 (September 2008), pp. 363–385.
43 Heath, Edward, *The Course of My Life: My Autobiography* (London: Hodder and Stoughton, 1998), pp. 428–429.
44 Ibid., p. 428.
45 Ibid., pp. 428–429.
46 Ibid., p. 428.
47 TNA, DEFE 70/214, R.J. Andrew to Graham Angel, 'Secret: Northern Ireland, 4 August 1971'; 'Draft Message to the Prime Minister of Northern Ireland from the Home Secretary'.
48 Iron, Colonel Richard, 'Britain's Longest War: Northern Ireland, 1967–2007' in Marston, Daniel and Carter Malkasian (eds), *Counterinsurgency in Modern Warfare* (Oxford: Osprey, 2008), p. 168.
49 Moloney, Ed, *A Secret History of the IRA*, second edition (London: Penguin, 2007), p. 101. One might also draw the conclusion that the presence of senior Provisional IRA commanders increased friction with the Army

at this time, leading invariably to an upsurge in violence in which a number of people lost their lives.

50 Interview with former senior Special Branch Officers, Belfast, 25 October 2010.
51 TNA, DEFE 13/838, Lieutenant-General Sir Frank King to Merlyn Rees MP, 16 April 1974.
52 Interview with former senior Special Branch Officers, Belfast, 25 October 2010.
53 Public Records Office of Northern Ireland (PRONI), GOV/3/3/1299, Headquarters Northern Ireland Operational Summary for the week ending 0700 hrs 28 January 1972.
54 Ibid.
55 PRONI, GOV/3/3/1299, Headquarters Northern Ireland Operational Summary for the week ending 0700 hrs 4 February 1972.
56 Heath, *The Course of My Life*, p. 430.
57 LHCMA, Cooper Papers, 1/1/3, Round-Up Reports, 18 September 1973.
58 McGrattan, Cillian, *Northern Ireland, 1968–2008: The Politics of Retrenchment* (Basingstoke: Palgrave, 2010), p. 39.
59 Interview with former senior Special Branch Officers, Belfast, 25 October 2010.
60 Ibid.
61 See the comments by General Sir Mike Jackson in his autobiography, *Soldier: The Autobiography* (London: Bantam, 2007); and those made by Bob Stewart MP in House of Commons Debates, 3 November 2010.
62 Even though conventional wisdom suggests that the Army did not have doctrine on Internal Security and counter-insurgency until after the 1980s, it did have huge stockpiles of doctrine on Internal Security operations in the twentieth century. The question, therefore, is not did it have doctrine; rather, the question is who read it? See War Office (WO), *Keeping the Peace: Part 1 – Doctrine*, WO Code No. 9800 (London: The War Office, 7 January 1963); WO, *Keeping the Peace: Part 2 – Tactics and Training*, WO Code No. 9801 (London: The War Office, 16 January 1963). MoD, *Land Operations: Volume III – Counter-Revolutionary Operations, Part 1 – Principles and General Aspects*, Army Code No. 70516, Part 1 (London: HMSO, 29 August 1969); MoD, *Land Operations: Volume III – Counter-Revolutionary Operations, Part 2 – Internal Security*, Army Code No. 70516, Part 2 (London: HMSO, 26 November 1969); MoD, *Land Operations: Volume III – Counter-Revolutionary Operations, Part 3 – Counter Insurgency*, Army Code No. 70516, Part 3 (London: HMSO, 5 January 1970); MoD, *Land Operations: Volume III – Counter-Revolutionary Operations, Part 1 – General Principles*, Army Code No. 70516, Part 1 (London: HMSO, August 1977); MoD, *Land Operations: Volume III – Counter-Revolutionary Operations, Part 2 – Procedures and Techniques*, Army Code No. 70516, Part 2 (London: HMSO, 1977).

63 House of Commons Debates (Hansard), 3 November 2010, Vol. 517, Col. 977.
64 Clarke, A.F.N., *Contact* (London: Secker and Warburg, 1983), p. 32.
65 Benest, David, 'Aden to Northern Ireland, 1966–76', in Strachan, Hew (ed.), *Big Wars and Small Wars: The British Army and the Lessons of War in the Twentieth Century* (Abingdon: Routledge, 2006), p. 130.
66 Interview with a former officer in the Ulster Defence Regiment/Royal Irish Regiment, 22 September 2010.
67 See Ryder, Chris, *The Ulster Defence Regiment: An Instrument of Peace?* (London: Methuen, 1991).
68 Dixon, Paul, 'Counter-Insurgency in Northern Ireland and the Crisis of the British State', in Rich, Paul B. and Richard Stubbs (eds), *The Counter-Insurgent State: Guerrilla Warfare and State Building in the Twentieth Century* (Basingstoke: Macmillan, 1997), p. 189.
69 LHCMA, Cooper Papers, Cooper 1/1/10, 'Verbatim Transcript of Interview with Mr Merlyn Rees on BBC Television Panorama, 8.10pm, 11/1974'.
70 LHCMA, Cooper Papers, Cooper 1/1/13, briefing paper (n.d.).
71 Rees, Merlyn, *Northern Ireland: A Personal Perspective* (London: Methuen, 1985), p. 302.
72 LHCMA, Cooper Papers, Cooper 1/1/13, briefing paper (n.d.).
73 Ibid.
74 LHCMA, Cooper Papers, Cooper 1/1/12, Radio Interview of the Rt. Hon. Merlyn Rees, MP, Secretary of State for Northern Ireland, broadcast on RTE on 2 March 1975.
75 Smith, M.L.R., *Fighting for Ireland? The Military Strategy of the Irish Republican Movement* (London: Routledge, 1997), p. 132.
76 LHCMA, Cooper Papers, Cooper 1/1/1, 'Notes by FC on the Island of Ireland' (n.d.).
77 Bew, Paul and Gordon Gillespie, *Northern Ireland: A Chronology of the Troubles, 1968–1999* (Dublin: Gill and Macmillan, 1999), p. 106.
78 Adams, Gerry, *Hope and History: Making Peace in Ireland* (Dingle: Brandon, 2003), p. 29.
79 Newsinger, John, 'From Counter-insurgency to Internal Security: Northern Ireland, 1969–1992', *Small Wars and Insurgencies*, Vol. 6, No. 1 (spring 1995), p. 99; Peter R. Neumann, 'Winning the "War on Terror"? Roy Mason's Contribution to Counter-Terrorism in Northern Ireland', *Small Wars and Insurgencies*, Vol. 14, No. 3 (autumn 2003), p. 50.
80 TNA, DEFE, 24/1618, Working Party on Law and Order in Northern Ireland: Draft Paper on Future Policing Policy – for Discussion, circulated on 9 June 1977.
81 Rees, *Northern Ireland*, p. 302.
82 Neumann, 'Winning the "War on Terror"?', p. 47.
83 TNA, DEFE 11/918, NI General, Secret: Directive for the General Officer Commanding Northern Ireland as Director of Military Operations, 29 June 1977.

84 Newsinger, 'From Counter-insurgency to Internal Security', p. 99.
85 TNA, DEFE 24/1618, Secret: The Future Role and Organisation of the UDR, HQNI, 22 September 1977.
86 Dewar, *The British Army in Northern Ireland*, p. 154.
87 Hamill, *Pig in the Middle*, p. 226.
88 Ibid., p. 202; Edwards, 'Misapplying Lessons Learned?', pp. 303–330. Interview with former Senior RUC Special Branch officers, 25 October 2010; and 4 April 2011.
89 TNA, DEFE 11/918, 'Correspondence from Roy Mason to Fred Mulley', dated 18 May 1977.
90 Ibid.
91 TNA, PREM 19/41, Cabinet Secretary's Incoming Brief for PM, 4 May 1979.
92 House of Commons Debates (Hansard), 24 May 1979, Vol. 967, Col. 1206.
93 Thatcher, Margaret, *The Downing Street Years* (London: HarperCollins, 1993), p. 57.
94 TNA, PREM 19/80, Letter from Humphrey Atkins to Francis Pym, 19 July 1979.
95 Ibid.
96 Hamill, *Pig in the Middle*, p. 232.
97 TNA, PREM 19/80, Secret briefing on Northern Ireland OD(79), 9 July 1979.
98 Ibid.
99 Interview with former senior Special Branch Officers, Belfast, 25 October 2010.
100 'Obituary of Sir Timothy Creasey', *The Times*, 7 October 1986.
101 TNA, PREM 19/13, Statement by the Prime Minister, the Rt. Hon. Margaret Thatcher MP, 27 August 1979.
102 Urban, Mark, *Big Boys Rules: The SAS and the Struggle against the IRA* (London: Faber, 1992), p. 90.
103 TNA, FCO 87/975, Letter from Sir Frank Cooper, MoD, to Ken Stowe CB, NIO, dated 24 September 1979.
104 TNA, FCO 87/975, undated telegram from London to Dublin.
105 House of Commons Debates (Hansard), 11 December 1979, Vol. 975, Col. 1094.
106 'Sir John Hermon – Obituary', *The Times*, 8 November 2008.
107 House of Commons Debates (Hansard), 6 March 1980, Vol. 980, Col. 651.
108 House of Commons Debates (Hansard), 8 May 1980, Vol. 984, Col. 510.
109 Fuller, Colonel J.F.C. *The Reformation of War* (London: Hutchinson and Company, 1923), p. 201.
110 Iron, Colonel Richard, 'Exploiting Doctrine . . . From the Other Side of the Hill', *British Army Review*, No. 132 (Summer 2003), p. 26.
111 'Sir John Hermon – Obituary', *The Times*, 8 November 2008.

112 For more information on this special unit and the formation of the RUC's elite counter-terrorist capability see Holland, Jack and Susan Phoenix, *Phoenix: Policing the Shadows* (London: Hodder and Stoughton, 1996); see also Urban, *Big Boys Rules*.
113 Interview with a founding member of the RUC's 'Special Support Unit', Belfast, 25 October 2010.
114 Gray, Colin S., *Explorations in Strategy* (Westport, CT: Greenwood Press, 1996), p. 173.
115 Neumann, Peter R., *Britain's Long War: British Strategy in the Northern Ireland Conflict, 1969–98* (Basingstoke: Palgrave, 2003), pp. 163–165.
116 Interview with Tommy Gorman, Belfast, 23 June 2010. Gorman was an operations officer for the Belfast Brigade of the Provisional IRA.
117 O'Doherty, Malachi, *The Trouble with Guns: Republican Strategy and the Provisional IRA* (Belfast: Blackstaff, 1998), p. 157.
118 Urban, *Big Boys Rules*, p. 247.
119 Kitson, Frank, *Directing Operations* (London: Faber, 1989), pp. 60–61.
120 Interview with former senior RUC/PSNI Special Branch officers, Belfast, 25 October 2010.
121 Ibid.
122 Ibid. For more on this controversial point see Edwards, Aaron, 'Deterrence, Coercion and Brute Force in Asymmetric Conflict: The Role of the Military Instrument in Resolving the Northern Ireland "Troubles"', *Dynamics of Asymmetric Conflict*, Vol. 4, No. 3 (December 2011) pp. 226–241.
123 Tendler, Stewart and Jill Sherman, 'MI5 to Lead Fight Against IRA', *The Times*, 9 May 1992.
124 Clarke, Liam, 'Minister's Secret Peace Plan with IRA', *The Sunday Times*, 22 August 1993.
125 Ibid.
126 Interview with General Sir Roger Wheeler, Warminster, 28 January 2011.
127 Ibid.
128 Interview with former senior RUC/PSNI Special Branch officers, Belfast, 25 October 2010 and 4 April 2011.
129 Interview with Patrick Mercer MP, London, 25 January 2011. A former British Army colonel, Mercer was posted to HQNI in the early 1990s and had intimate knowledge of the ProExComm.
130 Information taken from Edmunds, Russell, 'Obituary: Francis Thomas Murray', *Herald Scotland*, 23 March 1996 and from private information.
131 Adams, *Selected Writings*, p. 278.
132 McAuley, James W., Catherine McGlynn and Jon Tonge, 'Conflict Resolution in Asymmetric and Symmetric Situations: Northern Ireland as a Case-Study', *Dynamics of Asymmetric Conflict*, Vol. 1, No. 1 (2008), p. 99.

133 Angstrom, Jan and Isabelle Duyvesteyn (eds), *Understanding Victory and Defeat in Contemporary War* (Abingdon: Routledge, 2007).
134 Interview with a former Officer Commanding from the King's Own Scottish Borders, Sandhurst, 16 February 2011.
135 Interview with Tommy Gorman, Belfast, 23 June 2010.
136 Interview with Danny Morrison, Belfast, 23 November 2010.
137 Ibid.
138 Interview with a former Officer Commanding from the KOSB, Sandhurst, 16 February 2011.
139 Interview with former Senior Special Branch Officers, Belfast, 4 April 2011.
140 Interview with Lieutenant-General Sir Philip Trousdell, Sandhurst, 2011.
141 Defence: Second Report, dated 12 December 2001. www.parliament.the-stationery-office.co.uk/pa/cm200102/cmselect/cmdfence/348/34807.htm#a12. Accessed: 14 July 2011.
142 Jackson, *Soldier*.
143 Benest, 'Aden to Northern Ireland', p. 130.
144 Callwell, Colonel Charles Edward, *Small Wars: Their Principles and Practice*, third edition (London: HMSO, 1906), p. 68.
145 PRONI, GOV 3/17/3, Correspondence between Lieutenant-General Sir Harry Tuzo and the Governor of Northern Ireland, Lord Grey of Naunton, relating to the security situation in border areas, dated 4 and 7 September 1971.
146 Evelegh, Robin, *Peace-keeping in a Democratic Society: The Lessons of Northern Ireland* (London: Hurst, 1978), p. 110.
147 Ibid., p. 37.

7

Return to Mesopotamia: the politics of military intervention in Iraq

> Imperialism imagines that we do not know it, and I think it is legitimate for those responsible for leading a nation, trade union or a military unit, to allow their enemy to imagine that they are ignorant about him. Thus, when confronting the enemy they do not necessarily have to reveal all their knowledge to make him blunder and to fall under the impression that they do not know their next move while making preparation to confront him in a manner that may inflict upon him the heaviest of losses.[1]

> We saw ourselves, as indeed we were, as part of a multinational coalition which was American-led. We didn't see ourselves as a little England in the southeast doing a national effort. It just wasn't like that.[2]

> We do not operate in any sort of political vacuum – far from it![3]

Introduction

Britain's military intervention in Iraq from 2003 was one of the most controversial foreign policy decisions since the Suez crisis in 1956. It prompted heated exchanges between politicians at Westminster, resignations from cabinet ministers in Whitehall, and mass anti-war demonstrations in London and in other cities around the United Kingdom. Yet, New Labour remained undeterred in its decision to commit British troops to the US-led 'liberation' of Iraq. Shortly before he ordered 46,000 British combat troops into action, Prime Minister Tony Blair reminded the House of Commons that 'Iraq's weapons of mass destruction and long range missiles, and its continuing non-compliance with Security Council Resolutions, pose a threat to international peace and security'.[4]

Though few could have forecasted it at the time, the unfolding events in Iraq would rupture Britain's strategic outlook, undermine the *jus ad bellum* (i.e. law on the use of force) arguments for intervention, and lead to a serious underestimation of the rapid deterioration in the Iraqi security situation after the fall of Baghdad,[5] and place interminable stress on the armed forces to the point where they stared defeat in the face in Southern Iraq.[6] The ending of British combat operations in the summer of 2009 signalled an ignominious withdrawal from the country. Intervention in Iraq may have been designed to disarm the Iraqi regime, but, as Steve Hewitt concludes, the 'overselling of the threat of Saddam Hussein's Iraq represents a microcosm of the Blair government's approach to the domestic war on terror'.[7] In terms of Blair's legacy, writes political scientist Dennis Kavanagh, the Iraq war 'has further radicalized Muslims across the world and probably increased the threat of terrorism'.[8] Moreover, the 'ethical dimension', which had hitherto underpinned Labour's foreign policy, was by now synonymous with the doctrine of liberal interventionism.[9] With the benefit of hindsight, though, Britain's Mesopotamia adventure was more of a direct result of Labour's traditional foreign policy[10] than its turn to moralism, as well as a longer-term consequence of corrosion in the state's strategic culture.[11]

New Labour's support for the Israeli–Palestinian peace process and the eradication of the root causes of Islamist terrorism rang hollow when juxtaposed alongside its legacy of bayonet-cushioned diplomacy. In Iraq itself it exploded a potent mix of nationalism, Islamist extremism, terrorism and insurgency, which would fan the flames of sectarianism and push the country to the brink of civil war.[12] At home, the Labour government conceded its mishandling of the intervention. Tired and weary from his relentless battles with Tony Blair, new Prime Minister Gordon Brown moved quickly to establish an inquiry into the affair, appointing the former Permanent Under Secretary at the Northern Ireland Office, Sir John Chilcott, to consider 'the way decisions were made and actions taken', as well as 'to establish, as accurately as possible, what happened and to identify the lessons that can be learned'.[13] The ensuing public hearings would have far-reaching consequences, not least in that they prompted the release into the public domain of an unprecedented level of secret correspondence and intelligence reports, throwing into sharp relief Britain's maladroit intervention in the internal affairs of this highly combustible Middle Eastern state. In hindsight, Blair's decision to rid the world of Saddam Hussein and all that he represented would continue to haunt British politics 'like a phantom monster . . . with bloody fangs'[14] long after he stepped down from office.

'Blair's wars'

It is tempting to examine Britain's intervention in Iraq in historical and strategic isolation. Nonetheless, Iraq formed part of what John Kampfner brilliantly characterized as 'Blair's wars'; a litany of five conflicts – Iraq (1998), Kosovo (1999), Sierra Leone (2000), Afghanistan (2001–)

and Iraq again (2003–09) – that soon became synonymous with Blair's personal 'naivety and hubris'.[15] 'Blair's wars' were the direct consequence of the failure by the previous Conservative governments to intervene more robustly in places as diverse as Somalia, Rwanda and Bosnia. Britain's new ethical impulse, according to its chief proponent Robin Cook, owed much to the 'unethical' practices of John Major's government, which included, amongst other things, the arming of Saddam Hussein in the Iraq 'supergun' affair.[16] Compounding the dearth of ethical decision-making in Conservative foreign policy, according to Lawrence Freedman, was Major's 'unenthusiastic' approach to humanitarian intervention.[17] In advocating a much more activist-led policy in foreign affairs, writes Christopher Hill, 'Cook was changing at least the language of post-war British foreign policy' by placing respect for human rights, democracy and other British values at the heart of his programme for the Foreign and Commonwealth Office.[18]

Indeed, there was a degree of truth in Cook's criticisms of previous government policy. In his memoirs, Major made it clear that he 'often used overseas trips to combine foreign policy with British economic interest',[19] while Douglas Hurd displayed suspicion towards 'the straightforward, violent solution to international problems'.[20] However, that the Tories preferred diplomatic overtures ahead of plainly coercive measures is frequently overlooked by commentators when examining the legacy of New Labour's foreign and defence policies. If nothing else, Britain's role in Bosnia encapsulated the fraught attempts by military commanders, politicians and civil servants in Whitehall to respond robustly to a dangerously fluid situation in the Former Republic of Yugoslavia. For Brendan Simms, 'the presence of British troops in the war-torn country, provided Whitehall with a figleaf to conceal its politico-military unwillingness to confront Bosnian Serb aggression'.[21] Yet in many respects Simms critiqued Britain's position in Bosnia without asking probing questions about the responsibilities of other states, especially the US. One could argue that the international community was broadly complicit in standing idly by as ethnic-fuelled aggression gripped cities from Mostar to Srebrenica. Nevertheless, Labour proposed a 'wider, more "comprehensive approach" to international affairs, alongside both the Foreign and Commonwealth Office (FCO) and the newly created Department for International Development (DFID)'.[22] It was a course of action, moreover, that promised to be, above all, proactive. Politically, the direct genealogy of liberal interventionism in Labour's outlook can be traced back as early as 1995, when Robin Cook publicly chastised the world for not 'lifting a gun barrel to halt the genocide last year' in Rwanda.[23]

In a major foreign policy speech at the Economic Club in Chicago on 24 April 1999, Tony Blair vowed never to allow such narrow self-interest to jeopardize the lives of others and thought that 'our actions are guided by a more subtle blend of mutual self interest and moral purpose in defending the values we cherish'.[24] He singled out 'two dangerous and ruthless men' for special attention, Slobodan Milosevic and Saddam Hussein, who he claimed had 'been prepared to wage vicious campaigns against sections of their own community'. In relation to the Kosovo conflict, he reminded his audience how:

> This is a just war, based not on any territorial ambitions but on values. We cannot let the evil of ethnic cleansing stand. We must not rest until it is reversed. We have learned twice before in this century that appeasement does not work. If we let an evil dictator range unchallenged, we will have to spill infinitely more blood and treasure to stop him later.[25]

Britain, no more than the US, contended Blair and his coterie of cabinet ministers and unelected advisors, could afford to stand by as 'genocide', 'ethnic cleansing' and other atrocities were taking place, even if that meant potentially breaching the norm of non-intervention.

After winning the landslide general election in May 1997, Blair and New Labour set about the task of reconfiguring Britain's foreign and defence policy. Having formally committed themselves to a defence review in opposition, they commissioned a Strategic Defence Review (SDR) in May 1997, which had been envisaged to take only six months but would not be published until some fourteen months later in July 1998. The SDR was different from the earlier Options for Change Defence Review in 1990, which, according to one senior general[26] based in the Ministry of Defence (MoD) at the time,

> was an entirely arbitrary financial figure which the government of the day imposed on us and said the army was to be 125,000, including 20,000 recruits, which was the intake at that stage every year. It didn't tell us what we were for – any of the three services – and the Secretary of State at the time used to talk about 'small' and 'better' and 'peace dividend'. And that there was never going to be another war. And looking at what has happened since is a strange thing to say. And bear in mind for the past 30 years we had been fixed in central Europe . . . except for Northern Ireland.[27]

There is certainly evidence to suggest that in 1989–90, with the Berlin Wall crumbling, the government had not engaged in much of what today might be called 'horizon scanning'. Some Tory ministers seemed to completely miss the fact that an armed conflict involving Britain in the Middle East was a growing possibility. As General Wheeler remarked: 'We asked the government for a defence review and for some reason the Conservative government had a complete hang-up about a defence review and wouldn't do it.'[28]

New Labour, however, had other plans for defence, which it had outlined in its 1997 election manifesto:

> Labour will conduct a strategic defence and security review to reassess our essential security interests and defence needs. It will consider how the roles, missions and capabilities of our armed forces should be adjusted to meet the new strategic realities. The review we propose will be foreign policy led, first assessing our likely overseas commitments and interests and then establishing how our forces should be deployed to meet them.[29]

Blair appointed his Secretary of State for Defence, George Robertson, to lead the SDR process. As General Wheeler, who was by then Chief of the General Staff (CGS), recalled:

> [W]hen the government arrived in 1997 we hadn't had one [a Strategic Defence Review] for a while and we were now in a completely different strategic situation from where we had been in 1989. And the government arrived with a very clear idea that they needed a strategic defence review, and the first documents that were produced were produced by the Foreign Office, which said what our national interests were and then we had the defence review run by George Robertson, the Secretary of State, in a way that we had not had anything in a long, long time. There were 50 study groups – each one run by a one-star person – from the nuclear deterrent on one end of the scale to how do you deliver supplies to the chain of command in a deployed formation at the other end. And the Secretary of State chaired a meeting with the Chiefs of Staff twice a week from 3 January to the 29 March 1998.[30]

The SDR envisaged the armed forces being a 'force for good', a catchy by-line later formally incorporated into British defence policy,[31] and given prominence by an MoD eager to sink its teeth into this new form of expeditionary warfare and thereby free itself from the shackles of a strategic cul-de-sac in Europe. New Labour's concept of the armed forces as a 'force for good' would have profound repercussions in the post-9/11 world.

The role of the armed forces altered dramatically under the SDR, in so far as the emphasis for delivering strategic effect shifted towards what were called 'key enablers', such as signallers, engineers and logistical support troops. It was the foundations laid by the SDR that placed the armed forces, and the Army in particular, on a new footing, meaning that 'in the post-Cold War world', as Robertson stated in his preface to the SDR, 'we must be prepared to go to the crisis, rather than have the crisis come to us'.[32] This was something openly admitted by Roger Wheeler on the eve of the twenty-first century, when he told an audience at the Royal United Services Institute (RUSI):

> I should stress two points: first multinationality is here to stay either in formal alliances such as NATO or in coalitions of the willing. Secondly, although some people speak of 'wars of choice', where participation is discretionary because many of these operations do not threaten the UK directly, the fact is that if we want to maintain our position as a leading player in NATO and on the UN Security Council we may well have an obligation to contribute even when we would rather not.[33]

The SDR talked up the potential strategic edge which 'key enablers' could bring for Britain's projection of force. They were the new 'means' by which Britain's security ends could be achieved; and they were to be built on a new internal culture of 'jointery' within the armed forces – and eventually across the FCO and DFID – that could be harnessed to make force much more readily employable. That Britain owed much to its subscription to multilateral institutions, such as NATO and the UN, and to its involvement in 'coalitions of the willing' with the US, to deliver real strategic effect, is self-evident. However, while Operations Desert Fox in Iraq, Allied Force in Kosovo and Palliser/Barras in Sierra Leone established Britain in the front rank of states with an 'ethical dimension' to their foreign policies, the truth was that these short-term, one-off interventions were all limited in scope and – with the exception of Sierra Leone – were multinational efforts. The use of the military instrument in these three cases – for limited, clear-cut and popular ends – had nonetheless won New Labour plaudits from the international community, even if they demonstrated nothing more than the 'effortless superiority of Western conventional forces against third-rate opposition'.[34] Things were to change dramatically at the dawn of a new decade.

The terrorist attacks in New York and Washington on 11 September 2001 (known popularly ever since as 9/11) redefined the way Britain's military forces were to be utilized by the government. The origins of this brand of 'mass casualty' terrorism lie in the dying days of the Cold War, when Soviet imperial overstretch met with fierce resistance from the Afghan Mujahedeen, most of whose weapons had been spirited into the country by the US Central Intelligence Agency (CIA) and British Secret Intelligence Service (SIS).[35] Out of the embers of the ensuing Soviet defeat sprang the rekindled flames of Islamist extremism and, in 1988–89, the formation of Al Qaeda by Saudi playboy Osama bin Laden.[36] Although bin Laden declared war on the US and its allies in the late 1990s, few inside the US administrations of Bill Clinton and George W. Bush took the threat seriously until the attacks on 9/11. When the attacks came, the US won the immediate sympathy of people across the world. The decision by President Bush to target the Taliban regime in Afghanistan, which had harboured the terrorists, was met with unanimous approval. Nonetheless, the military operations undertaken by the US and Britain to topple the Taliban and rout Al Qaeda would set in train a process that Cook later warned would 'deliver the very divide between the West and the Islamic countries that Osama bin Laden had desired'.[37] The irony, of course, is that Cook was willing to countenance force without a UN Security Council mandate when it came to Kosovo.

Throughout 2002 and into 2003 the Prime Minister consistently articulated the view that Saddam Hussein's regime was 'despicable' and could not be left 'unchecked'; importantly, though, he did not yet publicly advocate action against the Iraqi dictator outside of the UN framework.[38] Peter Mandelson, Blair's close friend and confidant, made the telling observation that the Prime Minister often

> worked from first principles. Where Iraq was concerned, these soon overwhelmed everything else. They led to a kind of tunnel vision, which got in the way of dealing thoroughly with some of the political nuances, and practical implications, of the campaign against Saddam.[39]

In very real terms the tendency to overlook the 'policy detail' in favour of 'big concepts' meant that Blair always kept the flame of military action against Saddam's regime alive when he constantly reminded MPs how the Iraqi dictator presided over 'one of the most repressive, murderous and barbaric regimes in the world'.[40] His interjections to ongoing debates about Iraq and WMD were vintage Tony Blair, the 'master persuader with the silver tongue', as the *Guardian's* Polly Toynbee observed, who could 'cut seductively through complexity to belief'.[41]

The slow drum-beat of war

The decision to intervene in Iraq was taken by a Prime Minister who relied disproportionately on his unelected advisers – what Anthony Seldon has cleverly labelled the 'denocracy'[42] – and an increasingly presidential style, tempered by extraordinary self-confidence and what Jonathan Powell has called 'his messianic belief in other contexts'.[43] There is considerable truth in this interpretation, not least evidenced in Blair's own memoirs, that toppling Saddam was necessary, if for no other reason than his 'influence within the region was both poisonous and repressive'.[44] For President George W. Bush Iraq, however, represented something more immediately dangerous to American national security, as he later disclosed in his memoirs:

> For my first eight months in office, my policy focused on tightening the sanctions – or, as Colin Powell put it, keeping Saddam in his box. Then 9/11 hit, and we had to take a fresh look at every threat in the world. There were state sponsors of terror. There were sworn enemies of America. There were hostile governments that threatened their neighbors. There were nations that violated international demands. There were dictators who repressed their people. And there were regimes that pursued WMD. Iraq combined all those threats.[45]

The decisions which Blair and Bush took in authorizing the use of force against Saddam's regime were tortuous ones, reached through a complex mosaic of fact and conjecture. Yet, as we now know, they were taken largely because of intelligence obtained at the time that painted the Iraqi dictator as a real threat to international security, something elaborated in the UN Security Council's Resolution 1441, which recognized 'the threat Iraq's non-compliance with Council resolutions and proliferation of weapons of mass destruction and long-range missiles poses to international peace and security'.[46] The dilemma for London and Washington was whether they could secure a second resolution legitimizing the use of force by the only international organization able to do so. The evidence that Saddam possessed weapons of mass destruction (WMD) was said to have been a 'slam dunk' by the then CIA Director, George Tenet, who assured Bush that the US had strong and verifiable intelligence.[47] Nonetheless, some members of the UN Security Council remained impervious to British and American calls for intervention.

Had Blair scrutinized the detailed evidence presented in the intelligence reports more openly and objectively, he would have reached the somewhat prosaic conclusion that Saddam did not possess any viable WMD. Indeed, the London-based think-tank the International Institute for Strategic Studies (IISS) had had its report on the issue plundered in lieu of accurate and actionable intelligence from state agencies. The IISS report on Iraq's WMD capabilities made clear that: 'The retention of WMD capacities by Iraq is self-evidently the core objective of the regime, for it has sacrificed all other domestic and foreign policy goals to this singular aim.'[48] Yet Blair and his government marshalled the speculative findings of the IISS report as evidence of the Iraqi dictator's duplicity. As Blair concluded at the time:

> Saddam has used chemical weapons, not only against an enemy state, but against his own people. Intelligence reports make clear that he sees the building up of his WMD capability, and the belief overseas that he would use these weapons, as vital to his strategic interests, and in particular his goal of regional domination. And *the document discloses that his military planning allows for some of the WMD to be ready within 45 minutes of an order to use them.*[49]

While Blair may not have known the quality of the human intelligence (HUMINT) reporting back to Washington and London on Saddam's WMD programme, he nonetheless made a decision based on instinct.[50] Recruiting informers inside the Iraqi regime was difficult, if not close to impossible, for British and American intelligence services. As the head of SIS between 1999 and 2004, Sir Richard Dearlove, admitted to the Iraq Inquiry:

> But bear in mind, as I say, recruiting sources with access, with a regime like this – it's easy to recruit people who don't have access, but to get people who really know secrets or are close to the heart of the regime, this is tough, not impossible.[51]

The difficulty with the intelligence picture more generally, mused Dearlove's counterpart at Thames House, Eliza Manningham-Buller, was that it remained incomplete.[52] Politicians, however, deal with facts and presentation. Unfortunately, Colin Powell, Bush's Secretary of State, deployed what amounted to only a fragmentary picture of Iraq's WMD programme as a crutch in his representations to the UN. Powell, remarked chief weapons inspector Hans Blix, had 'the thankless task of hauling out the smoking guns that in January were said to be irrelevant and that, after March, turned out to be nonexistent'.[53] It later emerged that not only had Britain's intelligence product been unsound, but that the US had failed to review HUMINT provided by German intelligence, known by his code-name 'curveball'. In David Omand's opinion, '[t]here can be little doubt that in both the US and the UK the intelligence/policy relationship was put under huge strain by the intervention in Iraq'.[54] The issue of intelligence pointed towards the dearth of credible information upon which to make strategic choices. It would only get worse.

Debates in the House of Commons intensified over the weeks leading up to the invasion. In mid-February 2003 upwards of one million people marched in London against the prospects of war. It prompted one of New Labour's high-profile Cabinet Ministers, Robin Cook, to resign. Addressing the Commons from the backbenches he urged a rethink of the policy. Meanwhile, one of the most vocal anti-war MPs, Clare

Short, made herself unavailable rather than face questions from Labour backbenchers. On the occasion of the crucial eve of war debate she travelled to New York and Washington to co-ordinate humanitarian efforts for post-war reconstruction.[55] Despite her misgivings Short nevertheless chose to remain a cabinet minister, preferring to 'stay on throughout and use whatever influence I had to persuade Blair to stay with the UN'. 'This was an agonising time for me', Short later wrote, 'But I was also desperately worried about the consequences for Iraq, the Middle East and the authority of the UN. I was also worried about the consequences for the Labour government.'[56]

There were concerns raised among some backbenchers that the Cabinet had been overwhelmed by Blair's presidential style. Historically, this was a reoccurring problem in at least two of the post-1945 Labour governments. For instance, the former Deputy Leader of the Labour Party, George Brown, resigned in 1967 over the issue of Prime Minister Harold Wilson's presidential style, citing a closed decision-making process and tendency to engage in 'group think'. As Brown observed in his memoirs:

> You must have effective Cabinet Government if democracy is to survive. If you don't have it, and you have instead all the powers of patronage, of 'leaking', of manipulating the Parliamentary Party against whichever of your colleagues is for the moment out of favour, it doesn't seem to me that you can have effective democracy.[57]

Standing by his decision, as Brown had done almost 40 years before him, Cook chose his resignation speech in the Commons to highlight how Britain's 'interests are best protected not by unilateral action but by multilateral agreement and a world order governed by rules'.[58] Writing in *The Guardian*, Polly Toynbee noted how:

> As the monumental debate batted back and forth all day in the Commons, there was a strange disjuncture as the two arguments failed to engage with one another. The moral case on both sides grew increasingly specious and disingenuous, with the innocent Iraqi citizens tugged this way and that: one side stood for their freedom from tyranny, the other for their freedom from bombing.[59]

By now Blair 'was trapped in the logic of his own earlier positions'.[60] The sabre which Blair had become no stranger in rattling on the world stage would be dramatically unsheathed in Whitehall as he deployed the armed forces in what would later be called the greatest failure of British policy since the appeasement of Nazi Germany in 1938 and the Suez debacle in 1956.

That no second UN resolution was forthcoming meant that Blair essentially followed the same path that he had walked down with many of his senior cabinet colleagues before in relation to Kosovo. While he considered the legality of the use of force he was about to authorize, it became much more of a 'moral case for action', Blair later wrote, that was 'never absent from my psyche'.[61] The same, however, may not have been true of the Americans, who were not subject to the same constraints in the rules-based system, above all because of their pre-eminent position as the world's only superpower. Bush, and his allies in London, might well have thought of Hans Morgenthau's observation of the fledgling UN in 1945, when he asked, 'Which nation that feels itself strong enough to get what it wants by threat or actual use of force will invite an international court to tell the world that international law, as it exists, gives it no title to what it wants?'[62] The question on this occasion was, of course, rhetorical. Nevertheless, one could be forgiven for thinking that the US now asked itself the same question in relation to the Iraq War. For the most part, the Iraq crisis provoked what Thakur and Sidhu have characterized as 'a multiple assault on the foundations and rules of the existing UN-centred world order'.[63] They cite Kofi Annan, who famously declared the crisis to have been 'a fork in the road . . . a moment no less decisive than 1945 itself, when the United Nations was founded'.[64] In the end, the intelligence, however flawed, pointed to Saddam's duplicity and Blair became a willing participant in the process now moving ever closer to intervention: troops from the so-called 'coalition of the willing' were ordered to the Iraqi border with Kuwait.[65]

In light of these events it could be argued that the process by which British troops were committed to the US-led 'Operation Iraqi Freedom' is perhaps less important than the question: were they suitably prepared to participate in what turned out to be an enduring military intervention? Allegations abound that the Armed Forces were ill-equipped to mount full-scale combat operations in the country.[66] The Chief of the Defence Staff (CDS) at the time, Rear Admiral Sir Michael Boyce, later told the Iraq Inquiry that in the run-up to war he was 'not allowed to speak, for example, to the Chief of Defence Logistics', Air Chief Marshall Sir Malcolm Pledger, by the Secretary of State for Defence

> because of the concern about it becoming public knowledge that we were planning for a military contribution which might have derailed one thought [sic] it might have stopped [sic] or be completely unhelpful in the activity going on in the United Nations to secure what subsequently turned out to be UN Security Council Resolution 1441.[67]

Consequently, planning assumptions for the imminent invasion were hastily put together 'on the fly' and relied on scant intelligence and information about the country's complex human terrain.[68] There is even evidence to suggest that senior officers in the MoD were 'under pressure to find intelligence that could reinforce the case' for invasion, despite its 'sparse and inconclusive' nature.[69] To put it another way, observed Hew Strachan,

> British forces were committed to Iraq before the criteria for war proposed by British campaign planners were fulfilled, and in particular in the certain knowledge that there was no structure for the post-conflict phase of occupation, despite that being a key element of any 'three-block' war.[70]

The plan for post-war reconstruction was in fact non-existent; the emphasis was much more on liberating the country from the evil hold of Saddam and his sons.

That the visible build-up of military force would succeed in providing a deterrent effect was something completely lost on Blair. As it happened though the PM and his advisors were increasingly paranoid about the impression it might give to the British public, who they had left largely unprepared for a major military commitment. As the CGS at the time (subsequently the CDS), Sir Michael Walker, later revealed, 'I think all Chiefs knew that we were having great difficulty being allowed to talk about stuff, being allowed to order stuff, being allowed to do the sorts of things we felt were essential precursors to any activity of that sort.'[71] On this occasion the military instrument was firmly subordinated to New Labour's policy as Blair became evermore staunch in his public determination to rid the world of Saddam's regime. The PM urged Parliament to support tougher action, including, crucially, armed intervention:

> This is not the time to falter. This is the time not just for this Government – or, indeed, for this Prime Minister – but for this House to give a lead: to show that we will stand up for what we know to be right; to show that we will confront the tyrannies and dictatorships and terrorists who put our way of life at risk; to show, at the moment of decision, that we have the courage to do the right thing.[72]

The Permanent Under Secretary at the MoD during this period was Sir Kevin Tebbitt, who subsequently informed the Inquiry that committing troops to Iraq was now a foregone conclusion: removing Saddam had become 'a vital security issue' for the UK.[73]

The strain placed on the armed forces by the intervention became immediately apparent as invasion forces rumbled over Iraq's borders. An internal MoD memorandum even warned ministers that:

> It will be necessary to draw down our current commitment to nearer a third by no later than autumn in order to avoid long term damage to the Armed Forces. Keeping more forces in Iraq would be outside our current Defence Planning Assumptions.[74]

It was a viewpoint grounded in a defence posture geared towards a one-off, short-term intervention, not an enduring campaign, as the SDR's 'New Chapter' of 2002 made clear. Operations were becoming strained and it was felt that, in the wake of 9/11, 'several smaller scale operations are potentially more demanding than one or two more substantial operations. And there are now signs that frequent, smaller operations are becoming the pattern.'[75]

The evidence upon which the decision to invade Iraq was based remains questionable. Indeed, the so-called 'dodgy dossier' was punctuated with conjecture, baseless allegations and speculation. The second part of the dossier simply profiled the internal security apparatus responsible for repressing the Iraqi people. One extract reads:

> The Iraqi security organisations work together to conceal documents, equipment, and materials.
>
> The Regime has intensified efforts to hide documents in places where they are unlikely to be found, such as private homes of low-level officials and universities. There are prohibited materials and documents being relocated to agricultural areas and private homes or hidden beneath hospitals and even mosques.
>
> This material is being moved constantly, making it difficult to trace or find without absolutely fresh intelligence.[76]

Meanwhile, back in Downing Street, the campaign was being carefully managed for public consumption. The narrative of 'shock and awe' from 35,000 feet, precision guided-missile technology and decapitation soon gave way to a ground invasion.

'The cupboard is totally bare': the politics of occupation

For members of Britain's armed forces who crossed over the Iraq–Kuwait border in March 2003, their immediate priority was to overthrow Saddam and disarm Iraq of its WMD, which he was rumoured to possess in vast quantities. Yet, as Robin Cook later conceded, even he had 'overstated Saddam's weapons capacity. The cupboard is totally bare.'[77] Sidestepping the issue somewhat, President Bush announced an end to major combat operations. The Coalition now had the unenviable position of being legally responsible for an entire state under Common

Article 2(2) of the Geneva Conventions.[78] They immediately formed the Coalition Provisional Authority (CPA), an interim body that oversaw the day-to-day administration of Iraq while embarking on a state-building mission. The CPA was based in what became known as the 'Green Zone', a heavily fortified compound in Baghdad that also doubled as the headquarters of all multinational forces in Iraq. Now that the Saddam regime had been toppled, British and American diplomats and soldiers set about trying to fill the vacuum.

The chaos now developing in Iraq nevertheless provided the military with the opportunity to step into the breach, especially when the CPA's lack of imagination became palpable. Hillary Synnott, who was the British representative on the CPA responsible for the south east, claimed that:

> Without an operational plan or the resources to fulfil one, the civilian arm had little to contribute to military strategic or tactical planning. The Army therefore had no option but to try to deal with the challenges themselves, so as to reduce the damaging security side-effects . . . In essence, if the CPA, the designated instrument, were not up to the job, then the Army would take it on themselves. The collective military experience of civil-military operations in Northern Ireland and the Balkans, among other theatres, instilled in them a justifiable confidence that they could have a shot at it. Anyway, there was no other choice.[79]

As the army grappled with a deteriorating security situation, without much relevant strategic guidance from London, they overreached on their 'collective experience' by misapplying the lessons of the last campaign (i.e. Northern Ireland) to a completely new environment. Sir John Keegan noted enthusiastically: 'What had worked in Belfast could be made to work also in Basra, against another set of urban terrorists, with a different motivation from the Irish Republican though equally as nasty.'[80] Keegan's comments are symptomatic of the Polaroid snapshots of past operations that have informed British military thinking since 1945. However persuasive they might at first appear, these comments betray a much more sophisticated understanding of the processes that eventually produced the conditions that led to success in Britain's small wars. If we take the example of Northern Ireland, the case most enthusiastically cited by British officers in Basra at the time, there are grounds for justifiable criticism.

Unsurprisingly, intervention in Iraq soon stretched the armed forces to the limit. As the weeks and months of the occupation wore on, the situation changed, becoming more fluid and dangerous, and left the British Army on a Peace Support Operations footing. Ironically, few took the claims of a developing insurgency seriously.[81] British military operations were in a state of flux. While there is certainly evidence that counter-insurgency doctrine existed, albeit with some dispute over its origin and the weight given to it by military commanders, there was much less evidence that it was being read.[82] It was hopelessly unrealistic for British troops to maintain a PSO stance, albeit one based on counter-insurgency principles, amidst what had become a counter-insurgency war.[83] As Robin Cook noted in his diary at the time, Britain 'will never make a success of our presence in Iraq if we refuse to come to terms with reality'.[84] There was a complete refusal to concede that the hasty intervention cum occupation had fomented an insurgency on the one hand, while serving as a force multiplier for terrorists like Al Qaeda in Iraq, who thrived on people's uncertainties and fears, on the other.

Within a matter of weeks of the invasion Blair and Bush were holding a 'war summit' at Hillsborough Castle against the immediate backdrop of a crucial pinch-point in the Northern Ireland peace process. One observer noted how 'Both George Bush and Tony Blair have huge belief in their individual powers of persuasion. If their will is clearly seen – especially if the President's will is seen – even the hardest men of Ulster may take note.'[85] While Bush's presence may have persuaded the 'hardest men of Ulster' to take note, it had a negligible effect on the hardest men of Iraq. The faltering 'peace process' probably compared unfavourably with what Washington and London had intended. For historian Niall Ferguson, the US was continually haunted by the 'uninvited guest' of 'the ghost of empire past' at these and subsequent summits between the two leaders over the next twelve months.[86] As Bush outlined his plans for the rebuilding of Iraq, Americans sought to absolve themselves of any charge that their country 'bore more than a family resemblance to empires of the past', to paraphrase Professor Michael Cox.[87] Nevertheless, in Ferguson's opinion:

> The lessons of empire are not the kind of lessons Americans like to learn. It's more comforting to go on denying that America is in the empire business. But the time has come to get real. Iraqis themselves will be the biggest losers if the United States cuts and runs. Fear of the wrong quagmire could consign them to a terrible hell.[88]

The CPA immediately ran into problems, not least from Iraqis who saw few real benefits in the upheaval that followed. Writing in his political memoirs one former Iraqi minister recalled how:

> The USA and its allies, mainly Britain, after June 2004, had to navigate through the murky institutions of the Iraqi government, pushing, cajoling and warning, if necessary, while paying something more than lip service to the sovereign government.[89]

As politicians and diplomats talked, however, the security situation worsened. By now the political vacuum was being filled by a plethora of interest groups; from recently returned exiles wishing to carve out new political and criminal fiefdoms for themselves, to militias and private security contractors keen to exploit the country's misfortunes. For Gareth Stansfield, a 'product of this political uncertainty was the deterioration of security'.[90] Suicide bombings escalated, confidence in the political process suffered several body blows, as looters, Fedayeen Saddam fighters and Al Qaeda-affiliated terrorists were only too happy to exploit the ensuing vacuum caused by regime change.

The American-led coalition struggled to maintain a sense of order as bodies began floating down the Tigris in large numbers, sectarianism drove Shia and Sunnis apart and the troops responded to attacks with heavy-handed tactics that resulted in the deaths of Iraqi civilians. For its part, Britain applied a 'softly softly' colonial policing approach to the security situation in the Shia-dominated south east. 'Soft hat' patrols were everywhere to be seen in Basra province for, as far as the British armed forces were concerned, the root cause of violence was attributable to criminality and could be dealt with by reassuring the local population through a process of 'framework patrolling'. Lessons from PSOs in the Balkans and Internal Security operations in Northern Ireland had taught them the tactical and operational utility of such Tactics, Techniques and Procedures (TTPs). Lieutenant-General Sir Rob Fry captured the mood amongst high-ranking commanders, who tended to rely on hardened experience in lieu of genuine adaptation to this unique environment:

> You would also, had you visited Northern Ireland at any time over the last 20 years, have seen exactly the same mix of techniques there that you see in Basra at the present time. The answer to your question is that there are well worn, well worked procedures for this and the British Army is merely building on the experience it has had for a very long time.[91]

Moreover, British ministers drove the process at the strategic level by articulating the overly optimistic view that Iraqis would be in a position to confront criminality and terrorism on their own within a matter of months,[92] a view shared by their US counterparts.[93] The obsession of handing over to indigenous Iraqi forces was complicated by the CPA's decision to disband the Iraqi army, in large part because of the presence of members of the Ba'ath party, and the US Army's tendency to rely on the disproportionate use of force in lieu of strategy. This was an unwise decision, critiqued on a cross-party basis in Britain by respected politicians Robin Cook, Douglas Hurd and Menzies

Campbell, who penned a strongly worded letter to *The Times* warning of the consequences of the 'heavy-handed deployment of US firepower in urban areas, against repeated British advice, [which] has not weakened the insurgency but strengthened the ambition of most Iraqis for an end to foreign occupation'.[94]

Nonetheless, plundering the historical record for quick-fix solutions from recent operational experience also proved unhelpful in combating growing Iraqi resistance. New Labour claimed that lessons could be learned from Northern Ireland and grafted onto what was perceived to be a similar situation in Southern Iraq. This was a false comparison to draw, in many ways because it ignored the long, painstaking process which British Security Forces underwent in order to defeat the terrorists in Ulster. Nevertheless, the Secretary of State for Defence, John Reid (himself a former Northern Ireland Secretary), wrote at the time:

> Iraqis now have a genuine opportunity to live in freedom and determine their own future. The people of that nation have a chance of achieving a place in Middle Eastern history; free, democratic and prosperous. They will decide how that democracy unfolds, not us. But we have helped to give them the chance and we will stand shoulder to shoulder with them as they do it, and until they do it.[95]

Far from the violence having abated to a level comparable with the tail end of the Northern Ireland 'troubles', the Iraqis were nowhere close to gripping the security situation. Indeed, sectarianism in Iraq was reaching epic proportions. The elections to the Iraqi National Assembly in January and December 2005 were illustrative of the increasing polarization in voting behaviour. While votes were cast for a range of secular and nationalist parties in January; by the time the second election came in December 2005 there had been a hardening of support for Islamist parties.[96]

To a large degree, sectarianism had been fomented by the terrorist group Al Qaeda in Iraq (AQI). Under the command of the Jordanian-born Abu Musab al-Zarqawi, AQI directly targeted the Shia mosque in Samarra in February 2006 as a means of escalating inter-communal violence. It had the desired effect as the body count continued to mount. One study by a team from the Bloomberg School of Public Health at Johns Hopkins University in Baltimore estimated that, by the middle of 2006, 654,965 persons had died since hostilities began in March 2003. Of these, 601,027 died as a direct result of violence, the overwhelming number at the hands of gunmen and car-bombers.[97]

In terms of military operations, 'tweaking the Army's light footprint in Basra only made matters worse,' argued Jonathan Steele, 'something confirmed when attacks against troops began to escalate throughout 2005 and 2006'.[98] As casualty figures doubled in the second half of 2005 Britain's pull back from the provinces of Maysan, Dhi Qar and al Muthanna to Basra was facilitated by the politicians' obsession for a 'conditions-based approach'. However, the truth of the matter was that it had been largely due to pressure from Iraqi political figures and intense anti-war feeling at home that permitted the armed forces the political cover to withdraw to Basra. Meanwhile, Des Browne had taken over at the MoD from John Reid. He was determined to take a more 'hands-on' approach to the campaign than his predecessors, arguing that there was now 'a steady and secure direction of travel, towards democracy, the rule of law, and economic regeneration'.[99] This political methodology depended on the following criteria falling into place: first, that Iraq's security forces could take on responsibility for internal security; and, second, that they could defend state sovereignty and work with the international community in the fight against terrorism. Browne's optimism was all very well but it failed to take into account the changing dynamics of the conflict in Iraq at this time. As Browne argued in the *Sunday Telegraph* at the time:

> Moreover, we need to recognise that some of the problems Basra faces are genuinely different from the rest of Iraq. The terrorist threat in the south is cloaked in a mixture of Shia extremism and criminality. Most of the strikes against Coalition troops are delivered through disparate militia elements funded from outside the area. Sectarian violence provides a backdrop of intimidation, murders and kidnapping. Criminality and political violence pervade society and, arguably, it is this which poses the biggest long-term threat to peace and prosperity there.[100]

Holding fast to the narrative that most of the problems were the result of 'extremism and criminality . . . funded from outside the area' betrayed a more nuanced analysis of the dynamics driving the hostile feelings between the various communities in Iraq and the Coalition forces.

The top general overseeing Britain's operations from Whitehall, General Sir Richard Dannatt, lost no time in intimating that the presence of Britain's forces in the South 'exacerbates the security problems'. His criticism extended deep into the political realm and to his predecessors who were responsible for deploying troops. 'I think history will show that the planning for what happened after the initial successful war-fighting phase was poor,' he said, 'probably based more on optimism than sound planning.'[101]

To counteract the growing resistance to the Coalition's presence and to reduce the effects of Al Qaeda attacks, military commanders invested heavily in Special Forces to deliver a strategic effect in Iraq that conventional troops could not hope to have alone. Beyond stabilization of the security situation the black operations missions overseen by three-star General Stanley McChrystal point to the input of industrial counter-terrorism and its contribution to constraining the options open to AQI.[102] The contribution of Special Forces, in the view of Colin S. Gray, can only be assessed in the context in which they are employed. However, as Gray also reminds us, the utility of Special Forces may not be immediately apparent, particularly if he campaign in which they are involved does not end in an overall victory. In Gray's view, '[p]olitical decision makers and military planners therefore must be aware of the need for special operations to be approached as a component of a broad strategic design'.[103] Beyond a definite operational strike capability against AQI, it is difficult to ascertain the real strategic impact of Special Forces on terrorism and insurgency in the country.

Military operations mounted by Britain's Armed Forces in Iraq pointed to the difficulty of fighting an insurgency when political masters in London were convinced that violence was largely attributable to a steady stream of foreign fighters crossing into the country from elsewhere. Fundamentally, the British had been forced to abandon Maysan province without first eliminating it as a sanctuary for the insurgency. The lessons of counter-insurgency operations in the past were simply ignored and a softer approach – rather than a muscular response – actually made future operations much more difficult for Coalition forces. As one fierce critic of the political–military strategy observed, 'The Army was taking a downstream solution leaving the pipeline open – mopping the floor without first turning off the tap. This was a major strategic error, which was to cost the British the entire campaign.'[104] The British Army was eager to get to grips with Basra, and Malaki's decision to force a hand-over in Maysan provided the opportunity for the retrenchment further south. Operation Sinbad was planned as a way to shift the militias back onto the defensive. However, there were a number of problems with it, as Dan Marston points out:

> Operation SINBAD did not achieve clear, hold, build due to the lack of resources, from both Whitehall and MNC-I, and a lack of political will to see the operation through. The change to countering 'criminality in Basra' in January 2007 did not help the internal debate for a change of strategy in MND (SE).[105]

This took place against the backdrop of a complex emergence of fledgling Iraqi sovereignty and the Iraqi Prime Minister's own political constraints, which made him reluctant to challenge the Shia militias in Sadr City, Baghdad, and in the predominately Shia city of Basra. Unfortunately, Britain's armed forces would continue to be plagued by the ever-present influence of PM Nouri al-Maliki for much of their deployment in Southern Iraq.[106]

The failure of strategy?

In the wake of Richard Dannatt's comments on the naïveté of 'hope' in bringing 'liberal democracy' to Iraq, Tony Blair moved to quash the developing Conservative critique that the government either lacked the nerve or the strategic direction in its handling of the 8,000-strong British force in Iraq:

> I hope that I have just explained very clearly what our strategy is. It is to withdraw progressively as the Iraqi forces build up their capability. For example, in the south of Iraq for the first time, there are 10,000 Iraqi troops who are trained to the fullest extent. They are very capable, and are doing an excellent job under the command of the Iraqi Army – [Interruption.] Yes, of course it is. As we are able to cede control, we do so, but to withdraw prematurely before the job is done would be disastrous.[107]

Despite Blair's assurances, however, Britain had by now settled on withdrawal from the south east before Iraqi security forces were ready to assume control of their own affairs. This premature withdrawal, however, had the adverse effect of creating a vacuum into which the Jaish Al Mahdi (JAM) and other armed groups now moved. As Dannatt himself recognized as early as October 2006:

> History will show that a vacuum was created and into the vacuum malign elements moved. The hope that we might have been able to get out of Iraq in 12, 18, 24 months after the initial start in 2003 has proved fallacious. Now hostile elements have got a hold it has made our life much more difficult in Baghdad and in Basra.[108]

Even amidst Dannatt's comments though there was recognition amongst some government ministers, including Browne, that the British mission was 'not to try to run the country for the Iraqis; nor to try to impose on them our ideal model of democracy – which inevitably reflects our traditions and our history, not theirs'.[109] Browne's comments pointed towards a limited strategy that had more to do with socio-economic transformation as a first step towards stabilizing the security situation. Britain's provincial efforts were to be welcomed, argues Carter Malkasian, 'gaining ground between 2003 and 2007 was a matter of fundamentally reorientating the whole American strategy [in security terms], not just learning new tactics or making a few wiser political decisions'.[110]

Hew Strachan reminds us that '[t]he problem of strategy is located along the fault line between policy and the operational level' of warfare. In this respect, it has not been unknown for politicians in Britain and the US to let military operations – the grammar of war – speak for themselves; consequently leaving 'strategy without a home'.[111] As the former Head of Britain's armed forces, Air Chief Marshal Sir Jock Stirrup, candidly disclosed in his evidence to the Iraq Inquiry, '[t]he problem was that any military approach [in Basra] could only succeed in a political context and we didn't have the political context'.[112] What Stirrup casually overlooked was that it had not specifically been a lack of political direction that was the problem, but the micro-management of British military forces on the ground in southern Iraq that had contributed to the fluid situation. This was amply evidenced by the Armed Forces Minister, Adam Ingram, who thought that the people of Iraq were 'no different from any other country: they want security, they do not want troops on the street; they do not want people being blown up', he argued. In tune with the socio-economic transformation argument, he claimed that most importantly 'they want jobs, they want employment and they want a future for their children – all of which we are seeking to deliver'. Ingram recognized that Britain was seeking to deliver that 'either through the agency of the Iraqi Government or through what we are seeking to do through the developing PRTs [Provincial Reconstruction Teams] or any other reconstruction efforts', but that it was difficult.[113] In perhaps the most galling reference to the alchemy of what now passed as knowledge and 'experience' of British counter-insurgency, Ingram further claimed that:

> This is, as we keep saying, about hearts and minds, and you do not win hearts and minds by military presence; you win it by all the other key ingredients. The hearts and minds are won by what we can do to ensure security, but the continuation of troops on the street is an indication that you are not winning in the other areas.[114]

Conflating a vague impression of Internal Security (and more specifically, MACA, or military aid to the civil authority) operations in Northern Ireland with the situation that had now developed in southern Iraq was a common misperception amongst Whitehall ministers, civil servants and military commanders. Rather than look to the tail end of Operation Banner for inspiration, they might have profitably examined the complex dynamics of the Iraqi state, particularly in evaluating the robust threat now gathering momentum in the back streets of Basra City and other epicentres of resistance to the occupation.

First, it is often assumed that COIN was the key strategy by which the armed forces 'won' in Northern Ireland. A much more rigorous analysis would reveal that the Army initially deployed on a peacekeeping mission to Northern Ireland in August 1969. The upsurge in inter-communal rioting between Protestant Unionists and Catholic Nationalists, several mishandled Internal Security operations to apprehend terrorists and uncover weapons, and the decision by the Provisional IRA in 1971 to move onto the offensive against the Security Forces, all prompted a decision in London to allow the military to conduct a counter-insurgency operation. However, COIN proved to be disastrous for the military. The new policy of 'police primacy' in counter-terrorist operations after 1977 eventually saw the successful defeat of the insurgents over a much longer period of time. During the remaining thirty years of Operation Banner the military played a supporting role to the police, effectively 'holding the ring' that enabled politicians to pursue a longer-term political solution to the crisis. Second, rarely is there any mention of the Security Forces' elaborate and highly clandestine fusion of intelligence about their opponents, which provided the vital lifeblood to the defeat of the IRA. In Iraq, this intelligence was lacking until the industrial counter-terrorism operations spearheaded by General McChrystal; ironically, these came up against considerable friction from British military commanders in Basra, allegedly because of their preoccupation with political constraints in London and Baghdad.[115] It was in this context that the British sought a truce with militant Islamists; effectively negotiating with their irregular enemy from a position of weakness, not strength, as in Northern Ireland, and facilitating the potent mixture of politics, violence and criminality in Shia-dominated areas. Synnott has challenged the criticisms levelled at the British, specifically that they somehow 'lost' Basra by 2007. In his opinion, this critique 'was based on serious flaws of misunderstanding and invalid comparisons between the different circumstances in Basra and the Baghdad region'.[116] Coalition tensions and British arrogance also had a part to play.

Compounding matters even further was a misperception that the security situation in the south was really about 'inter-faction rivalry, much of it then reflecting in non-judicial killing between rival Shia factions struggling for political and economic power'. The Chief of Joint Operations at Permanent Joint Headquarters, Lieutenant-General Sir Nick Houghton, told the Defence Committee at the time that '[i]n relative terms, vis-à-vis elsewhere in Iraq, the security situation there is still relatively low or modest'.[117] General Houghton later admitted to the Iraq Inquiry that he was 'aware of a sense of the politics of this, but had to properly maintain what I considered proper military advice as to where the balance of our forces should shift, as I saw it, in respect of the demands of the two operational theatres'.[118] Houghton's over-optimism and 'can do' attitude would lead him to make similar strategic decisions with respect to Afghanistan.

A softening in Britain's political strategy by 2006 has been noted by Steele, who argued that in a bid to avoid confrontation, they 'allowed the strongest political forces in the region, the Islamists, to have their way'.[119] The 'accommodation' with the militants, however, needed several criteria for success. First, a political plan was needed from ministers in Whitehall, London; second, a military plan had to be formulated by which to secure the Iraqi population; third, and above all, both political and military processes had to work hand-in-glove with American policy. The latter, claimed the senior American general, Jack Keane, was lacking.[120] In strategic terms, as Clausewitz would have recognized, without the necessary strategy in place all the tactical successes cannot produce a strategic effect. 'The core difficulty', argues Strachan, 'is that, although operational doctrine must be congruent with strategy, it is not strategy itself'.[121] By 2007 that strategy was increasingly being dictated by the US, not Britain.

Britain's further withdrawal from Basra City to an 'overwatch posture' at Basra International Airport in 2007 caused major political ripples and whipped up a media frenzy that placed great strains on the so-called Anglo-American 'special relationship'. It was completed against a backdrop of mutual animosity between politicians and military commanders and suffered from a complicated byzantine command structure, which meant that the disconnection between London and Basra – and Basra and Baghdad – ultimately stunted British military operations. This much is now clear, especially from the comments of those senior generals who commanded Multi-national Forces South. Here there were echoes of British policy in the Middle East during the post-war period, when failure in Palestine in 1948 and Aden in 1967 led to British withdrawal, followed by considerable flux and the seizing of power by the insurgents. Perhaps the main reason for this failure came when Britain announced its intention to withdraw, thus giving the insurgents the necessary fillip to continue their subversion in a largely political fashion. Yet both of these failures were absolute, at least in part because Britain had no Coalition partner to rely on to backfill the vacuum left by an impromptu departure. Reinforcements from the 81st Airborne in Basra in 2008 precipitated the end of Operation Telic.[122] Recognition that the armed forces remained overstretched came late in the day and was, arguably, the consequence of a well-established 'corporate decision-making culture'.[123]

It was becoming obvious that strategic malaise was now pervading the top echelons of government. Richard Dannatt delineated the problems well:

> The sad reality of that time was that much of the MoD, in its Byzantine way, was conducting business as usual, with equipment procurement and assessments of priorities continuing in a cocooned environment far distant from the harsh reality experienced by our soldiers on the front line of Helmand or Basra Palace.[124]

There is evidence that the lack of an overall strategic goal in London led to the backfilling of policy from within the operational theatre. There was a fundamental difficulty with that outlook, insofar as Britain remained the junior partner in the American-led Coalition. While the generals and senior commanders in Iraq recognized this, it was something ignored by London. As Betz and Cormack rightly point out:

> This attitude amounted to little more than a flight of strategic fancy that foolishly decoupled Basra from what was going on elsewhere. In other words, the overall national effort was uncoordinated and the British section of it was chronically under-resourced.[125]

London's failure to trust the professional advice they were receiving from their commanders on the ground created multiple problems and led invariably to an attempt to micro-manage the situation by providing what amounted to vague operational objectives, rather than a strategic vision. This was echoed by the Commander of Coalition forces in South East Iraq between August 2008 and March 2009, Major-General Andy Salmon, who told the Iraq Inquiry:

> Well, we had a set of objectives. There was no comprehensive strategic plan that I ever saw. So what we decided to do – when I say 'we', that is the Consul General, the head of the Provincial Reconstruction Team . . . and to a certain extent the head of US regional embassy office, decided to ensure that we had much more collective consensus, joined-up approach, because nobody was in charge.[126]

Interestingly, Salmon thought that the lack of an overall strategic vision was 'a learning point from this campaign'. A cursory glance over most of Britain's post-war military interventions would confirm that there is nothing new in this criticism. The initial absence of an overarching end goal has been the signature piece of most of Britain's 'small wars', wherein the Army and locally recruited forces have ensured success at the operational and tactical levels in order to permit (albeit) slow movement on the strategic front. That strategic opportunities can be occasioned by tactical and operational successes was no better illustrated in Operation Charge of the Knights.

The last hurrah: 'Operation Charge of the Knights'

Britain had a long history of training and equipping Iraq's military stretching back to the 1920s, when it was an ancillary part of the 'outer empire' under the League of Nations mandate. Intriguingly, under Britain's obligations to the Baghdad Pact in 1955, the British Military Mission to Iraq was based in Shaibah, southern Iraq. In the wake of the 2003 invasion the British once again established a training mission in the area. Yet, the negotiated truce with the militants did not signal the end of attacks against the Contingency Operating Base (COB) in Basra, which adapted its defences to counter daily bombardments from rockets and mortars. The strength of opposition within the city itself represented a microcosm of a much more widespread socio-political phenomenon that had grown up over many years. As Gilles Kepel argued:

> Twenty years earlier, the population explosion in the Muslim world had served the Islamist cause very well, by corralling in the peripheral slums of the great cities a corps of young men who would later rise up on the movement's behalf.[127]

The outrage amongst Iraqis who witnessed their sovereignty being violated, civilian losses spiralling out of control and the fledgling Iraqi administration absolving itself of blame only served to reinforce the hopelessness of it all. Britain's 'accommodation' with the JAM in 2007–08 only served to inflame hatred and apathy for the occupying forces. 'For many Basrawis', wrote Mark Urban, 'this withdrawal marked a final disappointment by the British.'[128] Secular systems of governance were replaced by gun-toting Islamist militias, who, Urban argued, were 'greatly aided in their ambitions by [t]he SIS in Basra', 'who played a central role in this'.[129] Echoes of Palestine and Aden are unavoidable here. In both historical cases, Britain's civil–military representatives were anxious to avoid damage to their prestige and lapsed into negotiation in order to ensure this did not happen. The withdrawal of Britain's forces to the relative safety of the COB pointed to the impoverishment of Coalition strategy. It was an imperfect position for British troops eager to deploy back onto the streets.

It was in the context of the negotiated truce with the militias that 'Charge of the Knights' came as such a surprise to Britain's civil–military hierarchy. The operation involved a major Iraqi-led clearance of Basra in which the senior Iraqi General for the region, Mohan al-Furayji, had nominal military command. Colonel (later Brigadier) Richard Iron, who served as the military mentor to General Mohan, told reporters at the time how:

> There's an uneasy peace between the Iraqi Security Forces [ISF] on the one hand and the militias on the other. There is a sense in the ISF that confrontation is inevitable. They are training and preparing for the battle ahead. General Mohan says that the US won the battle for Baghdad, the US is going win the battle for Mosul, but Iraqis will have to win the battle for Basra.[130]

Indeed, Prime Minister al-Maliki personally intervened to take overall command of the fast-paced operation. He asserted his authority by moving his cabinet down from the capital, behaving in the words of one British military officer very much 'like an 18th Century sovereign leading from the front and issuing orders to his senior commanders'.[131] In micro-managing his forces, though, Maliki risked alienating his newly trained-up forces.

General Sir Peter Wall, who was Deputy Chief of the Defence Staff (Commitments) responsible for Iraq, told the House of Commons Foreign Affairs Select Committee at the time that Charge of the Knights took the British by surprise. 'We found out about the operation at approximately the same time that General Petraeus discovered it', he claimed. His initial assessment was that:

> It was a hastily put together operation, as we all know. Fortuitously, it turned out to be very successful. I think that, as it unfolded, we were probably apprehensive that it would not work as well as it has. In fact, it has changed the landscape in Basra very considerably, and you have seen that for yourselves. We could get into a lengthy discourse about what happened on the day; the extent to which British people were bypassed and then pulled into the conduct of the operation, and the extent to which American people, who were mentoring the Iraqi formations that were brought down to Basra to increase the size of Iraqi forces there to make the operation a success, were actually outpaced by the speed at which the Iraqis themselves moved and took a bit of time to catch up. We could go into all of that. The fact is that, as the Secretary of State has articulated, we now have an extremely vibrant relationship between our forces and the Iraqi 14th Division and a number of other Iraqi agencies around Basra.[132]

As Wall openly admitted, the US remained in overall control of military operations from Baghdad. One of his subordinates, Barney

White-Spunner, who was GOC Multi-National Division South East in 2008, elucidated this rather complicated Coalition framework:

> I think it is important, particularly in the way Charge of the Knights developed, to realise that was a very close relationship and our operational command was very much exercised through the MNCI, through the MultiNational Corps Iraq, through General Austin. Obviously, there was a strong UK influence, as you would expect, and indeed as there should be, but it is absolutely clear that we fitted our operations into a pattern laid down by General Austin, not in some sort of little UK enclave separate to that. I think that's actually quite a key point.[133]

This was coalition military operations in their rawest form and would involve a revised counter-insurgency plan, summed up as follows:

> It was a systematic clearance of areas of Basra, followed by a sort of holding operation to hold the areas cleared and then to try and rebuild and reconstruct them. A lot was done by us, by the Iraqis, and, again, particularly a lot of American help on the reconstruction, on clearing the areas.[134]

The upbeat assessment of operations at the time betrayed a much more prescient view that the British had lost their nerve, something echoed in the work of Mark Urban and a number of other journalists at the time.[135]

The politics of withdrawal

With domestic political and public pressure mounting, Gordon Brown was faced with the dilemma of bringing the troops back home. Eager to break with the last vestiges of 'Blair's wars', Gordon Brown moved quickly to distance himself from some of the more unpopular policies of his predecessor. In a speech to the House of Commons on 8 October 2007, he moved to accelerate his government's strategy of reining in the military's combat role to one of 'overwatch'. This strategy itself involved two stages. The first stage was focused on security sector reform and included the following tasks:

- training and mentoring the Iraqi army and police force;
- securing supply routes and policing the Iran–Iraq border;
- and the ability to come to the assistance of the Iraqi security forces when called upon.[136]

Brown outlined the scheme of manoeuvre in relation to the timescale of Britain's drawdown, which, he envisaged, would move to its next stage in spring 2008. The Prime Minster then informed Parliament that the drawdown process would be 'guided as always by the advice of our military commanders'. For Britain's Armed Forces, he said, the focus would be on 'training and mentoring' he said, with the short-term aim of reducing troop numbers to 2,500:

> The first stage begins now. With the Iraqis already assuming greater security responsibility, we expect to:
>
> - establish Provincial Iraqi Control in Basra province in the next two months as announced by the Prime Minister of Iraq,
> - move to the first stage of 'overwatch',
> - reduce numbers in southern Iraq from the 5,500 at the start of September to 4,500 immediately after Provincial Iraqi Control and then to 4,000,
> - and then in the second stage of 'overwatch', from the spring – and guided as always by the advice of our military commanders – reduce to around 2,500 troops, with a further decision about the next phase made then. In both stages of 'overwatch' around 500 logistics and support personnel will be based outside Iraq elsewhere in the region.[137]

He concluded by stating how: 'At all times [we will be] achieving our long term aim of handing over security to the Iraqi armed forces and police, honouring our obligations to the Iraqi people and to their security, and ensuring the safety of our forces.'[138] Nine months later, in July 2008, Brown informed MPs that the criteria he had set were well on their way to being fulfilled. Training and mentoring of 14th Division would be complete by the end of the year; Basra's airport was to be handed over to civilian control; and economic investment was being pushed forward. 'As we complete these tasks, and as progress continues in these different areas,' he told the Commons, 'we will continue to reduce the number of British troops in Iraq'. Again, reassuring MPs, he said that 'future decisions will, as always, be based on the advice of our military commanders on the ground'. An end to Britain's intervention in Iraq was in sight as Brown proudly observed how the move from a combat role to 'overwatch' would lead ultimately to a transformation in the security situation, and allow Britain to 'make the transition to a long-term bilateral relationship with Iraq, similar to the normal relationships that our military forces have with other important countries in the region'.[139]

Interestingly, the criteria for success had changed. Giving evidence to the Iraq Inquiry, the Permanent Under Secretary at the MoD, Sir Bill

Jeffrey, said that a range of variables, including the intervention in Afghanistan and the MoD's inability to sustain two medium-scale operations, had affected the tempo of withdrawal:

> So I don't feel that we departed from our driving instinct on what would be the proper conditions for our withdrawal from Iraq, but it is undoubtedly the case that, over that whole period, other things being equal, we would have liked to have drawn down from Iraq as early as possible, both for Afghan military reasons and because operating what was, in effect, two medium-scale operations for that period of time is very stretching for defence.[140]

Meanwhile, in Basra, events on the streets were overtaking policy assumptions in MNF-I Headquarters in Baghdad. Colonel Richard Iron, who served as a military adviser based in Basra, was particularly candid in his admission that:

> We have treated Basra more like Palermo than Beirut as if the problems were more about a few criminal tribes and families than religious groups. Baghdad thought Basra was easy to solve and didn't fully understand the extent of the problem, plus the Americans, with their obligations in Mosul and elsewhere, believed Basra could look after itself. It was compounded by having little guidance from above as to whether we were right to accept the deal.[141]

Ironically, Britain had withdrawn from Basra city to the COB according to a similar time-scale to what it had employed for the 1948 evacuation from Palestine. Troops would continue to hold the line as the deadline set by the government drew ever closer. The main differences were that the process was much more ordered than it had been in the past, and, luckily, the US moved quickly to fill the gap left behind by Britain's armed forces.[142]

Conclusion

What does Britain's second war with Iraq tell us about its small wars strategy? Despite the dedication and professionalism of the armed forces in implementing government policy, the politicians failed the soldiers. Chronically under-strength and short of the necessary equipment, the Army bore the brunt of a protracted insurgency. In this respect, an unfortunate parallel could be drawn with British involvement in Aden, where, as Britain was the sole authority responsible for the colony, withdrawal took place against the backdrop of an immediate humiliation by nationalist insurgents and the long-drawn-out diminution in British power. Forty years later, Labour ministers again presided over what amounted to nothing short of British strategic malaise. Other misleading comparisons were drawn by troops themselves, who struggled to comprehend the mosaic of security challenges now confronting them, as they looked to their experience of military operations in Northern Ireland for inspiration. However, as this chapter has demonstrated, the comparisons were fruitless and ultimately led some officers in MND-SE to misapply lessons in the haste to backfill a dearth of civil–military strategizing from London.[143]

Admittedly, there were successes in Iraq on the security front, which could be attributed to the employment of Special Forces in covert strike operations against AQI and other militants. Commanded by the ruthless megalomaniac Abu Musab al-Zarqawi, AQI carried out numerous high-profile assassinations, no-warning car-bombings, indiscriminate suicide bomb attacks and the kidnap and brutal torture of non-combatants; AQI successfully fomented sectarian hatred between Sunnis and Shia. Meanwhile, a co-ordinated Sunni resistance spearheaded attacks against Coalition forces.[144] It had more than met its match in the person of General Stanley McChrystal, who, like General Norman Schwarzkopf in the first Gulf War, recognized the utility of its Special Forces, which included the Special Air Service, Special Reconnaissance Regiment and other highly clandestine Military Intelligence units. McChrystal successfully turned the tide on Islamist militants by mounting a sophisticated 'industrial counter-terrorism' operation from Baghdad.[145] This was, of course, supplemented by the efforts of General David Petreaus and a small team of advisers, including Lieutenant-General Graeme Lamb, who 'turned the tide' on the insurgency and co-opted Sunni militias into supporting the Coalition's security plan for Iraq.[146]

That Britain might have stayed out of the second war with Iraq is an intriguing counterfactual issue, not least in that a precedent of not following the US into conflict had been set by former Labour PM Harold Wilson in relation to Vietnam. Nonetheless, Wilson's actions could not have been further from Blair's mind, as he had already conflated Saddam's removal with the global war on terror in the aftermath of 9/11. Insofar as more immediate explanations for Blair's actions were at work, these could be found in his commitment to liberal interventionism forged in the peace enforcement missions in Iraq, Kosovo and Sierra Leone. 'Blair's wars' served to amplify New Labour's belief in the utility of the armed forces in achieving policy goals in the post-Cold War world.[147] What they almost certainly did not do was to persuade domestic public opinion of the need to expend 'blood and treasure' in wars of choice. Iraq, perhaps more than any other intervention in recent history, highlighted the requirement to frame interventions according to national interests, though they did so by means of emphasizing the altruistic goals of foreign policy. In the words of classical realist E.H. Carr, 'The necessity, recognised by all politicians, both in domestic and international affairs, for cloaking interests in a guise of moral principles is in itself a symptom of the inadequacy of realism.'[148] Iraq proved that even the most pressing threat to national interests could only be explained by reference to the interests of others, even if that was secondary to the task of WMD hunting or 'regime change'. While Iraq certainly ranks alongside British appeasement of Hitler in 1938 and the Suez Crisis of 1956 as one of the worst foreign policy debacles of the past century, it will have much more rigid implications for the British armed forces.

Notes

1 Hussein, Saddam 'Speech on the 27th Anniversary of the Arab Bath'ist Socialist Party, 8 April 1974' in *Saddam Hussein on Current Affairs* (Baghdad: Al-Thawra Publications, 1974), pp. 74–75. A copy of this book was presented to the Royal Military Academy Sandhurst Library by an Iraqi cadet in 1978.

2 Iraq Inquiry, *Oral Evidence of Lieutenant-General Barney White-Spunner on 'Basra: Operation Charge of the Knights'*, 7 January 2010, p. 53. Archived: www.iraqinquiry.org.uk/media/41732/100107am-white-spunner.pdf. Accessed: 12 April 2010.

3 Author notes on comments made by General Sir Mike Jackson at the Modern Warfare: Past Lessons, Future Conflicts Conference, Royal Military Academy Sandhurst, 6 May 2011.

4 House of Commons Debates (Hansard), 18 March 2003, Vol. 401, Col. 760.

5 Perhaps one of the most unprecedented consequences of the resulting Iraq War Inquiry was the release of highly classified documentation historians would generally have to wait over a generation to see. Of particular note are the reports compiled by the Joint Intelligence Committee, which have informed the British decision-making process on foreign, defence and security related issues throughout the post-war period. See 'Top Secret – *Declassified January 2011* – JIC Assessment, 19 February 2003, Southern Iraq: What's in Store?'. Archived: www.iraqinquiry.org.uk/media/50766/JIC-Assessment-19February2003.pdf. Accessed: 23 January 2011.

6 See Marston, Daniel, 'Smug and Complacent? Operation TELIC: The Need for Critical Analysis', *Australian Army Journal*, Vol. 6, No. 3 (summer 2009), pp. 165–180. Marston (p. 166) argues convincingly that 'the British Army was not on the verge of defeat in 2007, but Whitehall's and the Permanent Joint Headquarters' (PJHQ) strategy was flawed and close to failure'.

7 Hewitt, Steve, *The British War on Terror: Terrorism and Counter-Terrorism on the Home Front since 9/11* (London: Continuum, 2008), p. 120.
8 Kavanagh, Dennis, 'The Blair Premiership', in Seldon, Anthony (ed.), *Blair's Britain, 1997–2007* (Cambridge: Cambridge University Press, 2007), p. 13.
9 For more on liberal interventionism see MacGinty, Roger, 'Indigenous Peace-Making Versus the Liberal Peace', *Co-Operation and Conflict*, Vol. 43, No. 2 (2008), pp. 139–163.
10 Coates, David and Joel Krieger, 'The Mistake Heard Round the World: Iraq and the Blair Legacy', in Casey, Terrence (ed.), *The Blair Legacy: Politics, Policy, Governance, and Foreign Affairs* (Basingstoke: Palgrave Macmillan, 2009), p. 254.
11 For more on how Iraq is likely to 'shape wider thinking about Britain's strategic interests' see Ucko, David H., 'Lessons from Basra: The Future of British Counter-Insurgency', *Survival*, Vol. 52, No. 4 (August–September 2010), pp. 131–158.
12 Sectarian violence intensified to such an extent in 2006–07 that British academic Gareth Stansfield was claiming that there was not one civil war in Iraq, but *many* civil wars. See Stansfield, Gareth, *Accepting Realities in Iraq*, Middle East Programme Briefing Paper (London: Chatham House, May 2007).
13 Iraq Inquiry, *About the Inquiry*. Archived: www.iraqinquiry.org.uk/about.aspx. Accessed: 10 July 2011.
14 Hewitt, *The British War on Terror*, p. 120.
15 Kampfner, John, *Blair's Wars* (London: The Free Press, 2003), p. 351.
16 Ibid., pp. 7–8.
17 Freedman, Lawrence, 'Defence' in Seldon, *Blair's Britain, 1997–2007*, p. 618.
18 Hill, Christopher, 'Foreign Policy' in Seldon, Anthony (ed.), *The Blair Effect: The Blair Government, 1997–2001* (London: Little, Brown, 2001), p. 333.
19 Major, John, *John Major: The Autobiography* (London: HarperCollins, 1999), p. 511.
20 Hurd, Douglas, *Douglas Hurd: Memoirs* (London: Little, Brown, 2003), p. 476. Hurd also maintained a non-interventionist line on the Yugoslavian conflicts in the early to mid-1990s. He famously suggested that the parties in conflict must 'make peace between themselves' through the medium of negotiation and other peacemaking activities. See Hurd, Douglas, 'Averting a Balkan Tragedy', *The Times*, 3 December 1991. Hurd kept stringently to this line throughout his time in the Foreign Office, going as far as to proudly observe two years later that 'No government has ever advocated the use of military force to impose a political solution'. Hurd, Douglas, 'Our Chance to End a Bosnian Winter of Suffering', *Sunday Times*, 12 December 1993. He later admitted after leaving office that 'the doctrine of non-interference in internal affairs has now simply worn out'. Hurd, Douglas, 'Comment: Just Like the Book of Kings: Douglas Hurd

argues that the world has a chance to bring cataclysmic conflicts to an end', *Independent on Sunday*, 9 November 1997.

21 Simms, Brendan, *Unfinest Hour: Britain and the Destruction of Bosnia* (London: Penguin, 2002), p. 222.

22 Brown, David, 'Introduction: New Labour and Defence', in Brown, David (ed.), *The Development of British Defence Policy: Blair, Brown and Beyond* (Farnham: Ashgate, 2010), p. 2.

23 Cook, Robin, 'Robin Cook, shadow Foreign Secretary, on how Britain and the world share the responsibility for genocide', *Independent on Sunday*, 9 April 1995.

24 Blair, Tony, *Doctrine of the International Community: Speech by the Prime Minister to the Economic Club of Chicago on 24 April* (London: HMSO, 1999).

25 Ibid.

26 General Sir Roger Wheeler had been Vice-Chief of the General Staff at the time of the Options for Change exercise in 1990.

27 Interview with General Sir Roger Wheeler, London, 23 February 2011.

28 Ibid.

29 Labour Party, *New Labour Because Britain Deserves Better* (1997).

30 Interview with General Sir Roger Wheeler, London, 23 February 2011.

31 Codner, Michael, 'An Instrument of Honour? Britain's Military Strategy and the Impact of New Technologies' in Brown, *The Development of British Defence Policy*, p. 195.

32 Introduction by the Secretary of State for Defence, The Rt Hon. George Robertson MP in Ministry of Defence (MoD), *Strategic Defence Review*, Cm. 3999 (London: MoD, 1998).

33 Wheeler, General Sir Roger, 'The British Army after the SDR: Peacemakers Know that Britain Will Deliver', *RUSI Journal*, Vol. 144, No. 2 (1999), p. 5.

34 Freedman, Lawrence, 'Britain at War: From The Falklands to Iraq', *RUSI Journal*, Vol. 151, No. 1 (February 2006), p. 15. According to Andrew Dorman (p. 127) 'the British deployment of armed forces to Sierra Leone in May 2000 was one of the few successful uses of the military by the Blair administration'. Dorman, Andrew M., *Blair's Successful War: Britain's Military Intervention in Sierra Leone* (Farnham: Ashgate, 2009).

35 Coll, Steve, *Ghost Wars: The Secret History of the CIA, Afghanistan and Bin Laden, from the Soviet Invasion to September 10, 2001* (London: Penguin, 2004), pp. 53–54, p. 58. According to Coll (p. 569), 'Afghanistan after 1979 was a laboratory for political and military visions conceived abroad and imposed by force'.

36 Burke, Jason, *Al Qaeda: The True Story of Radical Islam* (London: Penguin, 2007), p. 2.

37 Cook, Robin, *The Point of Departure: Diaries from the Front Bench* (London: Simon and Schuster, 2003), p. 50. On the intellectual front this 'clash of civilisations' theory was gaining ground, especially amongst

Washington's so-called 'neo-conservatives'. It was propounded in the main by Samuel P. Huntington in his book *The Clash of Civilisations and the Remaking of World Order* (London: Free Press, 2002).

38 House of Commons Debates (Hansard), 10 March 2002, Vol. 383, Col. 23. Although not yet settled on 'regime change', Blair later said that 'it is very difficult to think of a situation where the Iraqi people most of all would not be better off without Saddam'. House of Commons Debates (Hansard), 24 September 2002, Vol. 390, Col. 20. However, it was not until February 2003 that Blair advocated military intervention, but only as a 'last resort' and within the framework of a UN Security Council Resolution. As Blair told the Commons, 'People sense that matters may come to conflict because they know that he has no intention of changing his heart or mind. However, that is his choice, not ours. Our choice, preference and desire are to resolve matters peacefully through the United Nations.' House of Commons Debates (Hansard), 25 February 2003, Vol. 400, Col. 135.

39 Mandelson, Peter, *The Third Man: Life at the Heart of New Labour* (London: HarperPress, 2010), p. 353.

40 House of Commons Debates (Hansard), 15 January 2003, Vol. 397, Col. 676.

41 Toynbee, Polly, 'Blair was wrong. He still is. But let's not fetishise the UN', *The Guardian*, 30 January 2010.

42 For more on the exuberant sofa-cushioned 'group think' that became synonymous with Tony Blair's style of leadership see Seldon, Anthony, *Blair* (London: Free Press, 2004), p. 692.

43 Powell, Jonathan, *Great Hatred, Little Room: Making Peace in Ireland* (London: The Bodley Head, 2008), p. 3.

44 Blair, Tony, *A Journey* (London: Hutchinson, 2010), p. 388.

45 Bush, George W., *Decision Points* (London: Virgin Books, 2010), p. 228.

46 UN Security Council, Resolution 1441 (8 November 2002). Archived: http://daccess-dds-ny.un.org/doc/UNDOC/GEN/N02/682/26/PDF/N0268226.pdf?OpenElement. Accessed: 9 July 2011.

47 Woodward, Bob, *Plan of Attack: The Road to War* (London: Simon and Schuster, 2004), p. 440.

48 IISS, *Iraq's Weapons of Mass Destruction: A Net Assessment. An IISS Strategic Dossier*, Press Statement Dr John Chipman IISS Director, Monday, 9 September, Arundel House, London. In his oral evidence to the Iraq Inquiry former SIS Chief Sir Richard Dearlove referred to the IISS report as a 'conservative estimate'.

49 Tony Blair writing in the preface to the dossier: *Iraq's Weapons of Mass Destruction: The Assessment of the British Government*, pp. 3–4. My emphasis.

50 Blair, *A Journey*, p. 412. Blair emphasizes that the Americans had made up their minds that 'Saddam was a threat, he would never cooperate fully with the international community, and the world, not to say Iraq, would

be better off with him out of power. My instinct was with them. Our alliance was with them. I had made a commitment after September 11 to be "shoulder to shoulder". I was determined to fulfil it.'

51 Iraq Inquiry, *Oral Evidence of Sir Richard Dearlove given in Private Hearing*, 16 June 2010, p. 53. Archived: www.iraqinquiry.org.uk/media/50694/20100616-Dearlove.pdf. Accessed: 21 January 2011.

52 Evidence by Baroness Eliza Manningham-Buller, Director-General of the Security Service, 2002–2007, to the Iraq Inquiry, 20 July 2010, p. 6. Archived: www.iraqinquiry.org.uk/media/48331/20100720am-manningham-buller.pdf. Accessed: 14 July 2011. Thames House is the headquarters of the Security Service, MI5.

53 Blix, Hans, *Disarming Iraq: The Search for Weapons of Mass Destruction* (London: Bloomsbury, 2004), p. 156.

54 Omand, David, *Securing the State* (London: Hurst and Company, 2010), p. 178.

55 House of Commons Debates (Hansard), 24 March 2003, Vol. 402, Col. 36.

56 Short, Clare, *An Honourable Deception? New Labour, Iraq, and the Misuse of Power* (London: Free Press, 2004), p. 188.

57 Brown, George, *In My Way: The Political Memoirs of Lord George-Brown* (London: Victor Gollancz, 1971), p. 182.

58 Cook, *The Point of Departure*, p. 378.

59 Toynbee, Polly, 'How this war could end up being Blair's LBJ moment', *The Guardian*, 19 March 2003.

60 Coates and Krieger, 'The Mistake Heard Round the World', p. 249.

61 Blair, *A Journey*, p. 439.

62 Morgenthau, Hans J., 'The Machiavelli Utopia', *Ethics*, Vol. 55, No. 2 (January 1945), p. 146.

63 Thakur, Ramesh and Waheguru Pal Singh Sidhu, 'Iraq's Challenge to World Order', in Thakur, Ramesh and Waheguru Pal Singh Sidhu (eds), *The Iraq Crisis and World Order: Structural, Institutional and Normative Challenges* (Tokyo: United Nations University Press, 2006), p. 3.

64 Ibid., p. 4.

65 For more on this point see Brown, David, 'Striking a Balance? Labour's Legacy and the Next Chapter of British Defence Policy' in Brown (ed.), *The Development of British Defence Policy*.

66 See Fairweather, Jack, *A War of Choice: The British in Iraq, 2003–2009* (London: Jonathan Cape, 2011).

67 Iraq Inquiry, Oral Evidence of Sir Kevin Tebbitt and Lord Boyce on 'Military Planning', 3 December 2009, p. 23. Archived: www.iraqinquiry.org.uk/media/40465/20091203-final.pdf. Accessed: 12 April 2010.

68 See David Kilcullen's book *The Accidental Guerrilla: Fighting Small Wars amidst a Big One* (London: Hurst, 2009).

69 Iraq Inquiry, Written Evidence of Major General Michael Laurie CBE, 27 January 2010. Archived: www.iraqinquiry.org.uk/media/52051/Laurie-statement-FINAL.pdf. Accessed: 27 May 2011.

70 Strachan, Hew 'Making Strategy: Civil-Military Relations after Iraq', *Survival*, Vol. 48, No. 3 (autumn 2006), pp. 59–60. On the 'three-block war' see Krulak, Charles, 'The Strategic Corporal: Leadership in the Three Block War', *Marines Magazine* (January 1999). Archived: www.au.af.mil/au/awc/awcgate/usmc/strategic_corporal.htm. Accessed: 25 March 2011.

71 Iraq Inquiry, Oral Evidence of Rt Hon General the Lord Walker of Aldringham, 1 February 2010, pp. 4–5. Archived: www.iraqinquiry.org.uk/media/45534/100201-walker-final.pdf. Accessed: 19 July 2011.

72 Tony Blair's contribution to the Iraq debate, House of Commons Debates (Hansard), 18 March 2003, Vol. 401, Col. 773–774.

73 Iraq Inquiry, Oral Evidence of Sir Kevin Tebbit.

74 Iraq Inquiry, Declassified extract from a letter to the Prime Minister sent jointly by the Foreign Secretary and the Defence Secretary: Iraq: UK Military Contribution to Post-Conflict Iraq, 19 March 2003.

75 MoD, *The Strategic Defence Review: A New Chapter* (London: MoD, July 2002), Cm. 5566, p. 14. Interestingly, as the MoD freely admitted in the same document, 'We would not, however, expect both deployments to involve warfighting or to maintain them simultaneously for longer than 6 months.' A similar point was made in the SDR, i.e. 'Supporting Essay 6: Future Military Capabilities' in the *Strategic Defence Review* (London: MoD, July 1998).

76 Number 10, *Iraq: Its Infrastructure of Concealment, Deception and Intimidation* (London: Cabinet Office, February 2003). Locating a copy of the 'dodgy dossier' is a complicated task, and it has long since been removed from government websites.

77 Cook, Robin, 'So many of us must shoulder the blame for this disastrous war', *The Independent*, 26 September 2003. Cook's comments should be seen in light of US Secretary of State Colin Powell's representation to the UN on the issue of Iraq's 'concealment' of its WMD. As he argued, 'What you will see is an accumulation of facts and disturbing patterns of behaviour. The facts and Iraq's behaviour demonstrate that Saddam Hussein and his regime have made no effort – no effort – to disarm as required by the international community. Indeed, the facts and Iraq's behaviour show that Saddam Hussein and his regime are concealing their efforts to produce more weapons of mass destruction.' See UN, 'Powell presents US case to Security Council of Iraq's failure to disarm', *UN News Centre*, 5 February 2003. Archived: www.un.org/apps/news/storyAr.asp?NewsID=6079&Cr=iraq&Cr1=inspect. Accessed: 25 March 2011. A Senate Committee commissioned to look into the pre-war intelligence found that the important human source 'curveball' was not 'sufficiently vetted and evaluated' prior to his information becoming 'actionable intelligence'.

78 On the laws of war relating to occupation, see Professor Daniel Thürer, *Current Challenges to the Law of Occupation*, 6th Bruges Colloquium,

20–21 October 2005. Archived: www.icrc.org/eng/resources/documents/statement/occupation-statement-211105.htm. Accessed: 31 May 2011.

79 Synnott, Hillary, *Bad Days in Basra: My Turbulent Time as Britain's Man in Southern Iraq* (London: I.B. Tauris, 2008), p. 140. Interestingly, the British government was spending an estimated £1,311 million (2003–04), £910 million (2004–05), and £1,098 million (2005–06) on operations in Iraq. Written answer from Adam Ingram to Rob Wilson, MP, House of Commons Debates (Hansard), Written Answer, 30 March 2006, Vol. 444, Col. 1153W.

80 Keegan, John, *The Iraq War* (London: Hutchinson, 2004), pp. 175–176.

81 Fairweather, *A War of Choice*, pp. 250–251.

82 Potts, Colonel David R., 'Principles for Waging Modern War', *British Army Review*, No. 130 (autumn 2002), pp. 10–16. From his reading of British COIN doctrine, Potts noted the following six fundamental principles: political primacy and political aim; co-ordinated government machinery; intelligence and information; separating the insurgent from his support; neutralizing the insurgent; longer-term post-insurgency plan. Gary Sheffield responded to Potts' article by reminding readers that the principles not only came from the writings of General Sir Frank Kitson and Sir Robert Thompson, but were also built on the much earlier writings of Charles Callwell, Charles Gwynn and Julian Paget. Sheffield argued, convincingly, that the Head of War Studies at Sandhurst, Dr John Pimlott, did more to actively articulate the concepts of COIN at a time when it was perhaps unfashionable to do so. The existence of doctrine on COIN, concluded Sheffield, 'casts doubt on the view that one sometimes hears expressed that before 1989, the British Army did not have any doctrine'. Sheffield, Gary, 'The Principles of War', *British Army Review*, No. 131 (spring 2003), pp. 76–77.

83 Allawi, Ali A., *The Occupation of Iraq: Winning the War, Losing the Peace* (New Haven, CT: Yale University Press, 2007), pp. 170, 187.

84 Cook, *The Point of Departure*, p. 332.

85 Stothard, Peter, *30 Days: A Month at the Heart of Blair's War* (London: HarperCollins, 2003), p. 223.

86 Ferguson, Niall, 'The Last Iraqi Insurgency', *The New York Times*, 18 April 2004.

87 Cox, Michael, 'From Empire to Decline', *The World Today*, Vol. 67, No. 8 (August/September 2011), p. 5.

88 Ferguson, 'The Last Iraqi Insurgency'.

89 Allawi, *The Occupation of Iraq*, p. 350.

90 Stansfield, Gareth, *Iraq: People, History, Politics* (Cambridge: Polity, 2007), p. 189.

91 Defence Select Committee, Oral evidence Taken before the Defence Committee on Tuesday 1 November 2005. Archived at: www.publications.parliament.uk/pa/cm200506/cmselect/cmdfence/556/5110103.htm. Accessed: 21 July 2011. General Fry's comments were in response to question 20 from the Committee.

92 Reid, John, 'Letter: Britain's Plan in Iraq', *The Guardian*, 16 July 2005.
93 Ricks, Thomas, *Fiasco: The American Military Adventure in Iraq* (London: Allen Lane, 2006), pp. 324–329.
94 Cook, Robin, Douglas Hurd and Menzies Campbell, 'Our troops must quit Iraq when the UN mandate ends in a year', *The Times*, 29 January 2005.
95 Reid, John, 'I promise you this: we won't cut and run', *The Times*, 19 August 2005.
96 Stansfield, *Iraq*, pp. 182–189.
97 Bloomberg School of Public Health, *The Human Cost of the War in Iraq: A Mortality Study, 2002–06*. Archived: www.jhsph.edu/bin/k/m/Human_Cost_of_WarFORMATTED.pdf. Accessed: 31 May 2011.
98 Steele, Jonathan, *Defeat: Why they Lost Iraq* (London: I.B. Tauris, 2009), p. 190.
99 Browne, Des, 'Future Challenges in Iraq', speech to the Royal United Services Institute, 24 May 2006. Archived: www.rusi.org/events/past/ref:E4475863D07F96/info:public/infoID:E44758F164291F. Accessed: 14 July 2011.
100 Browne, Des, 'With the butcher dead, Iraq has a hope', *Sunday Telegraph*, 11 June 2006.
101 *Daily Mail*, 12 October 2006.
102 For an insightful account of McChrystal's 'industrial counter-terrorism' drive see Urban, Mark, *Task Force Black: The Explosive True Story of the SAS and the Secret War in Iraq* (London: Little, Brown, 2010).
103 Gray, Colin S., *Explorations in Strategy* (Westport, CT: Greenwood Press, 1996), p. 168.
104 North, Richard, *The Ministry of Defeat: The British War in Iraq – 2003–2009* (London: Continuum, 2009), pp. 124–125.
105 Marston, 'Smug and Complacent?', p. 170.
106 See Hider, James, 'Raid on Militia drives wedge between allies', *The Times*, 9 August 2006. There is evidence, not least from Parliament's Defence Select Committee, that the MoD avoided the thorny issue of militias by stating 'We note the Committee's comments'. See HMG, *Iraq: An Initial Assessment of Post-Conflict Operations: Government Response to the Committee's Sixth Report of Session 2004–05* (London: HMSO, 27 July 2005), p. 11. Archived: www.publications.parliament.uk/pa/cm200506/cmselect/cmdfence/436/436.pdf. Accessed: 21 July 2011.
107 House of Commons Debates (Hansard), 18 October 2006, Vol. 450, Col. 868.
108 *Daily Mail*, 12 October 2006.
109 Browne, 'Future Challenges in Iraq'.
110 Malkasian, Carter, 'Counterinsurgency in Iraq, May 2003–January 2007', in Marston, Daniel and Carter Malkasian (eds), *Counterinsurgency in Modern Warfare* (Oxford: Osprey, 2008), p. 259.
111 Strachan, 'Making Strategy', p. 61.

112 Iraq Inquiry, Air Chief Marshal Sir Jock Stirrup, Oral Evidence, Monday 1 February 2010. pp. 21–22. Archived: www.iraqinquiry.org.uk/media/45320/20100201am-stirrup-final.pdf. Accessed: 6 March 2010.
113 PRTs began life in Afghanistan as a civil–military response to the problem of stabilization. The PRT in Basra, for instance, was tasked with redevelopment projects (such as Quick Impact Projects), which were designed to produce strategic effects that would contribute to the stabilization of the security situation. Interview with the Second-in-Command of the Basra PRT, MND-SE HQ, Basra, 25 September 2008.
114 Defence Committee, UK Operations in Iraq, HC 1241 (London: The Stationery Office, 10 August 2006), oral evidence taken before the Defence Select Committee on 20 June 2006. Archived at: www.publications.parliament.uk/pa/cm200506/cmselect/cmdfence/1241/1241.pdf. Accessed: 21 July 2011.
115 Urban, *Task Force Black*.
116 Synnott, *Bad Days in Basra*, p. 258.
117 Ibid. Oral evidence given by Lieutenant-General Nick Houghton, 20 June 2006, Ev. 3–4.
118 Iraq Inquiry, Oral Evidence of General Sir Nicholas Houghton on 'The Military Perspective from London, 2006–07', 3 December 2010, p. 37. Archived: www.iraqinquiry.org.uk/media/41897/20100105amhoughton-style-final.pdf. Accessed: 21 July 2010.
119 Steele, *Defeat*, p. 193.
120 Author notes on a lecture entitled 'The American Experience' by General Jack Keane at the Modern Warfare: Past Lessons, Future Conflicts Conference, Royal Military Academy Sandhurst, 5 May 2011.
121 Strachan, 'Making Strategy', p. 62.
122 The author saw this first-hand when he deployed to Basra in September 2008. The roar of American Blackhawk helicopters and Apache gunships across the Basra skyline contrasted sharply with the few bits of kit and equipment that the 'elements' in the British order of battle could muster. One got the distinct impression talking to British servicemen and women that Operation Telic would soon be drawing to an end, especially since Des Browne had announced in Basra in early September that the security situation had been 'transformed'.
123 For more on the legacy of federalized decision-making see Levene, Lord, *Defence Reform: An Independent Report into the Structure and Management of the Ministry of Defence* (London: The Stationery Office, June 2011), p. 78.
124 Dannatt, General Sir Richard, *Leading from the Front: The Autobiography* (London: Bantam Press, 2010), p. 248.
125 Betz, David and Anthony Cormack, 'Iraq, Afghanistan and British Strategy', *Orbis: A Journal of World Affairs*, Vol. 53, No. 2 (spring 2009), p. 324.
126 Iraq Inquiry, Oral Evidence of Major-General Andy Salmon on 'General Officer Commanding Multi-National Division (South East), 2008 to

2009', 20 July 2010, p. 27. Archived: www.iraqinquiry.org.uk/media/49279/20100720-salmon-final.pdf. Accessed: 24 July 2010.

127 Kepel, Gilles, *Jihad: The Trail of Political Islam* (London: I.B. Tauris, 2003), p. 364.

128 Urban, *Task Force Black*, p. 248.

129 Ibid., p. 249.

130 *The Observer*, 24 February 2008.

131 Ibid. Also, interview with Brigadier Richard Iron, 20 September 2011.

132 House of Commons, Foreign Affairs Select Committee, Oral Evidence by Lieutenant-General Peter Wall on Iraq and Afghanistan, 28 October 2008. www.publications.parliament.uk/pa/cm200708/cmselect/cmfaff/1145/8102802.htm. Accessed: 14 July 2011.

133 Iraq Inquiry, Oral Evidence of Lieutenant-General Barney White-Spunner, pp. 8–9.

134 Ibid., p. 19.

135 *The Times*, 2007.

136 House of Commons Debates (Hansard), 8 October 2007, Vol. 464, Col. 23.

137 Ibid.

138 Ibid.

139 House of Commons Debates (Hansard), 22 July 2008, Vol. 479, Col. 662–663.

140 Sir Bill Jeffrey, Transcript of oral evidence to the Iraq Inquiry, Permanent Under Secretary of State at the Ministry of Defence, 2005–2010, 8 March 2010, p. 10. Archived at: www.iraqinquiry.org.uk/media/45564/100308-jeffrey-final.pdf. Accessed: 20 June 2010.

141 Hanning, James 'Deal with Shia prisoner left Basra at mercy of gangs, colonel admits', *The Independent*, 3 August 2008.

142 In a visit to the COB in September 2008 the author witnessed first-hand how the Americans were moving in to take over from the British forces there. There was a feeling that Charge of the Knights had worked but that Britain's relationship with the US was under considerable strain.

143 Lieutenant General Sir Philip Trousdell who served as GOC Northern Ireland in 2003–05 recalled how HQNI received a phone call from a Brigade Major in Basra who asked for some workable lessons to be applied to a very different operational theatre. Interview with Lieutenant General Sir Philip Trousdell, Royal Military Academy Sandhurst, 28 March 2011.

144 See Hashim, Ahmed S., *Iraq's Sunni Insurgency* (London: IISS, 2009), Adelphi Paper No. 402.

145 Conversations with serving members of the UK Special Forces fraternity confirmed the author's view of the high regard McChrystal was held by their sergeant's mess. See Urban, *Task Force Black* for more.

146 Fairweather, *A War of Choice*, pp. 289–299.

147 Significantly, under Labour the UK's national rules of engagement were altered to permit intervention under the following circumstances:

'Overwhelming Humanitarian Catastrophe. A limited use of force may be justifiable without the United Nations Security Council's express authorization where that is the only means to avert an immediate and overwhelming humanitarian catastrophe. Such cases are likely to be exceptional and depend on objective assessment of the circumstances at the time and on the terms of any relevant decisions of the SC bearing on the situation in question'. Joint Doctrine Publication 0-01, British Defence Doctrine (Shrivenham: DCDC, August 2008), p. 1 B-2.

148 Carr, E.H., *The Twenty Years' Crisis 1919–1939: An Introduction to the Study of International Relations* (London: Macmillan, [1939] 1970), p. 92.

8

Building peace amidst conflict: Britain's changing strategy in Afghanistan

> It is a singular feature of small wars that from the point of view of strategy the regular forces are upon the whole at a distinct disadvantage as compared to their antagonists.[1]

> Military . . . [s]trategy is particularly concerned with the political consequences and advantages of the threat and use of force; it gives meaning and context to all operational and tactical actions. Its purpose is to balance the ways and means required to achieve stipulated ends, conditioned by the environment and prospective opponents.[2]

> [As for] the pull back in Basra and the deployment to Afghanistan, both events were highly politicised in their nature.[3]

Introduction

Britain's military campaign in Afghanistan has proven to be one of the most complex and enduring small wars of modern times. Initially deployed on a short-term mission in 2001, with the aim of toppling the Islamist Taliban regime from power in the Afghan capital Kabul, British forces soon found themselves re-deployed in the summer of 2006 to the southern province of Helmand on a stabilization and reconstruction mission, a deployment which encountered tremendous friction when faced with high-intensity insurgent opposition. Unlike the intervention in Iraq, military operations have been conducted under a United Nations (UN) sanctioned peace enforcement mandate from the outset. Indeed, the UN had already passed a resolution in the summer of 2001, which determined 'that the situation in Afghanistan constitutes a threat to international peace and security in the region'.[4] The warning was amplified exponentially when the United States (US) was attacked on 9/11 by Al Qaeda terrorists, who had been provided with a safe-haven by the Taliban in Afghanistan since moving their base of operations there from Sudan in 1996. The Taliban held a tight grip over most of the Afghan population from the mid-1990s, permitting their allies in the 'Al Qaeda hardcore' the space to recruit, train, plan and launch attacks from the lawless tribal areas straddling the porous border between Afghanistan and its neighbour Pakistan.[5]

British troops faced an arduous task when they deployed to Afghanistan alongside US forces within weeks of the 9/11 attacks. Prime Minister Tony Blair later claimed that the 'goal was not simply to remove the Taliban but to replace them with democracy, to rebuild the country',[6] arguably a much more ambitious and long-term project. As the senior service, the Royal Navy took the lead in operations against the Taliban and Al Qaeda in October 2001. Submarines based in the Gulf fired Tomahawk missiles at the Taliban's military infrastructure, while troops from 40 Royal Marines Commando Brigade spearheaded a vigorous ground assault several weeks later. British forces worked in harmony with their American and Afghan Northern Alliance allies as part of Operation Enduring Freedom, capturing Bagram airfield and destroying a bunker complex in the rugged Tora Bora mountain range.

The International Security Assistance Force (ISAF) was formed a few weeks later in December 2001 – in the wake of the Bonn Conference on Afghanistan – and was commanded first by Britain, then by Turkey, and subsequently by Germany and the Netherlands. NATO assumed responsibility for the ISAF mission in August 2003. In the interim half-decade, the resurgent Taliban, who 'were never quite broken', had time to regroup and lost no time in mounting a counter-attack against the international coalition.[7] Blair's rhetoric masked the reality that the Labour government had underestimated the challenge now ahead of them.[8] Nevertheless, Coalition troops were forced to adapt in light of the turn by the Taliban from semi-conventional fighting towards guerrilla tactics. Resurgent Taliban militants, who 'seemed convinced that the wind was definitely blowing in their favour'[9] – would soon prove to be a resilient adversary for British and ISAF troops.

While the operational experience of Britain's armed forces in Afghanistan must be situated amidst the evolving threat posed by their Taliban enemy, one must not lose sight of how this intervention fits into the broader historical context of Britain's other small wars since 1945. Of particular note are the lessons military commanders and defence policy-makers drew from Malaya and Northern Ireland in crafting anti-Taliban operations.[10] Continuing with the theme explored in the previous chapter, it was the misapplication of the tactical and operational lessons learned in previous campaigns that almost led to Britain's strategic defeat in Afghanistan.

It is only natural that Britain would draw upon this significant intellectual reservoir of military doctrine, given its long and distinguished history of combating terrorists and insurgents. The litmus test, as Paul Latawski rightly reminds us, 'is dependent on the ability of armed forces to learn and apply lessons to the conflict at hand'.[11] Latawski cautions us against overlooking the completeness of the past, for 'to ignore the past and not bring a historical perspective to military doctrine also carries the risk of replacing enduring principles of war with a mindset that marches to the drumbeat of intellectual fashion'.[12] In this respect, military doctrine and the lessons-learned exploitation process 'draws on the past, lives in the present, evolves, develops and, if necessary, gives way to a new thinking relevant to the present'.[13] While 'lesson learning' has undoubtedly fired the imaginations of defence professionals, with some even going as far as to claim that the British Army, in particular, has become a 'learning organisation',[14] it is the tendency to identify the wrong lessons that has often spelt disaster for Britain. It goes without saying that the Army can – and often does – legitimately draw from its long operational experience – uninterrupted thanks in large part to its longstanding 38-year deployment in Northern Ireland and peace support operations of the 1990s.[15] However, it is the overarching contention of this book that the lessons learned were often only snapshots of these small wars, which conveniently overlooked both their unique political context and the military failures that served as a prelude to success, if it came at all. Only by adopting a more empirically grounded perspective on the internal processes of change and innovation – as well as the shifting contours of the external international system – can we fully appreciate the British handling of its small wars.

In many respects, the deployment of Britain's Armed Forces in Afghanistan after 2001, like its involvement in the other campaigns scrutinized in this book, highlights the perennial difficulties facing governments in countering irregular adversaries. Moreover, it also illustrates both the effectiveness and inertia of government ministers, defence planners, and soldiers attempting to apply force in a conflict that is fast becoming 'increasingly hybrid in nature'.[16] As with Britain's small war in Iraq between 2003 and 2009, the ongoing commitment of its military forces in Afghanistan poses fundamental questions about how well the UK has been able to learn, adapt and 'transform in contact', while conforming to an Order of Battle (ORBAT) dictated largely by a US-led international coalition. Moreover, it throws into sharp relief the process by which military objectives in Afghanistan can be met by the artificial deadlines set by politicians in Whitehall. Over a decade of involvement in the Afghan theatre and five years of Helmand-centric warfare have exposed the difficulties encountered by Britain in developing a coherent strategy for fighting the small wars of the early twenty-first century, especially when operating as part of a broader alliance or coalition. And, apart from anything else, it points to the complex business of building peace amidst armed conflict.

In search of a strategy: from Blair to Brown

It has become something of a cliché to cite the observation made by then Secretary of State for Defence Dr John Reid, who opined that 'We hope we will leave Afghanistan without firing a single shot'.[17] Ironically, by January 2008, it was being reported that the British Army had expended almost 4 million bullets in the twelve months up until August 2007[18] in some of the most intense, close-quarter fighting since the Korean War of the early 1950s. By August 2009 that figure had trebled to 12 million.[19] In his polemical critique of New Labour's handling of the Afghanistan conflict, *A Million Bullets*, journalist James Fergusson informed us that '[t]he 'kinetic' nature of Operation Herrick 4 set the tone for Britain's Afghan engagement for, very probably, years to come'.[20] Arguably, a much bigger concern was not the underestimation of the type of operations British troops would be involved in but the dearth of intelligence on what the threat actually looked like. Bird and Marshal have given a damning portrayal of the lack of preparation prior to intervention in Afghanistan, going as far as to suggest that '[d]etailed knowledge of the Helmand security landscape appeared to be in short supply in London'.[21] This was no better evidenced than when Reid told Conservative MP James Arbuthnot in a debate prior to New Labour's deployment of the British mission to Helmand that '[t]he idea that there is already a huge presence or that there is a huge presence of, for instance, Taliban is not necessarily correct'.[22] In time, Reid would soon come to regret his words.

Politicians were therefore less cautious about deploying troops into Helmand province in 2006 than perhaps they should have been. Responding to questions about the mission that lay ahead of the Ministry of Defence (MoD) in Afghanistan, Reid delineated between the two concurrent operations involving UK forces:

> They will be reconciled through two separate missions: 'seek and destroy' against terrorists; and building and reconstructing Afghanistan's democracy, governance, economic development and security forces. However, only someone who is dreadfully naive would think that we will be allowed to carry out the second of those tasks – the NATO task, in which we will be involved when we go to the south – unhindered by any

> attacks. The House will expect us to say that if our troops are attacked while reconstructing Afghanistan, or helping and protecting the aid workers, or helping President Karzai's Government to extend, *we will robustly defend ourselves*. That is why I said that we cannot draw a complete distinction between the missions, but there will still be two. We will attempt to co-ordinate them, at a stage after phase 3, by establishing a double-hatted sequence in one General, so that there will be maximum co-ordination of two separate missions. We are not changing our mission to one of anti-terrorism. We are still there for the reconstruction of Afghanistan, but *we will defend ourselves* if attacked.[23]

Britain's largely defensive strategy, however, was confusing for military commanders on the ground in Afghanistan, some of whom doubted whether the objectives set by Reid and the civil–military hierarchy in London could be realistically met.[24]

Nevertheless, Blair's government pressed ahead with beefing up the re-deployment to Helmand. Hosting the London Conference on Afghanistan in 2006, Blair gave assurances that the UK would remain in Afghanistan for as long as necessary. The open-ended nature of the deployment exploded a potent cocktail, with the Chief of the General Staff (CGS), Sir Richard Dannatt, publicly arguing that the Army was 'running hot, certainly running hot' and questioning whether the armed forces were being properly resourced for such enduring operations.[25] Dannatt had arrived at the conclusion that the Army was 'doing most of the heavy lifting, the fighting and the dying' and he resolved to 'alert Tony's Blair's administration and my fellow chiefs of staff to the pressure building on the Army'.[26]

In contrast with the controversy over Iraq, the UN Security Council (UNSC) had already passed resolutions on the threat posed by Afghanistan to international security. These resolutions gave legitimacy to the initial US-led Operation Enduring Freedom and laid the basis for the continuing ISAF mission to Afghanistan after 2006. The force commitment promised by Prime Minister Blair and other world leaders after the London Conference was nurtured by the UN when it passed Resolution 1510, which laid the foundations for expanding operations beyond Kabul. UN Security Council Resolution 1662 clearly articulated the international community's view on what ought to happen:

> *Calls upon* the Afghan Government, with the assistance of the international community, including the Operation Enduring Freedom coalition and the International Security Assistance Force, in accordance with their respective designated responsibilities as they evolve, to continue to address the threat to the security and stability of Afghanistan posed by the Taliban, Al-Qaida, other extremist groups and criminal activities.[27]

Unfortunately, due to the pressures from other UNSC members, including China and Russia, the framework for delivering the mission had been largely fixed. This meant that when NATO took command of ISAF it had to operate from a disadvantage and 'had to deal with the consequences of actions over which it had little control'.[28]

One of the major problems with the resolutions and tight mandate was the autonomy they gave to states in terms of contributing troops to task. As Jennifer Medcalf has pointed out, 'The nationalising of operations in Afghanistan has also affected the effectiveness of the overall effort.'[29] Britain struggled with this more than any other state, particularly since the federalization of the MoD structure allowed for political interference at every level, from the strategic down to the tactical.[30] This was a problem of strategy that Clausewitz himself may well have recognized when he wrote:

> The only question, therefore, is whether, when war is being planned, the political point of view should give way to the purely military (if a purely military point of view is conceivable at all): that is, should it disappear completely or subordinate itself, or should the political point of view remain dominant and the military be subordinated to it?[31]

This was a conundrum facing senior military commanders, with the CGS between 2003 and 2006, Sir Mike Jackson, later admitting that the interventions in Iraq and Afghanistan were 'highly politicised' in their nature.[32] However, as this book has shown in relation to the other small wars it has profiled, Britain has always given a similar answer to Clausewitz's puzzle: the military instrument (the means) will always be subordinated to the political ends set by the government.

However, it does not excuse the underestimation of the challenge posed by Afghanistan in the corridors of power in Whitehall. This was nowhere better evidenced by the startling claim made by the MoD representatives, who boldly informed the parliamentary Defence Select Committee that '[i]t remains our assessment that the Taliban does not present a strategic threat to security in Afghanistan'.[33] In light of such an extraordinary claim, the question one must address, therefore, is to what degree this political interference has actually affected operations on the ground.

From what we now know, coherent strategy on Afghanistan was found wanting in the first years of Britain's re-deployment of forces to Helmand province. Some military commanders frequently complained of the lack of direction from their political masters. Nevertheless, these were compounded by the difficulties of working with a host nation and a more senior Coalition partner. Afghanistan in the early twenty-first century was not the same species of small war as Malaya had been in the middle of the twentieth century. Importantly, David Ucko has warned that Malaya is limited in its lessons for today's insurgencies:

> The key, however, lies in not focusing too closely on the actual methods employed in Malaya but in the underlying principles guiding the counter-insurgency effort as a whole. They centred on achieving a nuanced political understanding of the campaign, operating under unified command, using intelligence to guide operations, isolating guerrillas from the population, using an appropriate level of force necessary to achieve security and assuring and maintaining the perceived legitimacy of the counter-insurgency effort in the eyes of the populace.[34]

In reality, there were few similarities. The aim of 'winning the "hearts and minds"' of the local population was certainly present, albeit superficially speaking; however, a tighter civil–military command structure, with a firm civilian lead and a workable plan – based on the critical mass of troop numbers – to liberate areas under insurgent control was not. Moreover, it could be argued that the joining up of 'ink spots' of consent into a groundswell of support for the Kabul-based government proved almost impossible, particularly when the operational impetus seemed to be to spread the limited number of British troops thinly over an area half the size of England.[35]

Moreover, the faulty thinking[36] behind the defensive 'platoon house strategy', which pitted battle-hardened soldiers against a formidable enemy, challenged one of Britain's fundamental principles of war that concentration of force ought to brought to bear on the enemy. It did not help matters much, as Bird and Marshal maintain, when British officers insisted on harking back to the Army's distinguished COIN experience. By and large, these: '[f]ormulaic references to "winning hearts and minds" became embarrassing, given the destruction that was wreaked in the immediate vicinities of UK defensive positions'.[37] What made matters worse was the over-optimism displayed by government advisors, who argued that, despite the upsurge in violence and combat casualties, real progress was being made. Greg Mills, for instance, argued that the 'reality is different'; 'short-term reportage of security incidents remains only pixels in the wider mosaic of national progress'.[38] With advice like this, who could have blamed the military for their over-optimism? Foreign Secretary David Miliband's Special Representative to Afghanistan, Sir Sherard Cowper-Coles, singled out such advice for particular scrutiny when he described the 'very eager military with a laudable "can do" attitude offering politicians over-optimistic advice about what can be done and the resources needed to do it'.[39] General

Sir Nicholas Houghton, who was the Commander of Joint Operations in both Iraq and Afghanistan in 2006–07, later summed up this attitude when he said:

> I felt in Iraq, we could deliver the strategy, with risk, with the means that were available, but it became relatively quickly evident that within Afghanistan we were not militarily in a position of strategic coherence. We did not have the means to deliver on objectives, and, therefore, the requirement to rebalance, to make us strategically balanced in Afghanistan.[40]

As Operation Herrick 4 progressed, observed James Fergusson, 'it looked more and more as though the British had indeed chosen to pursue a purely military solution',[41] which ignored the lessons drawn from past experience in Malaya and Britain's other small wars. On a more basic military level, the dispersal strategy also ran counter to the Army's own principle of concentration of force.[42]

The strategic differences between Malaya and Afghanistan were stark. For one thing, Britain was now a junior partner in a much bigger US-led mission. Along with the smaller military presence, the diplomatic clout wielded from London was nowhere near as influential as it had been in colonial times, with the mission in Afghanistan teetering on the brink of failure.[43] Moreover, no matter how powerful the individual military and civilian leaders appointed by the US, Britain or the UN, the 'Briggs Plan' could not be re-created beyond some rather vague references to 'ink spots'. It was the legitimacy of the Afghan state – represented after 2004 by the administration of Hamid Karzai – that was at stake. Additionally, some of the tactical lessons from Malaya were not suitable for Afghanistan. The terrain, both human and physical, was completely different and overlooked how in Malaya (and Northern Ireland for that matter), the political process was seen as legitimate by the vast majority of the people. As one recognized authority on Malaya has concluded, 'It is naive to think that the blend of policies found at the optimisation phase of successful insurgencies will work well at the outset of a conflict.'[44] Other oversights included the need to initiate security sector reform, which meant co-operating (or partnering) with indigenous security forces while pursuing a policy of tackling criminality, such as the illicit drug trade. Bird and Marshal remind us how:

> Individual policy areas became disconnected from any sense of a co-ordinated whole. Each had its own internal dynamics, controversies, differences of emphasis and debates. Counter-narcotics, security sector reform, reconciliation, anti-corruption, counterinsurgency and regional

> engagement were all pursued to a greater or lesser extent, but in an unco-ordinated manner that produced often contradictory and mutually exclusive initiatives.[45]

Arguably, what made matters worse on the ground was the lack of co-ordination between the various government departments deployed as part of Britain's repertoire of civil–military support for the ISAF mission. By the closing months of 2010, however, convincing evidence emerged that these shortcomings had been addressed and that more focused policy had replaced the confusion.[46]

The involvement of Britain's armed forces in two operational theatres whipped up 'a perfect storm',[47] according to Richard Dannatt, who, in his first major interview as CGS, was 'apparently calling for a withdrawal from Iraq, criticising the government and making other disparaging remarks in an interview with the *Daily Mail*'.[48] Jonathan Powell, Tony Blair's Chief of Staff, revealed how '[w]e were getting pressure from Labour politicians to dismiss him, but to do that would turn him into a martyr'.[49] Instead, Blair later briefed the Chiefs of Staff and warned them that 'if commanders behaved in this political way they could guarantee that prime ministers in future would not put British troops in harm's way'.[50] Dannatt's interjections in the political debate only served to aggravate a deeper problem in British strategizing: namely, that fighting 'a war on two fronts' was not something defence planners envisaged ever having to do, certainly not for a period longer than six months; nor could it be realistically sustained, despite the termination of Operation Banner in the summer of 2007. It has been argued that, under New Labour, the armed forces were woefully underfunded and under-resourced – giving the impression that Britain remained content to simply muddle through in Afghanistan.[51] The pressure placed on the armed forces by fighting 'a war on two fronts' had placed the Military Covenant under pressure and he warned against the lack of support for troops on the ground.[52] As Dannatt pointed out to an audience in London:

> We *must* move from being a society that uses the military as a political and media football – and more towards seeing the military for what it is – the instrument of foreign policy conducted by a democratically elected Government acting in the name of the people.[53]

In Dannatt's mind this meant placing a greater premium upon soldiers in society and he actively sought a recalibration in Clausewitz's 'holy trinity' between government, army and nation, a position that almost cost him his job as CGS and in all probability sounded the death knell on his promotion to CDS.[54] In retirement, Dannatt has been acerbic about the way that Labour had handled defence, recalling at one public meeting how it was important while these conflicts were ongoing that someone could represent the interests of the Army at the highest political levels in London.[55] That Dannatt choose to do so in a more upfront and confrontational way, however, placed him on the same par as some of his Whitehall predecessors, most notably Field-Marshal Montgomery.

By their third year of their deployment to Helmand, British troops were making little strategic progress.[56] Their operations were likened to 'mowing the lawn', insofar as when they killed or captured insurgents, the Taliban simply sprouted up again. And at the tactical level British troops were being drawn into an increasingly brutal fight with their opponents, who were now using more sophisticated weapons against coalition forces based in forward operating bases. The number of attacks from Improvised Explosive Devices (IEDs) grew exponentially, killing and wounding more and more soldiers on the ground.[57] The most horrific injuries were being sustained, to the point where Britain was rumoured to have been experiencing a crisis in its battlefield casualty replacement system. In terms of casualties, the numbers of dead steadily rose from 39 in 2006, to 42 in 2007, 51 in 2008, 108 in 2009 and 103 in 2010. Remarkably, 1,746 had been wounded in action between 2006 and 31 July 2011. Of this total, 527 were very seriously or seriously injured.[58]

'Chickens coming home to roost': a change in priorities

The outcome of the British general election in May 2010 signalled a significant step-change in British policy towards Afghanistan. In the run-up to the election all three party leaders broadly agreed on the need to ensure that political and military efforts succeeded. Writing in the weeks running up to the election Conservative Party leader David Cameron accepted that:

> The strategy which has been in place since the end of last year is, I believe, broadly the right one; we must give it the necessary time and support to succeed. That is how we can continue to reverse the Taliban's momentum, build up the Afghan armed forces, and create the conditions for transition to Afghan control.[59]

Within days of his appointment as Defence Secretary, Dr Liam Fox accompanied his ministerial colleagues – International Development Secretary Andrew Mitchell and Foreign Secretary William Hague – on a joint trip to Afghanistan. It was a unique demonstration of the government's intent to place the war in Afghanistan at the top of its list of priorities, and in a joint statement all three ministers outlined the new Coalition government's policy:

> Afghanistan remains one of the poorest countries in the world. There are few countries where the combination of our moral commitment to development and safeguarding our national interest is so enmeshed. Building the capacity of the state to guarantee security and stability, deliver development and reduce poverty is central to defeating violent extremism and protecting British streets. Looking at ways to improve the quality and impact of our aid will be a key part of this visit.[60]

Shortly after its formation, the Conservative–Liberal Democrat Coalition announced that it would make Afghanistan its main effort. However, it would not be immediately drawn on a likely deadline for British disengagement from the country. As Hague made clear when challenged by a BBC reporter, 'of course sometimes things are tougher than you expected. And so you've got to try and make sure . . . the strategy's right and the progress is taking place, but not make the job harder of the people doing such hard work here by setting them an artificial deadline'.[61] Ironically, within a matter of months the British government had agreed on a deadline. Reaffirming its 'continued resolve and commitment' on Afghanistan, it set a date of 2015 for the withdrawal of combat troops,[62] although admitted that military training teams would remain behind to ensure the training of host nation forces, similar to what had been done after the termination of British combat operations in Iraq in 2009.

Arguably, it was the shift in policy towards Afghanistan between New Labour and the new Coalition government which has also exposed something more damaging. Under Labour, there was a woeful disconnection between political objectives and military ways and means. In the Clausewitzian sense, of course, the two are always closely interwoven and mutually dependent. Yet, as Sir Sherard Cowper-Coles noted, over six months into the Coalition government's term in office:

> Afghanistan needs a new political and regional settlement, which cannot be delivered by military force. Military force can contribute – there is no military solution but, equally, there is no non-military solution. Military force plays a part but, in my view and my experience, it should and must be a subsidiary part. That is why politicians like you – like this Committee – need to develop and encourage the vision of a political approach to solving the underlying tensions that are giving rise to the violence.[63]

Cowper-Coles' disgruntlement may have been personal, after all he had stepped down as Britain's Special Envoy to Afghanistan and Pakistan in June 2010, yet it was tempered with the experience that Britain's strategy may well have become self-defeating. In a scathing attack on the civil–military leadership in London, he claimed that the strategy guiding operations was driven more by resources available to the Army, than by 'an objective assessment of the needs of a proper counter-insurgency campaign in the province'.[64]

Interestingly, against the backdrop of a renewed focus on succeeding in Afghanistan was a complete absence of the promotion of democracy, the leitmotif which had previously driven New Labour's foreign policy. In contrast, Liberal Democrats and Conservatives had remained unconvinced of the merits of liberal interventionism, with Liam Fox publicly stating that he had little time for the 'ethical dimension in foreign policy'. While the media lambasted Fox for 'speaking off message', it seems that the Coalition government's approach to strategizing about national security issues 'was more "politics-led" than the government would have cared to reveal', which was, in another sense, also 'more "economics-led" than the government would have dared to reveal'.[65]

The Strategic Defence and Security Review

The Coalition government's rush to impose severe efficiency savings measures has been justified on the basis that Britain's economic well-being is just as important as its armed forces. The Strategic Defence and Security Review (SDSR), was published 24 hours after the National Security Strategy (NSS), promised to undertake root and branch reform of the MoD. The SDSR reinforced the Conservative's integrated approach to security, defence and foreign policy.[66] Already the ambitious and heady policy of the Labour government was being reversed. Fox went further than many of his ministerial colleagues by stating, categorically, that Britain was not in Afghanistan 'for the sake of the education policy in a broken 13th-century country. We are there so the people of Britain and our global interests are not threatened.'[67] This was in marked contrast to the Labour approach, which continually played up the altruistic ambition of helping the Afghan people emerge from the clutches of an oppressive insurgency.

Moreover, whereas New Labour had undertaken a foreign-policy-led defence review in 1997, the Coalition government had given much more authority for decision-making to the Treasury, even though decisions were officially to be taken by the National Security Council (NSC), a much more integrated mechanism for overseeing British security. In the Coalition government's inaugural NSS it argued that the world had changed and new threats had emerged, ridiculing the Labour government for not taking this into account. One of the defining features of the NSS was the delineation in the character of conflict since the Cold War and how 'Iraq and Afghanistan have placed huge and unexpected demands on Britain's national security arrangements'.[68]

The SDSR set a number of high-profile objectives for Britain. The main one, perhaps unsurprisingly, in relation to the enduring mission in Afghanistan, was to stabilize the state and prevent the return of Al Qaeda terrorists. British troops numbered approximately 9,500 by the end of 2011. However, the SDSR also placed a deadline on the involvement of British forces, which it anticipated would be withdrawn from a combat role by 2015. Interestingly, General Sir David Richards was regularly briefing the media that they would remain until the job was done. In many ways this parroted the line being taken by Richards' close friend and ally, General David Petreaus, who, as Commander of ISAF between 2009 and 2011, was uneasy with the prospect of pulling out before the job was done. That there nevertheless remained a time limit on military involvement signalled to the Taliban that all they needed to do was to keep a watching brief and then go all out once ISAF handed over to the Afghan National Security Forces (ANSF). There were uncomfortable echoes of Palestine, Malaya and Aden, which undoubtedly persuaded the insurgents to keep going until the foreign occupiers withdrew, thus heralding a strategic defeat. However, one might resort to even the most determined authority on counterinsurgency, Sir Robert Thompson, who argued that in a protracted engagement with an irregular opponent, one had a stark choice: withdraw or escalate. 'The only difference between the two', he wrote amidst the Vietnam War, 'is that, by withdrawing, you merely lose, but by further escalation, you lose stinking'.[69]

For a number of years Britain's armed forces were 'running hot', fighting what General Dannatt termed 'a war on two fronts', in many ways a metaphor for his own internal Whitehall battles against both his political masters in the Labour government and the terrorists and insurgents now ranged across the various theatres of the war on terror. As the SDSR noted:

> We must also confront the legacy of overstretch. Between 2006 and 2009 UK forces were deployed at medium scale in both Iraq and Afghanistan. This exceeded the planning assumptions that had set the size of our forces and placed greater demands both on our people and on their equipment than had been planned for.[70]

The SDSR's conclusions also pointed towards a deeper, more pronounced tendency within the previous New Labour government to employ force as one of the main options in dealing with threats to national security.

Under the Coalition government, the NSC has assumed overall responsibility for operations in Afghanistan. In the 'age of austerity' these interlinked problems cannot be solved without the concerted efforts of all instruments of power working in harmony. Moreover, the Chancellor of the Exchequer's mantra of 'Britain living within her means' has had a remarkable influence on military operations, as efficiency savings are sought out to plug the country's gapping deficit.[71] Andrew Dorman has cautioned us against buying into the assumption that defence spending can be adjusted to suit the economic outlook. Instead defence must be decided according to a more strategic calculus, taking into account the desired policy ends and balancing these with the ways and means:

> The idea that defence should be increased or decreased depending on economic performance makes no logical sense. As the first duty of government, the relative level of defence spending should be determined by the level of threat posed and the requisite armed forces needed to counter them.[72]

As the Coalition government's tenure wore on it was becoming increasingly apparent that the timescale for withdrawal of all combat forces would remain unmovable. The main effort of the NSC, Foreign and Commonwealth Office, DFID, MoD and the Armed Forces throughout 2011 remained Afghanistan. In the annual CDS lecture at the Royal United Services Institute, General Sir David Richards reviewed the year. Reaffirming the government's policy, he lost no time in following the PM's lead vis-à-vis the 2015 deadline, though he conceded how, 'Of course, we all recognise that the UK relationship with Afghanistan will continue for many years to come, including an enduring and highly supportive Defence relationship'.[73] Even under a new government, it seems that the MoD is eager to maintain the view that the conditions-based approach is dictating the withdrawal date.

By now military doctrine had evolved to capture the learning of how to handle the drawdown, bringing online what the MoD now referred to as 'security transitions'. As the military doctrine on this makes clear: '[t]he ultimate goal of security transition is sufficient stability for other processes of state-building and peace-building to mature without being dependent on an operational international military presence'.[74] Interestingly, the central focus of this process is support of the political process, something learned by operations in Northern Ireland over 38 years, but arguably important to all of Britain's small wars since 1945.

Conclusion

While the Coalition government moved away from the 'joined up' view of foreign, defence and security policy towards a more 'integrated' and 'whole of government' approach may appear somewhat cosmetic, it nonetheless marked a significant step-change in Britain's policy towards Afghanistan. Perhaps, unsurprisingly, the rhetoric of democracy promotion and the perpetuity of the 'ethical dimension' in Britain's foreign policy has since been dropped in favour of the more limited aim of stabilization. The focus, perhaps from as early as 2009, has been much more on Britain's homeland security and the need to establish a functioning state in Afghanistan that can meet the challenges of an armed opposition and deter terrorists from operating within its borders.

In terms of the Coalition government's revised counter-terrorist strategy, the role of defence has become only one piece of a co-ordinated civil–military effort to protect Britain's national interests. Nonetheless, just like in the past, the military continues to bear the brunt of overseas operations even amidst an to as the 'age of austerity' in British defence policy.[75] That David Cameron's government has tried to breathe new life into the Afghan small war during this 'age of austerity' has been ably assisted by the military's own internal housekeeping. The MoD's internal training regime has been overhauled in recent years in order to focus the minds of its servicemen and women on the main effort in Afghanistan. 'Operation Entirety' began under General Dannatt's watch, when General Sir David Richards was Commander-in-Chief, and has sought to place the British Army on a war footing, while attempting to articulate more clearly the principal reasons why Britain's presence in the country is needed. In Professor Anthony King's words, Operation Entirety has been 'notably partial in which bits of the army and which bits of the Helmand campaign have been put on a genuine war-footing'. As with previous campaigns, there has been little doubt in the insurgents' minds 'about whether they are at war or not'.[76]

Another key aspect of the war in Afghanistan, which had always featured to a greater or lesser degree in Britain's other small wars, was the increasing audibility of public opinion. Throughout the post-1945 period public opinion has factored more in the decision-making process of politicians and military commanders and has frequently been accredited with precipitating the withdrawal of British forces, particularly when the cost in 'blood and treasure' has been judged too high. The impact on domestic politics is all too obvious, as Richard Dannatt has warned, and it comes with 'the risk' of success 'being undermined by a precipitate reduction in our troop levels for domestic political reasons'.[77] Helping the public understand why the ISAF mission in Afghanistan is so important was vital and would help politicians keep a steady posture. Yet, one might add that the rush to withdraw according to a domestic political timetable risks leaving raising the stakes in terms of international politics. Premature withdrawal, in the eyes of other, more predatory, states risks sending a signal of weakness no amount of finessing public opinion at home can arrest.

Notes

1 Callwell, Colonel Charles Edward, *Small Wars: Their Principles and Practice*, third edition (London: HMSO, 1906), p. 85.
2 Ministry of Defence (MoD), *Joint Defence Publication 0-01: British Defence Doctrine* (Shrivenham: DCDC, August 2008), para. 113.
3 Comments by General Sir Mike Jackson at the 15th Whither Warfare Conference, Royal Military Academy Sandhurst, 6 May 2011.
4 United Nations Security Council (UNSC), S/RES/1363 (2001), 30 July 2001. Archived: http://daccess-dds-ny.un.org/doc/UNDOC/GEN/N01/473/97/PDF/N0147397.pdf?OpenElement. Accessed: 16 January 2011.
5 Burke, Jason, *Al Qaeda: The True Story of Radical Islam*, third edition (London: Penguin, 2007), p. 13. Burke cautions against viewing Al Qaeda as monolithic, arguing that it should be seen as a movement of radical Islamists. Al Qaeda's leader Osama Bin Laden was eliminated by US Special Forces in May 2011. It was reported that Bin Laden had been living in Abbotabad, several hundred kilometres south of Islamabad, between 2005 and his death at the hands of US forces in 2011.
6 Blair, Tony, *A Journey* (London: Hutchinson, 2010), p. 357.
7 Fergusson, James, *Taliban: The True Story of the World's Most Feared Guerrilla Fighters* (London: Transworld, 2010), p. 113; pp. 128–131.
8 Conversation with a former commander of British forces in Afghanistan, Sandhurst, December 2010.
9 Giustozzi, Antonio, *Koran, Kalashnikov and Laptop* (London: Hurst and Company, 2007), p. 71.
10 While it is impossible to say for sure what lessons were applied with any kind of authority, one can find traces of these lessons in the military's formal doctrine. There is evidence in Joint Defence Publication (JDP), 2/07, *Countering Irregular Activity within a Comprehensive Approach* (Shrivenham: DCDC, 2007).
11 Latawski, Paul, *The Inherent Tensions in Military Doctrine*, Sandhurst Occasional Papers, No. 5 (Camberley: RMA Sandhurst, 2011), p. 2.
12 Ibid., p. 1.
13 Ibid.

14 For more on this point see Kiszely, Lieutenant General Sir John, 'Learning about Counter-Insurgency', *RUSI Journal*, Vol. 151, No. 6 (December 2006), pp. 16–21; Alderson, Colonel Alex, 'The Army's "Brain": A Historical Perspective on Doctrine and Development', *British Army Review*, No. 150 (winter 2010/11), pp. 60–64; Newton, Paul, Paul Colley and Andrew Sharpe, 'Reclaiming the Art of British Strategic Thinking', *RUSI Journal*, Vol. 155, No. 1 (2010), pp. 44–50.

15 For a similar argument see Egnell, Robert, 'Lessons from Helmand, Afghanistan: What Now for British Counter-Insurgency?', *International Affairs*, Vol. 87, No. 2 (2011), pp. 297–315. For an outline of the military lessons learned by the British Army during Operation Banner see Edwards, Aaron, 'Misapplying Lessons Learned? Analysing the Utility of British Counter-Insurgency Strategy in Northern Ireland, 1971–76', *Small Wars and Insurgencies*, Vol. 21, No. 2 (June 2010), pp. 303–330 and Edwards, Aaron, 'Deterrence, Coercion and Brute Force in Asymmetric Conflict: The Role of the Military Instrument in Resolving the Northern Ireland "Troubles"', *Dynamics of Asymmetric Conflict*, Vol. 4, No. 3 (December 2011), pp. 226–241.

16 MoD, *Strategic Trends Programme: Future Character of Conflict* (Shrivenham: DCDC, February 2010), p. 1.

17 Cited in Wilkinson, Isambard, 'British take on Taliban in five days of Afghan fire fights', *Daily Telegraph*, 23 May 2006.

18 Harding, Thomas, 'A Year in Helmand: 4 Million Bullets Fired by British', *Daily Telegraph*, 12 January 2008.

19 Kirkup, James, 'British troops fire 12m bullets in three years', *Daily Telegraph*, 10 August 2009.

20 Fergusson, James, *A Million Bullets: The Real Story of the British Army in Afghanistan* (London: Bantam Press, 2008), p. 329.

21 Bird, Tim and Alex Marshal, *Afghanistan: How the West Lost its Way* (London: Yale University Press, 2011), p. 159.

22 House of Commons (Hansard) Debates, 23 January 2006, Vol. 441, Col. 1161.

23 Ibid., Col. 1159. My emphasis.

24 Conversation with a former commander of British forces in Afghanistan, Sandhurst, December 2010.

25 Cited in *The Guardian*, 4 September 2006.

26 Dannatt, General Sir Richard, *Leading from the Front: The Autobiography* (London: Bantam Press, 2010), p. 236.

27 UNSC, S/RES/1662 (2006), 23 March 2006. Archived: http://daccess-dds-ny.un.org/doc/UNDOC/GEN/N06/281/41/PDF/N0628141.pdf?OpenElement. Accessed: 9 November 2010.

28 Medcalf, Jennifer, *Going Global or Going Nowhere? NATO's Role in Contemporary International Security* (Oxford: Peter Lang, 2008), p. 177.

29 Ibid., p. 187.

30 On the point about the 'byzantine structure' of the MoD, see Levene, Lord, *Defence Reform: An Independent Report into the Structure and Management of the Ministry of Defence* (London: The Stationery Office, June 2011).
31 Clausewitz, Carl Von, *On War*, edited and translated by Michael Howard and Peter Paret (Princeton, NJ: Princeton University Press, 1989), p. 607.
32 Comments by General Sir Mike Jackson at the 15th Whither Warfare Conference, Royal Military Academy Sandhurst, 6 May 2011.
33 House of Commons Defence Committee, *UK Operations in Afghanistan: Government Response to the Committee's Thirteenth Report, 2006–07*, dated 9 October 2007, HC 1024 (London: The Stationery Office, 12 October 2007), p. 4.
34 Ucko, David, 'The Malayan Emergency: The Legacy and Relevance of a Counter-Insurgency Success Story', *Defence Studies*, Vol. 10, Nos. 1–2 (March–June 2010), pp. 34–35.
35 Troop numbers stood at 2,400 at the end of March 2006. The majority of these troops were not infantry. Written answer from Adam Ingram to Jim Cunningham, MP, House of Commons (Hansard), 30 March 2006, Vol. 444, Col. 1151W.
36 Egnell, 'Lessons from Helmand', p. 303.
37 Bird and Marshal, *Afghanistan*, p. 172.
38 Mills, Greg, 'Calibrating Ink Spots: Filling Afghanistan's Ungoverned Spaces', *RUSI Journal*, Vol. 151, No. 4 (August 2006), p. 25.
39 Cited in Harnden, Toby, *Dead Men Risen: The Welsh Guards and the Real Story of Britain's War in Afghanistan* (London: Quercus, 2011), p. 40.
40 Iraq Inquiry, Oral Evidence of General Sir Nicholas Houghton on 'The Military Perspective from London, 2006–07', 3 December 2010, pp. 35–36. Archived: www.iraqinquiry.org.uk/media/41897/20100105amhoughton-style-final.pdf. Accessed: 21 July 2010.
41 Fergusson, *A Million Bullets*, p. 153.
42 King, Anthony, 'Understanding the Helmand Campaign', *International Affairs*, Vol. 86, No. 2 (March 2010), p. 321.
43 Coghlan, Tom, 'Afghan mission is shaken up after Blair tells envoys of his frustration', *Daily Telegraph*, 22 January 2007. Soon after, Blair appointed Sherard Cowper-Coles as Ambassador to Kabul.
44 Hack, Karl, 'The Malayan Emergency as Counter-Insurgency Paradigm', *Journal of Strategic Studies*, Vol. 32, No. 3 (June 2009), p. 412.
45 Bird and Marshal, *Afghanistan*, p. 252.
46 House of Commons Foreign Affairs Select Committee, Corrected Transcript of Oral Evidence given by Rt Hon. William Hague and Karen Pierce CMG, The UK's Foreign Policy Afghanistan and Pakistan, 15 November 2010.
47 Dannatt, *Leading from the Front*, p. 236.
48 Powell, Jonathan, *Great Hatred, Little Room: Making Peace in Ireland* (London: The Bodley Head, 2008), p. 286.
49 Ibid.

50 Ibid., pp. 286–287. David Cameron's government has gone further by checking the power of Chiefs of Staff in Whitehall, excluding them from the Army board and opting instead to have their collective views aired via the Chief of the Defence Staff.

51 Betz, David and Anthony Cormack, 'Iraq, Afghanistan and British Strategy', *Orbis: A Journal of World Affairs*, Vol. 53, No. 2 (spring 2009), p. 336.

52 McCartney, Helen, 'The Military Covenant and the Civil–Military Contract in Britain', *International Affairs*, Vol. 86, No. 2 (March 2010), pp. 411–428.

53 Dannatt, Richard, *Address to the International Institute of Strategic Studies, 21 September 2007*. Archived: www.iiss.org/conferences/military-leaders-forum/general-sir-richard-dannatt. Accessed: 1 July 2010.

54 Smith, Michael, 'Gordon Brown pulls rank to stop General Sir Richard Dannatt heading forces', *The Times*, 15 June 2008.

55 Dannatt, General Lord, 'Morality in Public Life: A Soldier's Perspective', Public Lecture to the St Paul's Camberley Debating Society, 7 March 2011. Notes by the author.

56 See Holmes, Richard, 'Rupert should not have died for this', *The Times*, 7 July 2009. The late, great military historian Professor Richard Holmes argued that 'We need a real strategy, not a sequence of tactical ploys; winning battles will not necessarily win the war.' An article by Anthony Lloyd later in the same year argued that 'Sangin is the most glaring example of Britain's strategic bleed-out in Helmand'. Lloyd, Anthony, 'Weary troops are fighting a losing battle not a lost cause', *The Times*, 23 September 2009.

57 Rayment, Sean, *Bomb Hunters: In Afghanistan with Britain's Elite Bomb Disposal Unit* (London: HarperCollins, 2011).

58 Defence Analytical Services and Advice, MoD, figures released on 16 August 2011.

59 Cameron, David, 'The Conservative Party View of Future Defence and Security Policy', *RUSI Analysis – Commentary*, April 2010. Archived: www.rusi.org/analysis/commentary/ref:C4BCEC98CCE762. Accessed: 10 October 2010.

60 Department for International Development, Secretaries of State Visit Afghanistan, 22 May 2010. Archived: www.dfid.gov.uk/Media-Room/Press-releases/2010/Secretaries-of-State-visit-Afghanistan. Accessed: 31 May 2010.

61 Foreign Secretary William Hague speaking to the broadcaster Jon Sopel in Afghanistan on BBC1's Politics Show, 23 May 2010. Archived: www.fco.gov.uk/en/news/latest-news/?view=Speech&id=22268610. Accessed: 2 June 2010.

62 See HMG, *The National Security Strategy*, para 1.2 and box. Archived: www.direct.gov.uk/prod_consum_dg/groups/dg_digitalassets/@dg/@en/documents/digitalasset/dg_191639.pdf?CID=PDF&PLA=furl&CRE=nationalsecuritystrategy. Accessed: 18 October 2010.

63 Corrected Transcript of Oral Evidence to be published as HC 514-iii, House of Commons Oral Evidence taken before the Foreign Affairs Committee,

The UK's Foreign Policy towards Afghanistan and Pakistan, Tuesday 9 November 2010, Sir Sherard Cowper-Coles KCMG, Gilles Dorronsoro and Gerard Russell MBE.

64 Norton-Taylor, Richard, 'Army strategy in Helmand under fire from former top diplomat', *The Guardian*, 13 January 2011.

65 Cornish, Paul and Andrew M. Dorman, 'Dr Fox and the Philosopher's Stone: The Alchemy of National Defence in the Age of Austerity', *International Affairs*, Vol. 87, No. 2 (2011), p. 346.

66 Sylvester, Rachel and Alice Thomson, 'Liam Fox, new Defence Secretary, flies flag for our boys and Eurosceptics', *The Times*, 21 May 2010.

67 Adetunji, Jo, 'Liam Fox tells soldiers their operational allowance will be doubled', *The Guardian*, 23 May, 2010.

68 See HMG, *A Strong Britain in an Age of Uncertainty: The National Security Strategy* (London: Cabinet Office, October 2010), Foreword. Archived: www.direct.gov.uk/prod_consum_dg/groups/dg_digitalassets/@dg/@en/documents/digitalasset/dg_191639.pdf. Accessed: 12 July 2011.

69 Thompson, Sir Robert, 'Squaring the Error', *Foreign Affairs*, Vol. 46 (1968), p. 442.

70 HMG, *Securing Britain in an Age of Uncertainty: The Strategic Defence and Security Review* (London: Cabinet Office, October 2010), p. 15. Archived: www.direct.gov.uk/prod_consum_dg/groups/dg_digitalassets/@dg/@en/documents/digitalasset/dg_191634.pdf?CID=PDF&PLA=furl&CRE=sdsr. Accessed: 12 July 2011.

71 See the comments by George Osborne in his 'Speech at The Lord Mayor's Dinner for Bankers & Merchants of the City of London', Mansion House, 16 June 2010'. Archived: www.hm-treasury.gov.uk/press_12_10.htm. Accessed: 18 January 2011.

72 Dorman, Andrew, 'Providing for Defence in an Age of Austerity: Future War, Defence Cuts and the 2010 Strategic Defence and Security Review', *The Political Quarterly*, Vol. 81, No. 3 (July–September 2010), p. 380.

73 Richards, General Sir David, *11th Annual Chief of Defence Staff Lecture*, 14 December 2010. Archived: www.mod.uk/DefenceInternet/AboutDefence/People/Speeches/ChiefStaff/20101214 11thAnnualChiefOfDefenceStaffLecture.htm. Accessed: 20 January 2011.

74 MoD/Stabilisation Unit, Joint Doctrine Note 6/10, *Security Transitions: The Military Contribution* (Shrivenham: DCDC, November 2010), p. vi.

75 See Cornish and Dorman, 'Dr Fox and the Philosopher's Stone', pp. 335–353.

76 King, Anthony, 'A six-month command is not the way to beat the Taliban', *Parliamentary Brief*, 5 March 2011. Archived: www.parliamentarybrief.com/2011/03/a-six-month-command-is-not-the-way-to-beat#all. Accessed: 10 August 2011.

77 Dannatt, Richard, 'We must hold fast in Afghanistan, or we'll lose all we have fought for', *Daily Telegraph*, 1 January 2011.

Conclusion

> In a society of sovereign nations, military force is a necessary instrument of foreign policy. Yet the instrument of foreign policy should not become the master of foreign policy. As war is fought in order to make peace possible, foreign policy should be conducted in order to make peace permanent. For the performance of both tasks, the subordination of the military under the civilian authorities which are constitutionally responsible for the conduct of foreign affairs is an indispensable prerequisite.[1]

> While the politicians havered, while authority crumbled, the soldier tried to keep order. And when at last the British had gone, from country after country, it was found that the British army was the only British institution to leave a permanent mark – the mark of order and organization amid a carnival of collapsing parliamentary government.[2]

> [W]e have all but lost the capacity to think strategically. We have simply fallen out of the habit, and have lost the culture of strategy making.[3]

'War is a big and sprawling word that brings a lot of human suffering into the conversation, but combat is a different matter' wrote Sebastian Junger in his essay *War*, which paints a vivid and arresting picture of the rigours of warfare as experienced on a very individual level by US soldiers in Afghanistan.[4] Junger might also have added that war – in terms of the actual collective fighting between belligerents – is 'big and sprawling', not only because of the human and cultural effects of the bloodshed it often heralds but also because of the political context that weighs heavily on the minds of those who engage in it. Junger rarely delves into the political connotations of war, preferring to see the engagement between combatants as warfare in all its deceptively primal glory, a culminating point when 'combat stops being a grand chess game between generals and becomes a no-holds-barred experiment in pure killing'.[5] In this respect, Junger shares much in common with those who would dispute the enduring relevance of Clausewitz's political understanding of warfare. Notable amongst these critics has been the distinguished military historian Sir John Keegan, who has called into question the 'poisonous intoxication'[6] of Clausewitz's definition of war and suggested that perhaps there is 'an even greater wisdom in the denial that politics and war belong within the same continuum'.[7] This anti-Clausewitz fault-line in our understanding of the nature of war runs deep and perhaps manifests itself most acutely amongst those at the so-called 'crunchier end of operations', with the toms, bootnecks, jocks, rangers and sappers who have been called upon to implement government policy in some of the most hostile soldiering environments on earth.

As this book has endeavoured to illustrate, even if soldiers do not give politics more than a passing – and in the author's experience, often derogatory – thought in the everyday business of 'combat', their actions are directed by and, in turn, help shape, the principal political context of war.[8] In Clausewitz's immortal words, war is 'the continuation of political intercourse, carried on with other means'.[9] However, this statement has often been expressed by those, like Keegan, who see the Prussian philosopher of war and his present-day followers in the strategic studies camp as positively jingoistic and impervious to human suffering in war. While this may be true of some strategists, it is not true of all, for, as Colin S. Gray reminds us, 'strategy is impregnated with moral content'.[10] One must not lose sight of a reoccurring theme developed in this book, which is that while individuals might well be guided by morals, states are not.[11]

The classical realist scholar Hans Morgenthau, for instance, suggests that 'the degree in which the essence and aim of politics is power over man, politics is evil; for it is to this degree that it degrades man to a means for other men'.[12] Pursuing this logic further, therefore, the waging of war is perhaps to be seen as the purest form of the struggle for power. Moreover, politics, or international politics more precisely, involves maximizing and furthering a state's power for the business of securing its national interests. For Morgenthau, that most tough-minded of realists, international politics can be defined as 'a continuing effort to maintain and to increase the power of one's own nation and to keep in check or reduce the power of other nations'.[13] Morgenthau, like many classical realists, points to the zero-sum nature of power in the international system and the inevitable clash between human beings in securing the nation state's political ends. His view of human nature is broadly correct; competitiveness, selfishness and the 'security dilemma' make the international system the anarchic place it has always been. However, even Morgenthau has a blindspot in his thinking, choosing to concentrate his gaze more on the interplay between national interests and domestic political opinion in the pursuance of policy, though this crucial point must also be factored into our discussions of Britain's way of warfare.[14]

Arguably, nowhere has the zero-sum nature of power been as exacting as it has in Britain's small war in Afghanistan. There are several inter-connecting reasons why. First, the success of the long-term counter-insurgency and stabilization project is not yet certain. The Taliban may be on the ropes but they have not yet been defeated. Neither Britain nor any other state actor involved has been able to draw them out for a decisive military 'win'. Secondly, much hinges on the ability of Afghan National Security Forces (ANSF) to take increasing responsibility for the security transition on the ground. Finally, while Britain and the US insist that they are involved in the stabilization of Afghanistan to protect their homelands from terrorist attacks – that have been and may continue to be – launched from within Afghanistan, the truth is that war in Afghanistan involves overlapping, competing and mutually exclusive national interests that go well beyond the immediate project of stabilising the country. Since 2006, Afghanistan has become the crucible of a much wider conflict involving its neighbours: from the predatory ambitions of Iran to the malign influences of Pakistan's 'Janus-faced' civil–military establishment.[15] How the US and Britain define their strategic goals and the methodology they choose in dealing with these regional dynamics will determine their longer-term security, more so perhaps than prevailing victorious over a localized insurgency. While possibly a little too jingoistic to admit, it is not beyond the realms of possibility that 'the agents of order', to paraphrase Colin S. Gray, 'must be capable of imposing discipline on the agents of disorder. Sometimes, war is necessary.'[16] Yet even experts on the region itself have concluded how '[t]here is no more a political solution in Afghanistan alone than there is a military solution in Afghanistan alone'.[17]

That there must be a political *and* military solution in small wars has certainly been the conclusion reached by Britain somewhere in between the 'third' and 'fourth' Afghan wars, when an ailing Great Power sought to apply its will on resilient adversaries in some of the world's other harsh soldiering environments. In many ways, Britain's 'small wars' have helped to define the famous soldiering tradition with which it is renowned the world over. However, as this book has attempted to show, it was a reputation that was hard-won. For one thing, the lessons learned from these campaigns suggest that there has frequently been a disconnection in civil and military relations, so much so that failure – and risk of failure – has only been averted once these relations have been harmonized and unity of effort restored between Britain's political and military establishment. By taking a more strategic perspective on these conflicts, this book has demonstrated that Britain has typically misapplied force against its irregular opponents in the short term, before, finally, re-calibrating its approach for success in the long term. While there has been a tendency amongst politicians to forget these past failures, the British Army – as an institution – has been much more critical in its own assessment of what it could have done better.[18] The degree of intellectual agility evident amongst today's general staff is certainly welcome, but the lack of an effective mechanism for capturing *and* disseminating lessons learned from its institutional memory means that politicians are unlikely to follow suit.[19] It is, instead, much more likely that politicians will continue to rely on the military to fall back on its own institutional culture of doing what is expected from them in their service of the nation.[20] The indefatigable 'Tommy' of Rudyard Kipling fame will not unreasonably continue to bring 'order and organization', to paraphrase Correlli Barnett, amidst a 'carnival' of Britain's crumbling authority.

Re-imagining Britain's small war strategy

Addressing Officer Cadets at the Royal Military Academy Sandhurst Commissioning Parade in August 2010, Prime Minister David Cameron observed that 'as newly commissioned officers, you are all following in the footsteps of nearly 200 years of history'. He reminded them that many would soon be joining their chosen regiment or corps on operations in Afghanistan and that they faced tough times ahead. Nonetheless, the Army had loyally stood in the breach and, for him personally, he would 'never forget that defence of the realm is the first duty of any government'.[21] Cameron went on to say that in today's complex security environment, soldiers are 'also diplomats, because this is not about two armies facing each other. It is a war amongst the people.' The concept of 'war amongst the people' is not new, as General Sir Rupert Smith reminded us in his influential book *The Utility of Force* in 2005; indeed, the idea of the irregular grammar of warfare can be traced back to the early nineteenth century in the form of Napoleon Bonaparte's *levée en masse* and Carl von Clausewitz's 'people at arms'.[22] The view that soldiers are also diplomats, however, is not new either – though it is certainly a lesser well-known concept. As this book has detailed, it has become a recurrent skill, which the military has had to come to terms with in all of Britain's small wars since 1945.

On another level, David Cameron's speech illuminates the politician's understanding of how the military instrument can be utilized in order to win the clash of wills with one's opponents. It also recognizes, moreover, the Army's hard-won experience in interacting with the political end goals. As Hew Strachan reminds us,

> the military, which wages war in rogue states' or 'failed states', and so builds new states, is shaping and even formulating policy as it fights. Politics have the potential to permeate all military action, but in conflicts like Iraq and Afghanistan war and policy are even more deeply intertwined.[23]

The difficulty is that so often the political nature of a conflict can consume a small war from the lowest tactical level and actually influence strategy through to the highest civilian–military levels. Britain's experience of small wars campaigning suggests that politicians need reminding of the consequences of their decisions when they are prone to forget, something Major-General Sir Charles Gwynn would have readily approved of from his perspective of the inter-war period.[24]

Under Labour governments, the ideological baggage of their backbenchers meant that, whilst in power, they did not freely admit the extent to which national interests dictate their international policy. Conservative governments have tended to be much less quixotic about how Britain's national interest factor in their own decision-making processes. As Anne Deighton informs us, in the 1950s, 'the defining trait of foreign policy was to maintain Britain's place as a major global and imperial power in a rapidly changing period of fresh ideological and power-political challenges'.[25]

Moreover, the small wars in Palestine, Malaya, Kenya and Cyprus had undoubtedly taken their toll on Britain, militarily as well as politically and economically, with governments increasingly taking the view that responsible withdrawal from Empire was the best way to ensure good order and stability and avoid, above all else, damage to the country's prestige. It was part of an even more deceptively simple viewpoint, raised by Professor Sir Michael Howard: 'In any event, if we had attempted to retain our hegemonical position in any of these regions, how would it have been paid for?'[26] One might also add the views of one-time Colonial Secretary Oliver Lyttelton to this strategic debate. Lyttelton argued that 'the only practical course' open to the Conservative government was to support the process of decolonization, for, after all, 'we do not have the force to govern without the consent of the governed'.[27] Conservative politicians like Lyttelton, and also Churchill, nevertheless held fast to the idea of Britain as a 'great power'. In one of his final speeches as Prime Minister in 1955 Churchill said:

> Our moral and military support of the United States and our possession of nuclear weapons of the highest quality and on an appreciable scale,

> together with their means of delivery, will greatly reinforce the deterrent power of the free world, and will strengthen our influence within the free world. That, at any rate, is the policy we have decided to pursue.[28]

Although he would not have admitted publicly at the time, Churchill became more convinced that Britain's decline could only be arrested by an ever-closer alliance with the US.

While Churchill may have been hunkering down for the rigours of posterity, with his own reputation as a strong war-time leader now assured, of course, Labour's George Wigg challenged the government's defence posture more clinically: 'I said a year ago that I was quite sure that a year hence we would be weaker than we then were. If the present Government remain in office we shall be weaker a year hence than we now are'.[29] Within a decade unqualified support for the US relegated Britain to 'middle-ranking' status. Eden's tenure as Prime Minister marked the apogee of British imperial power. In Niall Ferguson's words, the Suez Crisis of 1956 'proved that the United Kingdom could not act in defiance of the United States in the Middle East, setting the seal on the end of empire'.[30] By the time Harold Macmillan succeeded Anthony Eden, his 'winds of change' had spread rapidly throughout the colonial periphery. Britain's 'age of hegemony was effectively over', argues Ferguson.[31] When Labour's Harold Wilson became Prime Minister in 1964 the eclipse of British power had become reality. For John A. Young, the Conservatives, beyond Churchill's term as PM, 'had failed to match their international ambitions to national resources'.[32] If this is true, it confirms Young's view on the bi-partisan nature of Britain's international policy in the 1960s.

Recurrent strategic trends

That the Cold War never developed into an all-out 'hot war' can be attributed to the reluctance of both blocs to follow through on their veiled threats. However, constant brinkmanship and the predilection for proxy warfare meant that they continually sought to undermine the other at arms length. The positions adopted by both sides were shaped by the effectiveness of intelligence machinery in providing warnings of pending threats to national security. As historian Christopher Andrew has remarked, 'Intelligence is probably the least understood aspect of the Cold War, sometimes sensationalised, often ignored.' And for those historians studying policy-making in East and West who 'fail to take intelligence into account are at best incomplete, at worst distorted'.[33] What this book has tried to do is to examine Britain's small wars in light of how intelligence, amongst other things, was used in civil–military relations to counter irregular adversaries.

Many of the civil–military measures explored in this book are frequently cited today as textbook examples of the British 'black art' of counter-insurgency. While it is one thing to claim lineage in terms of having been involved in small wars campaigning, it is quite another to claim a natural affinity for small wars strategy. As Robert Egnell rightly reminds us, it does not necessarily follow that the British Army has, 'as a result of these historical experiences, an almost natural talent for counterinsurgency'.[34] Arguably, there is perhaps more merit in examining more forensically the failures arising from these cases than their purported successes. As this book has outlined, there is limited evidence that doctrine was being followed by commanders in a consistent fashion. However, as Sir Robert Thompson has written, this is sometimes beneficial:

> The strategy is best defined as the deployment and application of the means, both military and civil, to achieve the aim. All the experience of war and history, including past counterinsurgencies, teaches that the strategic approach must be indirect rather than direct.[35]

Though Britain has good reason to regard itself as a market-leader in fighting small wars, its experience has been hard won and often prompted by the prospect or, to paraphrase Mack, the actuality of 'military stalemate or even failure'. The British Army's application of counter-insurgency principles, for instance, has been judged by some to be a model for best practice:

> The substance of the 'British Way,' if substance there be, lies not so much in the fact that it is theoretically unique, but that the British are perceived historically to have been more consistent than their peers in putting the theory into practice.[36]

In practical terms, as Betz and Cormack acknowledge, it was much harder for Britain to implement policies from the metropolitan centre – as decolonization soon proved. Innovative strategies were needed to ensure that newly independent colonies did not side with the Soviet Union. And, as Labour's Colonial Secretary Arthur Creech Jones argued in the late 1940s, the government hoped that they would 'obtain the good will of the local governments and the co-operation of the colonial peoples' in facilitating independence. 'Unless it is freely given,' he maintained, 'I fear that colonial development will not go far.'[37] Britain continually sought to guard against any damage to its prestige as it withdrew in orderly fashion from its East of Suez responsibilities in the post-war world. Those who sought a place in the Western sphere of influence were rewarded with socio-economic and political advancement; those who rejected it were ruthlessly suppressed through the medium of 'illiberal dirty wars'.[38]

Britain's colonial experience is still regarded today as having some relevance in the 'new wars' that we face. Yet, as Hew Strachan reminds us, 'although some expertise was imported from one area to another, the commanders on the ground developed their own responses independently and without reference to counter-insurgency campaigns being waged elsewhere'.[39] As this book has also demonstrated, there has not been such a clean-cut break as one might think. The operational plans put in place in Kenya followed a 'Malaya Plan' and the subsequent strategy in Cyprus followed both a Malaya and Kenya model, though not, surprisingly, a Palestine one. *Defending the Realm?* suggests that there is a recurrent tendency to ignore, at worst, or misapply, at best, lessons from other experiences. It is often failure or the prospect of failure that prompts a strategic recalibration and leads ultimately to either success or, indeed, repeated failure.

Plus a change: the enduring nature of war

Strategic theorist Colin S. Gray has remarked that 'in order to understand the 1990s, or the 2090s, study the 1890s, 1790s, and so forth. The future is the past in the ways that matter most.'[40] A common thread seems to run through much of the journalistic, academic and policy literature that war is different in character now from how it has been in the past. However, one must be careful not to overstate how dramatically warfare has changed. If anything, the nature of war has endured, though the character (in terms of the weapons and technology employed) may well have altered, in some cases, beyond all recognition. Cautioning against employing the present fashionable intellectual accessory in research on war today, Gray reminds us, in 'a practical subject like international relations, poor – which is to say impractical – theories are at best an irrelevance, and at worst can help get people killed'.[41] Being aware of historical precedence is important for tactical reasons too, as Thomas Mockatis points out: '[c]opying specific tactics from one campaign and applying them slavishly to another almost certainly will result in failure'.[42]

The painful lessons identified by Britain's Armed Forces in Iraq and Afghanistan after 9/11, have led to a process of continual reflection and circumspection, re-appraisal and adaptation, which the Army has always prided itself on, but is all too prone to forget. The story at the heart of *Defence of the Realm?* has been one of Britain's decline in world politics and the impoverished strategy that was employed by successive governments and their armed forces in arresting that decline. It is not about apportioning blame or recognizing the infallibility of the military instrument, but of looking honestly at the genesis of 'muddling through', which has, at times, seemed to emasculate more 'strategic' thinking.

Ultimately, the Army's experience of small wars during the post-war period was framed by the government, in the context of military aid to the civil power. In this respect it was unusual for the military to be given the lead in tackling irregular opponents.[43] While harsh tactics were at times deemed necessary, Britain's civil–military leadership preferred to emphasize the minimum use of force. Moreover, as the cases explored in this book also demonstrate, there is firm evidence to support the view that the military recognized this limited role. While the military objective may have been 'to kill or capture every gangster' or 'wipe the floor' with them, this was done as part of a wider strategic plan to restore law and order and facilitate political progress. As Major-General Charles Callwell pointed out at the beginning of the twentieth century, '[t]he enemy must be forced to understand that business is meant, that the regular army intends to accomplish whatever enterprise it engages in. Half measures are fatal.'[44] In Callwell's understanding of small wars, it was strategy which favoured one's opponent, while tactics favoured the organized armed forces. The challenge for the former though was to ensure strategic success by the appropriate application of force.

As the work of Callwell and others confirms, small wars have long had a place in the proud tradition of British soldiering. In seeking to disarm its irregular opponent, Britain was fully engaged in maintaining and in some cases maximizing its power, albeit it according to the logic of the wider strategic context, which included decolonization, Cold War and much later the so-called 'war on terror'. The prospect of success weighed heavily on the minds of Britain's soldiers and diplomats, for failure would have meant a diminution of power on the world stage. In the end, *Defending the Realm?* meant a fine balancing act in strategic terms.

Notes

1 Morgenthau, Hans J., *Politics Among Nations: The Struggle for Power and Peace*, brief edition (Boston, MA: McGraw-Hill, 1993), p. 387.

2 Barnett, Correlli, *Britain and Her Army, 1509–1970: A Military, Political and Social Survey* (London: Allen Lane, 1970), p. 479.

3 House of Commons Public Administration Select Committee, Who Does UK National Strategy?, First Report of Session 2010–11, 12 October 2010 (London: HMSO, 18 October 2010), p. 3.
4 Junger, Sebastian, *War* (London: Fourth Estate, 2010), p. 234.
5 Ibid., p. 140.
6 Keegan, John, *A History of War* (London: Pimlico, 1993), p. 385.
7 Ibid., p. 392. Keegan announces his intent at the outset of his magisterial account of the cultural dimension of war as by stating that 'WAR IS NOT THE continuation of policy by other means. The world would be a simpler place to understand if this dictum of Clausewitz's were true' (p. 3). Keegan's views are shared to an extent by another distinguished analyst of the British way of war, Captain Sir Basil Liddell-Hart, who disagreed with 'those who conceive the destruction of the enemy's armed forces as the only sound aim in war, who hold that the only goal of strategy is battle, and who are obsessed with the Clausewitzian saying that "blood is the price of victory".' Liddell Hart, Captain Sir Basil, *The British Way in Warfare* (London: Faber, 1932), p. 100.
8 Gray, Colin S., *Another Bloody Century: Future Warfare* (London: Weidenfeld and Nicolson, 2005), pp. 22, 24–25, 30, 62–63.
9 Clausewitz, Carl Von, *On War*, edited and translated by Michael Howard and Peter Paret (Princeton, NJ: Princeton University Press, 1989), p. 75.
10 See Gray, Colin S., 'Moral Advantage, Strategic Advantage?', *Journal of Strategic Studies*, Vol. 33, No. 3 (2010), p. 338. Gray, *Another Bloody Century*, pp. 338–339.
11 Gray, *Another Bloody Century*, p. 379. Or to put it another way, as E.H. Carr did on the eve of the Second World War, 'We shall never arrive at a political order in which the grievances of the weak and the few receive the same prompt attention as the grievances of the strong and many. Power goes far to create the morality convenient to itself, and coercion is a fruitful source of consent.' Carr, E.H., *The Twenty Years' Crisis, 1919–1939: An Introduction to the Study of International Relations* (London: Macmillan, [1939], 1970), p. 236.
12 Morgenthau, Hans, 'The Evil of Politics and the Ethics of Evil', *Ethics*, Vol. 56, No. 1 (October 1945), p. 14.
13 Morgenthau, Hans, 'The Twilight of International Morality', *Ethics*, Vol. 58, No. 2 (January 1948), p. 80.
14 There are those who dispute the utility of the 'inside-out pattern' as an understanding of the international system. Waltz, for instance, argues that 'It is not possible to understand world politics simply by looking inside of states. If the aims, policies, and actions of states become matters of exclusive attention or even of central concern, then we are forced back to the descriptive level; and from simple descriptions no valid generalizations can logically be drawn.' See Waltz, Kenneth N., *Theory of International Relations* (Boston, MA: McGraw-Hill, 1979), p. 65. In perhaps his most palpable observation Waltz argues that 'Each state arrives at policies and

decides on actions according to its own internal processes, but its decisions are shaped by the very presence of other states as well as by interactions with them.'

15 On Iran see Tisdell, Simon, 'Afghanistan war logs: Iran's covert operations in Afghanistan', *The Guardian*, 25 July 2010; comments by Mostafa Mohammad-Najjar cited in 'US-Afghan strategic treaty will endanger Iran's interests: minister', *Tehran Times*, 24 July 2011. On Pakistan see Lieven, Anatol *Pakistan: A Hard Country* (London: Allen Lane, 2011).

16 Gray, *Another Bloody Century*, p. 60.

17 Rubin, Barnett R. and Ahmed Rashid, 'From Great Game to Grand Bargain: Ending Chaos in Afghanistan and Pakistan', *Foreign Affairs*, Vol. 87, No. 6 (November/December 2008), p. 40.

18 As General Sir David Richards has pointed out, in many ways, 'Afghanistan is a signpost to the future: it is the testing ground for us and our enemies'. See Richards, David, 'A Soldier's Perspective on Countering Insurgency', in Richards, David and Greg Mills (eds), *Victory among People: Lessons from Countering Insurgency and Stabilising Fragile States* (London: Royal United Services Institute, 2011), p. 33.

19 Author's notes of comments by General Sir Peter Wall at the 15th Whither Warfare Conference, Royal Military Academy Sandhurst, 5 May 2011.

20 Kitson, Frank, *Bunch of Five* (London: Faber, 1977), p. 174.

21 Number 10, PM's Speech at Sovereign's Parade, Sandhurst, 13 August 2010. Archived: www.number10.gov.uk/news/speeches-and-transcripts/2010/08/pms-speech-at-sovereigns-parade-sandhurst-54519. Accessed: 20 August 2010.

22 Clausewitz, *On War*, pp. 479–483.

23 Strachan, Hew, 'Making Strategy: Civil-Military Relations after Iraq', *Survival*, Vol. 48, No. 3 (autumn 2006), p. 72.

24 Gwynn, Charles, *Imperial Policing* (London: Macmillan, 1934), pp. 13–14.

25 Deighton, Anne, 'Britain and the Cold War, 1945–1955' in Leffler, Melvyn P. and Odd Arne Westad (eds), *The Cambridge History of the Cold War*, Volume 1: *Origins* (Cambridge: Cambridge University Press, 2010), p. 113.

26 Howard, Michael, '1945–1995: Reflections on Half a Century of British Security Policy', *International Affairs*, Vol. 71, No. 4 (1995), p. 711.

27 Lyttelton, Oliver, Viscount Chandos, *The Memoirs of Lord Chandos* (London: The Bodley Head, 1962), p. 352.

28 House of Commons Debates (Hansard), 1 March 1955, Vol. 537, Col. 1897.

29 Ibid., Col. 1964.

30 Ferguson, Niall, *Civilisation: The West and the Rest* (London: Penguin, 2011), p. 303.

31 Ibid.

32 Young, John *The Labour Governments, 1964–70*, Volume 2: *International Policy* (Manchester: Manchester University Press, 2003), p. 220.

33 Andrew, Christopher, 'Intelligence in the Cold War', in Leffler, Melvyn P. and Odd Arne Westad (eds), *The Cambridge History of the Cold War*, Volume 2: *Crises and Détente* (Cambridge: Cambridge University Press, 2010), p. 417.
34 Egnell, Robert, 'Lessons from Helmand, Afghanistan: What Now for British Counter-Insurgency?', *International Affairs*, Vol. 87, No. 2 (March 2011), p. 301.
35 Thompson, Sir Robert, 'Squaring the Error', *Foreign Affairs*, Vol. 46 (1968), p. 449.
36 Betz, David and Anthony Cormack, 'Iraq, Afghanistan and British Strategy', *Orbis: A Journal of World Affairs*, Vol. 53, No. 2 (spring 2009), p. 322.
37 House of Commons Debates (Hansard), 8 July 1948, Vol. 453, Col. 599.
38 Grob-Fitzgibbon, Benjamin, *Imperial Endgame: Britain's Dirty Wars and the End of Empire* (Basingstoke: Palgrave Macmillan, 2011), p. 377.
39 Strachan, Hew, 'Introduction' in Strachan, Hew (ed.), *Big Wars and Small Wars: The British Army and the Lessons of War in the Twentieth Century* (London: Routledge, 2006), p. 8.
40 Gray, Colin S., 'Clausewitz Rules, OK? The Future is the Past – with GPS', *Review of International Studies*, Vol. 25, No. 5 (December 1999), p. 164.
41 Ibid., p. 165.
42 Mockaitis, Thomas R., *The Iraq War: Learning from the Past, Adapting to the Present and Planning for the Future* (Carlisle, PA: Strategic Studies Institute, February 2007), p. 15.
43 General Sir John Hackett argues that this dislike for martial law owes much to England's experience of Cromwell's rule in the seventeenth century. 'The harmonious relationship between civil and military power, which has persisted in Britain since then, in which the subordination of the military to the civil is fundamental, owes much to this salutary experience.' Hackett, General Sir John, *The Profession of Arms* (London: Sidgwick and Jackson, 1983), p. 174.
44 Callwell, Colonel Charles Edward, *Small Wars: Their Principles and Practice*, third edition (London: HMSO, 1906), p. 76.

Select bibliography

Primary sources

Newspapers and journals

Daily Chronicle
Daily Express
Daily Herald
Daily Mail
Daily Mirror
Daily Telegraph
Daily Worker
East Anglian Daily Times
Globe and Laurel (Journal of the Royal Marines)
Guardian
Independent
Independent on Sunday
Irish Times
New Statesman
New York Times
Observer
Palestine Post
Spectator
The Star
Sunday Express
Sunday Telegraph
Sunday Times
Sussex Daily News
The Thin Red Line (Regimental Journal of the Argyll and Sutherland Highlanders)
Time
The Times
The Wishstream (Journal of the Royal Military Academy Sandhurst)

Private papers

Imperial War Museum, Lambeth, London, Department of Documents

General Sir George Erskine Papers
Lieutenant-General Gordon Macmillan Papers
Lord Harding of Petherton Papers
Colonel C.R.W. Norman Papers
W.H. Thompson Papers

King's College London, Liddell-Hart Centre for Military Archives

Field-Marshal Lord Alanbrooke Papers
Sir Frank Cooper Papers
Major-General Anthony Deane-Drummond Papers
Major-General Sir Charles Dunbar Papers
Sir Charles Johnston Papers
General Sir Harold Pyman Papers
General Sir Hugh Stockwell Papers
Brigadier Denis Talbot Papers

London School of Economics and Political Science

Lord Merlyn Rees Papers
Lord George Wipp Papers
Peter Short Papers

Oxford University, Bodleian Library Special Collections

Clement Attlee Papers
Harold Wilson Papers

Interviews

Dr Anthony Clayton
Tommy Gorman
Brigadier Richard Iron
Jon McCourt
Danny Morrison
Former Commander, British Forces in Afghanistan
Former Royal Engineers Search Adviser
Former Senior RUC Special Branch Officers
Lieutenant-General Sir Philip Trousdell
David Ullah
General Sir Roger Wheeler
Former Ulster Defence Regiment Officer
Former Ulster Defence Regiment Soldier 1
Former Ulster Defence Regiment Soldier 2
Former Ulster Defence Regiment Soldier 3

Official papers

HMG, *Treaty of Friendship and Protection between the United Kingdom of Great Britain and Northern Ireland and the Federation of South Arabia and Supplementary Treaty providing for the accession of Aden to the Federation, September 1964* (London: HMSO, 1964), Cmnd. 2451.

House of Commons Defence Committee, *Operations in Afghanistan*, Fourth Report of Session 2010–12, HC 554 (London: The Stationery Office, 17 July 2011).

House of Commons Public Affairs Committee, *Who Does UK National Strategy?*, First Report of Session, 2010-11, HC 435 (London: The Stationery Office, 18 October 2010).

Levene, Lord, *Defence Reform: An Independent Report into the Structure and Management of the Ministry of Defence* (London: The Stationery Office, June 2011).

MoD, Joint Defence Publication (JDP), 2/07, *Countering Irregular Activity within a Comprehensive Approach* (Shrivenham: DCDC, 2007).

MoD, *Joint Defence Publication 0-01: British Defence Doctrine* (Shrivenham: DCDC: August 2008).

MoD, *Land Operations: Volume I – The Fundamentals, Part 2 – Command and Control*, Army Code No. 70458, Part 2 (London: MoD, 28 April 1969).

MoD, *Land Operations: Volume III – Counter-Revolutionary Operations, Part 1 – Principles and General Aspects*, Army Code No. 70516, Part 1 (London: HMSO, 29 August 1969).

MoD, *Land Operations: Volume III – Counter-Revolutionary Operations, Part 2 – Internal Security*, Army Code No. 70516, Part 2 (London: HMSO, 26 November 1969).

MoD, *Land Operations: Volume III – Counter-Revolutionary Operations, Part 3 – Counter Insurgency*, Army Code No. 70516, Part 3 (London: HMSO, 5 January 1970).

MoD, *Land Operations: Volume III – Counter-Revolutionary Operations, Part 1 – General Principles*, Army Code No. 70516, Part 1 (London: HMSO, August 1977).

MoD, *Land Operations: Volume III – Counter-Revolutionary Operations, Part 2 – Procedures and Techniques*, Army Code No. 70516, Part 2 (London: HMSO, 1977).

MoD, *Operation Banner: An Analysis of Military Operations in Northern Ireland*, Army Code No. 71842 (London: MoD, July 2006).

MoD, *Strategic Defence Review*, Cm. 3999 (London: MoD, 1998).

MoD, *The Strategic Defence Review: A New Chapter* (London: MoD: July 2002).

MoD, *Strategic Trends Programme: Future Character of Conflict* (Shrivenham: DCDC, February 2010).

MoD/Stabilisation Unit, Joint Doctrine Note 6/10, *Security Transitions: The Military Contribution* (Shrivenham: DCDC, November 2010).

RAF, *The Malayan Emergency, 1948–1960* (London: MoD, June 1970).
WO, *Keeping the Peace: Part 1 – Doctrine*, WO Code No. 9800 (London: The War Office, 7 January 1963).
WO, *Keeping the Peace: Part 2 – Tactics and Training*, WO Code No. 9801 (London: The War Office, 16 January 1963).

Public Records Office of Northern Ireland (PRONI)

CAB series
GOV series

National Archives, Kew

AIR series
CAB series
CO series
DEFE series
FCO series
FO series
KV series
PREM series
WO series

Secondary sources

Books and articles

Acheson, Dean, *Power and Diplomacy: The William L. Clayton Lectures on International Economic Affairs and Foreign Policy* (Cambridge, MA: Harvard University Press, 1958).
Adams, Gerry, *Hope and History: Making Peace in Ireland* (Dingle: Brandon, 2003).
Alderson, Colonel Alexander, 'Revising the British Army's Counter-Insurgency Doctrine', *The Royal United Services Institute Journal*, Vol. 152, No. 4 (August 2007), pp. 6–11.
Alderson, Colonel Alexander, *The Validity of British Army Counterinsugency Doctrine after the War in Iraq 2003–2009* (Cranfield: unpublished PhD thesis, November 2009).
Alderson, Colonel Alex, 'The Army's "Brain": A Historical Perspective on Doctrine and Development', *British Army Review*, No. 150 (winter 2010/11), pp. 60–64.
Aldrich, Richard J. and John Zametica, 'The Rise and Decline of a Strategic Concept: The Middle East, 1945–51', in Aldrich, Richard J. (ed.), *British Intelligence, Strategy and the Cold War, 1945–51* (London: Routledge, 1992).
Allawi, Ali A., *The Occupation of Iraq: Winning the War, Losing the Peace* (New Haven, CT: Yale University Press, 2007).
Anderson, David, *Histories of the Hanged: Britain's Dirty War in Kenya* (London: Phoenix, 2006).

Andrew, Christopher, *The Defence of the Realm: The Authorized History of MI5* (London: Allen Lane, 2009).
Andrew, Christopher and Vasili Mitrokhin, *The Mitrokhin Archive II: The KGB and the World* (London: Allen Lane, 2005).
Angstrom, Jan and Isabelle Duyvesteyn (eds), *Understanding Victory and Defeat in Contemporary War* (Abingdon: Routledge, 2007).
Aron, Raymond, *Democracy and Totalitarianism*, translated by Valence Ionescu (London: Weidenfield and Nicolson, [1965] 1968).
Aron, Raymond, *The Imperial Republic: The United States and the World, 1945–1973*, translated by Frank Jellinek (London: Weidenfeld and Nicolson, 1973).
Attlee, Clement, *As it Happened* (London: William Heinemann, 1954).
Barnett, Correlli, *Britain and Her Army, 1509–1970: A Military, Political and Social Survey* (London: Allen Lane, 1970).
Barnett, Correlli, *The Audit of War: The Illusion and Reality of Britain as a Great Nation* (London: Macmillan, 1986).
Barnett, Correlli, *The Lost Victory: British Dreams, British Realities, 1945–1950* (London: Macmillan, 1995).
Barthorp, Michael, *Crater to the Creggan: A History of the Royal Anglian Regiment, 1964–1974* (London: Leo Cooper, 1976).
Bass, Christopher and M.L.R. Smith, 'The Dynamic of Irwin's Forgotten Army: A Strategic Understanding of the British Army's Role in Northern Ireland after 1998', *Small Wars and Insurgencies*, Vol. 15, No. 3 (2004), pp. 1–24.
Bayly, Christopher and Tim Harper, *Forgotten Armies: The Fall of British Asia, 1941–1945* (London: Allen Lane, 2004).
Begin, Menachem, *The Revolt*, revised edition, translated by Samuel Katz (London: W.H. Allen, 1983).
Benest, David, 'Aden to Northern Ireland, 1966–76', in Strachan, Hew (ed.), *Big Wars and Small Wars: The British Army and the Lessons of War in the Twentieth Century* (Abingdon: Routledge, 2006).
Bennett, Huw, 'The Mau Mau Emergency as Part of the British Army's Post-War Counter-Insurgency Experience', *Defense and Security Analysis*, Vol. 23, No. 2 (2007), pp. 143–63.
Bennett, Huw, 'Erskine, Sir George Watkin Eben James (1899–1965)', *Oxford Dictionary of National Biography* (Oxford: Oxford University Press, 2008); online edn, January 2011. Archived: www.oxforddnb.com/view/article/97289. Accessed 21 June 2011.
Betz, David and Anthony Cormack, 'Iraq, Afghanistan and British Strategy', *Orbis: A Journal of World Affairs*, Vol. 53, No. 2 (spring 2009), pp. 319–336.
Bew, Paul and Gordon Gillespie, *Northern Ireland: A Chronology of the Troubles, 1968–1999* (Dublin: Gill and Macmillan, 1999).
Bird, Tim and Alex Marshal, *Afghanistan: How the West Lost its Way* (London: Yale University Press, 2011).
Blair, Tony, *A Journey* (London: Hutchinson, 2010).

Blaxland, Gregory, *The Regiments Depart: A History of the British Army, 1945–1970* (London: William Kimber, 1971).
Blix, Hans, *Disarming Iraq: The Search for Weapons of Mass Destruction* (London: Bloomsbury, 2004).
Blundell, Sir Michael, *So Rough the Wind: The Kenya Memoirs of Sir Michael Blundell* (London: Weidenfeld and Nicolson, 1964).
Branch, Daniel, *Defeating Mau Mau, Creating Kenya: Counterinsurgency, Civil War, and Decolonization* (Cambridge: Cambridge University Press, 2009).
Brinkley, Douglas, '"Dean Acheson and the Special Relationship": The West Point Speech of December 1962', *The Historical Journal*, Vol. 33, No. 3 (September 1990), pp. 599–608.
Brown, David (ed.), *The Development of British Defence Policy: Blair, Brown and Beyond* (Farnham: Ashgate, 2010).
Brown, George, *In My Way: The Political Memoirs of Lord George-Brown* (London: Victor Gollancz, 1971).
Bullock, Alan, *Ernest Bevin: Foreign Secretary, 1945–1951* (London: William Heinemann, 1983).
Burke, Jason, *Al Qaeda: The True Story of Radical Islam*, third edition (London: Penguin, 2007).
Bush, George W., *Decision Points* (London: Virgin Books, 2010).
Callwell, Colonel Charles Edward, *Small Wars: Their Principles and Practice*, third edition (London: HMSO, 1906).
Carr, E.H., *The Twenty Years' Crisis 1919–1939: An Introduction to the Study of International Relations* (London: Macmillan, [1939] 1970).
Carruthers, Susan L., *Winning Hearts and Minds: British Governments, the Media and Colonial Counter-Insurgency, 1944–1960* (London: Leicester University Press, 1995).
Carver, Michael, *Harding of Petherton: Field Marshal* (London: Weidenfeld and Nicolson, 1978).
Carver, Michael, *War Since 1945* (London: Weidenfeld and Nicolson, 1980).
Castle, Barbara, *The Castle Diaries, 1964–70* (London: Weidenfeld and Nicolson, 1984).
Chalmers, Malcolm, *Rethinking British Security Policy*, RUSI Discussion Paper (London: RUSI, 14 March 2008).
Chappell, Stephen, 'Air Power in the Mau Mau Conflict: The Government's Chief Weapon', *RUSI Journal*, Vol. 156, No. 1 (February/March 2011), pp. 64–70.
Clarke, A.F.N., *Contact* (London: Secker and Warburg, 1983).
Clausewitz, Carl Von, *On War*, edited and translated by Michael Howard and Peter Paret (Princeton, NJ: Princeton University Press, 1989).
Clayton, Anthony, *Counter-Insurgency in Kenya, 1952–60* (New York: Sunflower University Press, [1976] 1984).
Clayton, Anthony, *Frontiersmen: Warfare in Africa since 1950* (London: UCL Press, 1999).

Cloak, John, *Templer, Tiger of Malaya: The Life of Field-Marshal Sir Gerald Templer* (London: Harrap, 1985).
Coates, David and Joel Krieger, 'The Mistake Heard Round the World: Iraq and the Blair Legacy', in Casey, Terrence (ed.), *The Blair Legacy: Politics, Policy, Governance, and Foreign Affairs* (Basingstoke: Palgrave Macmillan, 2009).
Cohen, Eliot, *Supreme Command: Soldiers, Statesmen and Leadership in Wartime* (New York: Free Press, 2002).
Coll, Steve, *Ghost Wars: The Secret History of the CIA, Afghanistan and Bin Laden, from the Soviet Invasion to September 10, 2001* (London: Penguin, 2004).
Cook, Robin, *The Point of Departure: Diaries from the Front Bench* (London: Simon and Schuster, 2003).
Cornish, Paul and Andrew M. Dorman, 'Dr Fox and the Philosopher's Stone: The Alchemy of National Defence in the Age of Austerity', *International Affairs*, Vol. 87, No. 2 (2011), pp. 335–353.
Corum, James S., *Training Indigenous Forces in Counterinsurgency: A Tale of Two Insurgencies* (Carlisle, PA: Strategic Studies Institute, 2006).
Crawshaw, Nancy, *The Cyprus Revolt: An Account of the Struggle for Union with Greece* (London: George Allen and Unwin, 1978).
Crossman, Richard, *Palestine Mission: A Personal Record* (London: Hamish Hamilton, 1947).
Dalton, Hugh, *High Tide and After: Memoirs, 1945–1960* (London: Frederick Muller, 1962).
Dannatt, General Sir Richard, *Leading from the Front: The Autobiography* (London: Bantam Press, 2010).
Deakin, Stephen, 'Security Policy and the Use of the Military: Military Aid to the Civil Power, Northern Ireland 1969', *Small Wars and Insurgencies*, Vol. 4, No. 2 (autumn 1993), pp. 211–227.
Deighton, Anne, 'Britain and the Cold War, 1945–1955', in Leffler, Melvyn P. and Odd Arne Westad (eds) *The Cambridge History of the Cold War*, Volume 1: *Origins* (Cambridge: Cambridge University Press, 2010).
Dillon, Martin, *The Dirty War* (London: Arrow Books, 1991).
Dixon, Paul, 'Counter-Insurgency in Northern Ireland and the Crisis of the British State', in Rich, Paul B. and Richard Stubbs (eds), *The Counter-Insurgent State: Guerrilla Warfare and State Building in the Twentieth Century* (Basingstoke: Macmillan, 1997).
Dockrill, Michael, *British Defence Since 1945* (Oxford: Blackwell, 1989).
Dorman, Andrew, 'Viewpoint – The Nott Review: Dispelling the Myths?', *Defence Studies*, Vol. 1, No. 3 (2001), pp. 113–121.
Dorman, Andrew M., *Blair's Successful War: Britain's Military Intervention in Sierra Leone* (Farnham: Ashgate, 2009).
Dorman, Andrew, 'Providing for Defence in an Age of Austerity: Future War, Defence Cuts and the 2010 Strategic (Security and) Defence (and Security) Review', *The Political Quarterly*, Vol. 81, No. 3 (July–September 2010), pp. 376–384.

Douglas-Home, Charles, 'A Mistaken Policy in Aden: The Case for Union with the Yemen', *The Round Table*, Vol. 58, No. 229 (January 1968), pp. 21–7.

Douglas-Home, Charles, *Evelyn Baring: The Last Proconsul* (London: Collins, 1978).

Eden, Anthony, *The Memoirs of Sir Anthony Eden: Full Circle* (London: Cassell and Company, 1960).

Edwards, Aaron, 'Social Democracy and Partition: The British Labour Party and Northern Ireland, 1951–64', *Journal of Contemporary History*, Vol. 42, No. 4 (October 2007), pp. 595–612.

Edwards, Aaron, ' "Unionist Derry is Ulster's Panama": The Northern Ireland Labour Party and the Civil Rights Issue', *Irish Political Studies*, Vol. 23, No. 3 (September 2008), pp. 363–385.

Edwards, A., 'Abandoning Armed Resistance? The Ulster Volunteer Force as a Case-study of Strategic Terrorism in Northern Ireland', *Studies in Conflict and Terrorism*, Vol. 32, No. 2 (February 2009), pp. 146–166.

Edwards, Aaron, *A History of the Northern Ireland Labour Party: Democratic Socialism and Sectarianism* (Manchester: Manchester University Press, 2009).

Edwards, Aaron, 'Interpreting New Labour's Political Discourse on the Peace Process', in Hayward, Katy and Catherine O'Donnell (eds), *Political Discourse and Conflict Resolution: Debating Peace in Northern Ireland* (Abingdon: Routledge, 2010).

Edwards, Aaron, 'Misapplying Lessons Learned? Analysing the Utility of British Counter-Insurgency Strategy in Northern Ireland, 1971–76', *Small Wars and Insurgencies*, Vol. 21, No. 2 (June 2010), pp. 303–330.

Edwards, Aaron, 'Deterrence, Coercion and Brute Force in Asymmetric Conflict: The Role of the Military Instrument in Resolving the Northern Ireland "Troubles" ', *Dynamics of Asymmetric Conflict*, Vol. 4, No. 3 (December 2011), pp. 226–241.

Edwards, Aaron, *The Northern Ireland Troubles: Operation Banner, 1969–2007* (Oxford: Osprey, 2011).

Edwards, Aaron and Stephen Bloomer (eds), *Transforming the Peace Process in Northern Ireland: From Terrorism to Democratic Politics* (Dublin: Irish Academic Press, 2008).

Edwards, Aaron and Cillian McGrattan, *The Northern Ireland Conflict: A Beginner's Guide* (Oxford: Oneworld Publications, 2010).

Edwards, Aaron and Cillian McGrattan, 'Terroristic Narratives: On the (Re) Invention of Peace in Northern Ireland', *Terrorism and Political Violence*, Vol. 23, No. 3 (June 2011), pp. 357–376.

Egnell, Robert, 'Lessons from Helmand, Afghanistan: What Now for British Counter-Insurgency?', *International Affairs*, Vol. 87, No. 2 (2011), pp. 297–315.

Elkins, Caroline, *Britain's Gulag: The Brutal End of Empire in Kenya* (London: Jonathan Cape, 2005).

English, Richard and Michael Kenny, *Rethinking British Decline* (London: Macmillan, 2000).

Fairweather, Jack, *A War of Choice: The British in Iraq, 2003–2009* (London: Jonathan Cape, 2011).
Ferguson, Niall, *Empire: How Britain Made the Modern World* (London: Penguin, 2003).
Ferguson, Niall, *Civilisation: The West and the Rest* (London: Penguin, 2011).
Fergusson, James, *A Million Bullets: The Real Story of the British Army in Afghanistan* (London: Bantam Press, 2008).
Fergusson, James, *Taliban: The True Story of the World's Most Feared Guerrilla Fighters* (London: Transworld, 2010).
Fraser, T.G., *The Arab-Israeli Conflict*, third edition (Basingstoke: Palgrave Macmillan, 2007).
Fraser, T.G. and Donette Murray, *America and the World since 1945* (Basingstoke: Palgrave Macmillan, 2002).
Freedman, Lawrence, 'Order and Disorder in the New World', *Foreign Affairs*, Vol. 71, No. 1 (1992), pp. 20–37.
Freedman, Lawrence, *The Politics of British Defence, 1979–98* (Basingstoke: Macmillan, 1999).
Freedman, Lawrence, 'Britain at War: From The Falklands to Iraq', *RUSI Journal*, Vol. 151, No. 1 (February 2006), pp. 10–15.
Fuller, Colonel J.F.C., *The Reformation of War* (London: Hutchinson and Company, 1923).
Fuller, J.F.C., *The Dragon's Teeth: A Study of War and Peace* (London: Constable, 1932).
Gaitskell, Hugh, *The Challenge of Co-Existence: The Godkin Lectures, Harvard University* (London: Methuen, 1957).
Galula, David, *Counter-insurgency Warfare: Theory and Practice* (London: Praeger Security International, 1964, 2006).
Giustozzi, Antonio, *Koran, Kalashnikov and Laptop* (London: Hurst and Company, 2007).
Gray, Colin S., *Explorations in Strategy* (Westport, CT: Greenwood Press, 1996).
Gray, Colin S., 'Clausewitz Rules, OK? The Future is the Past – with GPS', *Review of International Studies*, Vol. 25, No. 5 (December 1999), pp. 161–182.
Gray, Colin S., *Another Bloody Century: Future Warfare* (London: Weidenfeld and Nicolson, 2005).
Gray, Colin S., 'War – Continuity in Change, and Change in Continuity', *Parameters: The US Army's Senior Professional Journal*, Vol. 40, No. 1 (summer 2010), pp. 5–13.
Gray, Colin S., 'Moral Advantage, Strategic Advantage?', *Journal of Strategic Studies*, Vol. 33, No. 3 (June 2010), pp. 333–365.
Grivas, George, *The Memoirs of General Grivas*, edited by Charles Foley (London: Longmans, 1964).
Grob-Fitzgibbon, Benjamin, *Imperial Endgame: Britain's Dirty Wars and the End of Empire* (Basingstoke: Palgrave Macmillan, 2011).
Gwynn, Charles, *Imperial Policing* (London: Macmillan, 1934).

Hackett, General Sir John, *The Profession of Arms* (London: Sidgwick and Jackson, 1983).

Hamill, Desmond, *Pig in the Middle: The Army in Northern Ireland, 1969–1984* (London: Methuen, 1985).

Hamilton, Nigel, *Monty: The Field Marshal, 1944–1976* (London: Hamish Hamilton, 1986).

Harding, Field-Marshal Lord, 'The Cyprus Problem in Relation to the Middle East', *International Affairs*, Vol. 34, No. 3 (July 1958), pp. 291–6.

Harnden, Toby, *Dead Men Risen: The Welsh Guards and the Real Story of Britain's War in Afghanistan* (London: Quercus, 2011).

Hashim, Ahmed S., *Iraq's Sunni Insurgency*, Adelphi Paper No. 402 (London: IISS, 2009).

Hastings, Max, *The Korean War* (London: Michael Joseph, 1987).

Hauser, Beatrice, *Reading Clausewitz* (London: Pimlico, 2002).

Healey, Denis, *The Time of My Life* (London: Penguin, 1990).

Heath, Edward, *The Course of My Life: My Autobiography* (London: Hodder and Stoughton, 1998).

Herzog, Chaim, *The Arab–Israeli Wars: War and Peace in the Middle East* (Bath: Book Club Associates, 1982).

Hewitt, Steve, *The British War on Terror: Terrorism and Counter-Terrorism on the Home Front since 9/11* (London: Continuum, 2008).

Hobsbawm, Eric, *Revolutionaries*, revised and updated edition (London: Abacus, 2007).

Hoffman, Francis G., 'History and Future of Civil–Military Relations: Bridging the Gaps', in Murray, Williamson and Richard Hart Sinnreich (eds), *The Past as Prologue: The Importance of History to the Military Profession* (Cambridge: Cambridge University Press, 2006).

Holland, Jack and Susan Phoenix, *Phoenix: Policing the Shadows* (London: Hodder and Stoughton, 1996).

Holland, Robert, *Britain and the Revolt in Cyprus, 1954–1959* (Oxford: Clarendon Press, 1998).

Holt, Maria, 'Memories of Arabia and Empire: An Oral History of the British in Aden', *Contemporary British History*, Vol. 18, No. 4 (2004), pp. 93–112.

Howard, Michael, *Clausewitz* (Oxford: Oxford University Press, 1983).

Howard, Michael, '1945–1995: Reflections on Half a Century of British Security Policy', *International Affairs*, Vol. 71, No. 4 (1995), pp. 705–715.

Howard, Michael, *The Invention of Peace: Reflections on War and International Order* (London: Profile Books, 2000).

Howe, Stephen, *Anticolonialism in British Politics: The Left and the End of Empire 1918–1964* (Oxford: Clarendon Press, 1993).

Huntington, Samuel P., *The Soldier and the State: The Theory and Practice of Civil-Military Relations* (Cambridge, MA: Harvard University Press, [1957] 1985).

Huntington, Samuel P., *The Clash of Civilisations and the Remaking of World Order* (London: Free Press, 2002).

Hurd, Douglas, *Douglas Hurd: Memoirs* (London: Little, Brown, 2003).

Hussein, Saddam, 'Speech on the 27th Anniversary of the Arab Bath'ist Socialist Party, 8 April 1974', in *Saddam Hussein on Current Affairs* (Baghdad: Al-Thawra Publications, 1974).

Hyam, Ronald, *Britain's Declining Empire: The Road to Decolonisation, 1918–1968* (Cambridge: Cambridge University Press, 2006).

Iron, Colonel Richard, 'Exploiting Doctrine . . . From the Other Side of the Hill', *British Army Review*, No. 132 (summer 2003), pp. 22–26.

Iron, Colonel Richard, 'Britain's Longest War: Northern Ireland, 1967–2007', in Marston, Daniel and Carter Malkasian (eds), *Counterinsurgency in Modern Warfare* (Oxford: Osprey, 2008).

Jackson, General Sir Mike, *Soldier: The Autobiography* (London: Bantam, 2007).

Johnston, Charles Hepburn, *The View from Steamer Point: Being an Account of Three Years in Aden* (London: Collins, 1964).

Jomini, Baron, *Treatise on Grand Military Operations or a Critical and Military History of the Wars of Frederick the Great as Contrasted with the Modern System Together with a Few of the Most Important Principles of the Art of War* (London: Trubner and Company, 1865).

Jones, Martin D.W., 'Young, Sir Arthur Edwin (1907–1979)', *Oxford Dictionary of National Biography* (Oxford: Oxford University Press, 2004), pp. 875–877.

Junger, Sebastian, *War* (London: Fourth Estate, 2010).

Kampfner, John, *Blair's Wars* (London: The Free Press, 2003).

Keegan, John, *A History of War* (London: Pimlico, 1993).

Keegan, John, *The Iraq War* (London: Hutchinson, 2004).

Kennedy, Paul, *The Rise and Fall of the Great Powers: Economic Change and Military Conflict from 1500 to 2000* (London: Fontana Press, 1989).

Kenyatta, Jomo, *Facing Mount Kenya: The Tribal Life of the Gikuyu* (London: Secker and Warburg, [1938], 1953).

Kepel, Gilles, *Jihad: The Trail of Political Islam* (London: I.B. Tauris, 2003).

Kilcullen, David, *The Accidental Guerrilla: Fighting Small Wars amidst a Big One* (London: Hurst, 2009).

King, Anthony, 'Understanding the Helmand Campaign', *International Affairs*, Vol. 86, No. 2 (March 2010), pp. 311–332.

Kiszely, Lieutenant General Sir John, 'Learning about Counter-Insurgency', *RUSI Journal*, Vol. 151, No. 6 (December 2006), pp. 16–21.

Kitchen, Martin, 'British Policy Towards the Soviet Union, 1945–1948', in Gorodetsky, Gabriel (ed.), *Soviet Foreign Policy, 1917–1991: A Retrospective* (London: Frank Cass, 1994).

Kitson, Frank, *Low Intensity Operations: Subversion, Insurgency, Peacekeeping* (London: Faber, 1971).

Kitson, Frank, *Bunch of Five* (London: Faber, 1977).

Kitson, Frank, *Directing Operations* (London: Faber, 1989).

Latawski, Paul, *The Inherent Tensions in Military Doctrine*, Sandhurst Occasional Papers, No. 5 (Camberley: RMA Sandhurst, 2011).

Lawrence, T.E., *Revolt in the Desert* (London: Jonathan Cape, 1927).

Leffler, Melvyn P. and Odd Arne Westad (eds), *The Cambridge History of the Cold War*, Volume 1: *Origins* (Cambridge: Cambridge University Press, 2010).

Liddell Hart, Captain Sir Basil, *The British Way in Warfare* (London: Faber, 1932).

Louis, William Roger, 'The Dissolution of the British Empire in the Era of Vietnam', *The American Historical Review*, Vol. 107, No. 1 (February 2002), pp. 1–25.

Lyttelton, Oliver Viscount Chandos, *The Memoirs of Lord Chandos* (London: The Bodley Head, 1962).

McCartney, Helen, 'The Military Covenant and the Civil–Military Contract in Britain', *International Affairs*, Vol. 86, No. 2 (March 2010), pp. 411–428.

MacGinty, Roger, 'Indigenous Peace-Making Versus the Liberal Peace', *Co-Operation and Conflict*, Vol. 43, No. 2 (2008), pp. 139–163.

McGrattan, Cillian, *Northern Ireland, 1968–2008: The Politics of Retrenchment* (Basingstoke: Palgrave, 2010).

McInnes, Colin, *Hot War, Cold War: The British Army's Way in Warfare, 1945–95* (London: Brassey's, 1996).

Mack, Andrew, 'Why Big Nations Lose Small Wars: The Politics of Asymmetric Conflict', *World Politics*, Vol. 27, No. 2 (January 1975), pp. 175–200.

Macmillan, Lieutenant-General G.H.A., 'The Evacuation of Palestine', *The Journal of the Royal United Services Institute*, Vol. 93, No. 571 (August 1948), pp. 609–613.

Major, John, *John Major: The Autobiography* (London: HarperCollins, 1999).

Mandelson, Peter, *The Third Man: Life at the Heart of New Labour* (London: HarperPress, 2010).

Marston, Daniel, 'Lost and Found in the Jungle: The Indian and British Army Jungle Warfare Doctrines for Burma, 1943–5, and the Malayan Emergency, 1948–60' in Strachan, Hew (ed.), *Big Wars and Small Wars: The British Army and the Lessons of War in the Twentieth Century* (London: Routledge, 2006).

Marston, Daniel, '"Smug and Complacent"? Operation TELIC: The Need for Critical Analysis', *Australian Army Journal*, Vol. 6, No. 3 (summer 2009), pp. 165–180.

Mawby, Spencer, *British Policy in Aden and the Protectorates 1955–67: Last Outpost of a Middle East Empire* (London: Routledge, 2005).

Medcalf, Jennifer, *Going Global or Going Nowhere? NATO's Role in Contemporary International Security* (Oxford: Peter Lang, 2008).

Mellersh, Air Vice-Marshal Sir Francis, 'The Campaign Against the Terrorists in Malaya', lecture delivered on 7 March 1951, *The Journal of the Royal United Service Institute*, Vol. 96, No. 583 (August 1951), pp. 401–415.

Mills, C. Wright, *The Causes of World War Three* (London: Secker and Warburg, 1959).

Mills, Greg, 'Calibrating Ink Spots: Filling Afghanistan's Ungoverned Spaces', *RUSI Journal*, Vol. 151, No. 4 (August 2006), pp. 16–25.

Mitchell, Lieutenant-Colonel Colin, *Having Been a Soldier* (London: Hamish Hamilton, 1969).

Mockaitis, Thomas R., *British Counter-Insurgency in the Post-Imperial Era* (Manchester: Manchester University Press, 1995).

Mockaitis, Thomas R., *The Iraq War: Learning from the Past, Adapting to the Present and Planning for the Future* (Carlisle, PA: Strategic Studies Institute, February 2007).

Moloney, Ed, *A Secret History of the IRA*, second edition (London: Penguin, 2007).

Montgomery of Alamein, Viscount, Bernard Law, *The Memoirs of Field-Marshal the Viscount Montgomery of Alamein, KG* (London: Collins, 1958).

Morgan, Kenneth O., *Labour in Power, 1945–51* (Oxford: Oxford University Press, 1984).

Morgenthau, Hans J., 'The Machiavelli Utopia', *Ethics*, Vol. 55, No. 2 (January 1945), pp. 145–147.

Morgenthau, Hans, 'The Evil of Politics and the Ethics of Evil', *Ethics*, Vol. 56, No. 1 (October 1945), pp. 1–18.

Morgenthau, Hans, 'The Twilight of International Morality', *Ethics*, Vol. 58, No. 2 (January 1948), pp. 79–99.

Morgenthau, Hans J., 'To Intervene or Not to Intervene', *Foreign Affairs*, Vol. 45, Nos. 1–4 (October 1966–July 1967), pp. 425–436.

Morgenthau, Hans J., *Politics Among Nations: The Struggle for Power and Peace*, brief edition (Boston, MA: McGraw-Hill, 1993).

Morris, Benny, *1948: A History of the First Arab-Israeli War* (New Haven, CT: Yale University Press, 2008).

Morrison, Lord Herbert, *Herbert Morrison: An Autobiography* (London: Odhams Press, 1960).

Nagl, John, *Learning to Eat Soup with a Knife: Counterinsurgency Lessons from Malaya and Vietnam* (Chicago, IL: University of Chicago Press, 2005).

Narinsky, Mikhail, 'Soviet Foreign Policy and the Origins of the Cold War', in Gorodetsky, Gabriel (ed.), *Soviet Foreign Policy, 1917–1991: A Retrospective* (London: Frank Cass, 1994).

Neumann, Peter R., *Britain's Long War: British Strategy in the Northern Ireland Conflict, 1969–98* (Basingstoke: Palgrave, 2003).

Neumann, Peter R., 'Winning the "War on Terror"? Roy Mason's Contribution to Counter-Terrorism in Northern Ireland', *Small Wars and Insurgencies*, Vol. 14, No. 3 (autumn 2003), pp. 45–64.

Newsinger, John, *British Counterinsurgency: From Palestine to Northern Ireland* (Basingstoke: Palgrave Macmillan, 2001).

Newton, Paul, Paul Colley and Andrew Sharpe, 'Reclaiming the Art of British Strategic Thinking', *RUSI Journal*, Vol. 155, No. 1 (February 2010), pp. 44–50.

North, Richard, *The Ministry of Defeat: The British War in Iraq – 2003–2009* (London: Continuum, 2009).

O'Balance, Edgar, *Malaya: The Communist Insurgent War, 1948–60* (London: Faber and Faber, 1966).

Omand, David, *Securing the State* (London: Hurst and Company, 2010).

Paget, Julian, *Counter-Insurgency Campaigning* (London: Faber, 1967).

Paret, Peter, *Clausewitz and the State* (Oxford: Oxford University Press, 1976).

Peng, Chin, *My Side of History* (Singapore: Media Masters, 2003).

Peterson, J.E., *Oman's Insurgencies: The Sultanate's Struggle for Supremacy* (London: SAQI, 2007).

Phythian, Mark, *The Labour Party, War and International Relations, 1945–2006* (Abingdon: Routledge, 2007).

Pickering, Jeffrey, *Britain's Withdrawal from East of Suez: The Politics of Retrenchment* (Basingstoke: Macmillan, 1998).

Popplewell, Richard, '"Lacking Intelligence": Some Reflections on Recent Approaches to British Counter-Insurgency, 1900–1960', *Intelligence and National Security*, Vol. 10, No. 2 (April 1995), pp. 336–352.

Porch, Douglas, 'The Dangerous Myths and Dubious Promise of COIN', *Small Wars and Insurgencies*, Vol. 22, No. 2 (May 2011), pp. 239–257.

Potts, Colonel David R., 'Principles for Waging Modern War', *British Army Review*, No. 130 (autumn 2002), pp. 10–16.

Powell, Jonathan, *Great Hatred, Little Room: Making Peace in Ireland* (London: The Bodley Head, 2008).

Purdie, Bob, *Politics in the Streets: The Origins of the Civil Rights Movement in Northern Ireland* (Belfast: Blackstaff Press, 1990).

Rayment, Sean, *Bomb Hunters: In Afghanistan with Britain's Elite Bomb Disposal Unit* (London: HarperCollins, 2011).

Rees, Merlyn, *Northern Ireland: A Personal Perspective* (London: Methuen, 1985).

Ricks, Thomas, *Fiasco: The American Military Adventure in Iraq* (London: Allen Lane, 2006).

Richards, David and Greg Mills (eds), *Victory among People: Lessons from Countering Insurgency and Stabilising Fragile States* (London: Royal United Services Institute, 2011).

Riley, Jonathon, *The Life and Campaigns of General Hughie Stockwell: From Normandy Through Burma to Suez* (Barnsley: Pen and Sword, 2006).

Rubin, Barnett R. and Ahmed Rashid, 'From Great Game to Grand Bargain: Ending Chaos in Afghanistan and Pakistan', *Foreign Affairs*, Vol. 87, No. 6 (November/December 2008), pp. 30–44.

Ryder, Chris, *The Ulster Defence Regiment: An Instrument of Peace?* (London: Methuen, 1991).

Schelling, Thomas C., *Arms and Influence* (New Haven, CT: Yale University Press, [1966] 2008).
Schmidt, Brian C., 'Realism as Tragedy', *Review of International Studies*, Vol. 30 (2004), pp. 427–441.
Seldon, Anthony, *Blair* (London: Free Press, 2004).
Seldon, Anthony (ed.), *Blair's Britain, 1997–2007* (Cambridge: Cambridge University Press, 2007).
Service, Robert, *Comrades: A World History of Communism* (London: Macmillan, 2007).
Seymour, William, *British Special Forces*, with a foreword by David Stirling (London: Sidgwick and Jackson, 1985).
Shinwell, Emanuel, *Conflict Without Malice* (London: Odhams Press, 1955).
Short, Anthony, *The Communist Insurrection in Malaya, 1948–1960* (London: Frederick Muller, 1975).
Short, Clare, *An Honourable Deception? New Labour, Iraq, and the Misuse of Power* (London: Free Press, 2004).
Simms, Brendan, *Unfinest Hour: Britain and the Destruction of Bosnia* (London: Penguin, 2002).
Sinclair, Georgina, *At the End of the Line: Colonial Policing and the Imperial Endgame, 1945–80* (Manchester: Manchester University Press, 2006).
Smith, M.L.R., *Fighting for Ireland? The Military Strategy of the Irish Republican Movement* (London: Routledge, 1997).
Smith, M.L.R., 'Strategy in an Age of 'Low-Intensity Warfare: Why Clausewitz is Still More Relevant than His Critics' in Isabelle Duyvesteyn and Jan Angstrom (eds), *Rethinking the Nature of War* (Abingdon: Frank Cass, 2005).
Smith, Rupert, *The Utility of Force: The Art of War in the Modern World* (London: Penguin, 2005).
Stansfield, Gareth, *Accepting Realities in Iraq*, Middle East Programme Briefing Paper (London: Chatham House, May 2007).
Steele, Jonathan, *Defeat: Why they Lost Iraq* (London: I.B. Tauris, 2009).
Stockwell, A.J., 'Gurney, Sir Henry Lovell Goldsworthy (1898–1951)', *Oxford Dictionary of National Biography* (Oxford: Oxford University Press, 2008).
Stothard, Peter, *30 Days: A Month at the Heart of Blair's War* (London: HarperCollins, 2003).
Strachan, Hew, *The Politics of the British Army* (Oxford: Oxford University Press, 1997).
Strachan, Hew, 'Making Strategy: Civil-Military Relations after Iraq, *Survival*, Vol. 48, No. 3 (autumn 2006), pp. 59–82.
Strachan, Hew, *Clausewitz's On War: A Biography* (New York: Atlantic Books, 2007).
Stubbs, Richard, *Hearts and Minds in Guerrilla Warfare: The Malayan Emergency, 1948–1960* (Oxford: Oxford University Press, 1989).

Stubbs, Richard, 'From Search and Destroy to Hearts and Minds: The Evolution of British Strategy in Malaya, 1948–60', in Marston, Daniel and Carter Malkasian (eds), *Counterinsurgency in Modern Warfare* (Oxford: Osprey, 2008).

Synnott, Hillary, *Bad Days in Basra: My Turbulent Time as Britain's Man in Southern Iraq* (London: I.B. Tauris, 2008).

Thakur, Ramesh and Waheguru Pal Singh Sidhu (eds), *The Iraq Crisis and World Order: Structural, Institutional and Normative Challenges* (Tokyo: United Nations University Press, 2006).

Thatcher, Margaret, *The Downing Street Years* (London: HarperCollins, 1993).

Thompson, Sir Robert, 'Squaring the Error', *Foreign Affairs*, Vol. 46 (1968), pp. 442–453.

Thompson, Robert, *Revolutionary War in World Strategy, 1945–1969* (London: Secker and Warburg, 1970).

Thompson, Robert, *Defeating Communist Insurgency: Lessons from Malaya and Vietnam* (London: Chatto and Windus, 1972).

Toynbee, Arnold, 'Britain and the Arabs: The Need for a New Start', *International Affairs*, Vol. 40, No. 4 (October 1964), pp. 638–646.

Trevaskis, Sir Kennedy, *Shades of Amber: A South Arabia Episode* (London: Hutchinson, 1968).

Tripp, Charles, *A History of Iraq*, third edition (Cambridge: Cambridge University Press, 2007).

Tuck, Christopher, 'Northern Ireland and the British Approach to Counter-Insurgency', *Defense and Security Analysis*, Vol. 23, No. 2 (June 2007), 165–183.

Ucko, David, 'The Malayan Emergency: The Legacy and Relevance of a Counter-Insurgency Success Story', *Defence Studies*, Vol. 10, Nos. 1–2 (March–June 2010), pp. 13–39.

Ucko, David H., 'Lessons from Basra: The Future of British Counter-Insurgency, *Survival*, Vol. 52, No. 4 (August–September 2010), pp. 131–158.

Urban, Mark, *Big Boys Rules: The SAS and the Struggle against the IRA* (London: Faber, 1992).

Urban, Mark, *Task Force Black: The Explosive True Story of the SAS and the Secret War in Iraq* (London: Little, Brown, 2010).

Vigor, P.H., *The Soviet View of War, Peace and Neutrality* (London: Routledge and Kegan Paul, 1975).

Walker, Jonathan, *Aden Insurgency: The Savage War in South Arabia* (Staplehurst: Spellmount, 2005).

Waltz, Kenneth N., *Theory of International Relations* (Boston, MA: McGraw-Hill, 1979).

Waltz, Kenneth, 'International Politics is Not Foreign Policy', *Security Studies*, Vol. 6 (1996), pp. 54–57.

Wheeler, General Sir Roger, 'The British Army after the SDR: Peacemakers Know that Britain Will Deliver', *RUSI Journal*, Vol. 144, No. 2 (1999), pp. 4–8.

Williams, Francis, *A Prime Minister Remembers: The War and Post-War Memoirs of the Rt Hon. Earl Attlee* (London: Heinemann, 1961).

Wilson, Harold, *The Labour Government, 1964–1970: A Personal Record* (London: Weidenfeld and Nicolson, 1971).

Wingen, John Van and Herbert K. Tillema, 'British Military Intervention after World War II: Militance in a Second-Rank Power', *Journal of Peace Research*, Vol. 17, No. 4 (1980), pp. 291–303.

Woodward, Bob, *Plan of Attack: The Road to War* (London: Simon and Schuster, 2004).

Young, John W., *The Labour Governments 1964–70*, Volume 2: *International Policy* (Manchester: Manchester University Press, 2003).

Index